REAL ESTATE FINANCING

FREDERICK E. CASE
JOHN M. CLAPP
UNIVERSITY OF CALIFORNIA, LOS ANGELES

A WILEY/HAMILTON PUBLICATION

JOHN WILEY & SONS, Santa Barbara • New York • Chichester •
Brisbane • Toronto

This publication is designed to provide accurate and
authoritative information in regard to the subject
matter covered. It is sold with the understanding that
the publisher is not engaged in rendering legal, accounting, or other professional service. If legal advice or
other expert assistance is required, the services of a
competent professional person should be sought.

*From a Declaration of Principles jointly adopted by a
Committee of the American Bar Association and a Committee
of Publishers.*

Library of Congress Cataloging in Publication Data:

Case, Frederick E.
    Real estate financing.

    "A Wiley/Hamilton publication."
    1. Real estate business—Finance. 2. Real estate
investment. 3. Mortgage loans. I. Clapp, John M.,
joint author. II. Title.

HD1375.C394   658.1'5   77-27938
ISBN 0-471-07248-6

Printed in the United States of America

10 9 8 7 6 5 4 3 2

PREFACE

Designed as a text for college courses, this volume is also intended as a reference for practitioners and a guide for borrowers seeking real estate investment funds and lenders who must evaluate such requests.

Real estate financing is shown to be a form of risk taking that must be related to lending terms and expected earnings. A systems approach is followed, describing the processes, the interrelationships, the progression of events, and the formal instruments that are required. Relevant theory from economics, managerial finance, investments, money and banking, and urban economics is reviewed with reference to the special problems of financing real estate.

The book's successive parts reflect the orderly sequence of events in the financing of a real estate transaction. Part I provides an overview and introduction to the elements of financing and investment procedures, and describes the real estate money markets. The first chapter should be reviewed carefully since it introduces the systems concept and charts the organization of the book as a whole. Part II analyzes the importance of government, particularly Federal government, to the financing of real estate transactions. We show how regulatory authorities constantly affect the sources and uses of mortgage funds through their influence over lenders, their activities in secondary mortgage markets, and their insurance and guarantee of mortgage loans. The increasing significance of Federal tax laws to both borrowers and lenders of mortgage funds is fully explored.

The principles of borrower analysis and property analysis are then applied to various kinds of real estate as well as special-purpose properties and construction financing. In the process we probe some critical issues which continue to plague the mortgage lending industry.

The legal aspects of lending are examined, and the book introduces the potential variations of mortgages and trust deeds and the range of alternatives that might be used or are being used to make the mortgage instrument fit more effectively with money market changes, inflation, and changing borrower objectives.

Change is the order of the day in mortgage lending. Consequently the final part of the book looks at some of the proposals for changing the character of thrift institutions which provide the bulk of mortgage funds. The discussion of mathematics of real estate finance presents the concepts and formulas that permit computation of the costs of using real estate capital with a hand-held calculator. The appendixes includes a glossary of the frequently arcane terms of real estate financing and a list of major source materials that will enable the reader to keep up to date on current changes in the economy and in the money and real estate financing markets.

FREDERICK E. CASE
JOHN M. CLAPP

Los Angeles
January, 1978

ACKNOWLEDGMENTS

We are glad to record the following acknowledgments not only to recognize our many debts to others, but also to demonstrate the high quality of assistance we have been privileged to draw upon in the preparation of this book.

Among the numerous UCLA colleagues who knowingly or unknowingly helped us shape this book are Frank Mittelbach, Benjamin Bobo, Leo Grebler, Jack Shelton, and Keith Smith. Visitors who have presented graduate courses and contributed to our thinking include Robert Fletcher, California State University, Bakersfield; Claude Elias, Jr., University of Southern California; and William Whitney, an independent consultant and former student.

The extensive network of California community colleges and state colleges and universities has offered continuing contact with outstanding teachers whose writings and discussions have proved most thought provoking. Of course, we must make special mention of William Hippaka, California State University, San Diego; and William Tsagris, California State College, Fullerton.

Colleagues at the University of California, Berkeley, have generated many new concepts and much useful data, and we are most pleased to recognize their contributions, particularly those of Wallace Smith, Albert Schaaf, Sherman Maisel, and Stephen Roulac.

Many practitioners have provided facts, ideas, and exhibits, and we are especially indebted to Edward Johnson, Richard De Smet, and Thomas O'Neil, officers of Financial Federation, Inc. Oliver Jones, who contributes so much to mortgage banking through the Mortgage Bankers Association, has been a constant source of guidance on current trends through his writings in the Association's journal. Equally important has been the flow of ideas and information provided by fellow academicians Edward Edwards of Reading, Pennsylvania, and Arthur Weimer of Indiana University, who have been highly effective proponents of the savings and loan industry. And, of course, we must recognize Sanders Kahn, the outstanding New York

City teacher and practitioner, who is coauthor of the text by Kahn and Case, *Real Estate Appraisal and Investment.*

The importance of the staff support from our graduate assistants, Larry Fink and David Tsai, cannot be overlooked, nor can the able assistance of our typists, editors, and overall critics, Rose Altman, Nancy Kawata, and Karen List.

However, despite the many obligations noted above, we wish to make clear that responsibility for content, presentation, interpretations of theory, and practical recommendations is ours alone.

F. E. C.
J. M. C.

CONTENTS

II GOVERNMENT IN THE FINANCING PROCESS

V   ADVANCED TOPICS

APPENDIXES

1

Elements of
Real Estate Finance

1

FINANCING AND INVESTMENT PROCESSES–AN OVERVIEW

To be effective as either a mortgage lender or borrower it is necessary to have a firm grasp of the basic elements in the financing process and the instruments associated with those elements. Real estate financing should be seen as a system of inputs, outputs, money flows, and information flows that are used by both the borrower and the lender to make decisions with respect to a particular real estate investment and its financing. Both the borrower and the lender must first determine what they wish to do and then select the appropriate legal processes and financing instruments to achieve those goals. This chapter describes real estate financing as a system that has interrelated processes and formal instruments. A brief case study is included to illustrate the kinds of problems that lenders and borrowers face in dealing with each other.

THE REAL ESTATE FINANCING PROCESS AS A SYSTEM

The system formed by the factors contributing to the real estate financing process is represented in Figure 1–1. The diagram helps to identify the sequence in which activities must take place and the interrelationships of each activity with the others. Within the dotted lines labeled "Mortgage Markets" are the elements that are actually operative in mortgage markets. It is on those that our emphasis will be placed, though we recognize that many external elements also exercise some effect on mortgage markets. War, depression, inflation, the general business environment, non-mortgage

3

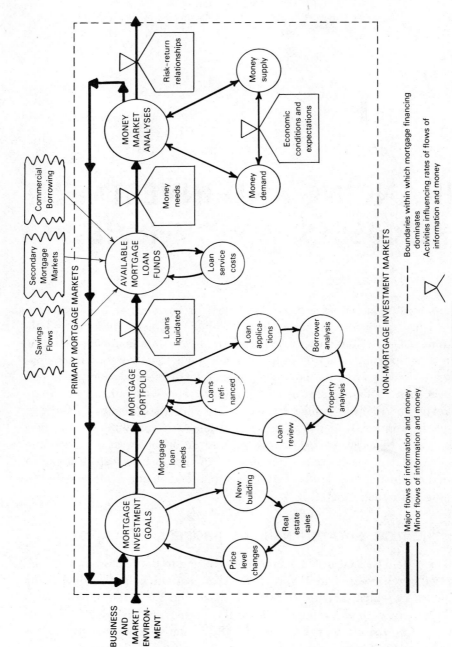

Fig. 1–1. A systems statement of the real estate financing process.

investment markets all influence the kinds and amounts of real estate financing that occur. However, detailed study of them is the subject matter of economics and will not be included in this text. We shall indicate in an elementary way how some of the principal elements outside of mortgage markets may influence what happens within those markets.

Mortgage Investment Goals. The real estate financing process begins because someone wants to borrow money in order to engage in some real estate related activity or someone who has some money wants to make it available to such a borrower. For this reason the first element in any real estate financing process is a determination of what is to be achieved through the mortgage investment process. The mortgage instrument is merely one of several ways in which persons can invest in real estate markets. The mortgage is desirable for those who want a reasonably assured rate of return and security for the recovery of their unpaid loan during the entire period of the investment process. Setting mortgage investment goals therefore means that the lenders decide what rate of return they wish to earn, how long they want to allow their money to remain in the mortgage investment, how much risk they are willing to take, and what kinds of real estate activity they will emphasize in their mortgage lending processes.

As presented in Figure 1–1, lenders who have identified their mortgage investment goals investigate the construction market to determine what new building is going on and how this may affect the demand for funds. From the real estate sales market they learn what kinds of lending opportunities exist among properties that are already built, and they then study price changes and general trends in the marketplace. The examination of market trends comes last in this particular subprocess because only the most current information is of value in deciding whether to make large loans or small loans, whether to require borrowers to provide large down payments or small down payments. The circular flow of the arrows indicates that these steps form a continuing process that originates with selection of investment goals and leads back to their confirmation or rejection.

Lenders then decide what kind of mortgage lending will fulfill their goals. In Figure 1–1 a gate or valve labeled "Mortgage Loan Needs" is located between the investment goals and the mortgage portfolio. Although the lenders may want to achieve a particular rate of return or to engage in a particular kind of mortgage lending, the markets or the borrowers may not allow it. The lenders must then change their goals; they cannot add to their mortgage portfolios. The rate at which mortgage portfolios increase or decrease depends upon the number of persons who want to borrow, the terms on which they wish to borrow, and the kinds of property they are offering as security.

The Mortgage Portfolio. As the lenders proceed in the mortgage lending process, they slowly build up portfolios of loans on which they are receiving interest and which they are administering. The creation of a mortgage portfolio is indicated in the cyclical flow that begins with loan applications. Lenders try to encourage a larger volume of loan applications than the number of loans they expect to make, in order to be able to select the best lending opportunities. Loan applications usually originate with the borrowers, who are required to state briefly what kind of loan is wanted, the terms expected, the intended use of the proceeds of the loan, and, in general, a description of current financial condition. If a loan application indicates potential for a good mortgage, the lender asks the borrower to complete forms which permit a deeper analysis of the borrower's monetary status.

Borrower analysis in its simplest terms consists of analyzing what the borrower owns, what the borrower owes to others, and how much net income is available to pay off the loan on a periodic basis. Also, if the borrower should fail to earn the income expected, are sufficient assets available for liquidation if necessary to meet the mortgage payments? In an extreme case, the lender may be legally entitled to take the borrower's assets to satisfy loan requirements.

There is considerable discussion among lenders as to which is more important in a decision to make a mortgage loan—the borrower, who must meet the terms of the loan and is the source of the loan's profitability, or the property, which stands as ultimate security against any failures or weaknesses on the part of the borrower. For this reason some lenders look at the property first. However, this is primarily a policy decision; legally the lender must look at both the borrower and the property.

Property analysis consists of estimating the current value of the property and the extent to which its value will continue to be in excess of the amount not yet paid on the loan.

If the borrower and the property appear to be acceptable, the loan process is initiated through a series of legal forms and processes which will be discussed later. The primary goal of the lender at this time is to create a loan agreement in which the loan will be repaid automatically according to the stated terms and without the need for administrative review or legal processes for collection of overdue funds. Review of the loans goes on constantly while the mortgages are in the portfolio of the lender.

Other sources of mortgages for lenders are loans that have been made earlier and have to be refinanced. Most refinancing is required because borrowers are unable to meet the loan terms that were agreed upon originally. However, in good markets, where borrowers are often interested in improving or enlarging their properties, loans may be refinanced for larger amounts and on terms that are usually more favorable to the lenders but permit the borrowers a range of activity that would not otherwise be possible.

Monitoring the mortgage portfolio, finding new and more profitable loans, and selling or liquidating loans which are not profitable are the heart of the real estate financing process.

Loans can be liquidated in a number of ways. Most mortgage loans are liquidated according to the terms of the mortgage and are paid off well before the final due date. Some loans are liquidated through renegotiation with the borrower; the lender accepts the property without going through the legal process of foreclosure and sells the property to recover the investment. The most disastrous way of liquidating a loan is through the foreclosure process. Foreclosure is costly and time-consuming and usually means a loss to both the borrower and the lender. The process is complicated, involves numerous legal safeguards for both the borrower and the lender, and therefore is resorted to only under the most extreme conditions.

Available Mortgage Loan Funds. Lenders have several sources for money that can be made available for mortgage loans. The most common and continuing sources are loans that have been made previously and are now being paid off, and some of the funds that are received as costs in connection with making loans and foreclosing on properties. Loans made for 20 or 30 years are frequently paid off in one-third or less of the negotiated period because the borrower is trying to buy a better property or is seeking a better real estate investment opportunity.

Savings, a primary source of mortgage funds, flow into the mortgage markets from savings and loan associations, commercial banks, mutual savings banks, and insurance companies—the principal institutional lenders. Funds are also secured from private persons, real estate brokers, real estate investors, mortgage brokers, bankers, and federal sources. (There has been and probably always will be a direct relationship between the amount of savings nationwide and the volume of mortgage lending. This relationship is examined in some detail in Chapter 5.)

Another source of funds is secondary mortgage operations. Lenders who have made loans and have opportunities for making additional loans offer some of their loan portfolio for sale to those operating in secondary mortgage markets. For example, savings and loan associations can use their loans as security and get additional funding by borrowing from the Federal Home Loan Bank. (We will discuss this later.) Loans can also be sold to various federal housing or mortgage lending agencies, to other mortgage lenders who want to avoid the costs and problems of making loans but are quite willing to enjoy the profits accruing from regular payments. Many lenders who sell loans to others retain a *servicing privilege:* they continue to administer the loan and collect the payments, for a loan service fee of one-quarter to one-half per cent of the amount of the loan.

When it appears that short-term borrowing rates are lower than the long-term rates at which mortgage loans can be made, lenders can also turn to commercial banks or to the commercial money markets and borrow on either a short-term or a long-term basis. In recent years the persistence of short-term money rates at levels above those of long-term money rates has made commercial borrowing almost prohibitive as a source of mortgage loan funds. However, some lenders have engaged in commercial borrowing when they had a need for liquidity or cash, or when they wished to expand or to secure a dominant position in the mortgage markets even though it meant some loss in their mortgage lending processes.

When lenders have accumulated funds for mortgage loans, the extent to which they can use those funds is directly related to the need for mortgage money. The greater the need for mortgage money, the greater the demand for funds; typically, the higher the mortgage interest rates, the higher the profit potential for mortgage lenders. In depressed economic conditions or depressed money markets, money for mortgage loans may be easily available but there may be small need for it. Terms of loans become favorable to the borrowers but somewhat less than profitable to the lenders.

Money Market Analyses. The final major step in the real estate financing process consists of a continuous monitoring of money markets. Mortgage lenders must be much more aware of money market trends than of mortgage market trends. Actually, mortgage lending is merely another form of money market operations. Any mortgage lenders who think that they can be successful by looking only at the mortgage markets will soon find that they are losing their loan potentials and their sources of funds. In the same way, well-informed borrowers must keep current on the market and understand what is happening to money costs in order to decide whether the funding they need can be obtained most advantageously through mortgage borrowing or through other forms of borrowing.

Money market analysis is usually nothing more than evaluating the demand for money, the supply for money, and the extent to which economic conditions and expectations of economic change are affecting either the demand or the supply. In Figure 1–1 the arrows below "Money Market Analysis" go two ways, which means that at times it may be important to look at the demand for money as related to economic conditions, and at other times it will be important to look at the money supply. Both are important and, depending upon economic conditions, one should not be given precedence over the other. We shall discuss this at some length in later chapters.

The final factor that determines the extent to which mortgage loans are made or the extent to which mortgage lenders may go outside the mortgage markets to invest funds relates to the amount of risk the lenders see in the mortgage loans they can make and the amount of return they can expect from these loans. If there is a wide spread between return and risk, with risk low and return high, lenders will turn more and more to mortgage investment, and the flow of funds will then be from money market analysis back into mortgage investment goals. On the other hand, if the analyses suggest certain downturns that will increase risk and lower return, mortgage lenders who would normally be expected to emphasize mortgage loans will turn to other forms of investment until the risk–return relationships becomes more favorable.

To summarize, Figure 1–1 is a systems statement and requires an understanding of the basic elements of a systems process. In any systems process there are major levels of activity—in this case, mortgage investment goals, the mortgage portfolio, available mortgage loan funds, and money market analyses—and there must be a flow among them which causes the levels to change over time. The flow among these elements is usually monitored through various influences or valves, which are identified here as mortgage loan needs, loans liquidated, money needs, and risk–return relationships. Each of the major levels is in a process of constant change because of inputs coming from other levels and because of its own internal events. For example, changes occur in mortgage investment goals because of inputs from the business and market environment, from money market analyses, and from activities within the goals themselves which are related to the lenders' understanding of new building activities, sales of existing properties, and changes in price levels.

The essence of the systems approach, then, is a feedback process in which the end results of a particular activity (in this case, money market anlyses) flow back into the system's goals (real estate/mortgage investment) so that the goals can.be reinforced or changed.

"Mortgage Markets" in Figure 1–1 encompasses all of the elements necessary for a thorough understanding of the real estate financing process. However, since this process does not operate within a vacuum, its boundaries are shown as dotted lines; other influences will inevitably change the real estate financing process. These influences are almost innumerable but for our purposes we shall concentrate on the business and market environment, savings flows, secondary mortgage operations, and commercial borrowing activities.

BASIC FINANCING INSTRUMENTS AND PROCESSES

This entire book contains discussions of the various instruments and processes that are related to real estate financing. However, at this point, discussion of only the more basic instruments and processes is appropriate. Mastery of these basics is essential to an understanding of the complexities and details which will be discussed in later chapters. Figure 1–2 provides a summary listing.

Process Step	Basic Instrument
Request for loan	Loan application form
	Credit report
Agreement to lend	Loan commitment
Examination of the security	Property appraisal
Making of loan	Promissory note
	Deed of trust or mortgage
	Title proof
	Mortgage insurance
	Title deed
Administration of loan	Payment record
Closing of loan as:	
Required by agreement	Request for reconveyance
	Recording of completion
Renegotiated	New note and deed of trust
Foreclosed because not paid according to agreement	Notice of default
	Foreclosure through sale
	New title deed

Fig. 1–2. Basic instruments in the real estate financing process.

Loan Application. The real estate financing process begins when a borrower approaches a lender for the purpose of securing a loan. Typically this step involves a personal interview and completion of a rather brief loan application form. The lender may ask the borrower to furnish credit references and may contact those references to determine whether the transaction should continue. At this point the lender will rarely indicate whether the loan will or will not be made. There will simply be discussion of the terms under which the loan is to be made, the standards which the borrower and the property must fulfill, and any other conditions that must be met by the borrower before the loan can be completed. If the borrower seems satisfied and the lender feels the process can continue, they proceed to a loan commitment.

Loan Commitment. If a lender is interested in making mortgage loans and if preliminary discussions lead to a belief that the borrower can meet the requirements for a satisfactory loan, the lender may indicate in some way to the borrower a willingness to make the loan. Where large sums are involved or where the borrower must get a preliminary lending commitment, the lender may prepare a written statement that, if the borrower and the property can meet certain standards set by the lender, a loan will be made on a given set of terms. This is a legal agreement and is usually prepared with the assistance of lawyers. Poorly prepared loan commitments can cause borrowers to lose prospective loans or can force lenders to make loans which they had not intended to make.

Security Evaluation. Once the borrower has completed a form which indicates an ability to meet the loan conditions, the lender will ask for an appraisal of the property being offered as security. Appraisal of a property for loan purposes is a complicated process and is surrounded by a number of legal requirements where the lender is a bank, a savings and loan association, or any other form of institution subject to government review and regulation. Fortunately, over the years the appraisal process for lending purposes has been standardized so that it is possible to review the process and gain an understanding of what almost any lender will require.

Loan Completion. When both the property and the borrower appear acceptable, the more detailed process of completing the loan is undertaken. Many kinds of forms and reviews are connected with this process but at this point it is sufficient to say that first the lender has the borrower sign a note which says, in effect, I wish to borrow (or I agree to borrow, or I am borrowing) a given sum of money and I agree to repay this amount on the following terms, making these kinds of periodic payments. Then a deed of trust or mortgage is created. This instrument pledges the property involved in the transaction as security for the repayment of the mortgage if the borrower does not perform according to the conditions set forth in the promissory note.

It is important at this stage in the lending process for the borrower to be able to prove clear title to the property or sufficient title rights to guarantee the amount of money being loaned. This title proof is usually related to the title deed, which sets forth in legal terms a description of the property and the rights which the borrower/property owner has. The borrower typically buys a search of the title from a title insurance company. If the company finds a clear title, it issues an insurance policy to compensate the borrower for any defects in the title that may have been missed in the search. If the company finds any problems, such as an easement, it can exclude the easement from the insurance policy.

The borrower can guarantee that the loan will be repaid in case of death or disability by taking out a form of mortgage insurance policy that will cover all payments to the lender if the borrower dies or suffers a disabling accident. A more common form of mortgage insurance now involves a small additional monthly payment on the mortgage, which guarantees that the lender will receive proceeds owed if the borrower defaults for any reason. However, this latter form of mortgage insurance covers only the lender's investment and does not protect the borrower's equity in any way.

Loan Administration.   Once the loan has been completed the borrower receives a payment book to be submitted each time a payment is made—monthly or periodically, depending on the terms of the loan. The amount of principal and the interest paid are recorded on the stubs in the payment book. Further, at the end of each year, lenders provide to borrowers a summary of all payments made, the amount of the payment that is applied against the principal of the loan, and the amount that is applied to interest on the loan. This payment record is vital to the borrower; it must be submitted as evidence that the mortgage has been paid according to terms, if the borrower wishes to close out the mortgage or make changes in it.

Loan Closing.   A loan can be closed in a number of ways. The preferred way is completion as required by the terms of the promissory note. When this is accomplished, the borrower can request reconveyance of any title that may have been given to the lender as security for repayment of the loan. The borrower should also make sure that the legal public records show completion of the mortgage, fully paid according to the terms of the agreement. This notice of completion will normally be filed by the lender, but it is the borrower's responsibility to see that this is done.

Another way of closing a loan is to renegotiate it through creation of a new promissory note and a new deed of trust. Typically, this happens when the borrower finds that the terms originally agreed to cannot be met. But it may also mean that the borrower has a better opportunity for additional investments or, faced with a need for additional funding, is taking advantage of a good credit record with the lender. Having built up some equity in the property, the borrower may be able to get a new and better mortgage loan.

The most disastrous way of closing a loan is through foreclosure, which occurs because the borrower has not paid according to the promissory note agreeemnt. Foreclosure is an expensive process in which neither the borrower nor the lender makes a profit. The lender must send the borrower a notice of default, and this may take from 45 to 90 days. The lender must then engage legal assistance in foreclosing on the property, securing sufficient title to it to have a sale, and paying the proceeds of the sale. Any residual funds are applied against amounts due the lender and any remainder is given to the borrower. The lender can then issue a new deed of title under which all the rights that had been secured to the loan agreement have now been passed on to whoever has purchased the foreclosed property.

TO LEND OR NOT TO LEND

To review what has been said and to illustrate what the lender faces in making a loan, Figure 1–3 presents data on two borrowers, A and B. If you were a lender, would you make a loan to either or both of these borrowers? You are free to make any assumptions you wish about your goals in lending or the return you are seeking on your investment. Assume that each borrower wants to secure a loan for the years, rates, and down payments that are prevalent under current market conditions. Analyze what each borrower is trying to do, the kind of security he is offering, and whether his assets in conjunction with what he owes, what he earns, and the value of the property are sufficient bases for making a loan.

Compare, for example, the property A wants to buy with the property being offered B. Does the price seem about right in terms of the size, the number of bedrooms and baths, and the age of the property? Consider the condition of each property. Is it satisfactory for loan purposes or should the entire process be rejected because the properties are not new and in superior condition? Are too many repairs needed? A must borrow $2,000 to pay for necessary repairs.

Theoretically, the value of the property relates to the quality of the neighborhood in which it is located. A is buying property in an old and stable neighborhood; B is buying in a neighborhood that is changing. This could mean that new kinds of property uses will be coming in, that a social or economic mix is developing which may influence the kinds of properties that are built and the degree to which they are maintained.

Notice also that A has been renting at $450 a month and owns nothing. B's house has a value of $30,000 and he now has an equity of $8,000 in it; he wants to move into a better house. Should A be rejected because he has

	A	**B**
The Property		
Price	$55,000	$45,000
Size	2,500 sq. ft., 3 br, 2 ba	2,000 sq. ft., 3 br, 1 3/4 ba
Age	30 yrs	15 yrs
Condition	Good	Good
Needed Repairs	$2,000	$750
Neighborhood	Old, stable	New, changing
Present Housing Rent	$450 per mo.	
Own (value)		$30,000
(equity)		$ 8,000
The Borrower		
Occupation	Stockbroker	Department head
Company	Dean Witter	Hughes Aircraft
Income (previous year)	$18,500	$18,000
Family	Wife, 1 child	Wife, 3 children
Other Income	Bonus: $4,200	Overtime: $2,000
		Wife (part-time work): $8,000
Assets		
Securities (market value)	$10,000	None
Life Insurance (amount)	$20,000	$25,000
Savings (cash)	$ 1,000	$ 3,000
Recreation Vehicle		2 years old: $8,000
Sailboat		$3,000
Auto	New: $3,700	3 years old: $1,300
Debts		
Mortgage Payments (annual)	None	$3,000
Auto Payments	$85 per mo.	$120 per mo.
Personal Loans	$200 per mo.	$125 per mo.

Fig. 1–3. Borrower and property analysis—information memo. Should a loan be made? On what terms?

no experience at home ownership and may be trying to buy more than he can afford? Is B a good risk even though he does have an $8,000 equity? He is trying to buy a house which is 50 per cent higher in value than the one he now owns. Will he be outreaching himself?

The Borrower. What do you think about the occupations of A and B? A is a stockbroker. Under current conditions, does a stockbroker have a sufficiently secure earning potential? Notice that A works for a highly reputable brokerage firm. B is a department head at Hughes Aircraft, which probably means that he has worked his way up the line and has a reasonably secure job. But the aircraft industry is notoriously unstable, and employees are being laid off and rehired constantly. Both borrowers have about the same income level, but A has one child whereas B has three children. Does this heavier financial burden mean that B should not be allowed to buy a more expensive house? A has one child; there is a possibility that he may have more children.

Would you count the extra income or not? Last year, A earned a $4,200 bonus—25 per cent more than his basic income of the previous year. B earned $2,000 in overtime. In the aircraft industry this may mean that he is one of the people who is retained regularly; when layoffs occur, B simply works less overtime. Apparently B's children are sufficiently grown that his wife can work part-time. She earned $8,000 during the previous year. Should this $8,000 be counted as an additional source of income toward the mortgage, or does the wife's part-time work indicate she is doing it reluctantly and will quit as soon as she can?

Assets. What have these borrowers managed to accumulate in the years since they have been working? They both own automobiles. A owns a new model valued at $3,700; B owns an older one valued at $1,300. Does this mean that A is a better risk or simply that he buys news cars frequently and is always in debt for car payments? Does it mean that B is thriftier, uses his car carefully and for as long as possible, and keeps his auto payments down?

A has managed to acquire $10,000 in securities and B has none. A has life insurance equal to $20,000; B's life insurance is equal to $25,000. But is the amount of insurance carried by each of these men sufficient with respect to their family responsibilities? Would you want them to have more life insurance and would you want the life insurance to serve as additional security for the mortgage?

A, in spite of his income, has only $1,000 in savings in cash, whereas B has managed to accumulate $3,000. Also, in spite of his financial obligations, B owns a recreation vehicle which is two years old and has a value of $8,000, and a sailboat valued at $3,000. Does this mean that B is a better financial manager, that whatever his income level he can manage his debts and still get the things he wants? Would he then be a better manager and a better risk for the mortgage loan contemplated?

Debts. What borrowers owe is frequently a good measure of what they will be able to repay. A, who rents, has not had to make mortgage payments and is therefore perhaps unaccustomed to periodic repayments of the size required for a mortgage. On the other hand, B has been buying property and he has a $3,000 annual debt. Apparently he has repaid regularly on the mortgage and has shown the capacity for handling a mortgage debt. A has auto payments of $85, B's are $120. B's payments may reflect his debt on the recreational vehicle, which has been partially paid for. As for personal loans, does the $200 a month debt indicate A is unusually extravagant? Are he and his wife perhaps buying too much furniture, too many appliances, too much clothing? Or is $200 about right? B is spending only $125 a month even though he has heavier responsibilities. Does this mean he is better able to control his budgets?

Other Information. Turn back to Figure 1–1 and review other elements which must be considered in the real estate lending process. Assuming that this loan is to be made immediately, under current conditions, what additional information would you want, or have you now enough information to make the loan? If you have enough information, what terms would you want? For how many years would you make the loan? What down payment would you require? What interest rate would you charge? Would you want to charge some additional points for administering or closing the loan?

As you can see, the process of deciding to make a loan is complex and involves many kinds of judgments, few of which can be based on hard data or on careful objective analysis. This point will be emphasized throughout this book. Although a scientific approach can be made to mortgage lending, at some point lenders have to use their own judgment in determining what loans to make and the terms on which they shall be made. History shows that even the best of lenders make some mistakes. Lenders are aware of this and are always asking: Where are the weak spots that might cause mistakes? What risks are involved that cannot be identified or measured at the present? How much should be charged in order to cover these risks? The process of identifying risks and adjusting to them in order to make a profit is the focus for the next chapter.

There is no absolute answer as to loans to borrowers A and B. When you have finished reading this text you will be able to make much more informed judgments, but a good deal of your own personal value system will still be involved. This personal value system is built up through experience and through a better understanding of the whole process of real estate economics. You may want to use the examples of A and B to illustrate topics covered in other chapters.

SUMMARY

Money is the principal raw material which must be fed into the mortgage lending process. Mortgage lenders get most of their money from loan repayments and the deposits of many small savers. Some money is acquired from commercial bank loans. No matter what the source, the availability of mortgage money depends heavily on the general level of economic activity, the demand for money, and the alternative investments available to financial institutions.

If money is available, a loan application leads to investigation of the borrower and the property. Information considered by the lender includes the quality and age of the property, the prospects for the neighborhood, the borrower's age, income, occupation, years on the job, and family obligations. The borrower's previous indebtedness, previous repayment record, financial assets, and current liabilities are given heavy weight in borrower analysis.

QUESTIONS

1. Figure 1–1 indicates four steps in the real estate financing process: (a) mortgage investment goals, (b) mortgage portfolio, (c) available mortgage loan funds, and (d) money market analyses. Suppose you are the mortgage loan officer of a commercial bank or savings and loan association and are asked to indicate the relative weight of each step on a scale of one to ten. How much importance would you place on each step and what reasons can you give for your selections?
2. Indicate how each of the following might affect the availability of money for home lending purposes: (a) demand for business loans, (b) demand for construction funds, (c) decrease in personal savings, (d) increase in funds placed in the stock market, (e) rising unemployment rates, (f) rising prices generally.
3. What kinds of mortgage lending goals might a savings and loan association have?
4. What basic elements do mortgage lenders look for in evaluating borrowers and why do they need to know these things?
5. Identify each basic element in the real estate financing process and indicate how it is used.

2

FINANCING RISKS

Both borrowers and lenders in the real estate financing process are faced with the problem of balancing their opportunities for making profit against the chances that they will lose not only the profit but the amount they have invested. Both operate on the principle that as the risk increases, the rate of return should increase. However, even with this principle, they must consider the variety of risks involved and assign to them some order of priority based upon the objectives of the investment or the financing. Unfortunately, the process of balancing risk against return has not been sufficiently developed to permit precise formulation; the process continues to be based primarily upon the judgment of the loan officer and the loan committee and their views of the borrower. The potential sources of risk are summarized in Figure 2–1. At the end of this chapter we shall suggest some ways of dealing with risk which have resulted from empirical research into the problem.

BORROWER RISKS

There is no agreement among lenders as to which is more important: the risk of the borrower's failing to repay the loan or the risk that the property may not be equal to the security required. Typically, however, an evaluation of risk begins with the borrower. There are many things which the lender wants to know about the borrower, but essentially they can be summarized in four categories: credit reputation, motivation, stabilized income, and assets.

Risks of Financing Real Property

Borrower Risks	_____	Investment Risks	_____
Credit Reputation	_____	Mortgage Pattern	_____
Motivation	_____	Ratio of Loan to Value	_____
Stabilized Income	_____	Term of Mortgage vs. Life of	
Assets	_____	Property	_____
		Total Housing Costs vs. Rental	
Property Risks	_____	Payments	_____
Structural Qualities	_____	Portfolio Pattern	_____
Functional Qualities	_____	Diversification	_____
Mechanical Equipment	_____	Location	_____
Architecture and Appearance	_____	Kinds of Properties	_____
Location Risks	_____	Return	_____
Appearance of Neighborhood	_____	On Capital	_____
Age and Location for City Growth	_____	Of Capital	_____
Shopping, Churches, etc.	_____	Availability of Funds	_____
Inhabitants	_____	Market Reactions	_____
Transportation	_____	Property Prices	_____
Utilities and Services	_____	Money Rates	_____
Taxes and Assessments	_____	Value of the Dollar	_____
Economic Background Risks	_____	Level of Economic Activity	_____
Industry Size	_____	Real Estate Activity	_____
Industrial Diversifications	_____		
Cyclical Trends	_____		
Employment Trends	_____		
Loan Administration Risks	_____		
Accurate Record Keeping	_____		
Property Appraisal and Inspections	_____	1 = Decreases risk	
Property File Information	_____	0 = Neither decreases nor increases risk	
Loan Closing Information and Costs	_____	−1 = Increases risk	
Loan Servicing Costs	_____	✓ = Reject	

Fig. 2–1. Summary of risks in mortgage lending.

Credit Reputation. Presumably, a borrower who has borrowed in the past and repaid according to schedule while providing few, if any, problems for the lender is the best sort of risk. An evaluation of credit reputation therefore means that the lender must seek information from those who have provided financing to the borrower for other purposes or at other times. Typically, this information is obtained through a central credit bureau. In recent years, considerable controversy has surrounded these bureaus because the information they have collected has not always been accurate or relevant to the borrowing process; when included, it may injure the borrowers' reputations. As a result, borrowers now have the right to ask that all information about their credit be furnished to them and that they have an opportunity to correct mistakes. When adverse material remains, the borrowers can place letters of explanation with the records.

Borrowers who have never used credit or have used it only sparingly are sometimes in as difficult a position as those who have bad credit reputations. It is important therefore for borrowers who intend to use credit consistently in the real estate investing process to start the use of credit early and to maintain a good credit reputation. For example, borrowers who have resorted to bankruptcy because of a failure to meet certain obligations may have great difficulty obtaining later loans. At the same time, borrowers who have always paid cash and never subjected themselves to the discipline of loan repayments may be equally suspect.

The general rating system shown in Figure 2–1 is typical of those used by lenders. For example, in evaluating the borrower, the loan officer may be asked merely to make a check to indicate whether the credit reputation decreases risk or chance of loss, does not affect risk, or increases risk. Or, the loan officer may determine whether the borrower has a risk quality that warrants rejection of the loan.

Motivation.   Motivation is perhaps the single most important element in borrower risk analysis. A family with children which has been renting for some time and now needs more space that it can control and use according to family needs is probably the best form of risk, all other forms being equal. On the other hand, a young, newly married couple seeking a home only as a means of reducing their cost of living may be the most poorly motivated family in terms of repaying the loan. Motivation is complex and involves many considerations. For example, if a family is required to make a large down payment, does this motivate it to continue to repay the loan according to schedule? Might a family which has only a small amount invested have less concern about repaying the loan than one with a higher down payment?

Normally, motivation would relate to the need for the housing. A borrower who really needs the housing, or a borrower who is depending on the investment in order to earn the income, is probably the best borrower, i.e., the most strongly motivated. Motivation can be summarized simply as having a sufficient personal stake in the investment to want to repay it and having a reason for making the investment which necessitates continuous, perhaps early, repayment of the loan itself.

Stabilized Income.   Today's American family increasingly has more than one source of income. For example, the husband works, the wife works, and even some of the children work; all of them contribute to the family income. If the family has savings accounts, life insurance policies, or other forms of investment, the dividends or returns from these invest-ments are also a part of the income. If some family members are employed in industries that have overtime, there may be a considerable amount of overtime pay. Sales-related employment frequently produces regular bonuses.

The problem of the lender in evaluating income is to try to determine the average annual stabilized income a family is now receiving and is likely to receive over the period of the loan. Theoretically, housing expenses should not take more than 20 to 30 per cent of that stabilized income.

Recent legislation and court decisions have required that lenders give equal weight to the husband's income and the wife's income. In the past, the wife's income was usually discounted on the assumption that either she would not be working regularly or for very long, or she might become preg-nant and have to quit. Stabilized income therefore requires full and equal treatment of any earnings which the wife is contributing to family income.

Assets. Assets are considered important in borrower analysis for two reasons. First, assets can be used to produce additional funds in case in-come is interrupted and the family still has mortgage payments to make. Secondly, the accumulation of assets indicates a capacity on the part of the family to acquire things over time through some form of savings or periodic payment. Finally, assets are important because the lender will want to know what additional expenditures the family may have to make if it does acquire the property. For example, a newly formed family may have no furniture or other furnishings for the home. In evaluating their capacity to borrow, the lender must consider not only the loan but the other expendi-tures necessary to make the house livable. Either these expenditures can be considered independently of the loan, or the family can be encouraged to borrow enough funds to cover such things as new furniture, mechanical equipment, landscaping, or costs of providing additional improvements or rehabilitation to the housing.

Recent equal rights legislation is changing lenders' analyses of borrowers. Although practices are not standardized nationwide, "equal opportunity lenders" do not inquire about the marital status, the age, or the race of the borrower. Theoretically, all borrowers are evaluated on a common ground that gives an equal opportunity to secure the funding which the lenders have available. No borrowing is to be disapproved on the basis of the wife's income, or the sex, age, or race of the borrower. The information obtained from borrowers has been narrowed and, in an increasing number of cases, the questions which lenders ask are subject to review. Lenders must be prepared to prove that the information requested of the borrowers is pertinent to the lending decisions.

PROPERTY RISKS

Most lenders would put property risks secondary to borrower risks. Lenders are primarily interested in having loans repaid according to schedule and do not want to assume the risks or the costs of foreclosing on property in order to recover unpaid balances on loans. Typically, analysis of property risks is left to an appraiser, who is supposed to determine the market value of the property independently of any loan considerations. For this reason, appraisers are typically expected to be independent in their research and to have no role in determining whether a loan should or should not be made. Nor are appraisers supposed to be evaluated or compensated on the number of completed appraisals which result in approved loans. Considerable difficulty has arisen in the past because some lenders made appraisers a part of the loan process and evaluated the performance of appraisers on the basis of the loans which were produced as a result of the appraisals. Although this practice still exists to some extent today, on the whole it is condemned by reputable mortgage lenders.

Structural Qualities. A later chapter discusses in some detail the appraisal of a property for loan purposes. At this point, we are simply emphasizing some of the principal items which an appraiser would investigate. The type of construction, the durability of the house, its safety, its capacity for good family living—all are subsumed under structural qualities. Basically, the appraiser is asking two questions: "Were the materials used in this house of a good quality? Was the workmanship comparable to the materials?" A house with good materials but not adequately constructed may be less of a risk than if the reverse is true. Poor construction can usually be overcome, but poor materials present an impossible situation without considerable rehabilitation and renovation.

Functional Qualities. Functional analysis emphasizes the capacity of a house to meet family living requirements. Is the house arranged for privacy, for example? Is it possible to use the sleeping quarters without being annoyed by activities in the living quarters? Is the house arranged in such a way that traffic can flow through the house without interfering with normal daily functions? Is there adequate storage space? In other words, can the anticipated uses of this property be fulfilled satisfactorily, functionally, and economically?

Mechanical Equipment. Mechanical equipment includes refrigerators, stoves, freezers, air conditioning, clothes washing and drying equipment, electronic devices for clearing the air, alarm systems, and similar equipment which is intended to promote ease or safety in living. In some houses, mechanical equipment may account for almost 25 per cent of the value of the house. For this reason, the lender will want to know whether the equipment is working, whether it is of a capacity to meet the needs of the family, and whether it has been maintained in such a way that it can be expected to operate during the life of the loan. Typically, lenders will require that every item of equipment be identified in the loan agreement by name, serial number, model number, and manufacturer, and the loan will require that equivalent equipment be maintained on the property during the entire life of the loan. With the new emphasis on energy conservation, more and more lenders can be expected also to evaluate mechanical equipment in terms of its demands upon energy: will the energy cost be too high to warrant the use of the equipment, or will the equipment be so wasteful that it is a detriment to value and should not be used at all?

Architecture and Appearance.   These two items are probably the most subjective of any that appraisers have to consider in evaluating homes for financing purposes. Usually subjectivity is balanced against objectivity by comparing the architecture and general appearance of the home with other properties in the area. If the size, appearance, and architecture of the property seem to conform with the neighborhood, the property is usually given a high rating. On the other hand, if it is unique in some way, the appraiser is faced with the problem of determining whether the uniqueness adds to the value of the property and represents a new trend in the neighborhood, or whether it is so different as to warrant some kind of penalty in terms of loan value.

LOCATION RISKS

Appraisers have long considered the neighborhood of a property the principal determinant of its value. Certainly a good borrower who lives on a good property in a deteriorating neighborhood represents more risk than if the property and the borrower were in a better neighborhood. Neighborhood influence is such a strong determinant of the value of any property that location risks probably should receive almost the same weight as the borrower and the property. The indiscriminate evaluation of all properties because of a neighborhood characteristic has been roundly condemned and made illegal in many places. Lenders therefore can still consider neighborhood, but they cannot as a general rule refuse to make loans primarily because of neighborhood without evaluating the individual property and borrower.

Appearance of the Neighborhood.   The quickest clue as to the loan risk in a neighborhood in found in its appearance.   Are the properties maintained? Is there an absence of trash? Is there an absence of old cars, either along the street or in the lots? Do the houses appear to have been kept painted and repaired and do they look reasonably neat? Again, appearance is a subjective basis for evaluating a location, but it is the basis that borrowers use in deciding whether to buy in a particular neighborhood. Some of the most pioneering work in the evaluation of neighborhoods has been done by the Federal Housing Administration; the discussion in the remainder of this section follows some of the guidelines which the FHA has developed.

Age of Neighborhood and Location with Respect to City Growth. Neighborhoods pass through cycles. Typically, a neighborhood's age from its beginning to its maturity is about 25 to 40 years. At the end of its period of growth, the neighborhood may then stabilize and become a long-term good residential neighborhood or it may change from single-family to multi-family, commercial, or industrial, depending upon what is happening in the city. Older neighborhoods therefore are suspect unless there is clear evidence that they have stabilized into a particular kind of land use which enhances the value of the properties in the neighborhood.

Cities are in a constant process of growth and change. Some of the most rapid growth of cities occurred during the 1960's, but this growth seems to have slowed during the 1970's. Most of the growth took place in the suburbs. Because of their newness and their many kinds of public restrictions, suburbs typically were equipped with shopping centers, churches, good streets, lighting, etc. As a result, lenders tended to make the greatest number of loans in the suburbs, on the most favorable terms.

Shopping, Churches, and Other Amenities.   Three things are important to a family in choosing a neighborhood: access to jobs, access to schools, and access to shopping. Access can be thought of in terms of walking, short-distance driving, or public transportation.

Since most families have time for leisure, of almost equal importance in judging a neighborhood is access to churches, recreational sources, beaches and lakes, golf courses, and parks.

Inhabitants.   The quality of a neighborhood derives primarily from the people living in it. In the past, lenders tended to place heavy emphasis on homogeneity in a neighborhood: the families living in it were expected to be of the same race, religion, and income bracket. Legislation and court decisions have outlawed considerations of race and religion as bases for evaluating loans. Further, the question of whether homogeneity is really good when it is carried to excess has been raised. Lenders today tend to ask, "Who are the people living in the neighborhood and do they, as a group, have the qualities which will enhance property value during the period of the loan?"

Transportation. The energy crisis has brought new emphasis on evaluating neighborhoods with respect to access, preferably by public transportation, to important locations within the city. No longer can access be measured in terms of time or distance. It must be measured in terms of the amount of gasoline which will be used or the quality, costs, and convenience of the public transportation available.

Utilities and Services. When neighborhoods are created in areas in which utilities cannot be easily provided, many of the houses will be built with wells as the source of water and septic tanks as the means for sewage disposal. These may be owned and operated communally or independently. Most utilities and services provided on an independent basis will ultimately have to be consolidated and provided through publicly owned corporations. For these reasons, lenders will tend to discount areas which do not yet have access to public water, power, and sewage disposal. Since the cost of adding any of these is usually quite high, the value of a property will be adjusted in anticipation of the fact that the property owners will have to pay for these at some time in the future.

Taxes and Assessments. Although properties are supposed to be assessed uniformly throughout a city, so that owners of the same kinds of properties pay the same amount in tax bills, this practice is frequently not followed. Sometimes assessors find themselves so overloaded with work that instead of assessing regularly, they assess only as they are able to. This may mean that neighborhoods are underassessed or overassessed in comparison to the current market rates or to the way in which other neighborhoods are assessed. It is important, therefore, for the lender to determine what the levels of assessments are, how recently these assessments were made, the likelihood that the assessments will be changed, and the amount of property taxes resulting from the assessments and the operations of the city. Lenders will sometimes attempt to protect themselves against a potential loss caused by changes in taxes by requiring the borrower to pay monthly a small amount which is placed into a special account and used to pay taxes at the end of the year.

ECONOMIC BACKGROUND RISKS

The three risks mentioned above are typically those which a property owner can influence. For example, debts can be paid, the quality of a house can be improved, or a joint effort with neighbors can improve a neighborhood. But the risks described below are beyond the scope of the borrower and may be beyond the influence of the lender. Of these, the most important risks are the economic background risks: the lender analyzes the economic area within which loans are being made, to determine whether there will be continuous employment, stability in price levels, and other economic and business conditions which will guarantee that people can repay their loans according to schedule.

Industry Size. One of the most important elements in producing a solid economic base for an area is to have industry which is diversified. A large volume of manufacturing in a variety of industries is preferable to the dominance of one large manufacturer in the area. Lenders are inclined to make better loans in an area in which no single industry is so dominant that its decline would have a serious impact on the whole local economy. For example, in Detroit, which is so closely tied to the automobile industry, lenders must consider the impact of any possible change in automobile industry conditions upon any borrowers. The effects of dominance of a single industry are not peculiar to evaluation by lenders.

Industrial Diversification. The presence of many kinds of industries— manufacturing, assembling, mining—creates a diversity of sources of employment, which is as important as having large-scale industries that are not easily influenced by a small change in local economic conditions. Diversification insures that most of the population will be employed except during deep economic recessions.

Cyclical Trends. Some industries are subject to predictable cyclical change, either on a short- or a long-term basis. Lenders will want to know, therefore, whether the borrowers whom they are evaluating are subject to changes in employment and income because of cyclical industrial trends. In making loans where cycles are involved, the lender may want to shorten the loan, require more down payment, or compensate in other ways for predictable cyclical events during the period of the loan's existence.

Employment Trends. Consistently depressed economic areas have high unemployment rates as compared to the general economy. There is much discussion as to what is an appropriate unemployment rate, but most experts would say that an area which has only a 5 to 6 per cent unemploy-

ment rate over the long run is probably the best area in which to make
loans. High unemployment rates are usually found in economic areas
where the industries are obsolete or subject to wide fluctuation. Metropolitan centers which attract large numbers of unemployables also are
subject to high unemployment rates. However, unemployment rates can
be misleading. A general unemployment rate is less informative than an
unemployment rate which is related to industry types. It may be possible
therefore for a neighborhood to have an overall unemployment rate of 10
per cent and yet have many industries in which employment opportunities are available, especially if the industries are new or growing but not
of a sufficient size to influence changes in the local unemployment rate.

LOAN ADMINISTRATION RISKS

Loan administration risks are under the direct control of lenders, but
borrowers or even the property itself may create unanticipated problems
which will increase the risks or costs of administering a loan. The risks may
arise because the property is located in an area where the lender has no
other loans; visiting the property and checking on it may therefore become
difficult. The borrower may become unavailable as payments lapse or the
loan defaults. These are possible loan administration risks, but the five
elements discussed in the following sections are those on which lenders
place emphasis.

Accurate Record Keeping. Lenders prefer to have loans repaid in
level periodic payments, usually by a certain day of each month. Most
lenders set up their loan administration records on this basis. Such regu-
larity also permits programming of the loans on computers and the lender
obtains automatic records of payments and debts and automatic preparation
and mailing of any notices of payments due. The advent of computers has
reduced the risks associated with accurate record keeping. Nevertheless,
lenders find it necessary to conduct periodic sampling audits to determine
the extent to which errors may have been made or, more importantly,
whether some kind of fraud may be connected with the records.

Property Appraisal and Inspections. A property is appraised only at
the outset of a loan, but the lender will want to review the property from
time to time to be sure that it is being maintained in ways which protect
the investment. For this reason, the lender sets up a loan file which includes
the original appraisal and a periodic inspection plan. Lenders like to make
most of their loans in adjacent areas so that an inspector can visit several
properties on a single trip, thus reducing inspection costs.

Property File Information. A lender's file on a property includes the borrower's application, the lending agreement, the appraisal report, the title insurance and property insurance policies, and any other items which are necessary to administer the loan correctly and close it out according to schedule. The contents of property files may be regulated because most lenders are in supervised industries. For example, the property files of life

Disclosure/Settlement Statement

SETTLEMENT CHARGES		PAID FROM BORROWER'S FUNDS	PAID FROM SELLER'S FUNDS
SALES BROKER'S COMMISSION based on price $ @ %			
Total commission paid by seller Division of commission as follows:			
$ to			
$ to			
ITEMS PAYABLE IN CONNECTION WITH LOAN,			
Loan Origination fee %			
Loan Discount %			
Appraisal Fee to			
Credit Report to			
Lender's inspection fee			
Mortgage Insurance application fee to			
Assumption/refinancing fee			
ITEMS REQUIRED BY LENDER TO BE PAID IN ADVANCE,			
Interest from to @ $ /day			
Mortgage insurance premium for mo. to			
Hazard insurance premium for yrs. to			
yrs. to			
RESERVES DEPOSITED WITH LENDER FOR:			
Hazard insurance mo. @ $ /mo.			
Mortgage insurance mo. @ $ /mo.			
City property taxes mo. @ $ /mo.			
County property taxes mo. @ $ /mo.			
Annual assessments mo. @ $ /mo.			
mo. @ $ /mo.			
mo. @ $ /mo.			
mo. @ $ /mo.			

Fig. 2–2. Disclosure and truth-in-lending statements.

insurance companies, commercial banks, and savings and loan associations must conform to the regulations under which these lenders operate.

Loan Closing Information and Costs.   Recent legislation now requires lenders to provide full information on closing costs and closing activities. Figure 2–2 summarizes some of the information which must now be revealed to the borrower and kept as a part of the loan file. The information is

TITLE CHARGES:		
Settlement or closing fee to		
Abstract or title search to		
Title examination to		
Title insurance binder to		
Document preparation to		
Notary fees to		
Attorney's Fees to		
(includes above Items No.:		
Title insurance to		
(includes above Items No.:		
Lender's coverage $		
Owner's coverage $		
GOVERNMENT RECORDING AND TRANSFER CHARGES		
Recording fees: Deed $; Mortgage $; Releases $		
City/county tax/stamps: Deed $; Mortgage $		
State tax/stamps: Deed $; Mortgage $		
ADDITIONAL SETTLEMENT CHARGES		
Survey to		
Pest inspection to		
TOTAL SETTLEMENT CHARGES		

Notes: 1. Under certain circumstances the borrower and seller may be permitted to waive the 12-day period which must normally occur between advance disclosure and settlement. In the event such a waiver is made, copies of the statements of waiver, executed as provided in the regulations of the Department of Housing and Urban Development, shall be attached to and made a part of this form when the form is used as a settlement statement.

Fig. 2–2.   Continued.

Federal Truth-in-Lending Statement
(as part of Disclosure/Settlement Statement)

I. A. Cash price (contract sales price) $ _____

       1. Less any cash downpayment $ _____
       2. Less any trade-in $ _____
       3.   Total downpayment $ _____

    B. Equals unpaid balance of cash price $ _____

    C. Plus any other amounts financed:

       1. Property insurance premiums $ _____
       2. _____ $ _____
       3.   Total other amounts financed $ _____

    D. Equals unpaid balance $ _____

    E. Less any prepaid FINANCE CHARGES:

       1. Origination fee or points paid by borrower $ _____
       2. Loan discount or points paid by seller $ _____
       3. Interest from _____
                    (specify date)
           to _____ $ _____
                    (specify date)
       4. Mortgage guaranty insurance $ _____
       5. _____ $ _____
       6.   Total prepaid FINANCE CHARGE $ _____

    F. Equals amount financed $ _____

II. The FINANCE CHARGE consists of

    A. Interest *(simple annual rate of _____ %)* $ _____

    B. Total prepaid FINANCE CHARGE (I.E.6.) $ _____

    C. _____ $ _____

    D.   Total FINANCE CHARGE $ _____

III. A. The ANNUAL PERCENTAGE RATE on the amount financed is _____ %

    B. If the contract includes a provision for variation in the interest rate, describe _____
    _____

IV. The repayment terms are: _____
    _____

V. The FINANCE CHARGE begins to accrue on _____
                                 (specify date)

VI. In the event of late payments, charges may be assessed as follows: _____
    _____

VII. *(Use either A or B as appropriate)*

    A. Conditions and penalties for prepaying this obligation are _____
    _____

    B. Identification of method of rebate of unearned FINANCE CHARGE is _____

VIII. Insurance taken in connection with this obligation: _____

IX. The security for this obligation is _____
    _____

2. The Real Estate Settlement Procedures Act of 1974 (Public Law 93–533) requires use of a standard form for advance disclosure of settlement costs and to record actual charges incurred at settlement in all mortgage transactions involving federally related loans.

3. *Indicates a date, rate or amount that is estimated and may be subject to change.

Source: U. S. Department of Housing and Urban Development, "Settlement Costs and You" (Washington, D. C.: American Bankers Association, 1975).

Fig. 2–2. Continued.

useful to the lender in determining all of the costs connected with making a loan. These costs are amortized over the life of the loan, so that the actual profitability of the loan can be calculated. Lenders do not charge all of a loan's costs against the first years' payments because this would distort their actual average earnings on the loan.

Loan Servicing Costs. Loans have to be serviced, that is, borrowers must be notified, payments received, and properties inspected. The process of recording payments and providing notifications when they are not made according to schedule is costly and lenders are turning more and more to automated systems to accomplish these activities in an efficient manner. Unfortunately, few lenders have a reasonably accurate evaluation of what loan servicing costs really are. For example, in amortizing loan costs, part of the cost of the rent of the building and of other overhead expenses must be included.

INVESTMENT RISKS

The ultimate purpose in mortgage lending is to earn a return that is sufficient to cover the costs of managing the investment and of using other people's money, while yielding some profit to the investor for the risks undertaken. This is true for a home owner buying a house, an investor buying an apartment unit or income-producing property, or a lender making a mortgage loan. However, the risks which the lender faces are somewhat unique. Lenders must be concerned not only about the borrower, the property, and general conditions of the market, but about the combination of loans made and the yields they are producing both individually and overall. Investment risk analysis therefore requires that lenders monitor mortgage patterns, portfolio patterns, and reactions in the market to mortgage loans.

Mortgage Pattern. Three things are of special concern to lenders. First, when loans are made, lenders want to be sure that the value of the property which is pledged as security is maintained in a ratio that is favorable to the unpaid balance of the loan; that is, if the property were sold, after all costs of sale had been paid could the lender recover the money still owed? This would seem to require a considerable amount of forecasting on the part of the mortgage lender, since most mortgages are made for terms of anywhere from twenty to thirty years. However, most mortgages are paid off in eight to ten years, so mortgage lenders tend to concentrate on the first ten years of the anticipated life of a property. If the property promises to hold its value during this period, there is a better chance that it will maintain it during the rest of its life.

Mortgage Term.   The second concern for mortgage lenders is the property's continued value during the entire term of the mortgage. As we have mentioned, the first ten years of the life of a property are of primary concern, but since the life of a mortgage coincides approximately with the number of years in the life of a typical neighborhood, lenders will ask whether the neighborhood can sustain the property and whether the property's economic, functional, and physical qualities permit it to have some value during the entire life of the mortgage.

Housing Costs.   Lenders of mortgage loans are always concerned about the buyer's total costs of operating a house—the normal expenditures beyond the mortgage payments. If the buyer of a home finds that it costs more to own and operate the house than it would to rent an equivalent property, there may be an inclination to abandon the property. The introduction by the federal government of insured or guaranteed loans which permitted purchasers to move into properties with little or no down payment has produced a high risk of foreclosure. In our recent inflationary period, persons on limited income have found the rising costs of owning a house more than their incomes could accommodate. And so they frequently abandoned the houses. In 1974, for example, it was estimated that the FHA owned over 300,000 abandoned or foreclosed properties.

A general principle can be stated for all kinds of investment properties: The cost to the investor of owning a property and using it for designated purposes should be less than the costs of an equivalent investment or of another type of property. Any owner-investor wants a purchased property to earn a better return on an investment than would be yielded by renting an equivalent property. Comparative calculations are related to appraisal and to other considerations regarding a property. They are discussed in some detail in later chapters.

PORTFOLIO PATTERN

Mortgage investors like to maintain a mix of loans that will produce an average yield equal to the yield that can be earned on long-term funds under current market conditions. Since one-eighth to one-tenth of a typical mortgage portfolio is repaid each year, mortgage lenders have approximately that amount of funding, plus new funding, to invest each year. If they anticipate that mortgage rates may be going up, they will tend to hold the funds, put them in short-term investments, and wait until they can put them out at a higher rate. On the other hand, they may wish to make loans immediately in anticipation of a future drop in mortgage rates. This fluctuation in yield potentials on mortgages has given rise to the variable rate mortgage (VRM). More will be said about it in later chapters, but the principle of the VRM is that periodically the lender is allowed to change the mortgage rate to reflect a fluctuating cost of money. There are also some advantages to the consumer or borrower in that the VRM offers the opportunity of paying less on a loan if rates go down, and the borrower can always be sure that payments will never be more than the market rate if the rates go up.

An increasing number of mortgage lenders are putting their loan records on computers. When combined with computerized reports on monies received and loans repaid, these records allow daily measurement of the yields on an overall portfolio and lenders can determine the exact rate at which they should be loaning money. Some lenders, in fact, follow the principle that any monies received for mortgage loan purposes should be loaned out immediately at 1.5 to 2 per cent above the cost of that money. These lenders feel that a reasonable profit will result from maintaining such a spread between what the money costs and the rate at which it is loaned. There is, of course, considerable dispute among mortgage lenders as to what the percentage of the spread should be.

Diversification. In order to maintain a uniformly high yield, diversification is essential for most mortgage lenders. Diversification means that loans are made in different areas, on different kinds of properties, for varied terms of years, and with varied loan-to-value ratios. Obviously mortgage lenders also diversify in terms of risk. Since they wish to maximize their return, they will undoubtedly be making some loans at higher rates and then balancing them by making some loans at assured rates. For example, the Federal Housing Administration for a small fee will insure a lender against loss because of default on the part of the borrower. The lender must, however, accept a somewhat lower mortgage rate. It is this balancing of mortgage rate against risk which is at the heart of diversification.

All investors, including mortgage lenders, wish to earn a return on their investment. Usually they prefer to recover some portion periodically as loan payments are made or income is earned. Some would call this profit, but essentially it is an interest rate which compensates for the use of the money, for the risks taken, and for the management problems connected with the investment.

Availability of Funds. The flow of funds to mortgage lending is almost as unpredictable and erratic as fluctuations in the house-building industry. It is not clear whether the fluctuations in funds cause the volatility of the housing industry or whether the reverse is true. In any case, from year to year and even from month to month the lender is never precisely certain of the amount of money that will be available for making mortgage loans. The lender may make commitments for loans, but these commitments must always be predicated on the availability of funds. In times of acute money shortage, with money rates extremely high and savings flow very low, few mortgage loans are made. Availability of mortgage funds seems to be directly related to economic conditions and the confidence of the consumers in the general economy. We will speak more about this in the next chapter.

Market Reactions. Since mortgages are all tied to various kinds of properties, the mortgage lender is required to monitor two kinds of markets, at a minimum—money markets and real estate markets. If there are disastrous downturns in the real estate markets which make property valueless, the lender will not only be losing the security behind the loans but may face a considerable number of property foreclosures or voluntary reversions of the properties for the value of the unpaid balances on the loans. Money markets are particularly important because changes in money markets determine changes in the borrowing rate on mortgages.

There are at least five things which a mortgage lender will monitor in order to determine what is happening in the market: (1) *Property prices,* particularly for those properties on which the lender has mortgages. (2) *Money rates*—the costs and reyields on long-term and short-term investments. Typically the base rate for short-term funds is set by the prime rate for the best business borrowers and the long-term rate is set by U.S. bonds. (More about this later.) (3) *The value of the dollar.* As inflation continues and the value of the dollar becomes less or, to put it another way, it takes more and more dollars to buy the same thing, the particular advantage of owning real estate is that the prices of the real estate will escalate accordingly. Unfortunately the costs of owning and operating the real estate will also change, but usually at a rate which is below the price change. It is necessary therefore for a lender to monitor constantly the inflationary trends in the economy to make sure that the properties on which loans are held are maintaining their value and that the costs of owning and operating the properties do not exceed the price changes. (4) *Level of economic activity.* The value of property is directly related to the general level of the economy. The amount of funding available for mortgage lending is also related to the economy as is the decision of borrowers to borrow more funds to buy real estate or to continue to rent and not to borrow. There are particular parts of the real estate market and the business activity market which mortgage lenders learn to monitor. For example, the saving rate on a national basis is an important clue to the availability of funds. The number of building permits being issued indicates whether properties will be available for sale approximately eighteen months ahead of the date on which building permits are recorded. (Economic activity will be discussed in greater detail in later chapters.) (5) *Real estate activity.* In order to follow real estate markets, the lender looks not only at building permits but at the number of deeds and the number of mortgage loans recorded. Since there is a direct coincidence between the number of properties bought and sold, as reflected in deed recordings, and the volume of mortgage lending being made available, as indicated in mortgage loan recordings, these two items are most important to a lender. Their peculiarities, cyclical characteristics, etc., will be discussed at some length later.

TREATMENT OF RISKS IN MORTGAGE LENDING

Most mortgage lenders have elaborate plans, policies, and programs for determining the amount of risk they face in mortgage lending, how they will treat that risk, and what financial yields they can expect as a result of this risk treatment. We will be discussing lenders' risks at some length throughout the book. Figure 2–3 presents a summary of some of the more important protections that lenders employ for the treatment of risk. This list is not exhaustive, but it does indicate some of the basic principles which mortgage lenders follow to assure that their investments will perform according to plan. Basically a lender protects against a borrower by requiring a substantial down payment and making sure that the borrower understands exactly the terms of the loan and has the capacity to repay the loan according to schedule.

Property risks are compensated for by loaning only on properties which are well-built and well-located, and on which accurate appraisals have been completed.

Administrative risks are being protected against more and more through the use of elaborate computerized systems which provide the lender with a daily report on how many loans have been made, the amount of funds received, the types of loans made, the types of loans repaid, and the spread between costs of administering the loans and costs of the money loaned out.

SUMMARY

Borrower risks depend on the ability and willingness of the borrower to repay the lender. Ability to repay is largely dependent on stabilized income, i.e., income from all sources adjusted for the possibility that the

Protection against borrower risks

Require a down payment of not less than 10 per cent and preferably up to 25 per cent of purchase price.

Limit any loan agreement so that monthly payments on principal and interest do not exceed 20 per cent of the total family take-home pay.

Limit any loan to properties whose sale prices do not exceed 2 1/2 times the borrower's yearly income.

Require an acceptable credit report on the borrower.

Place emphasis on stability of income, stability of employment, and stability of family life.

Require amortized repayments of principal, interest, taxes, and insurance.

Limit loans to first Total Debts on first mortgages.

Require complete and accurate loan application form.

Keep loan payments below or equivalent to rental value of property being purchased.

Verify ownership of sufficient assets to serve as partial reimbursement in case of foreclosure.

Protection against property risks

Obtain properties located in desirable neighborhoods.

Secure prior loan commitments—FHA, VA, or conventional.

Spread loans among properties that are in various price categories.

Provide for accurate appraisals using at least FHA appraisal standards.

Provide for maintenance of the property over the life of the loan.

Limit loan terms so as not to exceed 20 years at most.

Aim for minimum taxes and other assessments on the property.

Maintain a favorable comparison of the subject property to similar properties in the market.

Protect the property adequately against adverse influences.

Protection against administrative risks

Adjust loan terms so that all loans will not become due within the same period.

Provide in the loan agreement for automatic, amortized repayments.

Provide flexibility of terms for good credit risks.

Require higher down payments, shorter terms, higher interest for poor credit risks.

Organize loan repayments so that loans will be repaid well before the end of the life of the property.

Scatter loans over various sections of the city.

Provide for periodic inspections of the property over the life of the loan.

Provide for automatic payment of taxes and insurance during the life of the loan. Make record keeping automatic.

Approach loan analysis with a systematic plan.

Fig. 2–3. Treatment of risks in mortgage lending.

income from each source will be interrupted or terminated. Ability to repay is also indicated by assets, since assets help to bridge periods when income flows are interrupted. The assets accumulated by a family also give an indication of willingness to repay since they indicate a capacity or incapacity to acquire things over time through savings or periodic payment. The credit reputation of the borrower and the borrower's reasons for wanting the property also indicate willingness to repay.

The lender undertakes the difficult task of evaluating the quality of the property which serves as ultimate security for the loan. This involves evaluation of structural soundness, functional quality, the quality of mechanical equipment, and architectural quality. The age of the property gives one indication of quality, but the way it has been maintained can be more important. Features unique to a particular property are hard to evaluate: Do they increase or decrease value? Is there a market for these characteristics?

The lender must also evaluate the economic environment, a problem which is discussed at greater length in Part V of this book. This involves studying the industrial structure of the local area and the business cycles, past and future, for the country as a whole. The vulnerability of local industry to national recessions is an important source of concern to lenders. An area which depends heavily on one kind of industry, such as the production of automobiles, can present problems for lenders in the event of an economic recession.

QUESTIONS

1. Discuss the pros and cons of placing primary reliance on the buyer versus the property, to assure loan repayments.
2. Why is each of the following important in evaluating the borrower? (a) Credit reputation, (b) motivation, (c) stabilized income, (d) assets.
3. Indicate specifically what to look for in each of the following items associated with property risks in mortgage lending: (a) structural qualities, (b) functional qualities, (c) mechanical equipment, (d) architecture and appearance.
4. What kinds of evaluations of neighborhoods might be considered discriminatory for mortgage lending purposes?
5. What should be adjacent to a home to make the home a desirable mortgage loan security?

3

THE GENERAL ECONOMY
AND REAL ESTATE
FINANCING

Chapters 1 and 2 gave an overview of the process of real estate financing; this chapter returns for a more detailed study of the various subjects that were introduced in the first two chapters, especially the relationship between the general economy and the flows of funds into and out of mortgage capital markets.

Mortgage capital markets are a subsector of larger general capital markets, and the funds which flow into and out of the mortgage markets are determined by the general strength of the economy and the demands for and uses of funds in other capital markets. To gain some perspective on the importance of mortgage financing in the general economy and some understanding of how to use general economic data to anticipate the uses and sources of mortgage capital, let us examine the system of money flows in the general economy.

MONEY FLOWS IN THE ECONOMY

The relationships among general economic activity, the availability of mortgage funds, and real estate market activities are presented in a simplified version in Figure 3–1. Let us look at that diagram briefly. Remember that it is a simplified diagram which places emphasis on mortgages and real estate markets.

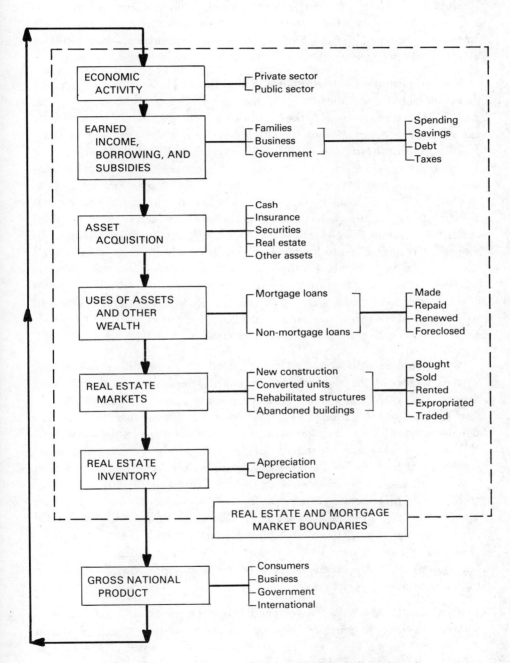

Fig. 3–1. The economy and money and mortgage market flows.

Economic Activity. Economic activity in the United States is generally divided into the activities of the private sector, which includes private businesses of all sizes and their consumers, and the activities of the public sector, which is essentially the federal, state, county, and local governments. Both sectors produce employment which yields income.

Earned Income, Borrowing, and Subsidies. The income produced by economic activity together with the money which can be borrowed by all sectors of the economy and the subsidies which are usually provided by government but may be provided by consumers or business are used by families, business, and government to carry on their daily activities. The flows of money with which we are concerned are spent usually for housing, clothing, recreation, capital investments, and similar items. Savings include deposits in financial institutions, purchases of life insurance, and the acquisition of various tangible assets. Some of the money which is spent or saved is derived through the creation of debt or the borrowing from others. Obviously, it is impossible to borrow from someone who has not accumulated savings, so debt is frequently the other side of the savings slope. Finally, income is used for the payment of taxes at all levels. Typically, a family may save up to approximately 10 per cent of its income, spend another 10 to 40 per cent for taxes, and use the remainder for other kinds of spending. When spending begins to outrun savings, debt is created.

Asset Acquisition and Use. The result of all spending is that the various sectors of the economy, but primarily the household sector, have assets which consist of cash, insurance (life insurance and property insurance), securities of various kinds, real estate, and other assets. We shall be concentrating on real estate acquired by the private and public sectors.

How are these assets used, particularly the cash, savings, and other wealth apart from the real estate? Assets and other wealth can be used to make mortgage loans or non-mortgage loans (automobile loans, personal credit, and similar debt-creating activities). As the economy prospers, loan activity tends to increase in volume so that assets and other wealth are created by the extent to which loans are made, repaid, renewed, or foreclosed. Foreclosure here means simply that an asset is transferred from someone who is trying to acquire it to someone who provided the funds for the attempt at acquisition.

Real Estate Markets. Assets and other wealth flow in considerable amounts to the real estate markets, which are a primary source of wealth for families, for business, and for government. As a result of the flow of these funds, a number of things happen in the real estate markets: new construction is begun; units are changed to different kinds of uses; structures are rehabilitated so that they are more economic in use; or buildings may be abandoned. To the extent to which units are abandoned, assets and other wealth are decreased. To the extent to which the other activities occur, assets are increased. Once the units have been acquired, they can be rented or sold; they can be bought by others; they can be traded or even expropriated. Expropriation involves the acquisition of a real estate asset through a legal process, when the public purpose for which it is to be used is judged more important than the private purpose of its present use.

Real Estate Inventory and GNP. From all of this real estate market activity a real estate inventory is created. Appreciation or depreciation of that inventory is measured in terms of continued interest in the real estate and mortgage markets. As the real estate inventory changes and is used, funds from this economic activity flow into the gross national product (GNP), which consists of the goods and services produced by consumers, business, government, and international transactions. This, in turn, creates a given level of economic activity and starts the cycle over again.

In the diagram, a dotted line indicates the elements with which we will be particularly concerned in real estate financing. We recognize that general economic activity has a considerable influence on what happens to mortgage markets and the flows in those markets, but we are not going to be concerned with these things in this text.

DEBT AND ECONOMIC ACTIVITY

The importance of debt in promoting economic activity can be judged from Figure 3–2. Since 1900 the fluctuations and general increase in gross national product have coincided very closely with the creation of new debt. Interestingly, in that 75-year period, debt as a ratio to the gross national product has not increased to any great extent. Depression periods clearly create a need for debt, but, except for the 1930's, debt as a ratio to gross national product has risen from an average of about 2½ to a little more than 3.

Does one sector of the economy owe more than it should so that if this sector were to collapse because of debt, the entire economy would be threatened? From the analysis in Figure 3–3 we learn that households owned approximately 39 per cent of the debt, business firms 9 per cent, governments 13 per cent, and financial institutions 39 per cent. In other words, debt is created because of activities by households and financial institutions. On the other hand, households owed only 16 per cent of the total

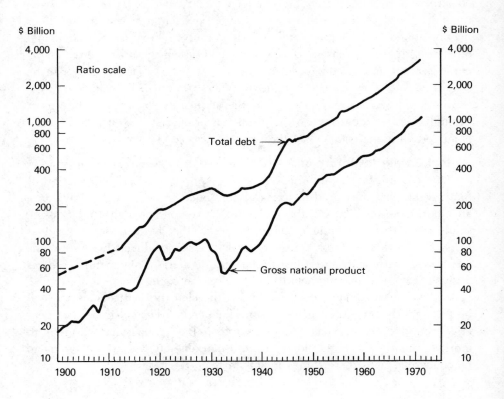

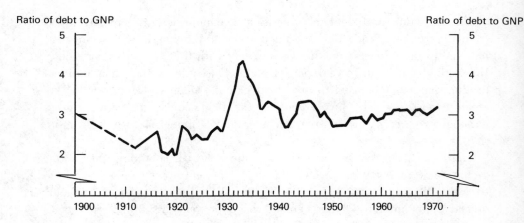

Source: Federal Reserve Bank of Chicago, *Two Faces of Debt* (October 1972), p. 26.

Fig. 3–2. Growth of debt and economic activity.

Total Debt in a Typical Year

Total Debt Owned	100%	Total Debt Owed	100%
By households	39%	By households	16%
By business	9	By business	22
By governments	13	By governments	25
By financial institutions	39	By financial institutions	37

Debt in the Household Balance Sheet

Total Debt Owned by Households	100%	Total Debt Owed by Households	100%
Owed by other households	1%	To other households	3%
Owed by business	6	To business	7
Owed by governments	21	To federal government (mortgages)	6
Deposits in financial institutions	72	To financial institutions	84

Source: Same as Figure 3–2, at p. 00.

Fig. 3–3.   Debt in the balance sheet of the economy.

debt, business 22 per cent, governments 25 per cent, and financial institutions 37 per cent. Households therefore provide a disproportionate amount of the money used for the creation of debt, as compared to the amount of debt they use for their own purposes. And financial institutions are overwhelmingly the key intermediaries in creating and owning debt.

On a household balance sheet in a typical year, the debt owned would be in the form of mortgages, promissory notes, or other commitments. Figure 3–3 shows that 1 per cent of the debts households own is owed to them by other households; 6 per cent is owed by business, 21 per cent by governments, and 72 per cent by financial institutions. Clearly then, households own debt by putting their money in financial intermediaries which then make it available to business, to government, and to other households. This again underlines the importance of financial institutions in money flows.

Of the debts owed by households, 3 per cent is owed to other households, 7 per cent to business, 6 per cent to the federal government (primarily in the form of mortgages), and 84 per cent to financial institutions in the form of mortgages, consumer loans, automobile loans, and furniture loans.

From this analysis it becomes clear that economic activity rests on the creation and use of debt and that the bringing together of those who wish to borrow money and those who have money to lend is accomplished primarily through financial institutions' acting as intermediaries.

GNP AND CREDIT MARKETS—A FORECAST

All of the previous analysis is essentially historic in character. The question is, can we expect these relationships to continue into the future. In order to determine this, the Federal Reserve System has created an elaborate system of analysis which is labeled Sources and Uses of Funds. Each month a report on the flow of funds in the economy is issued, and every quarter the flows of these funds are summarized. Some of these forms of analyses are presented at the end of the chapter; at this point it is sufficient that we review the material provided in Tables 3–1 through 3–4.

From an examination of Table 3–1 we find that in the period from 1955 to 1980 the gross national product is estimated to have increased by over 400 per cent, from $438 billion to $1,908 billion ($1.9 trillion). Much of this increase has been inflationary because, in terms of 1968 dollars, the increase is from $553 billion to $1.3 trillion or about two and one-half times. This comparison of real and current dollars suggests, then, that from 1968 to 1980 the increase in dollars due essentially to inflation is about 37 per cent.

Will this increase produce any substantial change in the real estate markets? Section B of Table 3–1, item 4, says that 5.1 per cent of the gross national product was spent annually for residential investment in 1955–1959 but this will drop to 3.7 per cent by 1980. If this is true, less mortgage money will probably be needed from the total gross national product to support residential markets. Section D, item 2, shows that personal savings are going to decline as a percentage of the gross national product. Since most funding for residential markets comes from personal savings, we can conclude that with the decline in residential construction there should be an adequate amount of savings.

Should we be worried about the 1980 period relative to the 1966–1970 period? Residential construction is scheduled to increase as a percentage of GNP while personal savings decline. Will this squeeze the mortgage markets? Probably not, since a similar relationship between savings and residential construction (both as a percentage of GNP) was observed in the 1961–1965 period.

Another way of anticipating where there will be a sufficient flow of funds to real estate markets is by examining mortgages as a percentage of the net borrowing in credit markets (Table 3–2). Housing mortgages in 1955 to 1959 represented about 2.7 per cent of the gross national product and this percentage changed very little between 1955 and 1970. There was a small decline in the 1966–1970 period, but by 1980 the typical percentage expected to prevail is about 2.6.

Table 3-1. GNP and Its Disposition, 1955-1980

	Annual Averages			
	1955-1959	1961-1965	1966-1970	1980
A. *Total GNP:*				
1. Current dollars (billions)	$438	$598	$863	$1,908
2. 1968 dollars (billions)	553	679	854	1,389
3. Implicit deflator (1968 = 100)	79.1	87.9	100.8	137.4
B. *Per cent distribution of expenditures:*	100.0%	100.0%	100.0%	100.0%
1. Personal consumption	64.1	63.6	62.3	61.4
2. Gross private domestic investment:	15.6	14.8	14.9	15.2
3. Nonresidential fixed	9.8	9.5	10.6	10.6
4. Residential	5.1	4.3	3.3	3.7
5. Inventories	.7	1.0	1.0	.8
6. Net exports	.7	1.1	.4	*
7. Federal govt. goods and services	11.3	10.7	10.9	9.6
8. State and local govt. goods and services	8.4	9.9	11.5	13.8
C. *Per cent distribution of income:*	100.0%	100.0%	100.0%	100.0%
1. Labor income	57.5	57.8	59.7	61.3
2. Proprietors' and rental income	13.5	11.6	10.0	7.2
3. Profits plus IVA[1]	10.6	10.2	9.6	10.2
4. Net interest	1.3	2.3	3.2	3.2
5. Total national income	82.9	82.0	82.4	81.9
6. Capital consumption allowance	8.3	8.8	8.6	8.4
7. Other charges[2]	8.6	9.8	9.6	9.8
8. Statistical discrepancy	.1	− .1	− .2	− .1
D. *Gross savings and investment (per cent of GNP):*				
1. Total private savings:	15.9%	15.8%	15.7%	15.3%
2. Personal savings	4.5	3.9	4.7	4.0
3. Undistributed profits and IVA	3.1	3.0	2.5	2.9
4. Capital consumption allowances	8.3	8.8	8.6	8.4
5. U. S. Govt. surplus	.1	− .3	− .5	− .1
6. State and local govt. surplus	− .3	.1	*	*
7. Statistical discrepancy	.1	− .1	− .2	− .1
8. Gross investment (1 + 5 + 6 + 7 = 9 + 10):	15.7	15.4	15.0	15.1
9. Gross private domestic investment	15.6	14.8	14.9	15.2
10. Net foreign investment	.1	.6	.1	*
E. *Other items (per cent of GNP or ratio):*				
1. Disposable personal income (DPI)	70.0%	69.1%	68.7%	67.0%
2. Business gross internal funds[3]	11.4	11.8	11.1	11.3
3. Excess of private investment over internal funds[4]	4.2	3.0	3.8	3.8
4. Personal taxes/personal income	11.9	12.5	14.1	14.4
5. Corporate profit tax rate	45.0	43.2	44.0	44.0
6. Personal saving/DPI	6.4	5.7	6.8	6.0
7. Unemployment rate	5.0	5.8	3.9	4.0

[1] Inventory Valuation Adjustment (IVA) accounts for value changes from inflation and other sources.
[2] Mainly indirect business taxes.
[3] Line D-3 plus line D-4.
[4] Line B-2 less line E-2.

Source: "Long-Term Prospects for Housing Finance—A Projection to 1980," Stephen P. Taylor, Chief, Flow of Funds and Savings Section, Division of Research and Statistics, Federal Reserve Board; a staff paper.

Table 3-2. Net Borrowing in Credit Markets, 1955-1980

	Annual Averages			
	1955-1959	1961-1965	1966-1970	1980
Total funds borrowed in credit markets by non-financial sectors, excluding corporate equities ($ billion)	$35.9	$58.2	$84.4	$161.7
A. *As per cent of GNP*:				
1. Total funds raised:	8.2%	9.7%	9.8%	8.5%
2. U. S. Govt.[1]	.3	.9	.9	.2
3. Other:	7.9	8.8	8.9	8.2
4. Municipals	1.1	1.0	1.0	1.2
5. Corporate and foreign bonds	1.1	.9	1.7	1.1
6. Housing mortgages	2.7	2.9	2.0	2.6
7. Other mortgages and loans	3.0	4.0	4.1	3.3
8. Sector totals	7.9	8.8	8.9	8.2
9. State and local govts.[2]	1.2	1.0	1.1	1.3
10. Households	3.7	3.9	3.0	3.0
11. Nonfinancial business	2.7	3.3	4.5	3.9
12. Foreign	.3	.5	.3	*
13. Memo: corporate equities not included above	.5	.2	.3	.6
B. *As per cent of total funds borrowed*:				
1. Total funds borrowed:	100.0%	100.0%	100.0%	100.0%
2. U. S. Govt.[1]	3.6	9.5	9.4	2.8
3. Other:	96.4	90.5	90.6	97.2
4. Municipals	13.9	10.2	10.3	13.8
5. Corporate and foreign bonds	13.0	9.0	17.7	13.5
6. Housing mortgages	33.1	29.9	20.5	30.7
7. Other mortgages and loans	36.3	41.3	42.1	39.1
8. Sector totals:	96.4	90.5	90.6	97.2
9. State and local govts.[2]	14.2	10.7	10.8	15.0
10. Households	45.6	40.2	30.4	35.3
11. Nonfinancial business	33.3	34.2	45.9	46.3
12. Foreign	3.2	5.4	3.5	.6
13. Memo: corporate equities not included above	6.6	1.9	3.2	7.3

[1] Includes budget agency issues but excludes issues by federally sponsored credit agencies that are not included in the budget.
[2] Includes loans from U. S. Govt.

Source: Federal Reserve Bank of Chicago, *Two Faces of Debt* (October 1972).

Looking at it another way, of all the funds borrowed, housing mortgages in 1955 accounted for about 33 per cent, declined gradually to 20.5 per cent in the 1966–1970 period, and are expected to increase again by 1980 to about 30 per cent of all funds borrowed. Summarizing, we can say that mortgage financing has historically been an important part of the gross

Table 3-3. Sources of Credit Demand (Percentage of GNP)

	Annual Averages			
	1955–1959	1961–1965	1966–1970	1980
A. *Housing*				
1. 1–4-family unit construction	4.51	3.18	2.28	2.25
2. Net increase in home mortgage debt	2.47	2.34	1.53	1.75
3. Net borrowing/construction (%)	55%	74%	67%	78%
4. Multifamily unit construction	.37	.91	.81	1.31
5. Net increase in multifamily mortgages	.23	.56	.48	.85
6. Net borrowing/construction (%)	62%	62%	59%	65%
B. *Nonresidential business*[1]				
7. Business internal funds	9.57	9.90	9.33	9.49
8. Capital outlays	9.88	9.74	10.87	10.69
9. Excess of outlays over internal funds	.31	−.16	1.54	1.20
10. Net funds raised, including corporate equities[2]	3.01	2.91	4.33	3.66
11. Funds raised/outlays (%)	30%	30%	40%	34%
C. *State and local governments*				
12. NIA surplus	−.30	.13	−.02	*
13. Less: transfers to retirement funds	.36	.45	.55	.65
14. Surplus after transfer	−.66	−.32	−.56	−.65
15. Financial asset acquisitions, net	.50	.72	.50	.62
16 Net funds raised in credit markets	1.16	1.04	1.06	1.27
D. *U. S. Government*				
17. NIA surplus	.06	−.32	−.50	−.07
18. Financial asset acquisitions, net	.35	.60	.42	.17
19. Net funds raised in credit markets[3]	.29	.92	.92	.24
E. *Other credit*				
20. Consumer durables	9.22	9.10	9.43	9.42
21. Consumer credit	.88	1.11	.85	.92
22. Consumer credit/durables (%)	9.50%	12.20%	9.10%	9.80%
23. Other domestic borrowing[4]	.39	.46	.59	.35
24. Foreign borrowing in U. S.	.26	.52	.34	.05
Total funds raised in credit markets by non-financial borrowers, including equities (2 + 5 + 10 + 16 + 19 + 21 + 23 + 24)	8.70	9.86	10.10	9.10

NIA = National Income Accounts.

[1] Nonfinancial business, including farm and nonfarm noncorporate.
[2] In Table 3-2, equities are excluded from total borrowing and shown separately on line 13.
[3] Borrowing from the public by the Treasury and agencies in the unified budget. Excludes borrowing from trust funds, which are consolidated in these tables, and borrowing by sponsored credit agencies.
[4] Policy loans to households and mortgage and bank loan credit to nonprofit organizations.

Source: Same as Table 3-2.

Table 3–4. Housing Expenditures in 1980

		1970	1980	Annual Rate of Growth (%)
	Private nonfarm housing:			
	1-to-4-family structures			
1.	New units (000)[1]	850[2]	1,340	4.65
2.	Average total outlays[3]	$22,700	$31,640	3.38
3.	Outlays for new units ($ billion)[4]	19.3	42.4	8.17
4.	Add: Rehabilitations ($ billion)	–	.6	
5.	Total outlays: $ billion	19.3	43.0	8.10
6.	Per cent of GNP	1.98%	2.25%	
	Multifamily structures			
7.	New units (000)[1]	500[5]	980	6.95
8.	Average total outlays[3]	$18,000	$24,900	3.30
9.	Outlays for new units ($ billion)[4]	9.0	24.4	10.50
10.	Add: Rehabilitations ($ billion)	–	.6	
11.	Total outlays:			
	$ billion	9.0	25.0	11.10
12.	Per cent of GNP	.92%	1.31%	
13.	Farm housing ($ billion)	0.6	0.4	−4.00
14.	Nonhousekeeping units ($ billion)	1.4	2.7	6.78
	Total residential construction:			
15.	$ billion	30.4	71.1	8.84
16.	Per cent of GNP	3.12%	3.73%	

[1] Excludes rehabilitations and mobile homes.
[2] Starts from mid-November 1969 to mid-November 1970.
[3] Outlays on following line, from NIA data, divided by new units on preceding line.
[4] Includes additions and alterations, brokerage and settlement fees, and other charges.
[5] Starts from September 1969 through August 1970.

Source: Same as Table 3–2.

national product and the creation of debt and that no significant changes in the historical trend are anticipated. This is the only assumption which is realistic, since there is little evidence to support any other assumption.

CONSTRUCTION AND REAL ESTATE MARKETS

Although real property is presumed to account for about two-thirds of the national wealth, annual residential and nonresidential construction does not account for a considerable portion of the gross national product activities. Some measure of the importance of construction can be found in Table 3–3. Notice that the basic unit of construction in the real estate market is the one-to-four-family dwelling unit. From 1955 to 1959 the net increase in home mortgage debt, a funds flow which is closely related to new housing construction (see Chapter 21), was 4.5 per cent of GNP. Since then, this percentage has been declining so that by 1980 it is expected to equal less than half of the 1955–1959 average. This means that the need for home mortgages is going to decline relative to GNP even though borrowing for construction will increase to approximately 78 per cent.

What does all this mean? It means that those who follow capital markets and their impact on construction believe that home buyers will rely more heavily on mortgage financing and less on equity. If they are right, home buyers will make smaller down payments and allow less equity to build up in their homes. However, people will not be able to afford as much home construction as in the past.

Inflation, the high cost of land, property taxes, and a multitude of other factors are expected to encourage more and more multifamily unit construction. Much of this will be for rent, but a good portion of it will also represent condominium construction. What the experts anticipate by way of change can be seen from Table 3–3, section A, item 4, multifamily unit construction. In 1955 to 1959 this accounted for approximately .37 per cent of the gross national product as a source of credit demand. But notice how rapidly that is expected to increase, and how consistently. By 1980 the demand for funds for multifamily unit construction is expected to more than quadruple. This will mean a corresponding net increase in multifamily mortgages, but notice that borrowing for the construction of multifamily mortgages is expected to equal only about two-thirds of the construction cost. Will there then be less real estate market activity?

Although Table 3–3 does not emphasize it, a considerable portion of outlays which business is expected to make will be for office buildings, industrial properties, and other kinds of real estate which are necessary for the operations of business. Business capital outlays have always constituted, in terms of credit demand, about 10 per cent of the gross national product; this ratio is expected to continue through 1980. Businesses can then be expected to invest in all kinds of nonresidential real estate. But notice also, in section B of Table 3–3, that corporations are not expected to raise any substantial amount of their funds through the issuance of corporate securities. This would suggest that borrowing by business for real estate purposes is going to continue as a fact of real estate and construction markets into the future.

Table 3–4 gives us a little better insight into how households will be functioning in future mortgage markets. The disturbing prediction is made that the average total outlay on a one-to-four-family house is expected to increase from about $22,700 in 1970 to about $32,000 in 1980. If the typical family were still investing approximately twice its annual income in housing, family incomes would have to increase to about $16,000 in 1980. Since family incomes hover at only about $12,000, a substantial increase in family income would be required in a brief period of time. It is more likely that families will be spending more of their income for housing—two and one-half to three times instead of twice its income. Where today it spends between 10 and 15 per cent of its income for shelter, in 1980 it will be spending between 15 and 30 per cent. All of this suggests again that borrowing will continue to be an important part of any real estate construction activity for residential units.

The same trends can be seen in the multifamily market. Average cost outlays are projected to increase a little less (at a 3.3 per cent annual rate instead of 3.38 per cent) from about $18,000 to almost $25,000 and the outlays for new units to increase from $9 billion to more than $24 billion. An interesting figure which may be underestimated is the prediction for rehabilitation of single-family and multifamily units. Although the table shows it increasing by only a small amount by 1980, if inflation prevails and if the costs of new buildings rise as a result of energy crises and other matters, families will turn more to existing structures and put money into them rather than into construction of new, more expensive housing. If this should occur, mortgage lending will have to concentrate on rehabilitation–conversion–modernization loans.

The bottom line in this analysis says that in 1970 residential construction accounted for about 3.12 per cent of the gross national product. In 1980 it will still account for only about 3.73 per cent.

THE TWO SIDES OF DEBT

Funds for mortgage lending come primarily from the financial sectors: savings and loan associations, commercial banks, mutual savings banks, and insurance companies. Households and government are presumed to be the nonfinancial sector of the economy. If the trends we have discussed so far prevail, what is likely to happen? In 1954 all housing mortgages outstanding equaled 24.2 per cent of GNP and 30 per cent (24.2/80.8) of debt owed by other than the U. S. Government (Table 3–5). Housing mortgages are expected to increase to more than 38 per cent of GNP by 1980. This increase reflects inflation as well as a real increase in the construction markets. Other mortgages and loans are expected to increase by about 50 per cent over the 1954 levels. The net result will be that where in 1954 housing mortgages constituted 16.9 per cent of the total debt, by 1980 they will account for 27 per cent, and other mortgages and loans will increase from 21.3 per cent to 33.4 per cent.

Table 3-5. Debt of Nonfinancial Sectors, 1954–1980
(Amounts Outstanding at Year End)

		1954	1959	1965	1970	1980
Total credit market debt owed by non-financial sectors:						
Current dollars		$525	$704	$1,032	$1,450	$2,730
A. *As per cent of GNP*:						
1.	Total debt	143.9%	145.6%	150.7%	148.5%	143.2%
2.	U. S. Government[1]	63.2	49.2	38.3	30.9	21.7
3.	Other	80.8	96.4	112.4	117.6	121.5
4.	Municipals	11.1	13.6	14.6	14.7	16.4
5.	Corporate and foreign bonds	14.7	15.9	15.8	18.5	18.8
6.	Housing mortgages	24.2	30.5	35.9	34.1	38.6
7.	Other mortgages and loans	30.7	36.5	46.1	50.3	47.7
8.	Sector debt totals	80.8	96.4	112.4	117.6	121.5
9.	State and local govts.[2]	11.3	13.8	15.1	15.2	17.0
10.	Households	32.2	41.1	48.7	47.3	47.8
11.	Nonfinancial business	32.8	37.2	42.9	50.0	53.1
12.	Foreign	4.5	4.4	5.7	5.2	3.6
B. *As per cent of total debt*:						
1.	Total debt	100.0%	100.0%	100.0%	100.0%	100.0%
2.	U. S. Government	43.9	33.8	25.4	20.8	15.2
3.	Other	56.1	66.2	74.6	79.2	84.8
4.	Municipals	7.7	9.3	9.7	9.9	11.4
5.	Corporate and foreign bonds	10.2	10.9	10.5	12.5	13.1
6.	Housing mortgages	16.9	21.0	23.8	23.0	27.0
7.	Other mortgages and loans	21.3	25.0	30.6	34.0	33.4
8.	Sector debt totals	56.1	66.2	74.6	79.2	84.8
9.	State and local govts.[2]	7.8	9.5	10.0	10.2	11.9
10.	Households	22.4	28.2	32.3	31.8	33.4
11.	Nonfinancial business	22.8	25.6	28.5	33.6	37.1
12.	Foreign	3.1	3.0	3.8	3.5	2.5

[1] Includes budget agency issues but excludes issues by federally sponsored credit agencies that are not included in the budget.
[2] Includes debt owed to U. S. Govt.

These projections reinforce the conclusions made previously about trends in construction and mortgage markets: Housing mortgages outstanding should increase faster than other mortgages as less equity is put into one-to-four-family houses. The summary in Figure 3-4 emphasizes that debt consists of two parts: investment or the sources of funds and consumption or the uses of funds. The figure provides a basis for analysis of the Federal Reserve reports on sources and uses of funds. For example, consumers acquire money, income, or assets through earnings, through savings, through gifts or other forms of non-earned income, and through transfer

Sources	Uses

Consumers

Earned income	Spending/Investing
Savings—interest	Housing
Non-earned income	Household goods
Transfer payments	Mortgage payments
Sale of assets	Securities
Borrowing	Spending/Consuming

Food Recreation
Clothing Education
Savings (acquisition of assets)
Checking Taxes
Deposits Insurance
Early retirement of debt

Business

Depreciation	Wages
Sales	Raw materials
Goods	Services
Services	Dividend payments
Short-term borrowing	Increase in assets
Stocks and bonds (long-term borrowing)	Decrease in liabilities
Sale of assets	

Government

Taxes	Equipment
Income and other	Services and purchases
Social taxes	Transfer payments
Security sales	Temporary deposits
Goods/services sales	Purchase of land or buildings
Manufactured money—gold	
Sale of public lands, buildings, or equipment	

Financial Sector

Savings—long term	Lending
Stock sales	Acquisition of securities
Bond sales	Operations
Earned income	Investment
Non-earned income	
Short-term deposits	
Business	
Government	
Consumers	

Fig. 3—4. Basic assumptions—sources and uses of funds.

payments (money received from social security or insurance). Income is transferred from one sector of the economy to another without any necessary relationship between what the sector has done to get that money and what it intends to use it for. Consumers use their money in spending and then investing. (In the Federal Reserve accounting system, purchases of substantial family assets such as refrigerators, stoves, mechanical equipment, and automobiles are considered part of the investing process. Gross national product treats them as part of the consumption process.) Through spending and investing, consumers acquire housing, household goods, mortgage payments, and securities; they also fulfill their needs for food, clothing, and recreation. But consumers also save part of their money through checking accounts, deposits in various kinds of institutions, taxes, and insurance. Taxes are considered to be savings in the sense that payments to the government may later result in social security payments, medical insurance payments, or similar benefits (the transfer payments mentioned above).

Study the other categories in Figure 3–4—where money comes from and how it is used. It will be helpful in understanding and forecasting mortgage money markets.

THE MORTGAGE MARKET AS A SUBMARKET

We wish to emphasize that mortgage markets are a minor part of the total economy of the United States. Innumerable happenings within the economy will affect mortgage markets, but many activities occurring in mortgage markets may have little impact on the total economy. For example, in 1973 when financing of construction was a problem business loan demand increased to more than $20 billion between January and December. The strong loan demand brought money market rates up considerably so that, from early 1972 to the end of 1973, the prime rate on the best kinds of business loans increased from about 4½ per cent to almost 10 per cent. The short-term borrowing by the Treasury on three-month bills went from about 3 per cent to almost 9 per cent. In order to get money, banks competed strongly for short-term certificates of deposits so that on large certificates of deposit they were paying as much as 10 per cent or more in 1973 as compared to about 3 or 4 per cent in 1972.

In the meantime, what happened in mortgage markets? As their deposits began to decline thrift institutions provided fewer and fewer commitments for mortgage lending. In the early part of 1972 they were committing about $28 billion for mortgages; by the end of 1972 that amount had declined to slightly more than $15 billion. Housing markets dropped sub-stantially and housing starts, which had an annual rate of 2.5 million in 1972, declined to only about 1.5 million in 1973. Outlays for housing, which had been climbing steadily and reached a peak of more than $60 billion in early 1973, declined to about $55 billion by the end of that year.

The net result of all this activity was that by 1974 outstanding mortgage monies had increased to almost $700 billion as compared with $100 billion in 1945. And, of the $700 billion, about two-thirds was for single-family homes. Where did this money come from? In 1968 federal agencies pro-vided about 5 per cent, commercial banks 15 per cent, savings and loans 44 per cent, mutual savings banks 14 per cent, individuals 10 per cent, and life insurance companies 12 per cent; but these percentages changed dras-tically by 1974. By mid-1974 federal agencies had increased their supply of mortgage funds by 87 per cent, commercial banks by 16 per cent, savings and loans by 12 per cent. On the other hand, mutual savings banks had decreased their supply by 21 per cent, individuals by 33 per cent, and life insurance companies by 53 per cent. Looking to the future, it would seem that any substantial changes in mortgage markets will come about primarily through what federal agencies and commercial banks decide to do. And what their decisions are related primarily to their evaluation of the general economy.

SUMMARY

Real estate financing occupies a small corner relative to all of the money flows in the economy. As a percentage of GNP, mortgage loans average between 5.0 and 10.0, and housing mortgages are only 2–3 per cent of GNP. Total expenditures for residential structures are not much larger, averaging 3–5 per cent of GNP. This gives insight into the forces which influence real estate financing, construction, and sales. Since real estate markets are a small part of the total picture, they are subject to influences which orig-inate in other parts of the economy.

Households are particularly important to the real estate market since they are principal suppliers of funds for the economy in general. Further-more, households were the only net suppliers of funds, except for a small amount advanced by financial institutions. For real estate markets, house-holds are particularly important since they supply savings capital to thrift institutions. From the demand side, changes in household behavior pat-terns, such as an increase in demand for multifamily structures, have im-portant implications for real estate financing and investing.

QUESTIONS

1. Discuss the relationships between debt and savings and the availability of mortgage funds.
2. What is the result of heavy flows of funds into real estate markets?
3. What kinds of debt are typically owed by households and what are the debts for?
4. If GNP grows more slowly in the future, what are some of the implications for housing financing?
5. Since residential construction never seems to account for more than 3 or 4 per cent of the total GNP, what does this imply for future mortgage lending?

4

PRIMARY SOURCES
OF MORTGAGE FUNDS

Investment in real estate is usually highly leveraged; most of the invested funds are provided by a lender rather than through equity. This is an important factor in making real estate attractive to equity investors who are willing to accept the risks associated with leverage. Federal regulations known as "margin requirements" attempt to prevent high leverage on purchases of common stocks. In recent years, margin requirements have largely prevented investors from putting up less than 50 per cent of the purchase price of financial instruments. Real estate, on the other hand, can be acquired with a typical down payment of 20–30 per cent; the amount of money put up by the investor can go much lower.

It is important to know where investors borrow mortgage money, how the sources of funds have changed over time, and how they are likely to change in the future. The purpose of this chapter is to investigate the sources of mortgage lending for various types of real estate investment. Likely future changes are the subject of Chapter 20.

AN OVERVIEW OF SOURCES OF MORTGAGE LENDING

Figure 4–1 is derived from the total amounts of mortgage money outstanding at four points in time from 1945 to 1974. The total was about $687 billion in 1974, up from $145 billion in 1956 and $312 billion in 1964. (Appendix A contains the sources of the data for 1964 and 1974 as well as

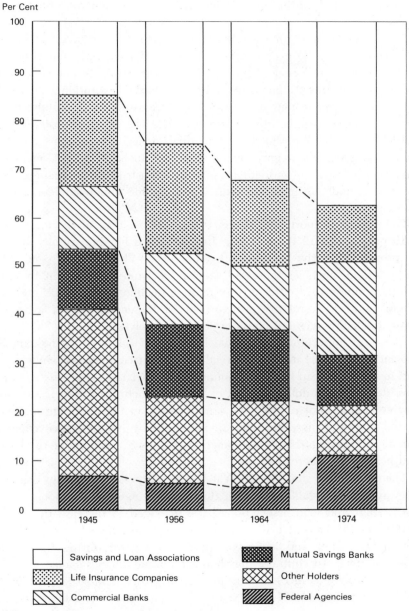

Fig. 4–1. Mortgages outstanding by type of holder, 1945–1974.

much more detail on the types of mortgage loans which were held by each lender.)

It is clear from Figure 4–1 that the sources of mortgage lending have changed dramatically over the past 30 years. For example, noninstitutional lenders held 41 per cent of mortgage funds in 1945, 23 per cent in 1956 and 1964, and only 21 per cent in 1974. Clearly, institutional lending has experienced an enormous growth, relatively as well as absolutely, particularly in the first decade after World War II. The other side of the coin is the decline in the importance of individuals as a source of mortgage funds. "Other holders," a category which does not include federal agencies, is composed primarily of individuals, although construction companies, finance companies, and mortgage companies account for somewhat less than half of the total.

Other holders' mortgages declined from 34 per cent of the total in 1945 to 19 per cent in 1956 and 1964. In 1974, a further precipitous drop sent the proportion in the hands of other holders to about 11 per cent. Meanwhile, federal agencies increased their share from 6.8 per cent in 1945 to 10.5 per cent in 1974, after a brief relative decline in the 1950's and 1960's (Figure 4–1). The relative growth of federal agencies is even larger when residential mortgages are considered by themselves.

The most important institutional lenders in 1974 were savings and loan associations (S&L's) and commercial banks, but commercial banks did not lend much more than half the amount lent by S&L's. (Appendix A contains more detail on the dollar amount of loans by each institution.) Life insurance companies lent roughly the same amount in the mortgage markets as mutual savings banks; the total amount held by life insurance companies and mutual savings banks combined was only $30 billion more than the total held by commercial banks.

The thirty years since World War II have witnessed enormous changes in the way the mortgage market is divided up among institutional lenders. The savings and loan associations have managed to increase their market share from 15 per cent in 1945 to 36 per cent in 1974 (Figure 4–1). The growth of savings and loans was particularly great during the 20 years ended in 1964. In contrast, the share of mutual savings banks was about the same in 1974 as in 1945, after a surge of growth from 1945 to 1956.

Between 1964 and 1974, the share of life insurance companies decreased while the share of commercial banks increased by an equal amount. Prior to 1964, these two institutions had maintained a remarkable stability in their shares of the market for mortgage loans.

These changes in the market shares of the mortgage lending institutions conceal large changes in the types of loans held by the institutions. Figure

4–2 indicates that residential mortgages became a larger part of the market immediately after World War II, and they have not lost much of that gain. Since 1956, multifamily mortgages have taken a larger part of the total amount lent on residential property. Figures 4–1 and 4–2 are related: a change in the demand for a given type of mortgage implies a change in demand for the services of the institutions which specialize in that type.

The institutional and economic factors which are responsible for the trends outlined in Figures 4–1 and 4–2 will be discussed below.

Savings and Loan Associations. In the post-World War II period, savings and loan associations (S&L's) have established a commanding position in the mortgage markets. This is more striking when one considers that S&L's are much smaller (in terms of assets) than commercial banks and about the same size as insurance companies. At the end of 1974, the assets of commercial banks were $916 billion, as opposed to $263 billion for life insurance companies and $296 billion for S&L's. Clearly, S&L's specialize in mortgage lending, whereas commercial banks and life insurance companies do not. About 85 per cent of the assets of S&L's are in mortgage loans, as opposed to 14 per cent for commercial banks and 33 per cent for insurance companies.

The same factor does not explain the dominance of S&L's over mutual savings banks, since mutual savings banks, with about 70 per cent of their assets in mortgages, also specialize in this area. With $110 billion in assets at the end of 1974, mutual savings banks are much smaller than S&L's. The reason is that S&L's, which expanded into the western states in the 1800's, have successfully prevented the legalization of mutual savings banks. Mutual savings banks are authorized in only 17 states and Puerto Rico, whereas S&L's are authorized in all 50 states, the District of Columbia, and Puerto Rico.

The dominance of S&L's in the mortgage markets is even greater if one looks at residential loans; S&L's tend to specialize their mortgage loans in residential property. In 1974, S&L's had 90 per cent of their mortgages in residential property as opposed to 49 per cent for insurance companies, 62 per cent for commercial banks, and 83 per cent for mutual savings banks. This specialization is partly responsible for the rapid growth in S&L's since the 1940's. The type of mortgage in which they specialize has grown (Figure 4–2), so the institution has grown (Figure 4–1).

The rapid growth of savings and loan associations is related to their insensitivity to the extensive foreclosures of mortgages during the Depression of the 1930's. S&L's were willing to aggressively expand their mortgages in the years immediately following World War II, when other lenders were

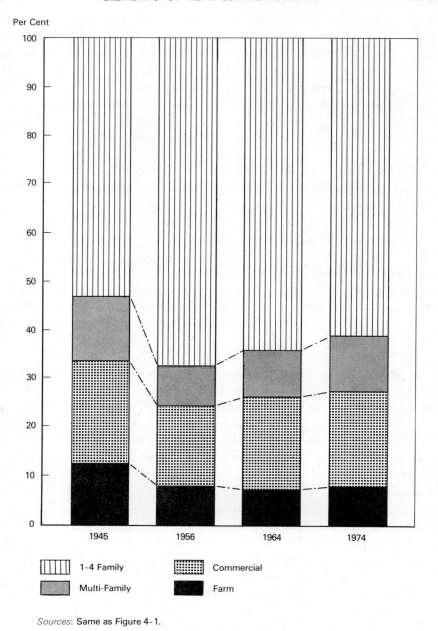

Fig. 4–2. Mortgages outstanding by type of property, 1945–1974.

reluctant to take on what appeared to be risky assets. The aggressiveness of S&L's is reflected in their willingness to acquire conventional loans (i.e., loans uninsured by the government). In 1956, 77 per cent of the mortgage loans of S&L's were conventional. Mutual savings banks had only 41 per cent of mortgages in conventional loans in 1956, despite the fact that the mutual savings banks were equal to S&L's at that time in size and in degree of specialization in the mortgage market. Life insurance companies, which lend on a national scale, had less than 40 per cent of their residential mortgages in conventional instruments in 1956.

The geographic distribution of the assets of S&L's helps to explain their rapid post-World War II growth. S&L's are concentrated in rapidly growing states and areas. These include California, where 17 per cent of the assets of S&L's reside; and Illinois, Ohio, and Florida, each of which has between 7 and 8 per cent of all S&L assets. Thirty-six per cent of assets are in the West or Central regions where relatively fast economic growth has accompanied rapid population growth.

The growth in the assets of S&L's was matched by growth in liabilities, primarily the deposits of many small savers. These deposits grew because of the increase of population and income in many of the states where S&L's do business. They also grew because the S&L's offered higher interest to their depositors than mutual savings banks and commercial banks. The higher yields available on the conventional loans which were aggressively sought by S&L's enabled them to pay more interest to depositors. This ability to bid aggressively for deposits was particularly characteristic of S&L's in the 1945–1955 decade.

The recent growth of S&L's is associated with the federal chartering of mutual associations: i.e., S&L's which are mutually owned by their depositors. The rapid growth of S&L's has undoubtedly been facilitated by the Federal Home Loan Bank system; Chapter 6 contains a full discussion of the FHLB. However, the stock associations—S&L's owned by stockholders—have been quite successful, even though all are state-chartered. Nearly 60 per cent of the assets of all stock-owned S&L's are held in California, a state which has grown rapidly since World War II.[1]

S&L's typically provide 20–25 per cent of all construction loans advanced by major lenders, less than the 35–40 per cent share of commercial banks. The lesser role of S&L's in this interim financing can be explained by the legal requirements which impinge on federally chartered S&L's. They may make construction loans not tied to permanent financing, but these must be accompanied by all of the complexities which accompany a mortgage loan: i.e., legal instruments, recordings, etc. Therefore, construction loans of all

[1] Roger Starr, *Housing and the Money Market* (New York: Basic Books, 1974), p. 109.

types, including those tied to permanent financing, amounted to only 17 per cent of mortgage lending by associations in 1974. This represented a decline from previous years.

Commercial Banks. Figure 4–1 indicates that commercial banks, the second largest mortgage lending group, expanded their share of the mortgage market during the 1964 to 1974 period. This expansion followed two decades of relative stability in the market share of commercial banks. A number of forces contributed to their success in the mortgage markets.

Figure 4–1 does not reveal many important facets of the mortgage lending activity of commercial banks. Historically, commercial banks have tended to specialize in short-term assets; certainly they hold a much smaller percentage of assets in mortgage loans than S&L's (14 per cent as opposed to 85 per cent). More importantly, commercial banks, true to their name, tend to concentrate their mortgage lending in commercial property. The maturity of commercial mortgage loans is typically less than for loans on residential real estate.

Commercial banks have always been an important source of mortgage loans on commercial property; in 1974 they were the largest lender, with 31.7 per cent of all commercial property loans. This reflected a substantial change from 1964 when they held only 20.3 per cent of commercial property loans, second to the life insurance companies.[2] Therefore, the fast growth in total mortgages held by commercial banks reflected, in part, an aggressive stance toward loans on commercial property.

Commercial banks are allowed more flexibility than other financial institutions in the types of assets and liabilities they can hold. This gives commercial banks a competitive edge in the commercial property loan market. Commercial banks can:

1. Package property loans with other financial services which they provide to businesses. The thrift institutions cannot provide financial services such as commercial loans (i.e., unsecured loans to businesses).
2. Make short-term construction loans (interim financing) which lead to permanent loans secured by a mortgage on the commercial property. Unlike the thrift institutions, commercial banks can make unsecured construction loans: i.e., they don't have to require that the borrower mortgage the property.

These unsecured construction loans (i.e., ordinary commercial loans which are for construction purposes) are important to commercial banks.

---

[2] See Appendix A, Table A–4, for the proportion of mortgage loans which are on commercial property.

Commercial banks provided about half of the *secured* construction loans on commercial property in 1973.[3] Their *unsecured* loans for construction purposes were estimated to be about 20 per cent of the secured loans. This amount is sufficient to give commercial banks a substantial lead in the competition for the rapidly expanding market for the permanent financing of commercial property. The expansion of commercial property loans can be seen in Figure 4–2.

Surprisingly, the activity of commercial banks in the market for residential loans goes far to explain the growth in the slice which they cut from the total mortgage market. The pie chart in Figure 4–3 tells the story, as do Appendix Tables A–1 and A–2. In one decade, commercial banks went from 14 to 18 per cent of the market for mortgages on 1–4-family homes. And this performance was from an intermediary which was expanding its share of multifamily and commercial mortgages even faster!

The activity of commercial banks in the mortgage market must be kept in perspective. Commercial banks, which have about 46 per cent of the assets of all financial intermediaries, are the giants of the financial world; they held nearly $1 trillion in assets by mid-1975. Their participation in the mortgage market is small relative to their size, but a small flex of their financial muscle can send their market share skyrocketing. Since commercial banks find short-term assets suited to the short-term structure of their liabilities, they limit their participation in the mortgage market. Also, their unique ability to make large business loans to blue-chip corporations reduces their interest in mortgage markets. Commercial loans offer greener fields, literally as well as figuratively.

The relative attractiveness of mortgage loans is greater for small commercial banks than for large banks, because the former do not have the resources to make multimillion-dollar loans to businesses. Therefore, they find the green pastures of business loans somewhat yellowed, and they turn to residential loans as a substitute. This is confirmed by data which suggest that small commercial banks carry a larger percentage of assets in residential loans.

Regulators serve to reduce the activity of commercial banks in the mortgage markets. They limit commercial banks in terms of the maturity of loans and the loan-to-value ratio. Bank examiners generally prefer to see assets which are easier to evaluate and easier to liquidate. A more lenient attitude on the part of regulators provides one explanation of the commercial banks' increasing market share in the residential mortgage market. The Federal Reserve Board ("the Fed") has been criticized for taking actions

[3] National Association of Real Estate Investment Trusts, *REIT Fact Book 1974* (Washington, D. C.: The Association), pp. 34–35.

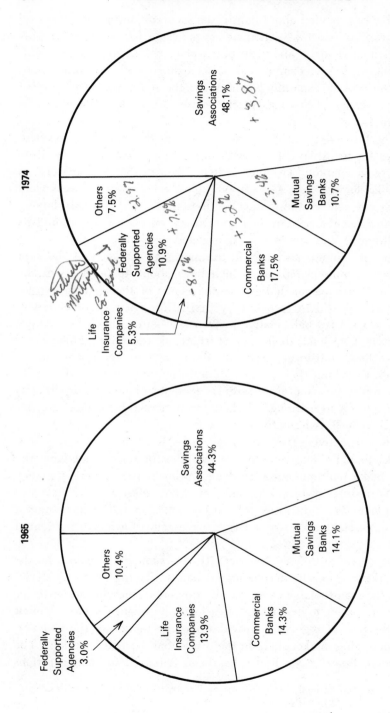

Source: Federal Home Loan Bank Board; Federal Reserve Board; U.S. League of Savings Associations, *Fact Book 1975,* p. 28.

Fig. 4–3. One-to-four-family nonfarm home mortgage loans outstanding, by type of lender, year-end 1965 and 1974.

which raise interest rates and produce housing slumps. In particular, the Fed has been criticized for the long decline in housing starts which began in 1972 and continued into 1975. The Fed has responded to this criticism in a number of ways, one of which is more lenient inspection of the mortgage loans of commercial banks.

Insurance Companies. In terms of the residential mortgage market, life insurance companies have gone in a direction opposite from that of commercial banks. Life insurance companies reduced their 1–4-family mortgages by more than $6 million during the decade ended in 1974 (Appendix Table A–3). In an inflationary period, an actual reduction in holdings represents a dramatic shift in lending policy. By 1974, the insurance companies provided only 5 per cent of all 1–4-family mortgages (Appendix Table A–2), down from 20 per cent in 1956 and 14 per cent in 1964.

The types of mortgages favored by life insurance companies are on large structures and developments: multifamily structures, office buildings, shopping centers, and other commercial or rent-producing projects. This emphasis in the lending of life insurance companies has held true throughout the past thirty years, but it was particularly noticeable in the last decade. In 1974, the proportion of life insurance company mortgages invested in residential real estate dropped below 50 per cent for the first time, while the proportion in 1–4-family dwellings was only 26 per cent (Appendix Table A–4).

Why did insurance companies favor multifamily and commercial projects to such a high degree during the 1964–1974 period? Most of the story can be read in the impact of inflation on the mortgage markets. A mortgage on 1–4-family property is fixed in dollar amount, so its value declines during a period of inflation. The holder of the mortgage is repaid with cheap dollars, i.e., dollars which won't buy nearly as much as the dollars which were lent out. Unless the interest rate on these mortgages is high enough to compensate the holder for the declining value of the dollar, the mortgage is not very attractive.

Mortgages on 1–4-family properties have usually provided enough interest to compensate lenders for inflation, but without much left over. Suppose, for example, that a life insurance company loans $1 million at a current market rate of 9½ per cent. The typical mortgage is outstanding for 8–10 years before it is paid off, usually because the owner moves. Therefore, the "real" rate of return on the $1 million depends on the amount of inflation over the next 10 years. If inflation averages 4.6 per cent, as it has over the past 10 years—or even 6.5 per cent, as it has over the past three years—the real rate of return will lie between 5 per cent and 3 per cent.[4]

Insurance companies have tended to emphasize mortgages on rent-producing properties because they can often expect to get a higher real rate of return on these mortgages. The reason is that the insurance companies can usually arrange to participate in the success of the property. For example, a participation loan might provide that the insurance company get a percentage of rents (net or gross) above a certain level. Or the insurance company might get part of the increased value of the property at the time it is sold. Further discussion of the financing arrangements which give the lender a piece of the profit action can be found in Chapter 12.

If insurance companies find rent-producing property, particularly commercial property, more attractive than 1–4-family property, why doesn't the same logic apply to thrift institutions? The answer is that legal and regulatory restrictions tend to keep the thrift institutions focused on residential property. For example, federal tax law gives them a strong incentive to keep 80 per cent or more of their assets in residential mortgages.

Commercial banks have more flexibility than thrift institutions, so they seized the same profit opportunity which was noted by the insurance companies. Insurance companies increased the proportion of their mortgage portfolio held in commercial mortgages from 27 to 44 per cent during the 1964–1974 period, while commercial banks moved from 28 to 33 per cent (Appendix Table A–4).

Life insurance companies enjoy a unique flexibility in the type of assets which they can hold. For example, they can hold equity investments in real estate, an avenue which is closed (for the most part) to other financial institutions. This is what allows insurance companies to participate in the growth of a rent-producing project. This flexibility extends to the geographical distribution of mortgage loans; the life insurance companies are the only truly national lenders.[5]

The national lending of life insurance companies is sometimes accomplished through their network of branch offices, but this involves maintaining a staff of mortgage specialists at each branch. It is often more profitable for the insurance company to rely on a mortgage banker acting as a correspondent. The mortgage banker originates and services the mortgages —for a fee, of course. The insurance company then purchases the mortgage from the mortgage banker. The mortgage banker does much of the clerical

---

[4] The rate of inflation, 1964–1974 and 1971–1974, was measured by the GNP deflator as reported in *Annual U.S. Economic Data* (St. Louis: Federal Reserve Bank of St. Louis, May 12, 1975).

[5] There is an exception to this. Commercial bank holding companies have recently purchased companies which specialize in mortgage lending in the national market.

work and provides the specialized knowledge of local housing markets which is necessary to choose high-quality loans; the insurance company simply provides the financing. Thus, there is a specialization of functions which benefits all concerned.

Unlike other financial institutions, insurance companies are not subject to withdrawal on demand. A large part of their assets serves as reserves against liabilities which might arise under insurance policies. But since the amount of premiums collected each year is more than adequate to pay claims, the "reserves" are really part of the wealth of the insurance companies. This large pool of wealth is well suited to long-term investment in real estate.

The attentive reader may have noticed an apparent contradiction in our discussion of life insurance companies. On the one hand, we have argued that they are uniquely suited to long-term mortgage lending on a national scale and that they have moved aggressively into mortgages on rent-producing properties. On the other hand, Figure 4–1 indicates that life insurance companies have had a declining share of the mortgage markets. Furthermore, Appendix Tables A–1 and A–2 indicate that their share of the mortgages on commercial properties has increased, but not nearly as much as the share of commercial banks. Why?

The question is especially difficult when one considers that commercial banks, with their short-term liabilities, are not suited to long-term mortgage lending to nearly the same degree as life insurance companies. But commercial banks, with about 15 per cent of their assets in mortgages in 1974, had much larger mortgage holdings than life insurance companies, even though the insurance companies had about 32 per cent of their assets in mortgages and another 3 per cent invested directly in real estate.

The holdings by life insurance companies of mortgage-backed bonds issued or guaranteed by federal agencies partly explain their declining share. Several federal agencies buy residential mortgages and issue mortgage-backed securities to financial institutions. Or the mortgage-backed securities issued by private firms can be guaranteed by federal agencies. When life insurance companies acquire these mortgage-backed securities, they are investing (indirectly) in the residential mortgage market. But these mortgage-backed securities are not included in the total dollar amount of mortgages held; they are included with holdings of corporate bonds or government securities. The holdings of these securities by insurance companies grew from approximately zero to several billion dollars during the 1964–1974 period. Still, they represented a very small investment relative to the total of $86 billion which insurance companies had in mortgages at the end of 1974.

Mutual Savings Banks. In some respects mutual savings banks are the poor relations of the financial institutions which invest in real estate. They not only have the smallest market share, but their share has declined over the thirty-year period ended in 1974 (Figure 4–1). This is perhaps surprising, considering that mutual savings banks, like S&L's, specialize in making mortgages. In 1970, 70 per cent of their assets were in mortgages, down from 73 per cent in 1965 but substantially higher than the 37 per cent which mutual savings banks held in mortgages in 1950.

This poor relation image should not be overemphasized. Mutual savings banks are very important in most of the 17 states where they are allowed to operate. Their relatively small size is due largely to legal restrictions which have prevented them from operating in most states, restrictions which can usually be traced to the S&L interests. Their declining market share can be traced to the relatively slow growth of the older eastern states where most mutual savings banks are located.

Mutual savings banks are showing some impressive signs of life; they could become much more important in the future. They are beginning to offer new types of deposit accounts such as the negotiable order of withdrawal (NOW). NOW accounts enable depositors to write checks on their interest-paying deposits, a privilege which depositors at commercial banks do not enjoy.

Mutual savings banks are not currently chartered by the federal government; they operate only under state charters, governed primarily by state banking regulators. However, they can join the Federal Deposit Insurance Corporation and most do so. This subjects them to some federal supervision. Also, savings banks can voluntarily join the Federal Home Loan Bank system (FHLB); this enables them to participate in the mortgage support programs of the Federal Home Loan Bank. A few have joined the FHLB in the past; in the future, many more will follow.

The geographical restriction of mutual savings banks has confined them largely to older states which have surpluses of capital. The amount that the mutual savings banks get in deposits exceeds the amount which they can profitably lend within their own states. This has led to their participation in the secondary mortgage market, through which they lend in other states. On the secondary market, mutual savings banks buy mortgages which were originated by other institutions (e.g., S&L's or mortgage banks) in other states.

The magnitude of the out-of-state mortgages made by mutual savings banks is large, making these mortgages an important aspect of the mortgage markets. One observer has put it as follows:

In 1970, 39% of savings bank mortgage loans were on out-of-state properties; only about one-quarter of these were made by savings banks in other states where savings banks are legalized. The remaining three-quarters of the out-of-state mortgages, amounting to about 30% of all savings bank mortgages, were made in states where no savings banks exist.[6]

Mortgage Banking. The mortgage bank is neither a bank, since it does not accept deposits, nor a mortgage lender, since it does not permanently invest money in mortgages. What, then, does it have to do with banking and mortgages, and why is it discussed in this chapter?

The mortgage bank, also called a mortgage company, is very important to mortgage lenders, and it is the fastest growing private institution which is actively involved with the major mortgage lenders. About 50 per cent of all mortgage banks have been formed in the post-World War II period; their growth has been accelerated by federal government participation in the mortgage market. A very large proportion of all mortgage loans originates with mortgage bankers—one source puts the proportion at 80 per cent of FHA and VA loans [7]—even though their holdings of mortgages are so small that they are lumped in with the holdings of other investors in Figure 4–1. The reason is that mortgage bankers sell their mortgages to other investors, usually shortly after the mortgage is originated.

The Take-Out Commitment. When the mortgage banker originates a mortgage, the ultimate objective is to be taken out of the deal. Unlike the institutions discussed above, the mortgage banker is not equipped to make long-term debt or equity investment in real estate. For the mortgage banker, which does not have deposits or insurance reserves, the primary source of capital is short-term loans from commercial banks. The commercial banks which provide this capital will not allow the mortgage banker's assets to be tied up with permanent mortgage loans. Therefore, the mortgage banker seeks an investor to buy the newly originated mortgage.

The mortgage can be sold to a government-related agency such as Fannie Mae or Ginnie Mae or to private institutions such as insurance companies, mutual banks, etc. In this chapter we focus on sales to private institutions. In either case, the mortgage banker has a problem: how to pay the mortgagor. The mortgage banker needs interim financing, to be able to carry the mortgage during the period before the mortgage is sold.

For the mortgage banker, interim financing is usually a commercial bank loan collateralized by the mortgage. This loan is typically for the full

[6] Starr, *op. cit.*, p. 102.
[7] Robert H. Pease and Lewis O. Kerwood (eds.), *Mortgage Banking* (2d ed.; New York: McGraw-Hill Book Co., 1965), p. 5.

value minus a few percentage points if the commercial banker thinks that the market for mortgages will decline. Even with the collateral, the commercial bank won't make the loan unless it has some assurance that the mortgage can be sold by the mortgage banker. Thus, the mortgage banker seeks a commitment, in advance, from the permanent investor. This is known as a "bankable commitment," since it provides the basis for the commercial bank loan.

The mortgage banker gets these advance commitments from institutions with which there is a correspondent relationship, as well as from government-related agencies. Correspondent relationships are formed with permanent investing institutions such as S&L's, commercial banks, savings banks, life insurance companies, pension funds, retirement systems, and endowment trusts. The commitments provide the mortgage banker with a certain amount of assurance that the mortgage can be sold. More important, it gives commercial bankers the confidence to make a collateral loan to the mortgage bank.

Three types of commitments can be given to correspondents of investing institutions. One is the regular take-out commitment, often called "an advance commitment." With these, the investing institution agrees to buy mortgages on specific types of properties at specific locations. The sale from the correspondent to the investor takes place as soon as possible after the mortgages are originated. The sale is contingent on the investor's acceptance of the property and the mortgagor, but the terms of this acceptance are so well known to the mortgage banker that few mortgages are rejected.

The second type of commitment is the allocation commitment, which is a forward commitment allocating a certain dollar amount for the investor's purchases from the mortgage bank. It is less specific than the regular advance commitment, although the investor still reserves the right to reject mortgages which don't meet acceptable standards. The advance commitment can be exercised at the investor's option within a specific time period, usually six months.

The third type of commitment is the standby commitment. With the standby commitment, the investor is given a longer time period (e.g., 6–9 months) within which to exercise the agreement to purchase. Furthermore, the purchases are to be made at such a deep discount that the correspondent (i.e., the mortgage banker) cannot ordinarily be expected to demand fulfillment of the commitment. Nevertheless, the mortgage banker will pay a fee for a standby commitment (e.g., .5 per cent of the dollar amount of the commitment) in order to have something to show its commercial banker. The commercial banker will make collateral loans to the mortgage banker if a standby commitment is available.

The Warehousing Process. When the commercial banker makes a loan collateralized by mortgages, it is said to warehouse the mortgages. The entire origination, commitment, and warehousing process is shown in Figure 4–4. As indicated in Figure 4–4, the loan documents which are signed by the mortgagor are passed from the mortgage banker to the commercial bank, along with information pertaining to the commitment from the investor. When the investor actually purchases the mortgage, the funds are usually paid into the mortgage banker's account at the commercial bank. This enables the commercial bank to release the mortgage documents to the investor; i.e., the mortgage is taken out of the warehouse.

The warehousing of mortgages has evolved into a more sophisticated arrangement known as a revolving line of warehousing credit. Under this arrangement, the mortgage banker has a right to put mortgages in the warehouse and draw collateralized loans up to a predetermined maximum amount. The commercial banker may review the maximum periodically. The interest rate on the revolving line is usually close to the prime rate, i.e., the rate charged the "best" (safest) borrowers.

The Economic Functions of a Mortgage Banker. We have seen that the mortgage banker specializes in originating mortgages, leaving the short-term and long-term financing of the mortgages to other institutions. More importantly, the mortgage banker services most of the mortgages after origination. Servicing involves the clerical functions related to billing the customer, collecting payments, and accounting for the payments. The accounting function separates the payments into principal, interest, insurance premium (if any), and real estate taxes (if any are included in the regular monthly payment). The servicing agent must keep track of the outstanding balance on the mortgage and the amount of interest due on the outstanding balance.

The servicing agent has to handle late payments, defaults, and foreclosures. This may require knowledge of local legal procedures. Similarly, local knowledge is required in the origination process. This is one of the principal reasons for the success of the mortgage banker, who can offer local expertise to large institutions which are not locally based.

The servicing function is compensated with a fee of a few tenths of one per cent of the outstanding balance on the mortgage. This has been sufficient to make the servicing contract highly profitable; it is one of the mortgage bankers' most profitable lines of business. Mortgage bankers are will-

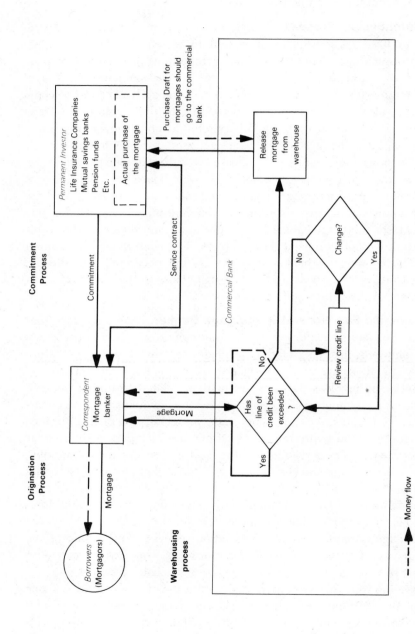

Fig. 4—4. The role of the mortgage banker in the private lending process.

Note: The role of the governmental agencies has been left out of this diagram. See Chapter 8 for a discussion of federal agencies.

ing to take a loss on their origination activities in order to get the servicing contract.

In recent years, the mortgage banker has served many other economic functions. These include the brokering of real estate, property appraisal, property management, serving as the leasing agent for commercial property, making construction loans, providing escrow services, and acting as an insurance agent. Also, mortgage bankers will use their own capital to make installment loans for the purchase of house trailers, vacation homes, etc.

NONINSTITUTIONAL SOURCES OF FUNDS

Mortgage banks are not institutional lenders; the small amount of mortgages which remain outstanding on their books at year end is included with "other holders" in Figure 4–1 and Appendix A. The same is true of real estate investment trust (REITs), and REITs also depend on other financial institutions (e.g., commercial banks) to supply most of their capital. The "other holders" category also includes pension funds, endowment funds, state agencies, and individuals, all of which can be classified as noninstitutional sources of funds. Finally, noninstitutional sources of funds include the federal agencies. Except for the Farmer's Home Administration, the federal agencies involved in the area are designed primarily to promote the secondary market for mortgage loans.[8]

Real Estate Investment Trusts (REITs). REITs have their roots in nineteenth-century mutual associations for investment in real estate; their modern development stems from a 1960 change in the tax law which exempts their earnings from federal taxation, provided that at least 90 per cent of earnings are passed through to investors. From 1961 through 1968, about $350 million of new REIT securities were sold to the public, bringing the total number of REITs to over 50.

Most of the early REITs were relatively small in terms of asset size and they specialized in investment in real property; only a few specialized in construction and development loans. During the 1969–1970 tight-money period, the traditional real estate lenders (savings and loans, commercial banks, and life insurance companies) were forced to greatly curtail their mortgage lending activities. REIT mortgage lending, on the other hand, grew rapidly during this period as stock market conditions permitted REITs to raise large amounts of funds through the sale of REIT equity securities. The formation of new trusts and the growth of existing ones pushed total REIT assets from $1 billion at the start of 1969 to about $5 billion by the end of 1970.

During 1971 and 1972 the monetary situation eased considerably, while REIT

---

[8] For a full discussion of these agencies, see Chapter 8.

assets continued their growth, reaching about $14 billion at the end of 1972. Several factors were responsible for the strong growth of REIT holdings of mortgages during these two years:

REITs were able to provide developers with the types of financing and service that were in demand;

Many REITs were actively making innovative types of loans and investments not sought after or not made by most traditional real estate lenders;

Strong growth in new construction activity enabled all real estate lenders to show increases in outstanding loans and investments.

REIT ownership of properties has also been increasing. Since 1971 a number of new REITs were formed to make such investments and many existing mortgage REITs have used their investment flexibility to acquire ownership interests in properties. Existing trusts which specialized in property ownership have continued to add to their holdings.

During 1973 the monetary climate changed to a much tighter one with the prime rate moving as high as 10 per cent. REIT assets continued to grow, however, reaching more than $20 billion by year-end.[9]

Most REITs do not specialize in holding mortgages. At the end of 1973, only 8 per cent of all REIT assets were in long-term mortgages, with another 8 per cent in short- and intermediate-term mortgages. Most of their assets were in construction or development loans (53 per cent) and property ownership (18 per cent). When they do acquire a mortgage, it is often with the help of a mortgage banker.

Endowments and Pension Funds. Like REITs, these funds hold a relatively small proportion of their assets in real estate mortgages. This is difficult to understand since the long-term nature of their liabilities is ideally suited to debt or equity investment in real estate. But the bull market in corporate equity securities was alluring to the endowment and pension funds. During most of the 1950's and 1960's, those funds with a large percentage of assets in stocks got excellent capital appreciation. Therefore, many funds increased their holdings in stocks and decreased the percentage of their assets in mortgages.

The generally poor performance of the stock market in the 1970's has changed the picture. Many endowment and pension funds are currently trying to explain how institutions with fiduciary responsibilities could allow 40–50 per cent of their assets to disappear. These institutions will be looking for more conservative investments which offer a reasonable rate of return and reasonable security of the principal amount invested. Mortgages and other real estate investments typically offer these characteristics to investors interested in the long-term outlook. Thus, endowment and pension funds

[9] The preceding is excerpted from the *REIT Fact Book 1974, op. cit.,* pp. 23–24.

will probably be a more important source of mortgage lending in the future. When they do lend, they usually do so through the secondary market and through correspondent relationships with mortgage bankers.

State and Local Financing Agencies.   These agencies typically specialize in providing housing to low-to-moderate-income families. They issue mortgages to private corporations which have agreed to certain conditions, such as limited dividends to shareholders and below-market rents for low-to-moderate-income families. In return, the private corporation gets reductions in real estate taxes and/or low-interest loans from the agency. The agency finances its mortgage holdings with seed money appropriated by the state or local government and through the issue of low-interest tax-exempt bonds.

Another approach is characterized by agencies designed to build public housing. New York's Urban Development Corporation provided an example during its brief life (1968–1975). It could issue bonds—it had more than $1 billion outstanding at one point—to finance the construction of developments which contained at least some housing for low-income groups. Even though the bonds were not backed by the full faith and credit of New York State, they were exempt from federal and New York state income taxes.

Agencies issuing tax-exempt bonds for the purposes of investing in real estate are competing to some extent with private mortgage lenders in the sense that they are displacing private construction and borrowing. Studies have yet to yield a convincing estimate of the number of publicly built units which would have been built by the private sector.

The volume of activity at state and local housing agencies is indicated by the $9 billion of tax-exempt funds they had outstanding at the end of 1974. This total grew at an 8.4 per cent annual rate during the 1964–1974 decade, a growth rate somewhat faster than the 7.6 per cent registered by mortgages at private financial institutions.

Individuals.   Since World War II, the participation of individuals in the mortgage lending process has been reduced to a very small level. There are several good economic reasons for this. Individuals have alternative investments such as savings certificates insured by the federal government, savings accounts, and bonds. Most individuals lack the expertise to evaluate the mortgage market, let alone the prospects for any particular piece of property. Finally, few individuals can contemplate an investment which matures in 30 years, almost half of a normal lifetime.

Before the Great Depression, individuals held a much larger proportion of residential mortgages than they do today. The loan-to-value ratio was about two-thirds then, so individuals could feel that they had enough collateral to eliminate most risk. At today's loan-to-value ratios of 75–80 per cent, more expertise is required in choosing a mortgage loan. Also, many earlier mortgages had maturities of about five years, with all of the periodic payment being to interest. Therefore, the mortgagee was not facing a long investment (the mortgagor generally planned to refinance at maturity).

At the end of 1972, individuals held $37 billion in mortgages, about 6 per cent of the total mortgage debt. Considering the arguments against mortgage holdings by individuals, how did they come to hold $37 billion? Some individuals who deal in real estate will make judicious investments in mortgages. Many others will make mortgage loans to friends and relatives. Often individuals find that they must take a mortgage in order to sell a piece of property. This can happen in declining neighborhoods where institutional mortgage lenders refuse to lend, i.e., "redlined" neighborhoods. Sellers in these neighborhoods may be required to take part of the purchase price in the form of a mortgage rather than cash. This is known as a purchase money mortgage.

Direct Federal Lending. The Veterans Administration (VA) and the Farmer's Home Administration (FmHA) will extend loans directly to eligible individuals. Applicants for direct loans must show that loans from private lenders were unavailable. The VA has designated geographical areas where direct loans will be made; the FmHA won't make direct loans in towns with more than 20,000 residents. This greatly restricts the overall size of direct federal lending, but it can be significant in specific rural areas. During the early 1960's, about $150 million per year has been authorized for VA direct lending.

The VA direct-lending program began with the Housing Act of 1950, which was an attempt to help veterans who lived in areas where loans would ordinarily be unavailable. It has been amended several times since then. The question which needs to be addressed now is whether any area of the United States, with the possible exception of parts of Alaska, is so remote that private lending is unavailable. If the answer to this is negative, the VA and FmHA are competing directly with private institutions. It is difficult to see how that kind of competition, in which the federal government necessarily has an enormous advantage, can be in the public interest.

Figure 4–5 summarizes the net flow of mortgage funds, extensions minus repayments, during the 1964–1974 period. It differs from Figures 4–1 and

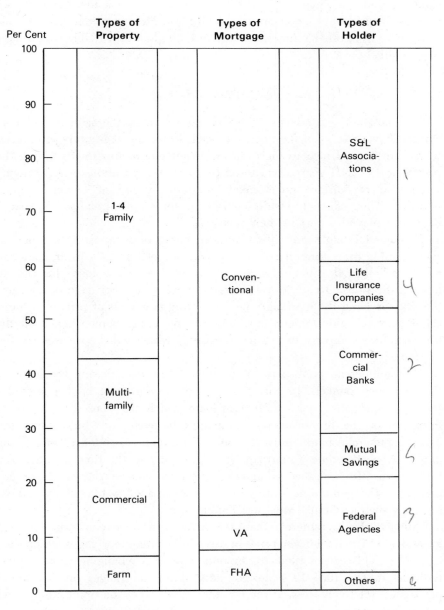

Source: See Appendix A.

Fig. 4–5. Changes in mortgages outstanding by type and type of holder, 1964–1974.

4–2 in that it shows what is happening in terms of activity rather than outstanding dollar amounts. For example, it shows that a mortgagor would
be most likely to use a conventional loan at an S&L or a commercial bank.
Borrowing from other sources, such as an individual or a REIT, would have
been unlikely.

SUMMARY

The most active lenders in the mortgage market, the savings and loan
associations (S&L's) make most of their loans on 1–4-family properties
which are located near to their offices. Their enormous growth during the
post-World War II years was caused by their concentration in fast growing
states and by various government programs in aid of owner-occupied
housing. Their efforts to legally restrict the spread of mutual savings banks
have also played a part in their success.

Commercial banks and life insurance companies concentrate much of
their lending in multifamily or commercial properties. Life insurance companies rely heavily on mortgage bankers who originate loans for sale to
other institutions. In addition to origination fees, the mortgage banker gets
fees for servicing the mortgage: i.e., collecting payments of principal, interest, insurance, and property tax. But the mortgage banker relies on the
life insurance company to provide the funds which will be invested in the
mortgage.

The commercial bank plays a role in this by warehousing the loans of
the mortgage banker. In this function, the commercial banker provides
the mortgage banker with short-term loans which are secured by the commitments of the life insurance companies to eventually buy mortgages.
Thus, commercial banks provide some of the money needed to bridge the
gap between the time a mortgage is originated and the time it is actually
sold to the life insurance company. Often the role of the life insurance
company, the commitment to permanent financing, is played by federal
agencies such as Ginnie Mae and Fannie Mae.

Unlike S&L's, commercial banks and life insurance companies have a
great deal of freedom in the types of assets other than mortgages which they
can hold. This causes them to respond quickly to changing profit opportunities. In the 1964–1974 period, both found mortgages on 1–4-family
properties relatively less attractive than mortgages on multifamily and
commercial properties.

The structure of life insurance companies is ideally suited to long-term
debt or equity investment in real estate. Commercial banks, on the other
hand, tend to favor short-term business loans, including loans for construc-

tion. These construction loans can lead commercial banks to extend long-term financing on the property, especially if it is a commercial property. Thus, commercial banks appeared to have an edge over insurance companies in the competition for these lucrative mortgages on commercial property.

QUESTIONS

1. What is the concept of "leverage" as used by mortgage lenders?
2. Discuss the major reasons why savings and loan associations make proportionately more loans than commercial banks.
3. Why do commercial banks not make more mortgage loans?
4. What kinds of mortgage loans would you expect insurance companies to favor and why?
5. Why are mutual savings banks not classified as savings and loan associations?
6. Review Figure 4–2 and the discussion of the mortgage lending activity of insurance companies. Can you think of reasons why the insurance companies have had a declining share of the mortgage market (Figure 4–1)?
7. Do you think that REITs will challenge S&L's for a larger share of new mortgage loan commitments? Why?
8. What are the benefits of the correspondent relationship to the insurance company? The mortgage banker? What do you think some of the problems are for both parties?

5

FLOWS OF
REAL ESTATE CAPITAL

We have already stressed the relationships among economic activity, employment, and personal savings. This chapter traces the flow of those savings into the institutional lenders who make possible the existence of the mortgage markets and therefore the housing markets. Some appreciation of the importance of savings to the housing industry can be obtained from Figure 5–1, in which annual changes in savings deposits are compared to annual expenditures on new residential structures. Notice how closely the two factors have moved since 1956. An upward or a downward trend in savings deposits is usually accompanied or followed slightly by a corresponding trend in the dollar volume of residential construction. On a long-term basis, the two trends have a rough similarity.

This relationship between savings and housing carries over into the mortgage market activity. Savings are made available primarily through the activities of the institutional lenders. Figure 5–1 highlights annual changes in construction, mortgages outstanding, and over-the-counter savings. (Over-the-counter savings are passbook savings or time accounts held by institutional lenders.) Notice again the close relationship among the amount of savings, the mortgages made, and the amount of construction. This relationship is the key to understanding what happens in mortgage lending markets, and is the subject of this chapter.

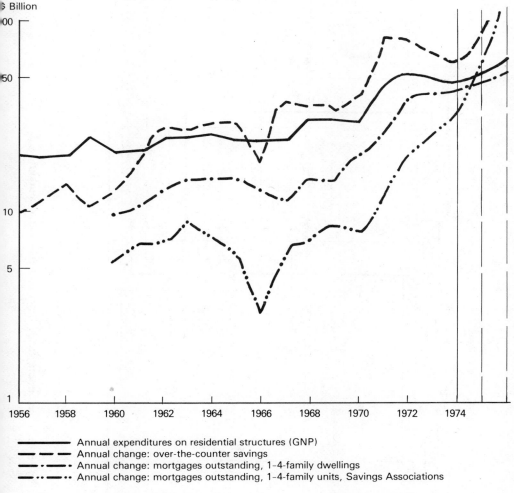

Fig. 5–1. Principal influences on housing starts, 1956–1975.

SAVINGS AND MORTGAGE FUNDS FLOWS

The system statement in Figure 5–2 emphasizes the relationships between personal savings and the availability of mortgage money. Let us look at the figure briefly. After goods and services are produced and an allowance is made for capital replacement and other items, the result is net national income. Net national income, in effect, is the money which is available to business, to consumers, and to the government for spending,

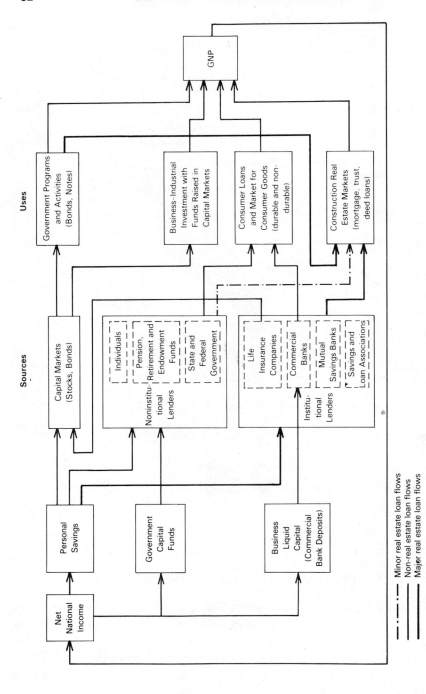

Fig. 5–2. Real estate funds flows and real estate markets.

Source: Based on Fred E. Case, *Real Estate Economics* (Calif. Assoc. of Realtors, 1975). Exhibit III–1, p. 30.

investing, or other uses. We are concentrating here on that portion of the net national income which flows to the consumer and which the consumer uses for both consumption and investment. Personal savings are, in effect, that portion of their income which families find they do not need for immediate use and which they therefore place somewhere in order for it to be secure or to earn interest.

Personal savings, therefore, flow essentially to three different places. Not many consumers put their money in the securities market, but for upper-income families with a considerable excess of income over consumption, securities markets represent a continuing form of investment. Consumers who wish to invest their money in tax-sheltered, income-producing investments may buy tax-exempt bonds, which are usually issued by government agencies. The securities market is then used to finance the activities of business firms and governments. We are not particularly interested in this section of the capital market.

Our concern is with the portion of the money market that flows to non-institutional and institutional lenders. Noninstitutional lenders are only a minor part of the mortgage market. They include individuals, pension funds, consumer loan companies, and other nonfinancial institutions which collect money and make it available for some reason. In recent years, because of the high rates on mortgages, consumer loan companies have been using a considerable portion of the money which they collect to invest in mortgage loans; but the amount of their lending for mortgages, even when combined with loans made by life insurance companies, is not an important part of the mortgage market.

Institutional Lenders. Loans made by insurance companies, banks, savings and loans, and mutual savings banks make up lending by institutional lenders.

INSURANCE COMPANIES. Insurance companies collect their money through premiums. Their heaviest inflow of savings from consumers comes usually at the beginning of the year and at midyear; smaller amounts flow in monthly. Since the insurance companies can use actuarial tables to estimate how much of this savings inflow will have to be paid out at a later date as insurance policies become due, they are able to invest large blocks of money in long-term mortgage loans. For this reason, insurance companies provide mortgage funding for the larger-scale investments which extend over periods of time. Many of the insurance companies not only provide loans but also invest portions of their funds as partners in various kinds of real estate investments.

The typical home buyer will probably not use a life insurance company loan primarily because the companies are very selective in the properties and the borrowers to whom they will make loans. They prefer borrowers who show every promise of providing no risk, who wish to borrow reasonably large amounts of money, and who may be a source of insurance sales. Similarly, pension funds prefer to loan to members.

At one time, insurance companies and pension funds were a quite important force in residential mortgage lending. But since 1955, residential mortgages have represented a decreasing proportion of their total credit market activity. In fact, between 1955 and 1975, as a percentage of all home mortgages, they declined to about one-fourth of their previous activity (Table 5–1). Although some increase in their activity is expected by 1980, it is not predicted to be large.

COMMERCIAL BANKS.   The bulk of the savings flow is to three kinds of institutional lenders: commercial banks, mutual savings banks, and savings and loan associations. Commercial banks and savings and loan associations may be chartered to do business by either the federal government or a state government. State-chartered institutions are usually limited in their lending and borrowing activities to the state within which they are chartered, but this depends upon state law. Mutual savings banks originated in the northeastern part of the United States, basically in the thirteen original colonies; because of a series of historical events, they have never extended their chartering beyond the limits of their original markets.

Commercial banks collect funds primarily in order to make consumer or business loans. They prefer short-term loans—30-, 60-, or 90-day or one-to-two-year loans—because these loans turn over quickly and their rate of return is higher than that of longer-term mortgage loans. When commercial banks do make loans, many of them prefer to do the bulk of their lending on short-term construction loans. These are mortgage loans which are used to finance the construction of a property, but the borrower is required to find some other lender to provide long-term funding once the construction is completed. Only a relatively small proportion of commercial bank assets is invested in mortgage loans.

The importance of residential mortgage markets in the scheme of overall economic activity can be appreciated from a review of Table 5–1. Of the net funds which were raised for residential mortgages, the total comprised only about 2–3.5 per cent of the gross national product; and of this, approximately 75–90 per cent has consistently been for home mortgages. This relationship is expected to continue with some small amount of increase through 1980. Of the funds advanced for mortgages, however, commercial

Table 5-1. Residential Mortgage Markets, 1955-1980[1]

	Annual Averages					
	1955-1959	1961-1965	1966-1970	1971-1975	1976	1980
A. *Net flows of credit, per cent of GNP:*						
1. Net funds raised:	2.70%	2.90%	2.01%	2.90%	3.76%	2.60%
2. Home mortgages	2.47	2.34	1.53	3.01	3.70	1.75
3. Multifamily	.23	.56	.48	−.11	.06	.85
4. Net funds advanced:	2.70	2.90	2.01	4.18	3.49	2.60
5. U. S. Government and sponsored agencies[2]	.20	−.02	.40	.51	.73	.31
6. Commercial banks	.28	.39	.32	.98	.58	.48
7. Savings institutions	1.59	2.00	1.06	2.31	2.48	1.40
8. Insurance and pension funds	.47	.46	.19	.24	−.21	.36
9. Others (REITs, finance companies)	.16	.07	.04	.14	−.12	.05
10. Memo: FHLB advances[3]	.06	.14	.10	.11		.08

	1954	1959	1965	1970	1975	1976	1977	1980
B. *Balances outstanding:*								
1. Billions of dollars	$88	$148	$248	$335	$492	$661	$678	$737
2. Per cent of GNP:	24.1%	30.5%	35.9%	34.0%	37.0%	38.0%	38.0%	38.6%
3. Home mortgages	20.5	26.6	30.5	28.2	31.0	32.0	32.0	29.1
4. Multifamily	3.7	3.9	5.4	5.9	6.0	6.0	6.0	9.5
Distribution of outstandings, by holder								
5. Home mortgages	100.0%	100.0%	100.0%	100.0%	100.0%	100.0%	100.0%	100.0%
6. U.S. Government and sponsored agencies[2]	3.7	4.2	3.1	7.4	13.0	12.0	12.0	10.0
7. Commercial banks	17.6	14.9	14.4	15.2	16.0	16.0	16.0	18.8
8. Savings institutions	45.6	51.9	59.8	59.4	61.0	56.0	56.0	59.6
9. Insurance and pension funds	20.6	19.1	15.8	11.2	4.0	3.0	3.0	5.2
10. Others	12.5	9.9	6.9	6.8	6.0	13.0	13.0	6.4
11. Multifamily residential mortgages	100.0%	100.0%	100.0%	100.0%	100.0%	100.0%	100.0%	100.0%
12. U. S. Govt. and sponsored agencies	2.0	4.8	2.8	5.8	27.0	22.0	22.0	12.4
13. Commercial banks	6.3	6.0	5.3	5.7	6.0	6.0	6.0	7.2
14. Savings institutions	34.8	38.8	48.8	45.6	39.0	41.0	42.0	43.7
15. Insurance and pension funds	27.1	24.9	33.8	39.6	19.0	19.0	19.0	34.8
16. Others	29.8	25.4	9.2	3.4	9.0	12.0	11.0	7.9

Note: 1977 estimated, based on first quarter rate.

[1] Excludes loans in process at savings institutions and U. S. Government liabilities for home loan mortgages. These are netted against the respective sector holdings.
[2] Includes mortgage pools backing GNMA-guaranteed securities.
[3] Credit to savings institutions.

Sources: Data for 1971-1975 and year-end 1975 are from Board of Governors of the Federal Reserve System, "Flow of Funds" for 1945-1972 and for second quarter 1975. All other data, including the 1980 projections, are from Stephen P. Taylor, "Long Term Prospects for Housing Finance," in *Ways to Moderate Fluctuations in Housing Construction*, published by Board of Governors of the Federal Reserve System (December 1972).

banks accounted for .63 per cent of the gross national product in the 1971–1975 period, whereas savings institutions (mutual savings banks and savings and loan associations) accounted for more than three times this amount. Insurance and pension funds provide only about one-third of the net funds which are advanced by commercial banks. Table 5–1 presents the residential mortgage market rather than the nonresidential market because the residential mortgage market is the primary market in which mortgages are created. Among other forms of mortgages to be discussed later are commercial mortgages, which typically equal one-fourth to one-third of the residential mortgage volume, and farm mortgages, which equal about one-tenth of residential mortgage flows.

Table 5–2 contains an analysis of the flows of funds to commercial banks, expressed as a percentage of the gross national product. In the period from 1966 to 1970 the total credit market advances of commercial banks equaled 3.17 per cent of the gross national product but residential mortgages ac-

Table 5–2. Commercial Banks, 1955–1980 (Per Cent of GNP)

	Annual Averages						
	1955–1959	1961–1965	1966–1970	1971–1975	1976	1977	1980
A. *Flows*:							
1. Total credit market advances:	1.60%	3.40%	3.17%	4.44%	3.4 %	3.0 %	3.23%
2. U. S. Government and agency securities	−.51	.13	.20	.67	1.14	.41	.24
3. Municipal securities*	.19	.70	.69		.50	.15	.04
4. Residential mortgages	.28	.39	.32	.96	.80	.89	.48
5. Other	1.64	2.18	1.96	2.30	1.32	1.67	2.05
6. Private demand deposits	.29	.60	.75	.91	.64	.40	.59
7. Domestic time deposits	.83	2.32	1.94	3.40	2.43	2.46	2.31
8. Other credits, net	.48	.48	.48	.91	.64	.40	.33
B. *Balance, end of period*:							
1. Total credit market assets:	38.9%	43.7%	44.6%	54.90%	45.6 %		47.3%
2. U. S. Government and agency securities	12.8	9.8	7.7	7.48	7.37		7.6
3. Municipal securities*	3.5	5.6	7.1	7.45	6.07		9.3
4. Residential mortgages	4.2	4.7	4.6	5.03	4.74		6.2
5. Other	18.4	23.6	25.2	34.94	27.42		24.2
6. Private demand deposits	21.8	17.9	15.9	17.49	17.11		13.8
7. Time deposits	14.0	21.5	23.6	28.51	17.33		30.3
8. Other credits, net	3.1	4.3	5.1	8.90	18.3		3.2

*State and local obligations.

Note: 1977 estimated, based on first quarter rate.

Sources: Same as Table 5–1.

counted for only .32 per cent of GNP. During the 1971–1975 period, residential mortgage lending accounted for 10 per cent of all commercial bank lending, just as it did in the 1966–1970 period. Residential mortgage lending represented a more important part of GNP in the later period: .55 as opposed to .32 per cent. This again emphasizes the fact that residential markets are an important but not principal lending activity for commercial banks. Where did the banks get this money? They got it primarily from domestic time deposits and private demand deposits and, to some extent, from other forms of credit. Notice, however, that the accumulated credit market assets which were advanced by commercial banks amounted to 44.6 per cent of the gross national product in 1970 and 54.7 per cent in 1975. According to the forecasts given in Table 5–2, the relative importance of commercial banks may slip somewhat by 1980.

SAVINGS AND LOAN ASSOCIATIONS. Although the assets of all savings and loan associations are considerably less than the total assets of all commercial banks, savings and loan associations play a much more important role in the flows of residential mortgages. Compare the fact that in the period from 1966 to 1970 residential mortgages by commercial banks represented .32 of the annual gross national product (Table 5–2) whereas for savings

Table 5–3. Savings and Loan Associations (Per Cent of GNP)

				Annual Averages			
	1955–1959	1961–1965	1966–1970	1971–1975	1976	1977	1980
A. *Flows*							
1. Total credit market advances: *	1.36%	1.77%	1.00%	2.51%	3.18%	3.49%	1.26%
2. Residential mortgages*	1.15	1.47	.82	2.00	2.62	2.50	1.07
3. Other credit	.21	.30	.18	.01	.01	.11	.19
4. Savings capital	1.24	1.63	.85	2.16	2.97	2.86	1.10
5. FHLB advances	.06	.14	.10	.15	−1.18	1.17	.08
B. *Balances, end of period*							
1. Total credit market assets: *	11.9%	17.2%	16.5%				19.0%
2. Residential mortgages*	10.2	14.7	13.9	14.0 %	15.49%	n.a.	16.2
3. Other credit	1.7	2.5	2.6	0	0	n.a.	2.8
4. Savings capital	11.3	16.1	15.0	17.62	19.8	n.a.	17.2
5. FHLB advances	.4	.9	1.1	1.26	1.98		1.2

*Net of mortgage loans in process.

Note: 1977 estimated, based on first quarter rates.

Sources: Same as Table 5–1.

and loans they represented .82 of the annual gross national product (Table 5–3). The contrast is even greater in the 1971–1975 period when the corresponding percentages were .55 and 1.57. This emphasizes the fact that savings and loan associations were created primarily to collect savings from the local markets and to make them available for home mortgage loans. Savings and loan associations are the leaders, not only in making home mortgage loans but in making and servicing long-term loans.

MUTUAL SAVINGS BANKS. Mutual savings banks are located in the important northeastern section of the United States where much of the money market activity of the country is centered. Although their assets are not as large as those of commercial banks and savings and loan associations, they do represent a reasonably large portion of the mortgage flows, as shown in Table 5–4. For example, in the period from 1971 to 1975, their flows

Table 5–4. Mutual Savings Banks (Per Cent of GNP)

	Annual Averages				
	1955–1959	1961–1965	1966–1970	1971–1975	1980
A. *Flows*					
1. Total credit market advances:	.45%	.54%	.43%	.73%	.48%
2. Residential mortgages	.43	.52	.23	.14	.32
3. Other credit	.02	.02	.20	.59	.16
4. Deposits	.41	.53	.44	.68	.47
B. *Balances, end of period*					
1. Total credit market assets:	7.7%	8.0%	7.5%	7.87%	7.8%
2. Residential mortgages	4.7	4.9	5.1	3.43	4.9
3. Other credit	3.0	3.1	2.4	4.44	2.9
4. Deposits	7.2	7.7	7.3	7.63	7.7

Note: 1975 estimated from first two quarters.

Sources: Same as Table 5–1.

equaled about .14 per cent of the gross national product which means that their flows were about one-tenth those of savings and loan associations and about one-fourth those of commercial banks. Their balances in residential mortgages and other forms of credit represented only about 8 per cent of the gross national product. However, mutual savings banks, like commercial banks and savings and loan associations, make mortgages insured by the Federal Housing Administration (FHA) and Veterans Administration (VA). We shall discuss this form of mortgage later. It is sufficient to say at this point that because these mortgages are insured or guaranteed by a federal agency, lenders are allowed to provide funding anywhere in the United States. There are restrictions on the manner in which they can provide money for FHA and VA mortgages, but, nevertheless, this opportunity to engage in national mortgage market lending has enabled mutual savings banks to use their funds not only in their local market areas but throughout the United States, and for this reason, they are sometimes an important force in mortgage lending outside their local areas.

FEDERAL INFLUENCES ON MORTGAGE FLOWS

The federal government first began activities in mortgage lending in 1932 when it created the Homeowners Loan Corporation for the purpose of advancing funds to borrowers who were temporarily unable to meet their mortgage loan payments because of circumstances beyond their control. Soon thereafter, the Federal Housing Administration was created for the purpose of insuring lenders against loss on mortgage loans. A series of other kinds of housing programs followed thereafter and continued to be developed each year, with most of them centering around some form of mortgage lending activity. One of the most important forms of federal activity in mortgage lending has been to provide secondary mortgage support for the home mortgage market. This means that federal agencies such as the Federal National Mortgage Association, the Federal Home Loan Mortgage Corporation, and others are able to buy mortgages which have been made according to the standards of the Federal Housing Administration (FHA) and Veterans Administration (VA) from lenders who have used all their funds and have opportunities for additional mortgage lending. It is called secondary mortgage activity because, in effect, the federal government keeps mortgage lenders in funds by buying from them loans which they have already made. These loans are usually purchased at something of a discount so that the federal agency can make some money on its lending activity or at least not lose money, but the mortgage lenders are often given the opportunity to make some money by continuing to service the mortgage loans, that is, collect the payments and forward them to the federal agencies involved.

Some notion of the importance of federally sponsored credit agency activity in mortgage lending can be obtained from reviewing Table 5–5. In the period from 1955 to 1959, residential mortgage credit advanced by federal agencies amounted to about .09 per cent of the gross national product, but by the period 1971 to 1975, it had increased to 1 per cent of the gross national product. However, the total credit holdings in residential mort-

Table 5-5. Federally Sponsored Credit Agencies (Per Cent of GNP)

	Annual Averages				
	1955–1959	1961–1965	1966–1970	1971–1975	1980
A. *Flows*					
1. Total credit advanced:	.26%	.24%	.60%	.99%	.52%
2. Residential mortgages[1]	.09	−.01	.30	.64	.28
3. Advances to S&L's	.06	.14	.10	.04	.08
4. Other	.11	.11	.20	.31	.16
5. Net security issues[2]	.23	.20	.56	.88	.45
Memo: Federal Government residential mortgages in budget[3]	.05	−.03	.10	.12	.01
B. *Balances, end of period*					
1. Total credit holdings:	2.0%	2.7%	4.6%	6.09%	6.5%
2. Residential mortgages[1]	.4	.4	1.6	2.95	3.5
3. Advances to S&L's	.4	.9	1.1	1.03	1.2
4. Other	1.2	1.4	1.9	2.11	1.8
5. Securities outstanding[2]	1.5	2.0	4.0	5.40	5.8
6. Memo: Federal Government residential mortgages in budget[3]	.9	.5	.8	.78	.5

[1] Includes mortgage pools backing GNMA-guaranteed securities.
[2] Includes GNMA-guaranteed securities backed by mortgage pools.
[3] Net of Federal Government liabilities for home mortgages assumed by Defense Department and Coast Guard.

Note: 1975 estimated from first two quarters.

Sources: Same as Table 5-1.

gages, particularly by federal agencies, is expected to rise from about .4 per cent of the gross national product in 1959 to 3.5 per cent of the gross national product in 1980. This means that the federal government is playing an increasingly important role in the sources and uses of mortgage funds. Notice particularly its role in providing advances to the savings and loan associations so that they in turn can make mortgage loans.

To understand the importance of federal agency activity in supporting the private housing market, we must compare changes in federal agency support or residential debt with changes in private housing starts. Federal agency activity has tended to moderate both increases and declines in housing starts. In some years, in fact, it has been estimated that federal monetary support of the residential markets has accounted for as much as 40 per cent of all the building activity occurring. The chapters of Part II study in detail how the federal government operates to influence changes in the mortgage lending market.

SAVINGS AS A SOURCE OF MORTGAGE FUNDS

It should be evident by now that the mortgage markets must survive on the flows of savings which are made available to them through institutional lenders. This has been true in the past and undoubtedly will continue to be true for some time into the future. However, there are many proposals for changing the basic financial structure of the United States which might affect these flows. Historically, some of the important influences on these flows have been the introduction of various kinds of life insurance, health insurance, and pension plans which have reduced the necessity for families to place a portion of their savings in commercial banks, savings and loan associations, or mutual savings banks in anticipation of emergencies which might require the use of these funds. As a result, money which might have gone into time deposits and savings deposits is now diverted to various federal agencies and insurance companies. Unfortunately, these agencies and companies have not used their funds for mortgage lending purposes. Instead, they have sought more lucrative short-term investment opportunities. As a result, some would argue that the historical flow of funds into mortgage markets has been seriously threatened.

While the dollar volume of funds flowing from mortgage lending has increased appreciably, has it increased at a rate which will permit mortgage lending to keep pace with the anticipated population increases and demands for new housing? If there is to be some impediment in the flows of funds to mortgage markets and an increasing demand, then it is easy to forecast that mortgage funds are always going to be available at higher rates than have prevailed historically. In the 1930's, for example, mortgage lending at a rate of 3 to 5 per cent was common. Even after World War II, FHA and VA loans were being made available at 4 to 5 per cent. When, in the 1960's, the 8 per cent mortgage rate began to appear, many persons forecast that housing construction, housing sales, and mortgage lending would collapse. This has not been true. The 8 per cent mortgage rate continues to be accepted as a reasonably good rate for mortgage lending. In fact, consumers are urged to borrow when they can on an 8 per cent rate. As the pressure for more funds has increased, mortgage lending rates at times have approached 12 to 15 per cent.

To give the preceding discussion a practical basis, obtain a copy of *The Federal Reserve Bulletin* or turn to the financial pages of a periodical or newspaper which you read for business news. Ask yourself whether there is any indication that savings are increasing so that more money could be made available for mortgage loans. Is there any indication that savings and loan associations have greater opportunities to secure funds for mortgage lending? Or, do shortages seem to be developing which threaten the mortgage flows? Take the historical trends which have occurred, use them as a basis for estimating what's likely to happen over the next year in mortgage loans, and then make your own forecast of what is likely to happen to mortgage rates.

QUESTIONS

1. What are "over-the-counter" savings and why are they important?
2. Why was the Home Owners Loan Corporation created and why is it important?
3. What are the FHA and the VA and how do they differ?
4. What is meant by secondary mortgage market activity by federal agencies?
5. Are savings important only to the mortgage market or to the general economy? Why?

II

Government in the Financing Process

6

FEDERAL REGULATION OF LENDERS

Numerous state and federal laws govern lending in real estate. For example, state usury laws set a limit on the interest rate which can be charged on a mortgage loan. The federal truth-in-lending laws require disclosure of the effective annual interest rate on the loan. Antidiscrimination statutes are designed to prevent loan decisions based on race, religion, or national origin. These laws govern *all* lenders in the real estate market—individuals, pension funds, life insurance companies, mortgage companies, or banks.

For noninstitutional lenders, the enforcement of these laws depends primarily on the courts, which are an expensive and difficult remedy for most participants in the real estate market. Fortunately, the federal regulatory agencies—the Federal Home Loan Banks (FHLB), the Federal Reserve Board (FRB), the Federal Savings and Loan Insurance Corporation (FSLIC), and the Federal Deposit Insurance Corporation (FDIC)—enforce many of the laws and closely examine all activity of institutional lenders. State banking authorities perform a similar function for uninsured banks which are not covered by the federal regulatory agencies.

This chapter focuses on the federal regulation of lenders. The scope and some of the details of federal regulation are covered. The extensive benefits available to financial institutions which voluntarily submit to regulation are explored.

THE FEDERAL HOME LOAN BANK SYSTEM

The Federal Home Loan Bank (FHLB) system, established in 1932, is a group of twelve regional banks which are controlled by the federal government. Figure 6–1 indicates the geographic distribution of the banks. An institution desiring to join the FHLB system must seek a charter from the bank in its area. The system is devoted almost exclusively to regulating savings and loan associations: of the 4,316 members of the system at the end of 1973, 99 per cent were S&L's. Forty-one mutual savings banks and two insurance companies were members.

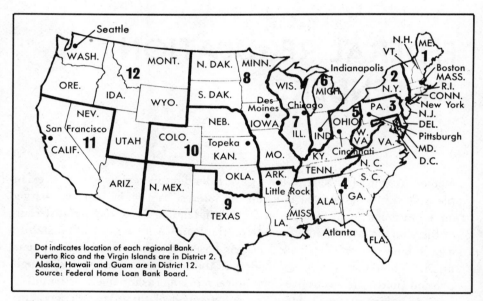

Dot indicates location of each regional Bank.
Puerto Rico and the Virgin Islands are in District 2.
Alaska, Hawaii and Guam are in District 12.
Source: Federal Home Loan Bank Board.

Fig. 6–1. Federal Home Loan Bank Districts. (U. S. League of Savings Associations, *1976 Fact Book,* p. 97.)

The Federal Home Loan Bank Board (FHLBB) is at the head of the FHLB system.[1]

The Board has three members, appointed for four-year terms by the President with the consent of the Senate. No more than two board members can be members of any one political party.

The Board, located in Washington, D. C., governs and regulates the Bank

---

[1] *1974 Savings and Loan Fact Book,* United States League of Savings Associations, p. 110. Since 1974, there have been no substantial changes in the structure and functioning of the FHLBB.

System. It is the chartering and regulatory authority for federal savings and loan associations. It also governs the Federal Savings and Loan Insurance Corporation. All federal associations must be FSLIC-insured; state associations may join if they qualify. The Board also directs the Federal Home Loan Mortgage Corporation, a secondary mortgage market facility authorized by the Housing Act of 1970.

The Board is an independent agency in the executive branch of the government, and submits an annual report to Congress. Its expenses are all met through assessments on the regional Banks and the Federal Savings and Loan Insurance Corporation, and assessments for examinations. None of the Board's expenses are paid out of federal funds, although Congress reviews them and may set limits on them. The Board's expenditures also are reviewed by the General Accounting Office.

The Federal Home Loan Banks have broad authority to regulate the most important lenders in the real estate market, the federally chartered savings and loan associations. The FHLB system charters S&L's, checks their liquidity, checks loan quality (percentage of loans with overdue payments or relegated to bad debt), and establishes limits on loan terms (maturity and amount of down payment). It also performs a number of services for member S&L's, including the gathering and distribution of industry statistics, and research on matters of importance to the industry. Lending to S&L's which are members of the FHLB system is one of the most important functions of the system.

The Federal Home Loan Bank system accomplishes a number of goals with its lending policies. For S&L's experiencing unusually large withdrawals of savings deposits, a temporary loan (called an "advance") from the local FHLB represents a dependable source of liquidity. This function has caused the FHLB system to be dubbed the "lender of last resort" for S&L's. When member institutions go to their FHLB for a loan, the situation is usually not desperate, but the ready availability of liquidity adds stability to the system. It insures against an unexpected failure whereby depositors discover that they cannot withdraw their funds.

The inability of a few depositors to withdraw funds can panic others, causing them to attempt withdrawals. This kind of run on the banks is disastrous, since banks keep much of their deposited funds in long-term illiquid assets. This is especially true with the thrift institutions, where assets are tied up in long-term real estate loans. Thus, the most important reason for federal regulation of financial institutions, whether they are thrift institutions or commercial banks, is to prevent a run on the banks.

The lending policies of the Federal Home Loan Banks can be used to subsidize member S&L's. In 1970, a special type of below-market interest rate advance was introduced by the FHLB system. It offered members a one-year advance for a variable rate which ranged from ¼ to 1¼ below the cost of funds to the FHLB system. This special advance was phased out of operation in 1973. During the same period, each of the twelve Federal Home Loan Banks was encouraged to use advances for its own purposes and to meet the needs of local members. This decentralized policy, which is still in effect, is reflected in a rate on advances which shows wide geographic variation. During 1973, the average rate on advances ranged from 6.8 per cent in Topeka to 8.3 per cent in Atlanta.

There are some restrictions on the use of advances by member banks. An FHLBB policy limits the amount borrowed to 25 per cent of deposits, except to meet sudden withdrawals in an emergency. This limitation is not very restrictive, and so usage of advances is heavy. During 1973 about 2,500 institutions, more than half of all FHLB system members, borrowed about $10 billion from the system. Since these are short-term loans, repayments were also large, so advances totaled about $15 billion at the end of 1973.

One of the functions of the FHLBB is to set the maximum interest rate which may be charged on savings deposits. This requires coordination with the Federal Reserve Board (discussed below) in order to maintain a reasonable relationship between interest rates paid by commercial banks and by savings and loans. Frequent adjustments are made in these ceiling interest rates.

The annual examination of members in the FHLB system is designed to determine whether fair and reasonable business practices are being followed. The examiners do not expect to find exorbitant interest rates on loans or unusually large loan defaults. They do expect adequate liquid reserves to back up savings deposits. A large number of detailed operating procedures are checked to determine whether they conform to accepted standards.

FEDERAL DEPOSIT INSURANCE CORPORATION (FDIC)

The insurance of bank deposits by the federal government is one of the most successful innovations in modern banking. The significance of deposit insurance goes far beyond banking; it provides an example of appropriate government intervention in business activity. The government has a legitimate interest in the safety and security of bank deposits, since the provision of currency and coin is one of the Constitutional obligations of the federal government. Today, this can be broadly interpreted to mean that the federal government has an interest in money in the form of demand and time deposits at banks. Clearly, a loss of confidence in these forms of money (or "near money" in the case of time deposits) would jeopardize the entire U. S. economy.

A general loss of public confidence in bank deposits did occur in 1933, and banks were forced to close their doors in order to prevent massive withdrawals. In the wake of this, the government decided to insure the payment of small deposits. The idea is that insurance will prevent panic, so the government will rarely have to pay depositors. Furthermore, the government has the resources to quickly pay millions or even billions of dollars when an individual bank fails. Later on, the assets of the failed bank can be liquidated in an orderly manner, preventing large losses to the government. In these activities, the government has enormous advantages over private insurance companies. People will readily place confidence in the government, and the government has the liquid reserves to meet emergencies.

FEDERAL SAVINGS AND LOAN INSURANCE CORPORATION (FSLIC)

Legislation enacted in 1934 established the Federal Deposit Insurance Corporation (FDIC) and the Federal Savings and Loan Insurance Corporation (FSLIC). The two have similar structures, purposes, and powers, but the FDIC insures commercial banks and mutual savings banks whereas the FSLIC insures savings and loan associations. Any bank, whether state- or federally chartered, may obtain insurance for a fee. Currently the fee is effectively about $\frac{1}{30}$ of 1 per cent of deposits. Almost all banks have taken the opportunity to get insurance. The FDIC covers commercial banks containing 99 per cent of all commercial bank deposits and the FSLIC covers S&L's which have 97 per cent of all association assets.

Not all deposits are insured, even at banks which join the FDIC or the FSLIC, because there is a limit on the size of the deposits which are covered. Figure 6–2 indicates how federal deposit insurance coverage has tended to increase over time. For example, corporate certificates of deposit in denominations of $100,000 or more are insured only up to the $40,000 limit. Since there were over $80 billion in these deposits in 1975, it should be clear that many deposits are not fully insured. However, at thrift institutions, which depend on deposits from many small individual depositors, most deposits are fully insured.

The federal government has always attached strings to its participation in the private sector, and federal deposit insurance is no exception. Members of the FDIC and the FSLIC are subjected to extensive regulation and supervision. This is presumably justified by the need to protect the govern-

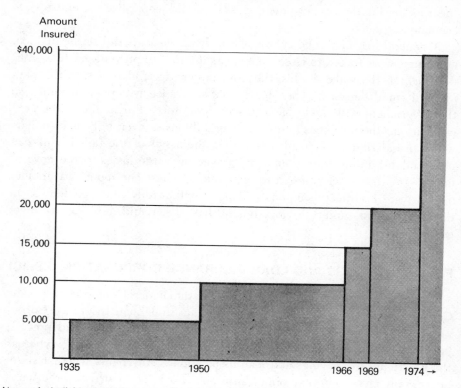

Notes: 1. Individuals holding more than one account in a bank receive insurance on each account.
2. Since December 1974, government deposits have been insured up to $100,000.
3. Only deposits at banks which are members of the FDIC and the FSLIC are covered.

Fig. 6–2. Insurance coverage on demand and savings accounts. (Each account insured to limit shown.)

ment from losses, but a private insurance corporation would not have the regulatory and supervisory authority granted to the FDIC and the FSLIC. The special public interest in financial stability justifies the broad powers of the federal insurance corporations.

The federal insurance corporations supervise state-chartered banks which are not members of the Federal Reserve system or of the Federal Home Loan Bank system.[2] Thus, the regulation of insured nonmembers is just an extension of the regulation of members; there are more similarities than differences in the regulation. The specifics of the regulation of banks and thrift institutions can be gleaned from the *Annual Report* of the Fed-

[2] The Federal Reserve System is the lender of last resort for commercial banks. Its structure and regulatory functions are similar to the FHLB system discussed above.

eral Deposit Insurance Corporation. There follow several excerpts from that report.[3]

Examinations. Examinations provide the Corporation with essential information for carrying out its supervisory responsibilities and for evaluating its risks as insurer of depositors. The Corporation regularly conducts examinations of all insured nonmember banks to determine their current condition, to evaluate bank management and to discover and obtain correction of unsafe or unsound practices or violations of laws and regulations. Although the Corporation is empowered under section 10(b) of the Federal Deposit Insurance Act to examine any insured bank for insurance purposes, it receives the reports of examinations conducted by other Federal supervisory agencies and thus rarely makes its own examinations of any Federal Reserve member bank.

At the present time, in 10 States the Corporation and State authorities conduct joint examinations, that is, examinations in which State and FDIC examiners work as a single team and make one report of examination. In three other States most of the examinations are on a joint basis. The Corporation has continued to encourage the use of joint examinations where State law lends itself to, and the State authorities are in agreement with, this procedure.

In addition to regular examinations, the Corporation conducts special examinations and investigations in connection with applications from insured nonmember banks for proposed new branches, proposed mergers, and various other actions requiring the Corporation's approval. In recent years, the numbers of these special examinations and investigations conducted each year have increased considerably faster than regular examinations.

o   o   o

Cease-and-desist and termination-of-deposit-insurance procedings. The Corporation usually attempts to gain correction of a violation of law or regulation, or of an unsafe or unsound banking practice on the part of an insured nonmember bank, by consultation with the bank's management and other appropriate supervisory authorities. The bank's failure to take the required corrective action may result in the initiation of cease-and-desist or termination-of-deposit-insurance proceedings. In certain instances, the Corporation and a bank may agree, in writing, on a specific corrective program to which the bank must adhere. Violation of a written agreement can itself be the basis for instituting cease-and-desist or termination-of-deposit-insurance proceedings.

o   o   o

Applications for deposit insurance. Nationally chartered banks, and State banks admitted to membership in the Federal Reserve System, become insured upon certification by the deciding Federal supervisory agency that the requirements for admission set forth by the Federal Deposit Insurance Act have been met. State-chartered nonmember banks apply directly to the Corporation for deposit insurance.

o   o   o

Applications for branches. Before establishing or moving a branch office, an

[3] The excerpts are from Federal Deposit Insurance Corporation, *Annual Report, 1972,* pp. 6–21. Today, the FDIC operates in substantially the same way as it did in 1972.

insured nonmember bank must have the approval of the Federal Deposit Insurance Corporation. In section 3(o) of the Federal Deposit Insurance Act, a branch is defined as ". . . any branch place of business . . . at which deposits are received, checks paid, or money lent." This definition includes tellers' windows and other limited-service facilities that may not be "branches" under the laws of some States. Excluding tellers' windows and other such limited-service facilities, Statewide or limited-area branching is prevalent in 35 States and the District of Columbia, while 15 States may be classified as unit-banking States. . . .

Branch applications approved by the Board of Directors of the Corporation totaled 716 during 1972. . . . Fourteen applications were denied. Nine of these denials were based primarily on management or financial condition, one was denied because of the applicant's very limited earnings prospects, and four were denied because they appeared substantially anticompetitive under the facts presented. An additional 132 applications for limited branch facilities were approved under delegated authority by the Director of the Division of Bank Supervision and the Corporation's 14 Regional Directors.

❖ ❖ ❖

Mergers. Section 18(c) of the Federal Deposit Insurance Act requires approval of the Corporation before any merger may be consummated in which the resulting bank is an insured bank that is not a member of the Federal Reserve System. This approval is also required in any merger of a noninsured institution into an insured bank.

The Act, as amended in 1966, provides further that, before approving any proposed merger of an insured bank, the deciding Federal agency must consider the effect of the transaction on competition, the financial and managerial resources of the banks, future prospects of the existing and proposed institutions, and convenience and needs of the community to be served. A merger that would result in a monopoly under the Sherman Antitrust Act may not be approved. A merger whose effect may be to substantially lessen competition in any section of the country, or tend to create a monopoly, may be approved, but only if the deciding agency finds that these anticompetitive effects are clearly outweighed in the public interest by the probable effects on the needs and convenience of the community to be served. Following approval of a bank merger by a Federal supervisory agency, the Justice Department may, within a 30-day period (or in emergency cases, within 5 days), bring action under the antitrust laws to prevent the merger.

❖ ❖ ❖

Truth-in-lending. The Truth-in-Lending Act (Title I of the Consumer Credit Protection Act) requires the disclosure of the terms of consumer credit used for personal, family, household, and agricultural purposes, and it regulates consumer credit advertising. The Corporation has the responsibility for administrative enforcement of the Act for insured banks that are not members of the Federal Reserve System.

Checking for compliance with the requirements of the Truth-in-Lending Act is a part of all regular examinations of State nonmember banks. When a violation is found, the Corporation ordinarily will seek voluntary corrective action. If it becomes apparent that voluntary compliance is not forthcoming, the Corporation has the authority to initiate administrative proceedings to issue a cease-and-desist order against further violations, and ultimately to terminate the deposit insurance of the bank. In addition, situations involving possible criminal violations of Federal laws are routinely referred to the Department of Justice. The Corporation refers Truth-in-Lending complaints and violations to other Federal and State enforcement agencies in accordance with established procedures.

The Act authorizes the Board of Governors of the Federal Reserve System to exempt from the requirements of disclosure any class of credit transactions within any State upon the Board's determination that applicable State laws are substantially similar to the Federal law, and that adequate provision for enforcement exists. In any State exempted from the Federal law under these provisions, while the Corporation continues its concern with the enforcement of Truth-in-Lending as a part of its regular examination procedures, primary enforcement rests with the State authorities.

Bank security. As provided by the Bank Protection Act of 1968, nonmember insured banks are subject to Corporation rules that establish minimum standards for installation, maintenance, and operation of security devices and procedures to discourage certain external bank crimes and to assist in apprehending persons who commit these crimes. In early 1969, the Corporation adopted Part 326 of its rules and regulations, which in part (a) requires the designation of a security officer for each insured State nonmember bank; (b) requires each bank to submit reports on security devices proposed for each banking office; (c) requires the development of a security program for each bank; and (d) requires each bank to develop a plan for installing, maintaining, and operating appropriate security devices in each banking office. The regulation also requires each bank to submit compliance reports as of the last business day of June of each calendar year, and to submit crime reports following the perpetration of a robbery, burglary, or nonbank employee larceny. During 1972, the Corporation received 627 crime reports filed pursuant to Part 326.5(d) of its regulations.

* * *

Nondiscrimination in lending for housing. Section 805 of Title VII of the Civil Rights Act of 1968 makes it unlawful for consumer lenders in granting real estate loans to discriminate on the basis of the loan applicant's race, color, religion, or national origin. In order to implement the fair housing provisions of Section 805 for banks under its supervision, the Board of Directors of the Corporation issued a Policy Statement on December 20, 1971. This statement, to become effective March 1, 1972, adopted certain minimum procedures that, in part, would require insured nonmember banks to publicize, by a prescribed logotype on loan service advertisements, and by lobby notices, that they are equal housing lenders. Following its analysis and evaluation of public comments received in the designated period ending March 1, 1972, the Corporation on April 25, 1972, issued an amended statement of policy. This amendment deferred the effective date of the nondiscrimination requirement from March 1 to May 1, 1972, and prescribed a redesigned logotype and lobby poster.

* * *

Corporation training activities. The Corporation's formal training programs for bank examiners, which are conducted at its modern training center, include three divisions of the Bank Examination School. These divisions consist of a basic course dealing with the fundamentals of banking and bank accounting, for new trainees; a second course emphasizing accrual accounting, audit techniques, and bank operations, with a portion devoted to examinations of computerized banks, for assistant examiners; and a program centering on credit analysis, asset appraisal, bank management simulation, and corporation policies and objectives, for senior assistant examiners. In addition, specialized training offered includes an advanced course in examining computerized banks and two courses (basic and advanced) in examining trust departments.

✿ ✿ ✿

Publications and statistical reports from banks. A report of assets and liabilities is submitted each quarter, and a report of income and expenses each year, by every insured bank to the appropriate Federal supervisory agency. The Corporation, which obtains this information from insured banks that are not members of the Federal Reserve System, has additional responsibilities for assembling and publishing the statistics for all banks. The Corporation obtains semi-annual information on assets and liabilities, but not income, of noninsured banks. A supplement to the midyear Report of Condition in 1972 gathered information on the maturity distribution of obligations of States and political subdivisions held by banks.

Data reported at midyear and at the end of the year are aggregated for the nation and each State and are published in *Assets and Liabilities—Commercial and Mutual Savings Banks*. Income data for insured banks are published in the issue of the booklet that contains the year-end Report of Condition.

Beginning with the December 1972 Report of Condition and the 1972 Report of Income, the Corporation makes available on request, at a nominal charge, the full reports of condition and income of insured nonmember commercial banks and FDIC-insured mutual savings banks. Previously, only the front of the Report of Condition—a simplified balance sheet—had been available for individual insured banks.

✿ ✿ ✿

During 1972, the Corporation continued its program of supplying a selected group of operating and report-of-condition statistics to each reporting bank. Comparative statistics are assembled for the year-end data in *Bank Operating Statistics*. Included are figures for the nation, States, different size groups of banks within each State, and smaller areas within States where branching is limited. Comparable summary data for mutual savings banks are available upon request to the Division of Research.

In conjunction with the Board of Governors of the Federal Reserve System and the Comptroller of the Currency, the fourth survey of trust assets held by commercial banks was conducted in 1972. The results of the survey were published in *Trust Assets of Insured Commercial Banks—1972*.

During the year, the Corporation continued its monthly surveys of mortgage rates and mortgage lending activity. The report form of the survey of interest rates on conventional 1-family nonfarm mortgages was revised in 1972, and the sample of banks updated. Another survey collects detailed data on acquisitions and dispositions, as well as outstanding balances, of construction and long-term mortgage loans of a selected panel of insured commercial banks and mutual savings banks.

Interest rates paid on savings and other time deposits held by individuals and businesses at insured nonmember commercial banks and FDIC-insured mutual savings banks were surveyed during 1972, as previously, on a quarterly basis. Information based on each of the surveys was sent to every reporting bank. The data were included in statistics that were published in summary form by the Board of Governors of the Federal Reserve System.

The Corporation sponsored independent research that resulted in publication of *Time-Sharing in Commercial Banks* in 1972. This 69-page book considers the current use of time-shared computers in both large and small banks.

During the past year, the Corporation encouraged research in banking and related fields by awarding four fellowships in banking and related fields to doctoral candidates. The successful applicants were selected on the basis of the importance of their proposed research, the relevancy of their research to the interests of the Corporation, and the expected ability of the applicants to complete their projects successfully.

Federal regulatory authorities—whether the FDIC, FSLIC, FHLBB, or the Federal Reserve Board—have extensive power to force their will on banks. They can force the reorganization or liquidation of a bank which is doing poorly. Thus, banks must be more conservative than other corporations, because the mere possibility of red ink jeopardizes the autonomy of bank management. The regulatory authorities can also suspend or remove bank officers in cases involving dishonesty or gross negligence.

SUMMARY

Federal regulation of the major real estate lenders is not compulsory. Rather, it is attached to voluntary membership in the Federal Home Loan Bank (FHLB) system, the Federal Reserve system, the Federal Deposit Insurance Corporation (FDIC), and the Federal Savings and Loan Insurance Corporation (FSLIC). Membership in these organizations provides substantial advantages to lenders. In return, they must accept detailed regulation and supervision of their activities.

One of the most important benefits of membership in the Federal Reserve and FHLB systems is the ability to borrow at the discount window. This form of borrowing is quickly available to lenders which are experiencing unusual demands on their liquid reserves. It may also provide a subsidy, since the rate charged (the "discount rate") is sometimes less than the rate on the other sources of funds.

Lenders which participate in the insurance programs offered by the FDIC and the FSLIC currently have each deposit account insured up to a maximum of $40,000, except for government accounts which are insured up to

$100,000. This is beneficial to the whole banking system, since confidence in the security of deposits prevents panic withdrawals. An individual deposit-taking institution has a strong incentive to participate in the government insurance programs since many depositors will not put their money in an uninsured account.

The extensive supervision of banks includes annual inspection of operating performance. Liquidity and loan quality are subject to close scrutiny, and loan terms (down payment and maturity) are checked. Merger and branching activity is supervised via applications which can be denied. Compliance with truth-in-lending and antidiscrimination laws is checked by the bank regulators. Day-to-day operating procedures, including training of personnel and processing of loans and deposits, are also examined.

Finally, the regulatory agencies require banks to submit voluminous statistics on every phase of the operation. These statistics provide early warning of operating difficulty. They are also compiled and made available to the public. This is an important source of information on the banking industry, and it is extensively used to facilitate planning at individual banks and thrift institutions.

QUESTIONS

1. The most important justification for heavy regulation of banks and thrift institutions stresses the public interest in preserving the stability of the financial system. But regulation often goes beyond mere preservation of stability.
   (a) What part of existing regulations do you think are necessary for preservation of financial stability?
   (b) What aspects of existing regulations go beyond the financial stability goal?
   (c) What might be the justification of regulations which go beyond stability? What are the drawbacks?
2. What are the powers and responsibilities of the three members of the Federal Home Loan Bank Board?
3. What are the goals of the system of cash advances from FHLB's to S&L's? How are these goals achieved?

7

FEDERAL TAX LAW INFLUENCES

Federal tax law, including the Tax Reform Act of 1976, gives favorable treatment to capital which is invested in real estate. Investors in real estate are particularly interested in four parts of the law and the regulations through which they are implemented: (1) the treatment of an owner-occupant's payments for interest and property tax; (2) the treatment of the profits of savings and loans and mutual savings banks; (3) the treatment of profits earned by syndicates and real estate investment trusts (REITs); and (4) the treatment of capital gains and losses in real estate, particularly the gains and losses of homeowners.

TAXES AND SUBSIDIES

These tax devices subsidize equity and debt capital which is invested in real estate. If the four tax provisions were abolished, investors in real estate would pay more than they now pay in federal taxes. Investment in real estate would be less attractive than it is now, so fewer dollars would flow to the real estate sector. From the U. S. Treasury's point of view, the taxes lost through the four provisions are as much a subsidy as an actual outlay of dollars. Thus, these tax provisions will frequently be termed "tax subsidies."

Any business can take depreciation on plant and equipment, so the depreciation which is allowed owners of real property cannot be considered a special tax subsidy to real estate. Nevertheless, the use of depreciation to shelter income from taxes does make investment in income-producing real property attractive. Few other investments available to individuals offer such a large amount of depreciation per dollar of gross income. A retail store, for example, has relatively few depreciable assets. The next section covers the way in which depreciation can be used to shelter income from a property and other income as well.

Federal tax law influences the risk associated with investment in real estate. For the most part, the tax law reduces risk. This chapter examines the way in which the various provisions of federal tax law alter risk.

Using Depreciation To Shelter Income.   Figure 7–1 illustrates an income-producing property which has been recently purchased for $1 million: $200,000 down and a first mortgage of $800,000. The purchase price is assumed to be about 7.7 times actual rental income of $130,000.

High interest rates (10 per cent in this example) mean that large payments must be made on the loan. With realistic property taxes of $20,000 and minimal other operating expenses of $20,000 (these expenses could well be 20 per cent of income, i.e., $26,000), the net cash flow to the investor is only $5,000. The investor has put $200,000 into the property, so the $5,000 net is not enough to justify the investment. This is especially true when risk enters the picture. A relatively small decline in income or increase in expenses could wipe out the positive net cash flow. If this were to happen, the investor might have to take cash from other sources (e.g., other assets or income from other sources) in order to operate the property.

There are a number of factors which compensate the investor for the small cash flow and the risk that additional cash will be required. One is equity build-up. In the first year, the interest expense is $80,000 (10 per cent of the $800,000 loan balance); since the loan payment is $85,000, the loan balance is reduced by $5,000. Another is appreciation in value. If the property can be sold at a price (net of selling costs) greater than $1 million, the investor will get the appreciation plus the equity build-up. However, the realization of appreciation and equity build-up is an uncertain future event. There is no way in which the investor can immediately benefit from these considerations.

A third factor, tax shelter, is of immediate value, assuming that the investor has income from other sources which can be sheltered. Figure 7–1 illustrates the amount of depreciation which can be taken under three different methods. In this example, the depreciable asset (the building, not the land) is assigned a useful life of 30 years with no salvage value. When the straight-line depreciation method is used, the annual depreciation is 3.33 per cent ($= \frac{1}{30}$) of the value of the asset. In this example, the value

Annual Revenues and Expenses

Rental income collected	$130,000
Operating expenses:	
Property taxes (2% of Market Value)	20,000
Other (15% of income; all are cash outlays)	20,000
Debt service (10%, 30-year loan of $800,000)	85,000
Net Cash Flow	5,000

Depreciation Shelter over First Five Years

Year	Straight-Line Method (assumes 30-yr. life)	Double-Declining-Balance (DDB) Method	Sum-of-the-Years'-Digits (SOYD) Method (the sum over 30 years is 465)
1	$33,333	$66,666	$64,519
2	33,333	62,221	62,366
3	33,333	58,074	60,215
4	33,333	54,202	58,065
5	33,333	50,589	55,914

Note: It is assumed that the market value of the depreciable asset, the building, is the same as cost, i.e., $1 million. For the purposes of this analysis land value is ignored.

Fig. 7–1. Depreciation shelter produced by an income property. (Assumed cost: $1 million.)

of the depreciable asset is $1 million, so the annual depreciation is a constant $33,333 per year. This is called straight-line depreciation because a graph of the book value of the building on the Y axis against time on the X axis would be a straight line. (Book value is the cost of acquisition, $1 million in this example, less cumulative depreciation.)

The double-declining-balance (DDB) method of depreciation starts at twice the rate used for the straight-line method. In the example given in Figure 7–1 the annual depreciation rate would be 6.66 per cent ($= 2 \times \frac{1}{30}$). However, this rate is applied to the book value (the "declining balance") of the building. Thus, the amount of depreciation in the second year is $62,221, 6.66 per cent of $933,334 ($= \$1,000,000 - \$66,666$). In the third year the amount of depreciation is $58,074, which is 6.66 per cent of $871,113 ($= \$1,000,000 - \$66,666 - \$62,221$).

The sum-of-the-year's-digits (SOYD) method begins by calculating the sum of the digits in the life of the asset. In our example, the sum of $1 + 2 + \ldots + 29 + 30$ is calculated. Fortunately, this sum, which is 465 in our example, can be calculated from a formula: The sum is $n/2$ times $n + 1$ where n is the total number of years in the asset life, 30 in our example. The next step is to divide the years of life remaining to the asset by the sum.

Thus, the sum of the year's digits is 15 (= 30/2) times 31 = 465. In our example, the depreciation rate for the first year is 30/465 = 6.4516 per cent. In the second year, the depreciation rate is 29/465 = 6.2366 per cent. These percentage rates are applied to the acquisition costs of the investment, the $1 million in our example.

It should be clear why the DDB and SOYD methods are called "accelerated" methods of depreciation. The amount of depreciation expense which can be deducted for tax purposes is larger in the early years of the investment than the amount which can be deducted under the straight-line method (Figure 7–1). But the amount of depreciation declines over time for both DDB and SOYD. At some point, the amount of depreciation allowed under the accelerated methods will drop below the amount allowed under the straight-line method.

Depreciation does not cause a cash outflow but it does cause an expense which is deductible for tax purposes. Suppose that the DDB method were being used for the income-producing property described in Figure 7–1. In the first year, depreciation expense would be $66,666 and there would be no corresponding cash flow. Thus, the income tax statement would have the following elements:

Gross income	$130,000
Operating expenses	40,000
Interest expense 10% on an $800,000 loan)	80,000
Depreciation expense	66,666
Total expenses	$186,666
Taxable income (loss)	($ 56,666)

This tax loss can be applied to reduce the tax liability from other, profitable lines of business. For a syndicate or a partnership the tax loss can be passed through to individual investors along with the positive cash flow. The individuals who own the property can then apply the loss against ordinary income from other sources.

Suppose that a wealthy individual has invested $200,000 of personal money in the investment described in Figure 7–1 and has chosen the DDB depreciation method. In the first year, the $200,000 investment returns a cash flow of only $5,000 but a tax shield of $56,666 is provided. If this wealthy individual were in the 40 per cent tax bracket (i.e., the government takes 40 per cent of every additional dollar of income), the tax shield reduces the tax liability by $22,666 (= .4 × $56,666). Thus, the yield of the investment in the first year is 13.8 per cent (= $27,666/200,000). Tax shields are even more valuable for individuals in higher tax brackets.

This is not the end of the tax story for this property. The tax authorities have the last laugh since they tax the appreciation in value at the time the property is sold; this is one thing the 1976 Tax Reform Act didn't change. Continuing with the above example, suppose that the property is sold at the end of five years for the amount put into the property, $1 million. The transaction is taxed at the difference between the sale price and the depreciated value of the property. In this example, the depreciated value of the property is $708,248 (= $1,000,000 − 66,666 − 62,221 − 58,074 − 54,202 − 50,589) so taxes are due on appreciation equal to $291,752 ($1,000,000 − $708,248). Clearly, taxes are due on the amount of the tax shelter, i.e., the sum of depreciation expenses. How has the investor benefited?

The benefit from a tax shelter comes in two ways. First, the appreciation, which is called capital gains, is taxed at a lower rate than ordinary income. In this example, part of the capital gains will be taxed at a 20 per cent rate rather than the 40 per cent rate for ordinary income; but only the part equal to straight-line depreciation (− $166,665) is eligible for the favorable capital gains treatment. The "excess depreciation" (total less straight line) is taxed at the ordinary income rate. Second, the tax liability on capital gains is generated after five years, while the tax savings were generated earlier. Thus, tax payments were deferred. This is equivalent to borrowing money from the taxing authorities, with zero interest charged by the authorities.

The 1976 Tax Reform Act reduced tax subsidies available from prepaid or construction period interest expenses. Suppose that the buyer of the property illustrated in Figure 7–1 had been required to pay two "points" to the lender. Since one point is 1 per cent of the loan amount, the buyer would have to pay the lender $16,000 in return for the privilege of getting the loan. Under the new law, this amount must be deducted from taxable income at the rate of $1,600 per year for ten years. The old law was much more liberal since the entire $16,000 could be deducted in the year paid. But the new law does make an exception for a home occupied as the principal residence; prepaid or construction period interest can be deducted in the year paid.

The simple example in Figure 7–1 has quickly gotten quite complicated, but it serves to illustrate the tax advantages of real estate. Shares of corporate stock and corporate bonds do not offer the same tax shield to investors.

The principles discussed here cannot substitute for the advice of a competent tax lawyer or accountant. These professionals can introduce further considerations, some of which we discuss below under the section on capital gains. Also, they can keep the investor informed on the latest IRS rulings and court decisions.

The Treatment of Interest and Property Taxes. Payments by home-owner-occupants for interest and property tax can be deducted from income in arriving at net taxable income. The deduction of interest and property tax is a subsidy to homeownership, but the way in which it provides a subsidy is not obvious. Landlords, like homeowners, can deduct interest and property taxes from their income. Furthermore, landlords can deduct an allowance for depreciation and for maintenance and operating expenses: i.e., landlords are treated like any corporation in that they can deduct the cost of doing business. Since the deductions available to landlords reduce the cost of the housing services which they provide, it would seem that families are being encouraged to rent rather than to own.

This apparent riddle can be solved in two ways. One is to note that the homeowner is sheltering outside income, unrelated to income earned from the property. The landlord, on the other hand, is usually unable to shelter nearly as much outside income as the homeowner. Another approach is to consider the homeowner's *implicit income* from a property. Implicit income is the amount of rent that the home would command on the open market. By foregoing the opportunity to rent the home, the owner is implicitly paying the rent from one pocket into the other. Clearly, this implicit income is not taxed, since it is not reported to the IRS, whereas the landlord's explicit rental receipts must be reported to the IRS.

Those who remain unconvinced that the deduction of interest and property taxes is a subsidy to homeownership may be persuaded by the following hypothetical situation:

1. A community consists of identical households occupying identical homes.
2. Each household head earns wages at the local factory.
3. Each household owns and occupies its own home, paying property taxes and interest on a mortgage.

Now a change occurs: the households play "musical houses," with each moving into a neighbor's house. After the change, the households pay each other identical rent. Clearly, the tax liability of each household has increased, because income has increased by the amount of the rent received, whereas deductions have increased only by the amount of depreciation and maintenance and operating expenses.

The amount of the federal tax subsidy of homeownership has been estimated at $2.9 billion for the entire U. S. in 1966.[1] In 1975 the subsidy was approximately $6.2 billion.[2] This does not include the subsidy of the *net* implicit rent. If the IRS attempted to make an estimate of the rental value of homes, it would presumably treat households as businesses: the implicit rental income would be reported as income, and expenses such as interest, property taxes, maintenance and operating expenses, and depreciation would be subtracted. The homeowner would be taxed only on the net implicit rent, after subtracting the expenses of homeownership. Relative to the existing tax procedures, this would increase homeowner taxes by $6.2 billion plus the tax on the net implicit rent.

The tax subsidy of homeownership is a *regressive* subsidy; i.e., it benefits the high-income family more than the poor. The reason is that the high-income family, in a higher tax bracket, gets a greater tax deduction—whether the deduction is measured in absolute dollars or as a percentage of income —than the low-income family. Also, high-income families are more likely to own than to rent. Aaron, using 1966 data, estimated that 70 per cent of the subsidy went to families with incomes above $10,000 per year and fully 90 per cent to families with incomes over $7,000.[3]

TAX SUBSIDIES TO LENDERS

Federal tax subsidies are available to lenders which are owned by depositors rather than by shareholders. This includes all mutual savings banks in the 18 states which permit them, all federally chartered savings and loan associations, and state-chartered savings and loan associations which are organized on a mutual basis.

Prior to 1951 these mutual lenders were free from federal profit taxation. Since that time, their federal tax burden has increased, but it is still substantially below the federal tax rate for nonfinancial corporations. More significantly, the tax law now specifically rewards investment of assets in real estate. Although these mutual institutions have always specialized in real estate finance, the tax law now explicitly recognizes the subsidization of real estate finance as a valid goal of national economic policy.

From 1951 through 1962 the mutual lenders paid no taxes on 100 per cent of additions to bad debt reserves, up to a maximum of 12 per cent of savings balances. For the period 1962 through 1969 only 60 per cent of additions

---

[1] Henry J. Aaron, *Shelter and Subsidies* (Washington, D. C.: The Brookings Institution, 1972), p. 56.

[2] The author has taken the growth in the subsidy to equal the growth in mortgage loans outstanding. This procedure involves a number of simplifying assumptions.

[3] Aaron, *op. cit.*, pp. 56–57.

to bad debt reserves, up to a maximum of only 6 per cent of savings, was tax-free. In 1970, pursuant to the 1969 Tax Reform Act, the tax authorities began a reduction of the 60 per cent figure toward a target of 40 per cent in 1979. In 1975, only 45 per cent of the additions to bad debt reserves were tax-free, up to a maximum of 6 per cent of savings.

This special tax subsidy is tied directly to the provision of mortgage money to the housing market. In the 1962 through 1969 period, the law required that 82 per cent or more of the institution's assets be held in residential mortgages, cash, government securities, and passbook loans. Otherwise the institution would lose the tax subsidy. Presently, the law has been liberalized; the institution loses only .75 per cent of its bad debt deduction for each 1 per cent by which it fails to meet the 82 per cent threshold. Thus, mutual associations are given an incentive to increase their holdings of mortgages or highly liquid assets up to the 82 per cent level.

The reduction in the tax subsidy to mutual lenders has been particularly sharp during the 16 years ended 1976. The profits tax rate of savings and loans can serve as an indicator. The rate was virtually zero in 1950, only 7 per cent in 1960, 16.1 per cent in 1965, and 27.3 per cent in 1972.[4] By way of comparison, the 1972 tax rate (i.e., profits taxes divided by profits before taxes) for mutual savings banks was 28 per cent. For commercial banks the rate was 23.5 per cent and for all corporations (including financial corporations) the rate in 1972 was 41.2 per cent.[5] Thus, the mutual institutions were given a substantial tax subsidy compared to all corporations but not compared to commercial banks.

The lower average taxation of commercial banks is significant in the light of the Hunt Commission proposals to tax all financial intermediaries on an equal basis and give them equal powers to accept deposits (including demand deposits) and to make all types of loans. These proposals, which are important even though they haven't been enacted into law, are discussed in Chapter 20. The tax subsidy of commercial banks is largely unrelated to the special tax treatment of additions to bad debt reserve; commercial banks don't benefit from this nearly as much as the mutual institutions. Rather, the subsidy stems from the tax-exempt interest on state and local bonds held by commercial banks. This points up the difficulty of achieving uniformity in the tax treatment of financial intermediaries. The differential tax treatment is related to a variety of causes and to the underlying differences in the functions of the intermediaries.

The quantitative significance of the special tax treatment of mutual lend-

---

[4] U. S. League of Savings and Loan Associations, *1974 Fact Book*, p. 104.

[5] The data for the last two sentences come from the FDIC, *1972 Annual Report*, pp. 265 and 271, from the *Survey of Current Business*, February, 1975, p. 5–2.

ers can be estimated by asking how much more tax they would pay if they were taxed at the same rate as manufacturing corporations. (This procedure ignores the fact that a change in taxation would change the size of before-tax profits and change the types of assets held by the mutual lenders). If this had been the case in 1972, the taxes of savings and loans would have increased by about $260 million whereas those of mutual savings banks would have increased by about $100.1 million. Thus, the federal government provided a subsidy, in the form of foregone tax revenue, of roughly $.36 billion. This subsidy is designed to encourage lending related to real estate.

TAX PREFERENCES FOR REITs AND OTHER SYNDICATES

The owners of most corporations, the stockholders, are taxed twice—once when the corporation figures its profits and once when a portion of the after-tax profits is paid in dividends. The profits are taxed at the corporate profit tax rate and the dividends are taxed as individual income.

The owners of REITs are taxed only once—when dividends are paid they are taxed at the rate on individual income. The profits of REITs are not taxed on that portion which is passed through to stockholders in the form of dividends. To take advantage of this tax preference, REITs must satisfy a number of conditions. The most important conditions are:

1. At least 90 per cent of profits must be paid out in dividends.
2. At least 75 per cent of assets must be invested in real estate, government securities, and cash.
3. The REIT must be managed by trustees for the benefit of owners of transferable shares.
4. The REIT must be a passive investor. It cannot engage in short-term speculation with equity positions in real estate, and it cannot engage directly in the management of real estate.

The tax treatment of REITs gives them a preferred position relative to the thrift institutions, commercial banks, and nonfinancial corporations. Federal taxes paid by REITs were virtually zero in 1972, as opposed to the substantial profits taxes levied against other institutions. Does this tax subsidy serve a public purpose? [6]

The tax subsidy is designed to give small investors an equity position in real estate. By buying shares of stock in REITs, the small investor can participate in a diversified portfolio of the construction loans, development

---

[6] The use of 1972 as a base line of comparison is necessary because of the subsequent deterioration in the position of REITs vis à vis other mortgage lenders.

loans, and mortgages on completed property which make up most of the typical REIT's holdings. In the absence of the tax subsidy, this type of investment presumably would not be attractive to small investors, so the supply of capital to the real estate industry would be reduced. On the other hand, many investors who use the tax subsidy would undertake the same type of investment even if the subsidy were not available. Thus, the amount of funds actually brought into the real estate sector by the subsidty cannot be estimated with any certainty.[7]

The tax subsidy is tied directly to the requirement that REITs invest in real estate. As a practical matter, almost 100 per cent of the REIT's assets are in real estate, cash, or government securities, not the 75 per cent minimum required by law. Thus, about $20 billion was made available to the real estate sector through REITs in 1972.

REITs are really a special type of real estate syndication. Other types of syndications (e.g., partnerships) enjoy tax privileges similar to those enjoyed by REITs: the portion of profits passed through to investors is not taxed before it reaches the investors.

The 1976 Tax Reform Act gave a special advantage to partnerships engaged primarily in real estate investment. Those partners whose liability is limited to the amount of their invesment can benefit from deductions based on the entire property value. Since a large part of property value is financed by a mortgage, the partners have bought large deductions with a limited investment. For example, suppose that the building illustrated in Figure 7–1 were owned by a group of partners. If the $800,000 mortgage had a nonrecourse provision—i.e., the lender cannot sue the partners—then all possible losses would be limited to the amount of their equity investment: This $200,000 would be the amount which the partners have "at risk." But under the 1976 law, the amount of depreciation which they can deduct is still $66,666 in the first year: over the life of the investment they could take deductions totaling $1 million even though their combined investment is only $200,000. The 1976 law denied this form of tax subsidy to partnerships not engaged in real estate investment.

TAX PREFERENCES FOR CAPITAL GAINS

Under the 1976 Tax Reform Act, investors with an equity position in any asset, financial or real, are usually eligible to receive preferential treatment of capital gains if they hold the asset for more than twelve months. Traders in real estate—i.e., those who make it their business to buy property and

[7] This same argument applies to all of the tax subsidies described here.

inventory it for later resale—must report gains as ordinary income, but the homeowner-occupant is always eligible for the preferential tax on long-term capital gains. The homeowner is further encouraged by a special tax provision which is not available to other investors: the homeowner can indefinitely defer all capital gains taxes if the gains are reinvested in another home within one year. To take full advantage of this provision, the cost of the new residence must be at least as much as the proceeds from the former residence, so the homeownr's opportunity to reduce the mortgage is restricted.

The homeowner who reinvests in a new residence is deferring tax liability. To calculate capital gains, the investor takes the sale price (excluding all costs of sale and of fix-up for sale) and subtracts the acquisition "basis" of the property. The basis for a new residence acquired by the homeowner becomes the purchase price of the old home, adjusted in several ways. The purchase price of the old home includes lawyers' and brokers' fees associated with the purchase, and it includes the cost of additional investment in the property. For example, a homeowner who panels a room or builds an addition can reduce capital gains by adding these expenses to the acquisition "basis." When the new home is sold, the capital gain is computed as the difference between the proceeds of the sale and the adjusted basis, but the basis was established by the cash outlay for the old property. Thus, the capital gain on the old property will become payable when the new residence is sold, provided that the proceeds of this sale are not again reinvested in a home.

A homeowner with a large capital gain on the sale of a house might choose to purchase a house which costs less than the cash proceeds of the sale. In this case, taxes are paid at the time of the transaction but only on that portion of the gains which was not reinvested in the new home. Or, the homeowner might choose to invest part of the proceeds from the sale of the home in a vacation home and part in a new place of permanent residence. In this case, taxes can be deferred only on that part of the capital gains which is reinvested in the new permanent place of residence.

For many homeowners, the deferral of taxes on gains which are reinvested in a new home is tantamount to a tax exemption. This is clearly the case for homeowners who are not required to move frequently. Those who do move frequently are discouraged from temporarily renting. If they rent for more than eighteen months, they will have to pay capital gains taxes on the sale of their former home. However, persons over age 65 can usually escape some taxation on capital gains, even if they sell their home and rent an apartment. To qualify, the home sold must have been occupied as the principal residence for five of the previous eight years. Only the gains on the first $30,000 of the adjusted sales price are exempt from capital gains when the homeowner is over age 65.

The calculation of the acquisition basis is different when a property is acquired through gift or inheritance. When this occurs, it is usually necessary to have a professional appraiser estimate the fair market value of the property. This fair market value plus any acquisition costs becomes the basis. When a property is acquired through exchange, the basis for the new property is the same as the basis for the old property.

Under the 1976 Tax Reform Act, investors in real estate can still indefinitely defer capital gains taxes by exchanging property rather than selling it. For example, if a warehouse worth $100,000 is traded for an apartment building worth $100,000 and both are owned free and clear, neither party to the transaction is taxed. The parties simply apply the tax basis associated with the old property to the new one. But assume this more complex exchange:

Property 1		*Property 2*	
Mortgage	$ 50,000	Mortgage	$ 50,000
Equity	50,000	Equity	60,000
Property value	$100,000	Property value	$110,000
Cash	$ 10,000		

In the exchange, the owner of property 1 has to put up cash—or other forms of "boot" such as a boat or automobile worth $10,000—in order to make the exchange fair. This boot is taxable for the person acquiring property 1.

The taxable portion of the exchange (the boot) is any property which is unlike real estate. But mortgages are unlike real property. Thus, any differences in the amounts of the mortgages must be boot. For example, consider the following exchange:

Property 1		*Property 2*	
Mortgage	$ 50,000	Mortgage	$ 30,000
Equity	50,000	Equity	60,000
Property value	$100,000	Property value	$ 90,000
Cash	$ 10,000		

The person acquiring property 2 and assuming the mortgage would now have a reduction in mortgage liability of $20,000. This boot received is netted against the boot given, the $10,000 cash: the result is a tax liability on the $10,000 net boot. This net boot received is equivalent to recognized capital gains.

Under the 1976 Tax Reform Act, what is the tax effect of this exchange for the person acquiring property 1? This person has net boot given of $10,000, the cash received less the extra mortgage liability assumed. The tax basis in property 1 can be increased by the net boot given. For example, if the basis in property 2 were $25,000 before the exchange, the basis in property 1 would be $35,000 after the exchange. Thus, if the person acquiring property 1 were to sell it for $100,000 the day after the exchange, a capital gain of $65,000 would be recognized. This is the same gain which would have been recognized if property 2 had been sold outright instead of exchanged.

The rules governing tax-deferred exchanges may seem complex, but there is an underlying logic: Taxes on capital gains can be deferred, never escaped entirely. The student should work through the examples given above with the added assumption that the basis in each property is $25,000 before the exchange. (This assumption can be changed; the results are always the same.) Compue capital gains before the exchange and after the exchange, remembering that there are two kinds of capital gains: gains recognized at the time of the exchange (net boot received) and gains unrecognized (property value less basis). The student will find that the sum of recognized and unrecognized capital gain is always the same before the exchange as after. Thus, exchanges are simply a technique for acquiring new property while deferring taxes on the unrecognized portion of capital gains.

The tax treatment of capital gains provides the investor in real property with an incentive to improve the property. The cost of these capital improvements is added to the acquisition basis of the property, reducing any capital gains or increasing capital losses. This is the only federal tax subsidy which specifically encourages the flow of new capital into existing property.

The tax subsidy which is given to real estate through the treatment of capital gains is a regressive subsidy; i.e., the amount of the subsidy is greater for high-income investors than for low-income investors. Capital gains are taxes at one-half of the rate for ordinary income. A typical family of four with a gross income of less than $22,000 will receive only a 12.5 per cent benefit, since the amount they pay on capital gains is one-half their marginal tax rate. (Of course, they will receive a 25 per cent benefit if they can defer the payment of the capital gains tax under the provisions outlined above.) Thus, this tax subsidy is primarily useful for high-income individuals; e.g., an individual in the 70 per cent bracket can get a 35 per cent benefit from the special treatment of capital gains, or a 70 per cent benefit if the gains can be indefinitely deferred as outlined above.

THE REDUCTION OF RISK THROUGH TAX SUBSIDIES

The tax subsidy helps mutual lenders to absorb the risk of losses on their mortgage portfolio. Additions to bad debt reserves are free from profits taxes (subject to the limitations discussed above) so these lenders have less to fear from defaults in mortgage payments than other lenders. This should encourage them to accept mortgages which would be too risky in the absence of the government's policy of reducing risk.

The effect of the tax subsidy afforded to REITs is to make a stockholder's investment riskier than it would be in another type of security. REITs cannot pass losses through to stockholders, and there would be little point in carrying losses forward since profits are passed through to investors without taxation. Thus, the stockholders must absorb 100 per cent of the loss, whereas the typical stockholder in a nonfinancial corporation absorbs only 57 per cent of any losses. On average, the other 43 per cent is absorbed through reduction in the nonfinancial corporation's tax liability.

Many REITs hemorrhaging red ink have discovered too late that their tax situation leaves them open to high risk. It is not at all certain that this aspect was carefully considered by investors contemplating the purchase of shares in a REIT. Some REITs have recently converted to ordinary corporations so that they can get the advantage of tax loss carryovers when good times return.

Figure 7–2 summarizes the total dollar amount of federal tax subsidy from three important sources. The total is $5.2 billion. The lion's share, 88.4 per cent of the total, goes to homeowners who occupy their homes. The remainder, 11.6 per cent or about $.6 billion, goes to the thrift institutions and to REITs. (The subsidy to REITs was vastly diminished in 1975 by their limited profitability.) The $.6 billion compares to a total corporate profit tax liability of $42.7 billion in 1972. The government sacrificed about 1.5 per cent of the total revenue it could have received from corporations in order to encourage the flow of capital into real estate.

SUMMARY

Homeowners can deduct from income the interest and property taxes paid on homes which they occupy. Since the income is unrelated to the property, they are receiving preferential tax treatment when compared to landlords. Also, the implicit net income after all expenses from the homeowner's property is exempt from taxes. This tax subsidy favors ownership over the rental of an apartment. The amount of the subsidy (in percentage

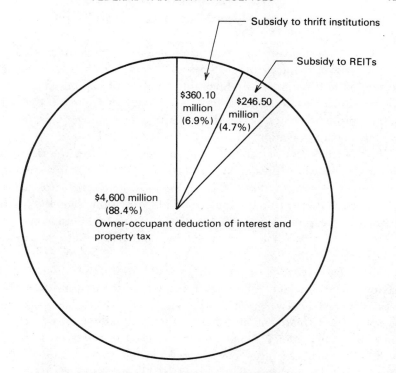

Subsidy to thrift institutions

Subsidy to REITs

$360.10 million (6.9%)

$246.50 million (4.7%)

$4,600 million (88.4%)
Owner-occupant deduction of interest and property tax

Total 1972 Tax Subsidy: $5,206.60 million

Notes: Owner-occupant subsidy based on Henry J. Aaron, *Shelter and Subsidies* (Washington, D.C.: The Brookings Institution, 1972).

Subsidy to thrifts and REITs based on assumption that an unexpected 1973 law forced them to pay profits taxes at the rate for manufacturing corporations (42.3 per cent). Subsidies omitted because of insufficient data: (1) Zero taxation of net implicit rent of owner-occupants, and (2) favorable tax treatment of capital gains.

Fig. 7–2. Tax subsidies to real estate, 1972.

terms) is greater for high-income than for low-income families; i.e., it is a regressive tax subsidy.

The profits of savings and loans and mutual savings banks are the subject of preferential tax treatment, provided that these institutions are organized on a mutual basis (without stockholders). These complicated tax provisions currently exempt from taxation a part of the profits which are transferred to bad debt reserves. On average, this gives these lenders to the real estate sector a substantial subsidy relative to nonfinancial corporations.

The profits of real estate investment trusts (REITs) are exempt from taxation if they are passed through to stockholders in the form of dividends.

Other corporations must pay taxes on profits regardless of the amount of dividends paid.

The tax treatment of long-term capital gains benefits real estate as well as equity investment in other types of assets. Furthermore, homeowners are singled out for especially favorable taxation of capital gains. They can indefinitely defer all taxation provided that they reinvest their gains in another principal place of residence. Homeowners over age 65 can permanently escape taxation on a part of their capital gains.

The tax treatment of capital gains and losses reduces the risk associated with investment in real estate, regardless of whether that investment is by a homeowner or someone else. This is because long-term capital losses can be deducted from ordinary income. This provision, like the preferential treatment of capital gains, is particularly useful to high-income investors.

The risk of real estate investment by mutual lending institutions is reduced through provisions of the federal tax law. These institutions are less fearful of bad debt losses than they would be in the absence of the reduction in taxes which follows a transfer to reserves for bad debt losses.

Economic difficulty recently experienced by REITs have disclosed that the special tax treatment afforded to them actually increases the risk assumed by stockholders. Losses cannot be used to reduce the stockholders' tax liability, whereas other corporations do get tax reductions when they incur losses. Thus, the stockholders in REITs must absorb 100 per cent of any losses. This has led some troubled REITs to convert to ordinary corporations.

QUESTIONS

1. Suppose that you are in the 60 per cent tax bracket and that you buy an income property for $1 million, 20 per cent of which is land value. Rental income collected, operating expenses, and debt service are the same as those given in Figure 7–1 (p. 109), but you use straight-line depreciation over a 25-year life for the improvements. (*Note:* Since the tax authorities assume that land has an infinite life, the straight-line depreciation rate is zero; i.e., no depreciation is allowed on land.)

   (a) What are the taxable income and the income tax shield during the first year of operation? (Show your work.)

   (b) How much does depreciation reduce taxes during the first year?

   (c) What is the first year's after-tax yield on the original equity investment?

   (d) Suppose that the property is sold at the end of the second year and that the capital gains are taxed at one-half the ordinary income tax rate. What is the income tax effect during the second year?

   (e) Continue with the assumptions made in (d). What is the present value of all the tax effects of depreciation, i.e., the reduction figured in (b) and the taxes on capital gains?

2. What is a "tax subsidy"?
3. Homeowners are allowed to deduct interest and property taxes from their income before paying income taxes. It is argued that this is a special tax subsidy given homeowners and only to homeowners, but landlords can also deduct these expenses. Explain in your own words how the homeowners are getting a special break.
4. Some people who have very nice houses in neighborhoods with rapid appreciation in value always seem to be "cash poor."
   (a) Explain how federal tax law encourages people with property appreciation to consume a lot of housing relative to other goods.
   (b) How does special consideration of the elderly allow them to recover at least part of their capital gains for expenditure on other goods?
5. What do REITS have to do to qualify for zero taxes on profits?
6. How does federal tax law reduce the risk associated with investment in mortgages by thrift institutions?

8

GOVERNMENT ACTIVITY IN THE SECONDARY MORTGAGE MARKET

Existing mortgages are bought and sold in a national market known as the secondary mortgage market. In the primary mortgage market, the new mortgage market, new mortgage loans are extended to the principals in a real estate deal—e.g., the buyer, whether the buyer is acquiring a new or existing property, and the builder or developer. In the secondary mortgage market, existing financial instruments are traded without consulting the principals.

The economic function of the secondary mortgage market is similar to that of secondary markets for stocks and bonds. The exchanges and the over-the-counter markets where stocks and bonds are traded provide liquidity to these investments. Thus, an investor who buys a new issue of stocks or bonds provides money to the issuing company or agency, but the secondary market gives that investor flexibility. If the secondary market is functioning normally, an investor can sell a financial security at any time; the investor isn't married to the issuing company or agency. This advantage carries over to the secondary mortgage market. But the secondary mortgage market has been slow to develop and most of its development has been carefully nurtured by the federal government. The special characteristics of the secondary mortgage market, many of which are not shared by secondary markets for other securities, are examined in this chapter.

Almost all activity in the secondary mortgage market is in residential mortgage loans because the federal government has attempted to encourage investment in residential real estate via stimulation of the secondary mortgage market. This chapter establishes the linkage between government programs to improve (and subsidize) the secondary market and the flow of mortgage money to the principals in real estate. The mechanics of the secondary market are examined in some detail.

THE FUNCTIONS OF THE SECONDARY MORTGAGE MARKET

Why has national policy nurtured the development of the secondary mortgage market? There are three reasons:

1. As a national market, the secondary mortgage market encourages the flow of funds from surplus areas of the country to deficit areas.
2. By providing mortgage lenders with liquidity, i.e., the ability to convert their mortgages into cash within a reasonably short period of time, the secondary mortgage market makes an investment in mortgages more attractive.
3. New money is attracted to primary mortgages by the separation of the risk-bearing, financing, and servicing aspects of mortgage extension.

Each of these reasons will now be examined in detail.

A National Market.   Buyers and sellers from all over the country effect transactions in the secondary mortgage market. This has enormous significance, because the primary mortgage market, unlike the market for newly issued stocks and bonds, is a local market. Savings and loan associations, for example, are required by regulators to make the vast majority of their loans on properties which are within 100 miles of their offices. Thrift institutions constrain themselves to a local market when making new loans to avoid properties which will be hard to reach if inspection, repairs, and maintenance become necessary. Insurance companies do lend on a nationwide basis, but only through trusted correspondents to the least risky borrowers.

The local character of the primary mortgage market is unique. New public issues of corporate securities are almost always distributed nationwide, and they may be distributed internationally. A new issue of corporate bonds, for example, is often distributed by an investment banking syndicate which has offices around the world. This method of distribution is rarely used in real estate finance—never for residential mortgage loans.

Therefore, the national character of the secondary market for mortgage loans is of particular significance.

Historically, mortgage lenders operating close to home have been limited by the amount of funds available in the local area. If deposits at thrift institutions were scarce in the area, the amount of money available for mortgage lending would also be limited and the scarcity of funds would make interest rates high. Areas with a relatively larger supply of loanable funds would have relatively lower interest rates. The development of a secondary mortgage market has changed these historical relationships.

Differences in regional interest rates indicate the extent of the development of a national mortgage market. Historically, regional interest rate differentials have narrowed since 1890, but some regional differences still exist. In 1960 the rate on conventional (i.e., uninsured) mortgages was 6.15 per cent in California and Texas but only 5.88 per cent in New York and other eastern states.[1] In December 1975 the West was still mortgage-deficient; the rate on conventional mortgages was 9.5 per cent in San Francisco, 9.1 in Houston, and 8.6 in New York.

Overcoming Regional Rate Differentials. Can regional interest rate differentials be explained by factors other than local capital deficiencies? Schaaf has investigated the possibility that regional interest rates are related to the riskiness of the loans.[2] His theory is that since financal institutions make riskier loans in certain parts of the country, they charge higher interest rates to compensate for the risk. When Schaaf measured risk by the loan-to-value ratio, he found a positive relationship to regional mortgage rates. But at the same time, he found that distance from a metropolitan area (Boston) is positively related to mortgage yields. Thus, regional capital deficiency appears to be an important cause of regional interest differentials, even after holding constant for regional differences in riskiness of loans.

In the mid-1960's, the west experienced such a deficit in mortgage capital that the California savings and loan associations began to advertise in the east. Their objective was to attract individuals with small deposits not needed for immediate use. Because of the shortage of capital in the west, the California S&L's could, for a time, offer higher interest rates than were available on savings deposits in the east.

The advertising campaign to attract deposits from many small individuals was a costly method of attracting funds. The prospective depositors required substantial compensation for sending their funds across the country.

[1] Jack M. Guttentag and Morris Beck, *New Series on Home Mortgage Yields Since 1951*, National Bureau of Economic Research, 1970, p. 69.

[2] A. H. Schaaf, "Regional Differences in Mortgage Financing Costs," *The Journal of Finance*, vol. 21, no. 1 (March, 1966).

These funds became illiquid; they could not be withdrawn simply by visiting the nearby branch of the local thrift institution or by writing a check. A delay of several days was required while a request for withdrawal crossed the country by mail. Consequently, most of the deposits were long-term time deposits and not day-of-deposit, day-of-withdrawal accounts.

The secondary mortgage market provides a much more efficient means of equalizing the regional imbalances in the supply of mortgage funds. Since the buyers of mortgages on the secondary market are generally large institutions—pension funds, insurance companies, thrift institutions, commercial banks, and so forth—large blocks of funds are involved. Professional intermediaries—mortgage brokers and governmental institutions—specialize in bringing together buyer and seller in the secondary market. These professionals are expert at ferreting out loanable funds wherever they exist. They can do this on a systematic basis, so the result is greater interregional dollar flows at less transfer cost per dollar than under the system of advertising for deposits at thrift institutions.

Aiding Regional Funds Deficits. The flow of funds from surplus to deficit regions is clearly advantageous to the deficit regions. They get more funds at less cost per dollar than they had before. With more funds flowing into the region, mortgage interest rates are lowered in the *primary* mortgage market. The primary market benefits from development of the secondary market, which stimulates construction and encourages home ownership.

The interregional flow of funds also benefits the surplus regions, but in a less obvious manner. Lenders in the surplus area clearly benefit; otherwise they wouldn't participate in the market. They get higher interest rates or they get less risk than they would in the absence of the secondary mortgage market. The economy of the surplus region benefits from greater trade with the deficit areas. To the extent that lower interest rates stimulate economic activity in the deficit region, trade is stimulated.

Improving Mortgage Liquidity. Liquidity is the ability to sell a financial instrument at small cost within a short period of time. The secondary mortgage market improves the liquidity of mortgages, although mortgages are still substantially less liquid than most stocks or bonds. The ability to sell on the secondary market assures the investor that cash can be raised to meet unforeseen future financial needs. Investors are willing to accept a lower rate of return on a more liquid investment; i.e., they pay for the convenience of being able to sell quickly by accepting lower interest. Thus, an increase in the liquidity of mortgages tends to lower interest rates throughout the market, even in the surplus region. The convenience of liquidity tends to lower interest rates in the surplus region, offsetting any increase caused by the diversion of funds to the deficit region.

Reducing Overall Mortgage Costs. When a bank extends a mortgage and then holds that mortgage, it is performing three distinct functions: financing, servicing, and risk bearing. As part of the financing function, the bank supplies funds. It is compensated with an interest rate which must be sufficient to cover the cost of acquiring the funds (e.g., paying interest to depositors and providing teller windows for the convenience of depositors) plus a profit. Financing can be logically separated from risk bearing; insurance can be purchased to pay the principal amount of the mortgage if the mortgagor defaults. The servicing function involves the clerical functions of billing, collecting payments, processing defaults, and sometimes handling payments for insurance and property tax.

The secondary mortgage market provides a mechanism for separating these three functions. Thus, specialists can develop expertise in each function, reducing the overall cost of extending a mortgage. As explained in the previous chapter, mortgage insurance is often available to absorb much of the risk of default. Insurance is important to the development of a national mortgage market; a distant investor does not want to get involved with evaluating the risk characteristics of a specific property. Federal insurance is particularly important in the private secondary mortgage market, i.e., the secondary market which operates without the interference of governmental organizations. These private market participants are more worried about default than the government.

Loan Servicing. The servicing function is uniquely important in the mortgage market, unlike the stock and bond markets where the servicing function is usually performed by a trustee or agent of the issuing corporation. In the stock and bond markets, the servicing function consists mainly of mailing dividends and paying coupons. In the mortgage market, payments must be collected from each individual mortgagor.

The servicing function is almost never traded on the secondary market. Instead, it remains with the financial institution which originated the mortgage loan, or with its agent. We turn, therefore, to a discussion of the various institutions which make the secondary mortgage market work.

ORGANIZATION OF THE SECONDARY MARKET

The servicing function is compensated with a fee, usually substantially less than .5 per cent of the outstanding amount of the mortgage.[3] Mortgage

---

[3] The average servicing fee in 1974 was .44 per cent on mortgages sold to GNMA and no more than .38 per cent on other mortgages.

bankers tend to become specialists in the servicing function: they rely on their ability to sell mortgages which they originate, retaining only the servicing function. For example, Colwell Company, a Los Angeles based mortgage company, reported that about one-third of its 1974 income came from servicing fees. This income was not subject to the cost–price squeeze which caused Colwell's 1974 earnings per share to decline 89 per cent from the 1973 level.[4] Without the servicing fees, Colwell would have reported a large loss in 1974.

Mortgage bankers become specialists in servicing mortgages by originating mortgages which are predestined to be sold immediately to a life insurance company or other institution. To accomplish this, the mortgage banker obtains a commitment from the other institution to purchase the mortgage but arranges to retain the servicing function in return for a fee. This unique arrangement allows insurance companies to make mortgage loans nationwide, without the network of branch offices which would be necessary to originate and service the geographically dispersed loans. In effect, the mortgage companies become agents (or "correspondents") of the insurance companies.

These commitments to purchase loans have certain strings attached. For example, the mortgage banker is usually obligated to search for the best properties and the most credit worthy mortgagors. In order to get these mortgagors, a relatively low rate of interest must be charged. (Thus, insurance companies generally receive less interest on their mortgages than the thrift institutions.) Because of the strings attached to commitments, the actual sale of the mortgage cannot be considered a true secondary market sale; i.e., it is not an arm's-length transaction involving nothing but the characteristics of a financial instrument.

Another type of secondary market sale involves an institution which originates a mortgage with the intention of selling it quickly. No commitment is obtained, but the originating institution has no intention of permanently lending funds. It should be distinguished from a true secondary market sale in which both buyer and seller view the mortgage as an investment.[5] With a true secondary market sale, the selling institution must sell its investment because it needs money for other purposes or because it feels that the terms of sale are particularly attractive.

The mortgage *broker* (not to be confused with the mortgage *banker*) receives all of its income from the secondary market. The mortgage broker brings buyer and seller together, holding real estate loans only as part of

---

[4] The Colwell Company, *Annual Report, 1974.*
[5] Saul Klaman, *The Postwar Residential Mortgage Market* (Princeton, N.J.: Princeton University Press for the National Bureau of Economic Research, 1961).

this brokerage function. The mortgage broker is analogous to the stock broker, and it receives income in the same way: by charging fees to buyer and seller or by taking a spread between the bid and asked prices. Under the latter method, the mortgage broker buys a real estate loan at one price and resells it at a slightly higher price. The buyer at the higher price is willing to pay the premium in order to avoid the costly process of finding a seller.

The Federal National Mortgage Association (FNMA). Mortgage brokers have a powerful competitor in the form of a government-inspired organization known as "Fannie Mae" (the Federal National Mortgage Association). As the nation's largest purchaser of residential mortgages, FNMA purchased $6.1 billion in 1973. As of year-end 1975, FNMA held $31.8 billion in mortgages.

In terms of both its history and structure, the Federal National Mortgage Association is a unique corporation. It first was chartered as a government corporation in 1938, then rechartered as a federal agency in 1954. The Housing Act of 1968 spun off Fannie Mae from the Department of Housing and Urban Development and authorized its establishment as a government-sponsored, stockholder-owned corporation.

The new organization was assigned the function of maintaining a secondary market for FHA and VA loans. Its former special assistance and management and liquidation functions were assigned to a new corporation, the Government National Mortgage Association. Although publicly owned, the organization's government ties are evident in a number of areas.

Five of Fannie Mae's 15 directors are appointed by the President. The Secretary of Housing and Urban Development has regulatory authority to set the corporation's debt limit and its ratio of debt to capital. He also may require the corporation to allocate a reasonable portion of its mortgage purchases to programs related to the national housing goals.

In an attempt to define its unique organizational structure and role in the economy, Fannie Mae declared that its combination of interests make it "a private corporation with a public purpose."

The basic function of the Federal National Mortgage Association is to provide a secondary market for residential loans. It fulfills this function by buying, servicing and selling loans. Prior to 1970, it was limited to buying and selling FHA-insured and VA-guaranteed loans. The 1970 Housing Act empowered the corporation to operate a secondary market for conventional loans.[6]

Fannie Mae meets the private sector in a weekly auction at which mortgages are sold by the mortgage lenders. The prices and terms of mortgages are submitted to Fannie Mae, so that Fannie Mae can fill a predetermined dollar quota with the most attractive mortgages. Fannie Mae typically

[6] United States League of Savings Associations, *1974 Savings and Loan Fact Book,* pp. 130–31.

purchases at a discount of ½ per cent and the selling institution may be required to hold shares of Fannie Mae's stock equal to 1 per cent of the unpaid principal. In terms of aiding the housing market, these weekly auctions are particularly important when mortgage funds are in short supply.

A vigorous secondary mortgage market would allow Fannie Mae to re-sell mortgages, especially during periods when funds are readily available. However, Table 8–1 indicates that the resale program has been relatively

Table 8-1. Federal National Mortgage Association Activity
(Millions of Dollars)

Year	Purchases	Sales	Total Loan Portfolio (Year-End)
1955	$ 86	–	$ 86
1960	980	$ 42	2,903
1961	624	522	2,872
1962	548	391	2,847
1963	181	780	2,062
1964	198	78	1,997
1965	757	46	2,520
1966	2,081	*	4,396
1967	1,400	12	5,522
1968	1,944	–	7,167
1969	4,121	–	10,950
1970	5,078	–	15,502
1971	3,574	336	17,791
1972	3,699	211	19,891
1973	6,127	70	24,183
1974	6,953	5	29,578

*Less than $500,000.

Note: All data adjusted to exclude special assistance and management and liquidation functions transferred to GNMA in 1968.

Sources: United States League of Savings Associations, *1974 Savings and Loan Fact Book*, p. 130, and *Fact Book, 1975*, p. 114.

unsuccessful. Thus, it appears that Fannie Mae has acquired a permanent loan portfolio and that the success of Fannie Mae in establishing a secondary market is open to question.

The Government National Mortgage Association (GNMA). There are three important differences between Fannie Mae and "Ginnie Mae." First, Ginnie Mae is owned entirely by the U. S. Government, operating as part of the Department of Housing and Urban Development whereas Fannie Mae is privately owned. Ginnie Mae was created by the Housing Act of 1968, the same Act which provided for Fannie Mae's acquisition by the private sector. Second, various programs to subsidize interest rates (the so-called "special assistance programs") are carried out through Ginnie Mae. Thus, Ginnie Mae gives money away whereas Fannie Mae must be self-supporting.[7] Since Fannie Mae is largely separate from the federal government, its purchases and sales do not show up in the federal budget.[8]

Third, Ginnie Mae guarantees securities backed by pools of FHA, VA, and Farmer's Home Administration mortgages. Since the payment of principal and interest is guaranteed, these mortgage-backed securities—of two types, mortgage-backed bonds (bonds secured by a pool of mortgages) and pass-through securities (the mortgage principal payments are passed to the bondholders)—are attractive to investors who would not otherwise be interested in mortgages; the mortgage backed security is very liquid. Through these securities, insurance companies and pension funds can invest more than otherwise in mortgages.

Ginnie Mae receives applications from mortgage lenders desiring to issue securities backed by a pool of government-guaranteed mortgages. If the application is approved, the forthcoming security has Ginnie Mae's guarantee that principal and interest will be paid. Table 8–2 shows Ginnie Mae's activity in this area. Clearly, the mortgage-backed security is of growing importance in the development of a secondary market for mortgages.

The success of the mortgage-backed security in attracting new funds to

Table 8–2. Government National Mortgage Association
Mortgage-Backed Security Program
(Millions of Dollars)

| | Pass-through Securities | | |
Year	Applications Received	Securities Issued	Bonds Sold
1970	$1,126.2	$ 452.4	$1,315.0
1971	4,373.6	2,701.9	300.0
1972	3,854.5	2,661.7	–
1973	5,588.0	3,294.4	–
1974	6,203.0	4,784.0	–

Sources: Same as Table 8–1, at pp. 131 and 114 respectively.

---

[7] The money given away by Ginnie Mae shows up as part of the governmnte deficit.
[8] This was an important reason for selling Fannie Mae to the private sector; formerly, all mortgages purchased by Fannie Mae added directly to the deficit.

the mortgage market can be measured by the extent to which nontraditional lenders—such as credit unions, retirement and pension funds, bank trust funds, corporations, and insurance companies—acquire the securities. Prior to 1973, only about 20 per cent of the mortgage-backed securities were acquired by these institutions.[9] The rest were acquired by commercial banks and thrift institutions, the traditional lenders in the mortgage market. Since then, the nontraditional lenders have actively acquired mortgage-backed securities only sporadically. Thus, the success of Ginnie Mae in creating a vigorous secondary mortgage market is still debatable.

Ginnie Mae works in tandem with Fannie Mae to subsidize interest rates on previously unoccupied homes of eligible home buyers.[10] Financial institutions desiring to make these subsidized loans can obtain a commitment from Ginnie Mae, provided that funds are available and the deal meets certain criteria. The private institution then makes the loan at a below-market interest rate and immediately sells it to Ginnie Mae. The originating institution gets servicing and origination fees.

Ginnie Mae cannot continue to hold the subsidized mortgage, because the entire dollar amount spent on the mortgage would show up as an addition to the government deficit. Under the tandem arrangement, Ginnie Mae can resell the mortgage to Fannie Mae, which is technically a private institution, but the price at resale is set to yield a market rate of interest to Fannie Mae. Since the market rate is above the subsidized rate, Ginnie Mae must sell at a discount. This discount is the total amount of the subsidy to the home buyer; it adds to the government deficit.

Tandem mortgages have been of growing importance in the housing market. Ginnie Mae issued commitments totaling about $10 billion in the two years ending in December, 1975, as opposed to about $3.1 billion in the previous two years.[11] Extravagant claims have been made for the success of the tandem subsidies. In June, 1975, when the Ford Administration released $2 billion in funds authorized for tandem purchases, the total amount of the subsidy involved was estimated at $60 million. Carla Hills, Secretary of the Department of Housing and Urban Development, claimed that this would produce the sale of 65,000 housing units and create as many as 130,000 new jobs.[12]

---

[9] This is based on George M. von Furstenberg, "The Economics of the $1.6 Billion Tandem Mortgages Committed in the Current Housing Market Slump," delivered at the Western Finance Association Meetings, San Diego, Calif., June, 1975.

[10] A small amount of interest subsidy has been made available for purchase of existing homes. Tandem arrangements with FHLMC will be discussed below.

[11] In 1974 FHLMC and FNMA issued another $5 billion of commitments on behalf of GNMA; von Furstenberg, op. cit.

[12] "President Vetoes Housing Bill but Frees Aid Funds," Los Angeles Times, June 25, 1975, pp. 1 and 11.

These estimates were obtained by dividing the average price of a new home which would be purchased under the program (about $30,770) into the $2 billion. This produced the expectation that the sale of 65,000 housing units would be aided under the program. Since it was estimated that two years of labor would go into each house, the claim was made that 130,000 new jobs would be created. All of this for a government expenditure of only $60 million, or less than $1,000 per home. The Secretary's claim was clearly extravagant; a more realistic appraisal of the relationship between the tandem program and the housing market can be made as follows.

The subsidy of about $1,000 per housing unit is a shallow subsidy: the interest rate charged home buyers is reduced by only 1 per cent or less under the existing program.[13] (Interest can be no less than 7¾ per cent.) Thus, a home buyer with a $25,000 mortgage will save $250 in the first year and less in later years as the mortgage is paid down. How many home buyers, offered that kind of subsidy, will buy a home which they would not have bought otherwise? Clearly, some of the 65,000 homes financed under the tandem arrangement would have been bought anyway. On these purchases, the subsidy is not effective in stimulating the housing industry.

Sophisticated econometric estimates have been made by von Furstenberg of the effect of the tandem program on housing starts in 1975. These estimates, which have produced only crude figures that applied to conditions existing in 1975, indicated that about 10,000 housing sales would be added by the $2 billion in tandem purchases—less than one-sixth of the sales estimated by Secretary Hills. The effect of these sales on employment was even more dubious: it could well be zero if the housing market were so overbuilt that no additional housing starts would be initiated because of an increase in sales.

The Federal Home Loan Mortgage Corporation (FHLMC). "Freddie Mac," like Ginnie Mae, is a government-owned corporation. It was created in 1970 by the Emergency Home Finance Act, with the objective of fostering a secondary mortgage market, particularly for conventional (i.e., uninsured) home mortgages. Table 8–3 indicates that Freddie Mac has been successful in reselling mortgages which it acquires.

Freddie Mac helped to pioneer the tandem mortgage program. In 1974, it purchased $3 billion in conventional home mortgages under tandem arrangements. It also purchases participations in conventional, FHA, and VA mortgage loans.

---

[13] Any home costing less than $42,000 ($55,000 in Alaska) is eligible under the 1975 tandem arrangements. There are no income limits, unlike the earlier programs (221 d-3, 235, and 236) administered by GNMA.

Table 8–3. Federal Home Loan Mortgage Corporation Activity
(Millions of Dollars)

| Year | Mortgage Transactions | | Loan Portfolio (End of Period) | | |
	Purchases	Sales	Total	FHA–VA	Conventional
1970	$ 325	–	$ 325	$ 325	–
1971	778	$113	968	821	$ 147
1972	1,297	407	1,788	1,502	286
1973	1,334	409	2,604	1,800	804
1974	2,190	53	4,586	1,961	2,625

Note: Components may not add to totals due to rounding.

Sources: Same as Table 8–1, at pp. 129 and 113 respectively.

Freddie Mac, like Ginnie Mae, sells mortgage-backed securities in the secondary market. Table 8–4 compares two kinds of securities issued by Freddie Mac—Guaranteed Mortgage Certificates (GMC) and Participation Certificates (PC)—to one kind of security, the modified pass-through, issued by Ginnie Mae. The securities differ in detail, but the securities issued under the auspices of Freddie Mac are backed by conventional mortgages whereas the Ginnie Mae security is backed by federally insured mortgages. The conventional mortgages can be partly or wholly insured by a private mortgage insurance company such as PMI or the Mortgage Guaranty Insurance Corporation (MGIC). The private mortgage originator gives mortgages to Freddie Mac to hold as trustee for the purchaser of the certificate. This reduces the risk to the purchaser; and, of course, the purchaser benefits from liquidity of GMC's and PC's.

Since Freddie Mac is not as old as Ginnie Mae, the amount of its mortgage-backed securities outstanding is far less. Table 8–4 indicates that Freddie Mac has a total of $1.3 billion outstanding whereas Ginnie Mae has $13.5 billion outstanding. Table 8–2 showed that Ginnie Mae issued $4,784,000 of pass-through securities in 1974 alone.

The last column in Table 8–4 shows a new kind of secondary market security which has recently been introduced by savings and loans, the mortgage-backed bond. It is significant that private institutions are beginning to follow the practices of the federal housing credit agencies in issuing secondary market certificates. This is a pattern which we will note in other areas of the mortgage market: conventional loans have acquired many of the characteristics of FHA-insured loans. Note that only two private issues, amounting to $65 million, were outstanding in October, 1975.

Table 8-4. Mortgage-Backed Securities—Criteria

	Government National Mortgage Association Modified Pass-Through Securities (GNMA's)	Federal Home Loan Mortgage Corporation Guaranteed Mortgage Certificates (GMC's)	Federal Home Loan Mortgage Corporation Participation Sale Certificates (PC's)	Savings and Loan Mortgage-Backed Bonds (MBB's)
Backed by	Pools of FHA/VA mortgages.	Pools of conventional loans.	Pools of conventional loans.	Pools of conventional or FHA/VA loans.
Term	Stated term—identical to mortgage pool—usually 30 years. Estimated average life is 12 years ±.	Stated term—identical to mortgage pool—usually 30 years. Estimated average life is 12 years. Investor has a Put to FHLMC at 15 years.	Stated term—identical to mortgage pool—usually 30 years. Estimated average life is 12 years.	Minimum effective term is five years. First issues at 10 and 15 years maturity.
Yield	Coupon = 1/2% below mortgage interest rates. Yield calculated on 12-year life. Yield approximates long-term Aaa corporates. Add 15 basis points when comparing GNMA's (with monthly payments of P & I) to corporate bonds paying interest semiannually and principal at maturity.	Coupon on Series A 1975 = 8.20%. Mortgage pool yield = 8.25%. Yield calculated on 12-year life. Yield has ranged between 10 and 20 basis points above GNMA's 8%'s.	Coupon has ranged from 7% to 9 1/8%. Yield calculated on 12-year life. Yield approximates GNMA's. Add 15 basis points when comparing PC's which have monthly payments of P & I to corporate bonds paying interest semiannually and principal at maturity. Deduct 12 basis points for 90-day delay in first payment. Prepayment fees passed-through to investor. Front-end fee paid on 120-day optional delivery commitments.	First issue by First Federal of Rochester, 9% coupon, January, 1975. Privately placed with pension funds and life companies. Second issue by Cal. Fed. 9 1/8% coupon, Sept. 1975. Public issue.

Risk:				
Underlying security	FHA-insured, VA-guaranteed or Farmer's Home Administration guaranteed loans.	Participation in pools of conventional loans. Private insurance on loans over 80% LTV.	Whole conventional loans. Participations in pools of conventional loans. Whole FHA and VA loans. Private insurance on loans over 80% LTV.	Conventional or government insured loans. First issues used government insured loans.
Collateralization	Mortgage pool is equal to outstanding securities.	Mortgage pool is equal to outstanding securities.	Mortgage pool is equal to outstanding PC.	Issues overcollateralized by mortgage pool. First of Rochester by 150%, Cal. Fed. by 175% measured by market value. Aaa rating on both issues.
Additional guarantees	GNMA guaranty = full faith and credit of U. S. Government.	FHLMC guaranty = $125 million net worth.	FHLMC guaranty = $125 million net worth.	Private or government mortgage insurance. Net worth and general credit of issuer. Debt obligations of issuing S&L. In case of default, bondholders become general creditors of the S&L. FSLIC has right of first refusal to purchase collateral.
Repayment Characteristics:				
Interest	Monthly; whether or not actually collected by servicer.	Semiannually	Monthly; whether or not actually collected by servicer.	Monthly or semiannually as accrued. (First of Rochester and Cal. Fed. were semi-annually.)
Principal	Monthly; whether or not actually collected by servicer.	Yearly, with guaranteed minimum payments.	Monthly as collected.	Monthly, semiannually, or annually. (First of Rochester was annual, Cal. Fed. one payment at 10 years.)

(continued)

Table 8-4. (continued)

	Government National Mortgage Association Modified Pass-Through Securities (GNMA's)	Federal Home Loan Mortgage Corporation Guaranteed Mortgage Certificates (GMC's)	Federal Home Loan Mortgage Corporation Participation Sale Certificates (PC's)	Savings and Loan Mortgage-Backed Bonds (MBB's)
Marketability:				
Amount outstanding 6/75	$13.5 billion.	$300 million.	$1 billion	$15 million = First of Rochester. $50 million = Cal. Fed.
Secondary Market	Very active market.	Active market.	FHLMC initiated trading desk 6/20/75.	Unknown.
Rating	Approximates a government agency.	None.	None.	S & P Aaa on both.
Legal Aspects:				
SEC Registration	Not required.	Not required.	Not required.	Not required if issued by a S&L.
Type Bond	Registered with GNMA.	Registered with FHLMC. Transfer agent is Federal Reserve Bank of New York.	Registered with FHLMC.	Private placement or public offering.
Minimum Denomination	$25,000.	$100,000.	$100,000.	$100,000 or $10,000 if issue is sold by registered securities dealer.
Qualifying Asset for S&Ls and MSBs.	Yes.	No.	Yes.	No.
Collateral Held by:	Commercial bank or trust company.	FHLMC as trustee.	FHLMC as trustee.	Commercial bank or trust company.

Restrictions on Issuer	Maintain net worth of 2% of first $5 million, 1% over $5 million. Maximum net worth = $250,000.			Variety of constraints regarding borrowing limitations, net worth requirements, scheduled items limits, an earnings test, etc.
Prospectus	Required on each new security—standard GNMA form.	Yes. Series A Prospectus dated 1/23/75.	None.	Although not required in regulations, issuing S&L must notify FHLBB of intent to issue MBB.
Reinvestment Restrictions	Pass-through security not applicable.	Any short-term security under "prudent-man rule."	Pass-through security not applicable.	S&L is constrained by the regulations in regard to the amount of reinvestment allowed and the terms under which substitution of collateral may take place.
Legality of Investment	National banks may purchase, deal in, and underwrite GNMA's with no limitation—legal investment for federally chartered credit unions.	National banks may purchase, deal in, and underwrite GMC's with no limitation—eligible as collateral for 90-day advances to member banks for FRB.	Not applicable.	National banks may not deal in MBB's.

Source: PMI Mortgage Insurance Company, October, 1975.

ARE THE MORTGAGE MARKETS BECOMING FEDERALIZED?

In discussing Fannie Mae, especially in Table 8–1, we said that Fannie Mae has been relatively unsuccessful in selling mortgages; a large portfolio of mortgage loans has been developing at Fannie Mae. How does Fannie Mae finance this portfolio?

Like private corporations—technically, Fannie Mae *is* a private corporation—Fannie Mae issues stocks and bonds in order to acquire funds for investment. Since Fannie Mae invests its funds in mortgages, it would appear to be channeling funds from other sectors of the credit market into mortgages. However, this is not always the case. Much of the stock is acquired by the thrift institutions; they have been required to invest in Fannie Mae's stock if they want to sell mortgages to Fannie Mae. Thus, they are purchasing Fannie Mae's stock with money which would otherwise have flowed directly into mortgage holdings!

Fannie Mae's bonds are attractive to individuals who get relatively high rates at low risk. These individuals may withdraw savings deposits from thrift institutions in order to buy the higher yielding notes of Fannie Mae. This is the process known as disintermediation. Here again, money is being diverted away from mortgage investment by thrift institutions toward mortgage investment by Fannie Mae.

The same arguments can be applied to the other federally related mortgage institutions. Thus, critics claim that the mortgage markets are becoming federalized as mortgage money is being diverted from private institutional lenders to the federal mortgage lenders.

The rapid growth of federal mortgage institutions has had a profound impact on the mortgage markets. However, all federally supported agencies held only 11.3 per cent of mortgages outstanding at the end of 1974. Therefore, it is certinly too early to raise the specter of a mortgage market in which the government participates in virtually every mortgage. Furthermore, the federally related institutions have helped to tap funds which would not ordinarily flow into the mortgage market. These newly opened channels are important; in the future they may be widened to yield a large stream of mortgages which would not have been made without the federal institutions.

Finally, have the private mortgage lenders been injured by the federally related lenders? Certainly the S&L's have grown strong during the period of expansion of federal mortgage lending. Indeed, the S&L's and the other private mortgage lenders have voluntarily participated in the programs of the federally related agencies, since the terms of those programs were attractive to private lenders.

The conversion of Fannie Mae to private status may be the key to this issue. Fannie Mae retains some ties to the government (the debt-to-equity ratio and participation in subsidy programs can be dictated by HUD officials) but private sector directors now sit with public sector directors. If the private sector gains a larger say in Fannie Mae's affairs, the federal government will have withdrawn significantly from the mortgage market. It will have left a new institution which the private sector finds helpful and valuable.

SUMMARY

The secondary mortgage market has developed with substantial support and encouragement from the federal government. Mortgage insurance, provided largely by the government, allows private parties in the secondary market to trade mortgages as investment securities which have little risk of default. The private secondary mortgage market, which utilizes the specialized services of mortgage brokers, relies on mortgage insurance.

Additional government support flows from Fannie Mae, Ginnie Mae, and Freddie Mac. All of these institutions buy and sell mortgages and hold a portfolio of mortgages. The portfolios have grown to the point where they appear to represent a permanent investment in mortgages. Thus, the extent to which these government-supported institutions have succeeded in nurturing the secondary mortgage market is debatable.

Securities backed by the portfolio of mortgages are issued by the government-supported institutions. These pass-through securities and mortgage-backed bonds provide pooling of risk—to the extent that risk is not washed out by government insurance. Pass-through securities consolidate many small financial instruments into a few large instruments. Thus, institutions with large blocks of funds—such as insurance companies, pension funds, trust funds, etc.—often seek to take advantage of mortgage-backed securities.

The tandem arrangement whereby Ginnie Mae purchases mortgages at high prices (i.e., below-market interest rates) in order to sell them at lower prices to Fannie Mae provides an important and growing subsidy to the mortgage market. The difference between the high and the low price is a subsidy which is absorbed by Ginnie Mae. The subsidy is only available to mortgagors with low incomes or properties with low to moderate values. At present, the only limitation is on the value of the property: it must be under $46,000 if the loan-to-value ratio is 90 per cent or less, and under $43,000 if the ratio is as high as 95 per cent. However, this subsidy is not large for any one home buyer, so the effect of the program on the housing market is small. Early predictions by the federal government overestimated the effect of tandem mortgages.

Mortgage bankers have tended to become specialists in servicing mortgages, in contrast to thrift institutions which are more likely to permanently invest money in mortgages which they service. The servicing function is complicated in the mortgage market by the need to collect monthly payments from many small mortgagors. The secondary market serves the valuable function of allowing investors to be free of the servicing function.

The secondary market for mortgages is a national market which facilitates the flow of funds from surplus regions of the country to deficit regions. This is important in keeping interest rates low in all parts of the country. Also, investors value the liquidity provided by the secondary market. They express their gratitude for liquidity by accepting a lower rate of interest than they would in the absence of a secondary mortgage market.

QUESTIONS

1. How does Fannie Mae reduce regional interest differentials? Why is the reduction in interest differentials considered an important objective of government policy?
2. How do Ginnie Mae and Fannie Mae operate to reduce interest rates for mortgages made on property in the low-to-moderate price range? What objections might be raised against this scheme?
3. What is the role of insurance companies in the secondary mortgage market?
4. Compare and contrast the various ways in which mortgage-backed securities reduce the risk to the investor.
   (a) List different types of risks which an investor in mortgage-backed securities faces.
   (b) For each type of risk, which security offers the most protection? Why?
   (c) Do you think that these risk differences are reflected in the secondary market transactions? If so, how?
5. What distinguishes Freddie Mac from Ginnie Mae? From Fannie Mae?
6. What is the role of mortgage bankers in the secondary market?
7. On the question of the federalization of the mortgage markets:
   (a) List some indications that the federal government has become more important as a mortgage lender.
   (b) What are the pros and cons of federal mortgage lending?

9

GOVERNMENT IN COMPETITION WITH PRIVATE MORTGAGE LENDERS

The various levels of government do very little direct lending in the mortgage market, although there is some direct lending by the Veterans Administration, the Farmer's Home Administration, and various state and local housing agencies, as noted in Chapter 4. The purpose of this chapter is to investigate some of the more important ways in which government, particularly the federal government, comes into competition with private firms operating in the mortgage market.

In the market for 1–4-family homes, the Federal Housing Administration (FHA) and the Veterans Administration (VA) insure about one-third of all the loans outstanding. While mortgage insurance does not bring the government into direct competition with the principal institutional lenders, it has profoundly altered competitive conditions in the private sector of the industry. Government insurance does come into direct competition with private mortgage insurers, who originate loans and participate in the secondary market. The private insurers have actively introduced innovative instruments which allow institutional lenders to participate more easily in the mortgage market. This activity can be traced, at least indirectly, to competition from government insurance.

Following the discussion of mortgage insurance, we will turn to private–public competition for loanable funds. During periods of credit stringency, the debt issued by the federal government and federally related agencies, including housing agencies, attracts funds which might have gone into financial intermediaries. The difficult term "disintermediation," introduced in Chapter 8, is widely applied to periods when investors bypass private intermediaries in favor of bonds or short-term government securities; i.e., they take deposits which might have gone to intermediaries and invest the money in securities, especially short-term government securities. These periods have a severe adverse impact on the availability and cost of mortgage loans, so disintermediation is a very pressing structural problem.

Federally related housing agencies such as the Federal Home Loan Bank (FHLB), the Federal Home Loan Mortgage Corporation (Freddie Mac), and the Federal National Mortgage Association (Fannie Mae) contribute to periods of disintermediation by issuing their own debt. Thus, they sometimes direct housing funds from the private sector to the new channels which they have recently opened up. This has naturally provoked some concern and even consternation among the private lenders, especially the thrift institutions. This important issue will be addressed in the last section of this chapter.

GOVERNMENT INSURANCE PROGRAMS

After the total collapse of a flourishing private mortgage insurance industry, the federal government entered the insurance field with the National Housing Act of 1934. The primary goal of the legislation was to revitalize the construction industry and provide employment in the building trades. The Federal Housing Administration (FHA) was designed as a temporary agency to combat depression, but unexpected consequences followed: the terms on which mortgages are offered were radically altered, not only for insured mortgages, but also for the uninsured (conventional) mortgages which compete with insured mortgages for the most desirable mortgagors. Partly because of these unexpected benefits, the FHA was given permanent life in 1946. The effects of the FHA on mortgage terms are discussed below.

The Mechanics of Government Insurance. The FHA, an arm of the Department of Housing and Urban Development (HUD), operates through approved lenders. Most lenders can qualify to participate in federal mortgage insurance, but the approval process serves to remind lenders of their dependence on the FHA for an important part of their business. Loss of approved status would have serious consequences for many lenders. The importance of FHA approval will become apparent when we discuss the adversary relationship which exists between the FHA and private mortgage lenders.

When a home buyer and a lender determine that an FHA-insured loan would be best, they fill out a lengthy application which emphasizes the borrower's income, a complete description of the property, other debt obligations of the borrower, and credit references (i.e., record of repayment of other debt). There are actually hundreds of different FHA insurance plans, many of which are for low-to-moderate-income families. One of the principal restrictions on the type of property is a limit on the amount of the mortgage which will be insured. On nonfarm property this limit has generally been under $50,000; many programs are for mortgages under $40,000. In any event, the specific rules and limits are changing all the time, so interested borrowers should contact the FHA or their lender.

The application, with an application fee which has usually been under $50, is forwarded to the regional office of the FHA. The FHA insists on its own standards of appraisal of the property, so days can elapse while the inspection and appraisal are performed. This "red tape" is often superfluous now that private lenders have adopted standards as strict as the FHA's; it is one of the objections to FHA insurance.

If the loan is approved it is subject to a limited term (years to maturity), a maximum loan-to-value ratio, and a maximum interest rate. The first two limits have had an important impact on industry practice by lengthening the maximum maturity and increasing the loan-to-value ratio. Under many FHA programs, the maximum maturity is 30 years or 75 per cent of the remaining economic life of the property, whichever is less. By pre-World War II standards, this is a lengthy maturity, but the FHA will even extend the maturity to 35 or 40 years in some cases if the longer maturity is needed to bring monthly payments into a reasonable relationship with income. Generally, the FHA wants the ratio of all housing costs to income to be less than 25 per cent.

The maximum loan-to-value ratio was originally 80 per cent, but it has been extended so that 90 per cent is now common and some programs go up to 97 per cent. With a 97 per cent loan, the borrowers have very little equity in the property—and little incentive to make sacrifices in order to continue mortgage payments if their incomes decline. Furthermore, the FHA has minimal protection against a decline in the value of the property. The equity may not even be enough to pay accrued interest, legal fees, and selling fees during the foreclosure process. Thus, the FHA is taking a significant risk with these properties.

Despite the liberalizing trends set by the FHA, it has lived up to its charter as a self-supporting institution. The insured borrower pays a substantial fee of ½ per cent per year of the outstanding balance of the mortgage. The part of this fee which is not needed for operating expenses is paid into a reserve fund known as the Mutual Mortgage Insurance Fund (MMIF). The FHA, like a private mutual organization, does not make a profit. Rather, it pools a large amount of risk, enabling many homeowners to be insured and imparting confidence in the insured mortgage to every participant in the mortgage market.

Confidence is naturally engendered by the fact that the FHA is an arm of the federal government and bolstered by the FHA's power to call on the U. S. Treasury to meet any obligations—a power it has not had to use. Although the FHA can also delay cash payments by issuing government bonds to cover its obligations, issuance of these bonds has not been necessary for many years. Instead, the FHA pays insurance claims in cash.

The FHA places a ceiling on the interest rate which can be charged on an insured loan. The ceiling is changed frequently; in 1975 it ranged between 8 and 9 per cent. However, this ceiling may be ineffective since lenders can charge fees to borrowers. (The way in which these fees raise the effective interest rate on the loan will be discussed in Chapter 22.) In some states, it is illegal to use fees to raise the effective interest rate, but there are usually ways around these technicalities. For example, the seller can offer to pay points, then raise the price of the real estate accordingly.

Even if FHA interest ceilings were adhered to, their effect would be to dry up the flow of insured mortgages. When market rates rise above ceilings, lenders will turn to conventional loans which pay a competitive return on invested funds. However, many investors prefer insured mortgages to conventional mortgages since the risk has been largely eliminated by the government. Thus, the interest rate on insured mortgages will usually be somewhat lower than market interest rates on conventional mortgages. From the borrower's point of view, this lower rate is more than erased by the ½ per cent insurance fee which must be paid to the FHA.

The other major insuring agency, the Veterans Administration, operates in a somewhat different manner. The first step for veterans who feel that they may be entitled to benefits is to contact a lender or a local office of the VA for the latest version of the complex regulations which cover the program. The VA has a guarantee program which covers 60 per cent of the deficiency after a loan is foreclosed and liquidated. It also has an insurance program which pays the entire loss to the lender. However, a lender who expects to receive compensation must have built up a sufficient balance with the VA. The lender's account with the VA is credited with 15 per cent of the loan amount whenever an insured loan is made. Thus, a lender who wants to get insurance coverage with the VA must have a sufficient volume of VA loans to have an adequate reserve with the VA.

The maximum amount of the mortgage insured by the VA is smaller than the maximum insured by the FHA (only about $27,000 on real estate loans), but some states offer more liberal benefits for veterans. California, for example, has an insurance program for veterans who were California residents at the time of their entry into the service and who want to buy a home in California.

Effects of Government Insurance on Private Mortgage Lending. In Chapter 19 we discuss the advantages and disadvantages of self-amortizing (or level payment) loans, i.e., loans which enable the borrower to make constant (level) monthly payments for a fixed number of months, after which the loan has been fully repaid. Use of this type of loan increased following the Great Depression; in recent years it has completely replaced the short-term real estate loan with a balloon payment at maturity.

All loans insured by the FHA and VA must be level payment (or direct reduction or self-amortizing) home mortgages. This requirement has led to the widespread use of this type of mortgage, and it is now extremely rare to find a balloon payment loan. Following the practice of the FHA and later of the VA, mortgage lenders making conventional (i.e., uninsured) loans have used level payment loans also.

Why have the mortgage lending institutions followed the FHA's example? They have responded to competitive pressure from the government insurance agencies. The level payment loan offers advantages to both borrowers and lenders, but especially to borrowers. Therefore, borrowers began to demand the level payment loan when they applied for a mortgage loan.

The level payment loan helps borrowers to budget their housing expenses so as to avoid default. This is in contrast to the balloon payment loan, which gives the borrower every incentive *not* to budget for repayment; instead, the borrower hopes that it will be possible to refinance at maturity. Furthermore, the borrower gets relatively low monthly payments with the level payment loan. This is because of the long term before maturity, another feature pioneered by the FHA. Thus, a monthly payment of $350 might include only $25 or $30 as repayment of principal. Clearly this monthly payment closely resembles payment of interest only.

The long term of the level payment loan eliminates the need to renegotiate the loan every few years. This substantially reduces the transactions costs—inspection, appraisal, recordings, and general paper work—which were incurred every five or ten years under the balloon payment loan. Thus, financing through the level payment loan is cheaper than through the balloon payment loan. Either fees are less or the interest rate is less or both.

High loan-to-value (L–V) ratios are another characteristic which the FHA and VA developed. They originally made loans at L–V's up to 80 per cent, then they went to 90 per cent, and they currently offer some loans to low-income families at an L–V of up to 97 per cent. The high L–V is extremely attractive to borrowers since it reduces the cash which must be provided as a down payment. It also virtually eliminates the need for a second (i.e., junior) mortgage. Since junior mortgages carry relatively high interest rates, the high L–V loan reduces the overall cost of borrowing.

With a high L–V, the lender assumes an additional risk in that the value of the property may not cover the balance due on the loan plus legal and clerical costs associated with foreclosure. The FHA was aware of this when it began use of the high L–V loans, so it introduced rigorous methods of borrower analysis. The methods discussed in Chapter 10 were extensively influenced by the competitive example offered by FHA- and VA-insured loans.

Recent experience indicates that the FHA has gone too far with the high L–V loan. A homeowner who has only a few hundred dollars invested in a home—e.g., under a 97 per cent L–V—has little incentive to avoid default. When default occurs, the lender has great difficulty in recovering the full amount owed plus foreclosure costs.

In the 1970–1975 period the general economy, particularly the housing sector, performed poorly. This led to a rise in defaults on mortgage payments, and nearly a hundred thousand homes which had high L–V mortgages passed into the FHA's possession. While precise figures are not available, it appears likely that the FHA's reserves (the MMIF) have been strained. Thus, after 40 years as a self-supporting institution, the future of the FHA has been clouded by excessively high L–V loans.

Mortgage Insurance and the Secondary Mortgage Market. FHA and VA mortgage insurance is tremendously important to the operations of the secondary market for mortgages. That market, with all of the benefits attendant to it (see Chapter 8), depends on reasonably standardized instruments. Traders buying and selling secondary market instruments for a profit cannot keep track of the numerous differences between mortgage instruments. The FHA and VA have standardized mortgages in two ways: (1) they have standardized terms and documents, and (2) they have eliminated most of the risk associated with default.

As explained above, most lenders have adopted the L–V and maturity which are most commonly offered by the FHA and VA. Furthermore, the documents associated with a mortgage have become more standardized as a result of FHA and VA activity. Thus, potential purchasers on the secondary market can concentrate most of their attention on the interest rate offered by the mortgage rather than on its terms.

The reduction of risk is the most important aspect of standardization. Since the FHA and VA eliminate most risk, the potential purchaser need not be concerned with construction standards, neighborhood characteristics, or borrower creditworthiness. Thus, most of the factors which make each mortgage somewhat unique cease to be relevant once the mortgage is insured.

There is some residual risk, financial as well as nonfinancial, associated with the FHA- or VA-insured loans. The financial risk is associated with the uninsured costs of foreclosure, including delayed cash flows and some loss of interest while a claim is processed. The nonfinancial risk is associated with the uncertainty as to when a claim will be paid. It has been proposed that mortgage insurance be improved by eliminating residual risk.[1] This would involve having the insuring agency pay the mortgagee while the mortgagor would make payments to the insuring agency.

GOVERNMENT IN COMPETITION WITH PRIVATE MORTGAGE INSURANCE

Private mortgage insurance flourished before the Great Depression, but most insurance companies closed their doors permanently during the bank holiday of March, 1933.[2] The field was preempted by government insurance until 1957 when the Mortgage Guaranty Insurance Corporation (MGIC) was formed. Private mortgage insurance proved to be profitable, despite competition from the FHA and VA. In 1972 privately insured mortgages totaled about $18 billion or 1.8 per cent of GNP; private insurance had amounted to 2.3 per cent of GNP in 1929.

The recent rapid growth of private insurance is more impressive than the dollar amount of mortgages insured. In 1972, MGIC, which has between 60 and 65 per cent of the private insurance market, increased its insured mortgages by 75 per cent. On the other hand, the dollar amount of $18 billion compares to $113 billion (about 11 per cent of GNP) insured by the

[1] This is described by Irwin Friend, "Summary and Recommendations," in *Study of the Savings and Loan Industry* (Washington, D. C.: FHLBB, 1969).

[2] This section draws on Chester Rapkin, *The Private Insurance of Home Mortgages* (Milwaukee, Wis.: MGIC, 1973). Copyright © 1973 by Chester Rapkin.

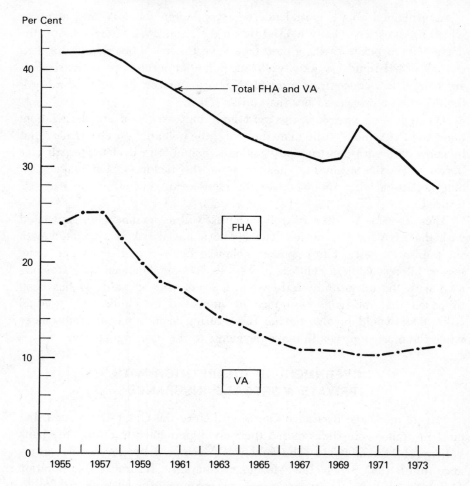

Note: FHA includes mortgages on multifamily projects as well as home mortgage loans. In 1974 the amount of residential mortgages outstanding stood at $506 billion.

Source: Leo Grebler, "The Role of the Public Sector in Residential Financing," prepared for the First Annual Conference, Resources for Housing, Federal Home Loan Bank of San Francisco, December 9-10, 1975.

Fig. 9–1. FHA-insured and VA-guaranteed mortgage loans as a percentage of all residential mortgage holdings, 1955–1974.

FHA and VA. But FHA and VA insurance grew only about 6 per cent in 1972. Figure 9–1 indicates that government insurance has actually declined precipitously relative to conventional residential mortgages outstanding.

Why has private mortgage insurance grown rapidly while government insurance has declined? First, private insurance has managed to offer somewhat different types of policies. MGIC has a plan which covers the top 20 per cent of a loan as long as the L–V is less than 90 per cent. This means that the mortgagee is protected for the 20 per cent decline in the total of: outstanding principal amount at the time of default, accumulated interest, legal costs, handling costs, and other charges. The cost of this insurance is ½ per cent in the first year but only ¼ per cent thereafter, as opposed to ½ per cent each year under the FHA plans. Furthermore, ten years' worth of insurance can be purchased for a single advance payment of 2 per cent of the amount of the mortgage.

Private mortgage insurance offers another great advantage over government insurance: speedy processing of applications. An application can be processed by MGIC within 24 hours, as opposed to several days for government insurance. Rapkin notes:

Policy considerations cause FHA to impose numerous statutory requirements and restrictions regarding property and borrower characteristics, which, in day-to-day lending practices, create much red tape for the institutional lender who operates in a competitive environment where efficient service may be as important a factor as mortgage terms in the successful closing of new loans. MGIC, on the other hand, imposes few procedural constraints on its lenders once they are approved and is usually able to offer same-day service on the telephone if the loan is acceptable.[3]

We have already commented on the importance of the loan standards set by the FHA in changing the character of all mortgages, uninsured as well as insured. The historical importance of FHA extends to property standards, where inspections and appraisals have set minimum construction standards. However, these procedures now often duplicate the procedures which have been adopted by most private lenders. Also, the requirement that time-consuming procedures be carried out on every property and every loan has limited the value of government insurance relative to private insurance. This, together with the high premiums, accounts for the declining importance of government insurance which is shown in Figure 9–1.

Insured loans are advantageous to financial institutions because they are considered "non-risk assets" by regulators who must compute ratios of risky assets to total assets and to liquid liabilities. The regulators limit financial institutions to maximum ratios of high-risk, high-yield assets. They also limit the L–V for commercial banks. The growth of private mortgage insurance has been aided by rulings in 1964 and 1971 classifying privately insured mortgages as non-risk assets.

Competition between government and private insurance has stimulated

[3] *Ibid.*, p. 46.

private concerns to come up with a new type of loan, the piggyback or joint loan. In this type of loan, as explained by Rapkin:

> . . . a financial intermediary, often a mortgage company, originates and services a high-ratio first mortgage, sells the bottom 70 or 75 percent to a life insurance company or some other institutional investor, and sells the remaining 15 or 20 percent to a secondary investor. . . . Under this procedure, private insurance is obtained on the entire mortgage, and the secondary investor is able to hold a high-yield investment risk free because his entire share, not exceeding 20 or 25 percent, is secured by MGIC mortgage insurance.[4]

PROBLEMS FACED BY MORTGAGE INSURERS

Mortgage insurance agents must guard against the possibility that lenders will take advantage of the fact that they are more familiar with the borrower and the property. For example, lenders might be tempted to ask for insurance on loans where the appraisal is high for the neighborhood, the neighborhood is beginning to decline, or the borrower's ability to repay is just a little doubtful. Rapkin calls this the process of adverse loan selection.

Lenders are not interested simply in insuring the most risky loans. They are also interested in earning high profits. Since risky loans will usually carry higher interest rates than less risky loans, lenders have an incentive to seek high-risk loans which will be acceptable to a loan insurance agent.

The FHA attempts to protect itself against adverse selection by conducting careful checks on the borrower and the property. This engenders the red tape which limits the value of FHA insurance to lenders and borrowers alike. MGIC protects itself against adverse selection by spot checks on the property appraisals of lenders. It also monitors claims made by lenders so that it can terminate business relations with lenders who take advantage of the situation.

A severe or extended decline in general economic conditions presents another problem to mortgage insurers. If unemployment were to become very high, mortgage defaults would be associated with declines in the market value of the property held as security. This is what happened during the Great Depression; the failure of private mortgage insurance companies resulted.[5] The best protection against this kind of problem is skillful application of monetary and fiscal policy. The success of mortgage insurance ultimately depends on the ability of the government to avoid an economic contraction as severe as the Great Depression.

---

[4] *Ibid.*, p. 52.
[5] Many other factors, described by Rapkin, contributed to the failure of mortgage insurance companies during the Depression.

Private mortgage insurers have to be more conservative than the FHA. If it has difficulty meeting claims, the FHA can fall back on the U.S. Government or delay cash payment of claims by making settlement with marketable government bonds rather than cash. Private insurers must always pay cash. FHA has another advantage: it can invest all of its assets in interest-bearing securities, whereas its competition must keep a certain amount in reserve accounts which do not pay interest. Thus, the FHA can afford to accept more risk than private mortgage insurers.

GOVERNMENT IN COMPETITION FOR LOANABLE FUNDS

The thrift institutions—savings and loan associations (S&L's) and mutual savings banks—depend on the deposits of individual households. Almost all of the funds available for mortgage loans come from these savings deposits. At S&L's, deposits provide 82 per cent of loanable funds and at mutual savings banks the corresponding figure is 90 per cent. That accounts for the close relationship between flows of deposits and flows of mortgage lending shown in Figure 9–2. The relationship is particularly remarkable because quarterly data were used. Mortgages followed deposits closely, despite large fluctuations in the flows of deposits. The association between change in deposits and change in mortgage lending is even closer if one looks at five-year periods. In this time frame, the lending of thrift institutions is usually within a few percentage points of deposit flows.

Figure 9–2 indicates that deposit flows are related to the business cycle. Shaded areas represent periods of contraction in the general level of business activity; unshaded areas represent periods of expansion. Deposits at thrift institutions, and therefore mortgage lending, generally begin to decline during periods of expansion and to rise during periods of contraction. In Chapter 8 we introduced the term "disintermediation," which is applied to periods of low and declining growth of deposits at financial intermediaries. What is the reason for this countercyclical (or half-countercyclical) pattern of disintermediation?

Causes of Disintermediation. The recovery from a recession in economic activity begins at the righthand edge of the shading in Figure 9–2. When recovery begins, all sectors of the economy increase their demand for funds so that they can increase their investment and other spending. This forces interest rates up, including the rate on home mortgages (Figure 9–2). Disintermediation occurs when interest rates are high or rising; a reverse flow of funds, with large deposits into thrift institutions, occurs when interest rates are low or falling.

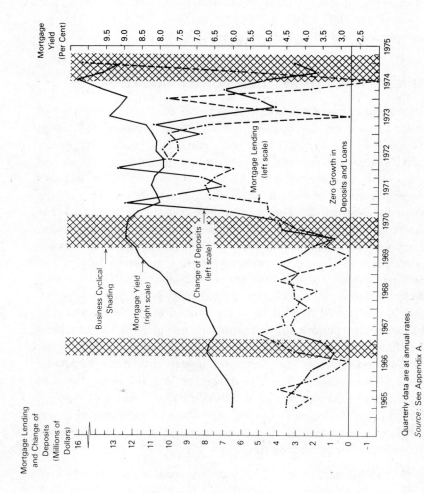

Fig. 9–2. Mortgage lending and change of deposits (sum of savings and loan associations and mutual savings banks) vs. mortgage yield (conventional primary market), 1965–1974.

The reason for disintermediation during periods of high or rising interest rates is that thrift institutions ("thrifts") cannot compete successfully with other sectors of the economy for the deposits of individual savers. The thrift institutions are locked into their holdings of long-term mortgages which carry fixed rates of interest. Thrifts can issue new mortgages at higher rates of interest, as indicated in Figure 9–2, but they can do nothing about the rate of interest they earn on their existing mortgage holdings. On the other hand, when they raise the interest rate which they pay to passbook depositors, *they must increase the rate for all depositors, not just new depositors.*[6] Therefore, they cannot earn enough money during periods of high and rising interest rates to allow them to compete for deposits.

Compare the situation of thrift institutions with that of insurance companies during periods of high and rising interest rates. Insurance companies get their loanable funds from accumulated premiums which are held as reserves against claims. These premiums are not subject to withdrawal, so insurance companies are relatively immune to rising interest rates.[7] They can take advantage of increases in interest rates to increase their return on assets without offsetting withdrawals or increased interest cost.

Commercial banks also have a better position than thrift institutions during periods of high and rising interest rates. Most of the assets of commercial banks are short-term business loans which can be renewed at higher interest rates. The loans which commercial banks make for intermediate terms, i.e., term loans, usually carry an interest rate which floats with the prime rate, so earnings are increased on this score also. Thus, commercial banks are in a position to raise interest rates to compete for deposits.

Regulatory authorities limit the ability of commercial banks to compete with the thrift institutions for deposits. They do this by placing ceilings, known as Regulation Q interest ceilings, on the rates which commercial banks can pay for deposits. With the Interest Rate Adjustment Act of 1966, Congress extended interest rate ceilings on deposits to thrift institutions. Since that time the regulatory authorities have always given the thrift institutions an interest rate advantage over commercial banks, but the amount of the advantage has been diminishing. In 1966, thrifts could offer savers .75 percent more than commercial banks; by 1977, the differential

[6] Thrifts can introduce new types of savings or time accounts. By making small adjustments in the terms of these accounts, they can offer higher rates only to new depositors or to depositors smart enough to transfer to new accounts.

[7] In the past, insurance companies gave some policyholders the right to take out loans (known as "policy loans") at fixed interest rates (e.g., 6 per cent). During periods of rising interest rates, many policyholders took advantage of this, subjecting insurance companies to an unanticipated and relatively unprofitable drain on their loanable funds. As new policies are written, this loophole is being closed.

had narrowed to .25 per cent, although thrifts can offer long-term time deposits at much higher rates than commercial banks.

Why did Congress extend interest controls through the Interest Rate Adjustment Act? To protect the S&L's and mutual savings banks from competing with each other by raising rates paid on deposits. It was feared that some thrift institutions would fail if forced by competition to pay high interest on deposits. The primary argument for protecting deposit institutions from failure is that failure shakes public confidence in the integrity of deposits. Thus, the government seeks to prevent loss of confidence in the banking system, since that could cause a run on banks and another bank holiday like the one experienced in 1933.

The reduction in the spread between rate ceilings for commercial banks and for thrifts has produced strong objections from thrifts. The United States League of Savings Associations argues that its share of the passbook savings market has been eroded. When the interest rate spread was .75 per cent in 1966, S&L's held 52 per cent and banks held 48 per cent of the total of S&L and bank passbook savings.

Since then the differential has been reduced to .25% on passbook savings, and as a consequence associations have seen their share of passbook savings shrink. At year-end 1974 associations held only 42% while the commercial bank share had grown to 58%.[8]

The federal government plays an important role in disintermediation since the short-term securities offered by the U. S. Treasury or by federal agencies attract most of the funds which would have gone into savings deposits. Savers have few alternatives for short-term, safe, liquid investments except government-related issues or savings deposits. The crucial question which we want to address here is the extent to which the agencies designed to help the housing market—primarily Fannie Mae, Ginnie Mae, and Freddie Mac (see Chapter 8)—contribute to disintermediation.

The Housing Agencies and Disintermediation. The federal housing credit agencies (FNMA, GNMA, FHLMC, and FHLB) issue a large part of the government bonds which compete with thrift institutions for funds. To get an idea of the importance of these agencies, it is necessary to include the Federal Home Loan Banks with Fannie Mae and Freddie Mac.[9] In the period 1965–1969, the housing credit agencies had net issues of debt securities (i.e., total issues less retirements) of $12.8 billion as compared

---

[8] U. S. League of Savings Associations, *1975 Fact Book*, p. 56.

[9] Ginnie Mae, which is an arm of HUD, draws on the U. S. Treasury for its funds. It is excluded in the calculations given here.

with direct U. S. Treasury issues of $19.4 billion. In the 1970–1974 period, the agencies had net securities issues of $32.8 billion as opposed to $61.9 billion for the U. S. Treasury.[10]

To what extent did the billions of dollars of securities issued by federally related housing finance agencies contribute to disintermediation? This is an important question. If they contributed to a great extent, they offset a large part of the results which they were intended to realize. During the difficult disintermediation periods, when the federal housing finance agencies should have been doing the most good for the housing industry, they may have been contributing to the problem!

Grebler has surveyed a number of studies of the extent to which these federal agencies make a net positive contribution to the housing market. These studies have employed the most sophisticated tools of economics and statistics to tackle this difficult question. Needless to say, different approaches to the problem turn up somewhat different conclusions. Nevertheless, Grebler remarks that "most models reveal positive short-run but no long-run impacts. On the whole, the FHLB System gets a better mark than does FNMA."

Grebler made his own estimates of the extent to which federally related housing credit agencies offset their own activities by causing disintermediation. For his estimates, the gross amount of funds which the agencies supplied to the housing market is distinguished from the amount after subtracting the estimated effects of disintermediation. The latter is termed the "net funds" supplied by the housing finance agencies. Grebler concludes:

The agencies did not supply any net funds in 1966. Their net contribution in 1969, 1970 and 1973–74 ranged from $4 billion to $8 billion, and it equalled about two-thirds of the gross amount supplied to the market in 1969 and one-half in 1973–1974. While these estimates indicate net benefits in terms of mortgage flows, disintermediation alone has reduced the funds available from federal agencies by substantial margins.[11]

Grebler was unable to make any estimates of the long-run effect of the finance agencies, but he concluded that a short-run positive impact is highly desirable. A short-run positive effect during periods of disintermediation would imply that the agencies have reduced the severity of cycles in the housing market. While this may be true, wide gyrations in mortgage flows

[10] Figures and discussion in this section are from Leo Grebler, "The Role of the Public Sector in Residential Financing," prepared for the First Annual Conference, Resources for Housing, Federal Home Loan Bank of San Francisco, December 9–10, 1975. See especially Appendix Table B–4.

[11] *Ibid.*, p. 30.

still characterize housing finance, and these gyrations extend to housing starts (see Chapter 21). Therefore, the building trades are still strongly affected by the cycles.

In the 1975 *Fact Book*, the United States League of Savings Associations expressed a great deal of concern over competition from the federally related finance agencies. The argument was carried a step beyond disintermediation to a contention that the agencies are squeezing the private sector by offering relatively low-interest mortgage loans:

> Although mortgage rates have slipped in relation to rates on utility issues ever since the late 1940's, the decline accelerated in recent years until, in 1974, mortgage rates actually dropped below utility yields. One reason for this drop has been the tremendous efforts made by the federal government to attract funds for mortgages through the use of its preferred borrowing positions. That is, mortgage credit has become available at lower rates than the private market could provide.[12]

This rechanneling of funds and relative decline in mortgage interest rates was seen as a threat to the private sector's ability to grow and maintain adequate reserves.

We find the position of the League of Savings Associations a little extreme, even though we have already cited evidence that the federally related finance agencies cause some disintermediation. It is somewhat contradictory for the League to argue that the agencies attract funds through high-yield securities *and* that they squeeze interest rates by using a "preferred" position to issue low-interest mortgages. How can the agencies have a preferred position if they must offer depositors relatively high interest rates in order to get their funds?[13] In fact, we doubt that any government instrument offered at the same rate as savings deposits can match them for liquidity and convenience. And, of course, the activity of the federal government has made savings deposits perfectly safe up to the $40,000 insurance ceiling.

Another factor may explain the extreme position taken by the League— the loss of a preferred income tax position (see Chapter 7). The League hopes to use this, and the development of federally related finance agencies, to bargain for another subsidy. They may well be successful; there has long been strong sentiment in this country for subsidies to the housing sector. Chapter 20 discusses a proposed tax deduction for interest earned from holding mortgages.

---

[12] U. S. League of Savings Associations, *op. cit.*, p. 73.

[13] We are aware that GNMA's tandem plan uses tax money to subsidize the interest rate paid by home buyers, but the amount involved here is not large. Furthermore, it does not involve use of a preferred borrowing position.

SUMMARY

The introduction of government mortgage insurance in 1934 has radically altered the lending practices of private financial institutions. Conventional mortgages—i.e., mortgages uninsured by the federal government—have been forced by competitive conditions to respond to the terms and conditions of insured mortgages, even though the latter make up only 34 per cent of all mortgages.

The influence of insured mortgages has extended to the establishment of minimum construction standards. Documentation of mortgages, analysis of the borrower, and analysis of the property have all been upgraded and standardized by the influence of insured mortgages.

The Federal Housing Administration (FHA) has increased allowable loan-to-value (L–V) ratios, and conventional mortgages have followed suit. This has been highly beneficial to borrowers since it allows the purchase of a home with relatively little accumulated capital. However, recent experience suggests that the FHA has gone too far in this direction. During periods of recession, an L–V of 95 or even 97 per cent gives homeowners little incentive to maintain their mortgage payments. In addition, the lender has almost no protection when default occurs. Tens of thousands of homes have recently passed through default and into the hands of the FHA.

Since 1955, the relative importance of government mortgage insurance has been reduced by several factors. The careful scrutiny by the FHA of borrower and property characteristics are time-consuming. Lenders complain that the FHA involves them in red tape which may jeopardize an impending loan. Since, over the past forty years, lenders have adopted the same standards as the FHA, they view the additional scrutiny by the FHA as superfluous. The FHA, on the other hand, must protect itself from a tendency of lenders to insure only the most risky loans.

After being wiped out by the Great Depression, private mortgage insurance has been able to reestablish itself during the past 15–20 years. Strong competition from the governmental insurance agencies has made the private insurers very innovative. They offer relatively low insurance rates and speedy acceptance of loans offered by approved lenders. They have introduced a joint (or piggyback) loan program in which the insured part of the mortgage is sold to one lender and the rest of the mortgage to another lender. This uninsured "bottom" of the mortgage is very safe, since it is protected against a large decline in the value of the property.

The government competes with private mortgage lenders for loanable funds. Most importantly, the housing agencies such as Freddie Mac and Fannie Mae issue debt instruments which attract funds away from savings deposits. This problem, known as "disintermediation," gets severe when interest rates rise above the rates which thrift institutions can pay for deposits. Most analysts believe that the efforts of housing credit agencies are partly offset by disintermediation, at least during the high interest period when federal help to the housing market is most needed. But there are many other advantages to these agencies, as outlined in Chapter 8.

QUESTIONS

1. The FHA introduced the self-amortizing, level payment mortgage during the Depression. It is now the most common form of mortgage, even for mortgages which are not insured by the FHA.
   (a) List some of the characteristics of this type of mortgage and discuss the ways in which it benefits borrowers.
   (b) Why does this type of mortgage now cause problems for thrift institutions?
   (c) Discuss one alternative to the level payment mortgage. Which characteristics of the level payment mortgage would be changed by this proposal?
2. How does mortgage insurance benefit the secondary mortgage market?
3. How does private mortgage insurance differ from FHA insurance? From VA insurance?
4. Define "adverse selection." Private mortgage insurance companies protect themselves against adverse selection by verifying the property appraisals on randomly selected properties (i.e., a spot check). This is done by hiring a second appraiser to estimate the property value. How does this help protect against adverse selection?
5. Define "disintermediation." How do the federally related housing finance agencies (FNMA, GNMA, and FHLMC) contribute to disintermediation? Does this conflict with their goals in the housing market?
6. How would you evaluate the argument of the savings associations that funds are being rechanneled through the federally related housing finance agencies?

III

The Borrower
and the Property—
Analysis and Application

10

BORROWER ANALYSIS

In determining whether to make a mortgage loan the lender gives careful consideration to the property which serves as security for the loan and to the borrower who will be expected to repay the loan. As noted below, there is considerable discussion as to which of these is more important for the lender's decision. Most lenders add a third item, the neighborhood; others include neighborhood factors in their analysis of the property.

The majority of lenders balance the three items against each other to determine whether some elements of risk in one might be acceptable because of advantages in another. For example, an older property which may not be quite adequate for loan purposes is being purchased by a borrower with an excellent credit reputation who is making a substantial down payment. This combination may make the loan acceptable. Although a great deal of research has been done with respect to the impact of the borrower, the property, and the neighborhood, there is as yet no reliable quantitative method for weighing these items against each other and selecting a single overriding factor for a lending decision.

A major controversy between lenders and borrowers is the extent to which the neighborhood should be considered in evaluating the loan. Some lenders take the attitude that although the borrower and the property may be fully credit worthy, a declining neighborhood is sufficient reason for refusing the loan. Their assumption is that the neighborhood will be the single most important factor in determining the value of the property in case of foreclosure. Further, they believe that a declining neighborhood tends to influence the borrower to neglect or abandon the property or even to abandon the loan. The practice of placing heavy emphasis on the neighborhood as a basis for making a loan is sometimes identified by the term "redlining." Various efforts are being made to overcome this practice, but it is difficult to alter a practice that is defended as being in the best interests of stockholders and depositors.

The major facts which a lender wishes to know about a borrower are:

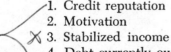

1. Credit reputation
2. Motivation
3. Stabilized income
4. Debt currently owed.
5. Assets

GUIDELINES FOR BORROWER ANALYSIS

Federal housing agencies have been particularly concerned about certain borrower analysis practices which result in the refusal of loans to a large segment of the borrower market. In January, 1974, the Federal Home Loan Bank Board issued rules or guidelines for the fair treatment of borrowers in making home loans. These rules affect the lending practices of more than 5,000 savings and loan associations which are regulated by the Bank Board. Unacceptable practices include: (1) discrimination against the borrower based on the racial composition of the neighborhood; (2) refusal to lend in a particular area because of the age of the homes or the neighborhood income level; (3) refusal to lend on the basis of the borrower's age, sex, or marital status. The Board issued these guidelines on the assumption that "the use of lending standards which have no economic basis and which are discriminatory in effect is in violation of law even in the absence of actual intent to discriminate." The Bank Board had earlier prohibited discrimination in home lending on the basis of race, color, or national origin; the guidelines were intended to add specific definition to these generalized rules.

The Bank Board informed the savings and loan associations that in evaluating borrowers they should consider part-time income, overtime income, and supplementary income, including income from a working wife, in evaluating a borrower's financial capacities to repay a loan. As we shall see below, this represented a significant change in former practices for evaluating a borrower.

The kinds of questions which are assumed to be pertinent to the evaluation of the economic capacity of the borrower are shown in Figure 10–1, which represents a composite of the information typically requested in a home loan borrowing situation. In essence, it consists of two major questions: (1) What does the home buyer own? and (2) What does the home

BORROWER ANALYSIS—MORTGAGE LOAN

A. Estimate of income available for repayment of mortgage loan: (monthly basis)

Income

1. Earned income:*
   Wage earner A: Gross_____
                 Deduction_____ $_____
   Wage earner B: Gross_____
                 Deduction_____ _____
   Wage earner C: Gross_____
                 Deduction_____ _____
2. Interest, dividends, royalties
   Savings interest _____
   Securities interest _____
   Securities dividends _____
   Royalties (source:) _____
3. Rents, property earnings (net) _____
4. Other income: (specify) _____

5. TOTAL INCOME _____
6. SUBTRACT: Anticipated total
   expenses _____

7. NET INCOME POSITION AFTER
   EXPENSES $_____

Expenses

1. Loan payments: $_____
   Automobile $_____
   Furniture _____
   Clothes _____
   Credit cards _____
2. Living expenses
   (specify) _____
   _____
3. Other expenses:
   (specify)
   Insurance (kinds)_____
   _____ _____
   _____ _____
4. TOTAL CURRENT EX-
   PENSES _____
5. Anticipated property expenses:
   Monthly loan
   payment (princi-
   pal and interest) _____
   Utilities, upkeep _____
   Property taxes _____
   Property insur-
   ance _____
   Other: (specify) _____
6. ANTICIPATED
   TOTAL EX-
   PENSES $_____

B. Estimate of assets available for additional security on the loan: (current totals)

	Market Value	Unpaid Loan Amt.	Net Value
1. Automobile (make and year)	$_____	$_____	$_____
2. Furniture	_____	_____	_____
3. Real estate (kind)	_____	_____	_____
	_____	_____	_____
4. Securities (specify)	_____	_____	_____
	_____	_____	_____
5. Business owned (specify)	_____	_____	_____
6. Other assets (specify)			
Savings	_____	_____	_____
	_____	_____	_____
7. TOTAL NET VALUE			$_____

8. Credit rating and evaluation (usually secured from credit rating bureau)

_____
_____

9. Pending suits, judgments, or litigation

_____
_____

10. RATIOS AND ANALYSES:
   Per cent of income remaining after all regular deductions (A−7) _____ %
   Per cent of income available for fixed and recurring expenses (A−5) _____ %
   Gross income (A−5) divided into home value _____
   Earned income (A−1) divided into home value _____
   Anticipated property expenses (A−5 expenses) as per cent
   of total income _____

Fig. 10–1. The prospective home buyer's balance sheet.

buyer owe? Presumably, the amount owned should be more than the amount owed and the borrower should have the capacity to meet the additional financial obligations imposed by the loan.

Credit Reputation.   Although we are discussing credit reputation first, there is no particular order of priority for the questions that are asked. No commonly accepted, quantifiable weights can be attached to the information, but income and indebtedness are probably accorded more importance than credit reputation. The purpose of looking into the credit reputation of the borrower is to determine whether money borrowed in the past has been repaid on schedule. This is the intent of the questions listed under "What Do I Own?" in Figure 10–1. If payments for autos or furniture or appliances or doctor bills have been made on a regular schedule, the borrower is presumed to be credit worthy. In addition, if most of these debts have been paid off, the borrower is in a better position to make larger payments on a home loan. Since the borrower is expected to be paying at least 20 per cent of income toward the purchase of a home, a sufficient portion of this income should be free from other debt obligations to permit such payments.

In essence, the lender is looking at the borrower's credit reputation for the purpose of determining what obligations the borrower has undertaken, what debts are unpaid, what assets are owned, and how they have been acquired. Were valuable assets acquired through some form of planned indebtedness and repayment? Finally, it is important that the borrower be able to furnish references from banks or other credit sources which indicate a reputation for repayment of debts according to schedule, without undue cost or administrative problems for the lender.

Borrower Evaluation Processes.   The following example indicates the way in which a lender might typically evaluate a borrower. Assume that a borrower is buying a home with a sale price of $18,700. The lender will make a loan for $16,500 and requires a $2,200 down payment. Annual costs of occupancy are: taxes $325, insurance $42, fuel and water $200, minimum maintenance $125, for a total of $692. The borrower wants a loan of $16,000 at 10 per cent for 20 years. This would mean annual payments on the loan of approximately $1,900, thus creating annual costs of financing and using the home of approximately $2,592. Since most lenders expect these costs to equal between 20 and 25 per cent of the borrower's annual income, the borrower, to qualify for the purchase of this home, would have to have an annual income of between $10,368 and $12,960. (In 1976, a typical new house was selling at a price of $48,000. Because of allowances for inflation, lenders were requiring a borrower to have an annual income of at least $19,000 in order to buy a home at that price.)

Bitter experience on the part of lenders and mortgage insurers has testified to the importance of income in determining the borrower's ability to repay. Table 10–1 indicates that borrowers with income below $8,400 were particularly prone to default in the 1969–1971 period. Adjusting for inflation, a comparable end-of-year figure for 1977 would be $12,500. Thus, borrowers with lower incomes must be considered relatively high risks, even if they are qualified in other respects. All other factors, of course, rarely remain the same. A family with a $9,000 annual income might seek a loan on a modest house which would not involve them in monthly expenses above 25 per cent of their income. Table 10–2 shows that financial institutions have had relatively good experiences with loans which do not involve the borrower in payments which are more than 25 per cent of income. Thus, it is important for lenders to consider not only income but all of the evidence with respect to ability to pay for housing.

Motivation. Lenders tend to put heavy emphasis on the motivation of the home buyer, presuming that the buyer who is most anxious to own a home is most likely to be a good home loan credit risk. For this reason, the borrower with a family who is buying a home to provide shelter for the family, is presumed to be a more strongly motivated borrower than one who is buying property for rental-income purposes. Motivation is, of course, very difficult to evaluate so lenders try in various ways to find out whether borrowers' reasons for buying homes are strong enough to encourage them to want to keep repaying on the loans, even when this involves some financial hardship.

Important clues to the motivation of borrowers can be found in a report of their activities in their communities. For example, memberships in local service organizations suggest a dedication to the local area and a willingness to meet debt obligations.

Stability of Income. Perhaps the single most important factor which will influence a lender's decision is the amount and stability of a borrower's income. Lenders will give greatest weight to income which is earned at a steady, full-time job or which comes from conservative investments such as federal government bonds. This type of income is likely to continue at a stable level during the entire period of the loan, assuming that the loan period is geared to the borrower's age. Jobs in which periods of unemployment are likely—e.g., blue-collar jobs in which the person does not have seniority—are undesirable from the lenders' point of view.

Table 10-1. Section 203(b), New Homes, Insurance Written 1968 and 1969; Defaults in 1969, 1970, and 1971

Mortgagor's Net Effective Annual Income	Defaults 1969–1971	Insurance Written 1968	Defaults 1969–1971	Insurance Written 1969	Ratio of Defaults to Insurance Written 1968	1969
Less than $ 3,600	.7	.2	.5	.1	3.50	5.00
$ 3,600 to 4,799	5.5	1.3	3.0	.8	4.23	3.75
4,800 to 5,999	14.8	6.8	8.1	3.6	2.18	2.25
6,000 to 7,199	23.7	16.6	19.2	11.5	1.43	1.67
7,200 to 8,399	18.6	18.3	24.9	17.1	1.02	1.46
8,400 to 9,599	15.5	17.7	15.7	18.1	.88	.87
9,600 to 10,799	9.6	14.4	12.2	16.6	.67	.73
10,800 to 11,999	4.1	9.5	6.3	11.8	.43	.53
12,000 to 14,399	5.1	9.9	8.1	13.4	.52	.60
14,400 and over	2.4	5.3	2.0	7.0	.45	.29
Total	100.0	100.0	100.0	100.0		

Source: Special tabulation of FHA data. From Chester Rapkin, *The Private Insurance of Home Mortgages*, copyright © 1973, by Chester Rapkin. Reprinted with permission.

Table 10-2. Percentage Distribution of Section 203(b), New Homes, Insurance Written 1968 and 1969; Defaults in 1969, 1970, and 1971

Housing Expense As Per Cent of Net Effective Income	Defaults 1969–1971	Insurance Written 1968	Defaults 1969–1971	Insurance Written 1969	Ratio of Defaults to Insurance Written 1968	1969
Less than 22	23	27	15	22	.85	.68
22 to 24	20	20	21	19	1.00	1.11
25 to 30	39	38	39	39	1.03	1.00
31 to 39	16	14	24	19	1.14	1.26
40 or more	2	1	1	1	2.00	1.00
Total	100	100	100	100		

Source: Same as Table 10-1.

Lenders have attempted to use various benchmarks for housing expenses as a percentage of income. Changing economic conditions and current emphasis on equality in home lending have meant that these benchmarks are no longer adequate and that other means must be used to measure the financial capacity of borrowers. Basically, lenders want to be sure that borrowers have a sufficient effective income to permit them to pay off their mortgage debt and to take care of the other obligations necessary to their life style. Present benchmarks assume that all expenses relating to housing should not exceed 33 per cent of a borrower's income and preferably should not be more than 25 per cent. A stable income stream from a secure job or from conservative investments allows the borrower to move toward the upper limit of the range.

These percentages might be exceeded if borrowers can show that they have been owning and occupying homes for which their total financial obligations have been beyond the range of the benchmarks, without any impairment of their ability to pay their debts. Borrowers may also be able to show that they will be increasing their financial capacities through savings or increasing their earned income so that the costs of housing will represent a continuously smaller proportion of their annual income.

Employment Record. Lenders will want to know where borrowers are currently employed, how long they have been employed on particular jobs, and what their prospects are for continued employment. Lenders will tend to give greater preference to borrowers who have been continuously employed, have shown a record of promotion, and are holding jobs in companies or industries in which there is continued prospect for employment.

The importance of income and job stability is indicated by Table 10–3. For example, borrowers with two or more jobs within five years of the loan application are more likely to become delinquent than borrowers who have held the same job for the past five years. In fact, the risk of delinquency drops significantly with length of job tenure.

Blue-collar jobs are particularly subject to periods of layoff or strike. Other jobs, in fields such as sales, experience slow periods with income interruptions and declines. These types of jobs are associated with higher loan delinquency rates (see Table 10–3). However, the importance of the type of job can be offset somewhat by long tenure on the job or by monthly payments that represent a relatively low proportion of income.

In determining how much income a borrower can apply to a home mortgage loan, a lender basically will ask: Does the borrower have additional sources of income from overtime pay, extra employment, family contributions, income-earning assets, or rental of other properties? The lender also may consider accumulated pension benefits. Finally, the lender

Table 10-3. Percentage Distribution of Mortgages and Delinquencies by Job Stability of Borrower; Savings and Loan Association Loans on Single-Family Homes, 1964

	All Loans	
	Current	*Delinquent*
(a) Number of jobs in past five years:		
None	1	1
One	75	68
Two	20	25
Three or more	4	6
Total	100	100
(b) Years on current job:		
Under one year	9	10
1–4	27	35
5–9	25	26
10–14	17	15
15 or more	22	14
Total	100	100
(c) Occupation:		
Self-employed	17	25
Executive	15	9
Salesman	6	9
White-collar	17	9
Skilled labor	28	29
Unskilled labor	8	13
Professional	1	1
Other	8	5
Total	100	100

Source: Leon T. Kendall, *Anatomy of the Residential Mortgage*, United States Savings and Loan League, 1964.

would be concerned about whether the borrower has insurance against temporary or permanent disability, with benefits large enough to allow the borrower, in case of personal health problems, to continue to make payments on the loan *and* provide for other needs. Finally, the lender will be favorably impressed by an opportunity to realize financial gain from the current transaction.

In January, 1975, *Mortgage Banker* magazine listed all of the potential income sources, other than the principal earned income, which a lender may want to consider in making a home mortgage loan:

1. Bonus income. Some employers pay bonuses regularly as a part of their overall compensation package.

2. Overtime income. This is normally not counted unless it has been earned consistently over a period of time.
3. Part-time income. Here the concern is whether the borrower has been working at a part-time job for some time or only temporarily.
4. Veterans' Administration benefits.
5. Wife's income. Since a greater number of wives are now working and contributing to the family's finances, this particular source of income is receiving increasing importance. If the wife is regularly employed and will continue to be employed, her income can be counted for 100 per cent of its value. However, some lenders have tended to discount some portion of this income. Lenders are no longer allowed to inquire with respect to the potential for having children, although some in the past have asked for statements or letters indicating that the family intended to have no children.
6. National Guard or military reserves income. Because of previous military obligations, many borrowers are still members of the reserves for some unit of the Armed Forces. This income can amount to several thousand dollars a year, is usually reasonably stable, and will continue for some time.
7. Child support and alimony. Lenders are not likely to accept this in considering financial capacity unless they have clear substantial evidence that it will continue.
8. Rental income. Some borrowers may have other income-producing real estate which could be considered as contributing to the income applicable to the current investment.
9. Investment income. The question here is the *sources* for the investment income. Some stocks and bonds, for example, may not be paying dividends and may have very little capital value in case they had to be liquidated to secure additional financing.
10. Income from commissions, fees, or royalties or other income which has been received regularly for some time.

The Mortgage Banker Association stresses that the process of borrower evaluation is a difficult one and there can be disputes among lenders with respect to the same borrower. The lender must be prepared to explain carefully the reasons for accepting or rejecting a particular borrower.

Some lenders place emphasis on what they call offsetting factors; perhaps the borrower is going to buy a property on which only a small loan is required or perhaps the borrower has an unusual job situation. As an example, assume that two borrowers have the same monthly income of $1,750. Borrower A has been on the job for two years and has monthly financial obligations totaling $600. This would represent approximately 34 per cent of total income. Borrower B has been on the job 15 years and has total monthly obligations of $700, or 40 per cent of income. Is either of the borrowers acceptable? Does the 40 per cent represent such a substantial increase over the benchmarks that Borrower B would not be acceptable? At this point, other information about the borrower would have to be considered. What is the age of the borrower? Does the borrower have a job from which increases in income can be expected? Is the property a good one? What is the nature of the current obligations? Will they soon be repaid? Have the obligations permitted the borrower to acquire assets which can be liquidated in case additional financial support is needed? Most lenders would tend to put considerable emphasis on determining whether the borrower had shown a history of responsible home ownership.

Before making a loan or asking that an application be filled out, the mortgage bankers recommend that an interview be conducted in which three things are to be determined:

1. Does the borrower understand the full terms of the mortgage contract and the rights and responsibilities inherent in the contract?
2. Does the borrower seem to be sincerely motivated to buy the property?
3. Can some form of personal, friendly relationship be established so that the borrower can be assisted in organizing and operating family finances to avoid a difficult financial situation; or, can the borrower be encouraged to keep the lender informed if financial difficulties arise so that both can work to assure that the loan will be paid according to schedule?

If the interview concludes favorably and the borrower seems a good risk, the lender asks that a loan application be filled out and the process of lending is put in motion. Figure 10–2 shows a loan application in use at a savings and loan association.

Current Debt and Current Assets. The purchase of a home always involves additional expenditures beyond those connected with merely the price of the home and the mortgage lending contract. Does the prospective homeowner already own the furnishings necessary to make the home livable or must they be purchased? This is one reason why lenders are most anxious to determine what the borrower currently owes and owns. Presumably, the borrower who has acquired all the furnishings necessary to make the home livable and has paid off these costs, or is in the process of paying them off and will soon have the obligation completed, is a much better risk than one who is faced with buying all of this property.

Lenders may have reservations about borrowers who have invested heavily in such things as campers, boats, or second homes. These all represent a financial drain which the borrowers may not be able to handle successfully if there is an economic downturn involving a temporary loss of income.

PROTECTION AGAINST BORROWER RISKS

Lenders have developed a series of devices which they use to protect themselves against the possibility that the borrower will not repay the loan according to schedule. Obviously, the most important protection is to require a substantial down payment. Preferably, the borrower should be paying down not less than 10 per cent of the purchase price. In times of credit stringency a 25 per cent down payment is frequently considered a minimum requirement for most borrowers. We have already mentioned that the lender will examine loan obligations and other payments necessary to own and operate the property and will try to insure that these total costs generally do not exceed 30 to 35 per cent of the total family take-home pay. A lender also will tend to limit the loan amount so that the borrower cannot buy a property which exceeds approximately two and one-half times the family's total annual "accountable" income (income available to pay the loan). Because of inflation in recent years, many lenders now restrict the price limit to not more than two times the borrower's income.

As further protection, the lender will require a complete credit report on everything the borrower has owed and paid for in the past and on what is now owed and being paid off.

Obviously, the stability of the borrower's total accountable income is considered along with stability of employment and family life. An older person with a family and an established job is usually considered an ideal borrower. On the other hand, a younger person who obviously has good prospects, works for a good company, and has started a family is an equally acceptable risk.

From the experience of the Depression period, lenders have realized that borrowers should be required to make periodic payments on the loan principal, interest, property taxes, and property insurance. For this reason, many lenders require borrowers to make a monthly payment which includes all of these items. In addition, many lenders insist that the borrower be limited to a single loan on the property. They feel that the borrower should acquire the property with only one loan, since a second loan may impose an undue financial burden. Typically, second loans are for shorter terms

LOAN APPLICATION

FINANCIAL FEDERATION INC BANK OF STRENGTH

The Federal Equal Credit Opportunity Act prohibits creditors from discriminating against credit applicants on the basis of sex or marital status. The Federal agency which administers compliance with this law concerning this savings and loan association is the Federal Home Loan Bank Board, 320 First Street, N.W., Washington, D. C. 20552.

This form shall be considered as an application for a loan only when it is **received by the Association at one of its offices** and, provided that it has been properly filled-in, signed and dated, and is accompanied by any documents or schedules requested by it or required by law. If married you may apply for a separate account if the real estate security is separate property.

TO: _____ SAVINGS AND LOAN ASSOCIATION

The undersigned hereby apply for a loan as follows: Loan No. _____

Loan Amount	Interest Rate	Reserve payment as required by Association	Term-Years	Principal & Interest Payment
$	%			$

The loan will be evidenced, on your usual forms, by a Promissory Note secured by a First Deed of Trust on the real property located in the State of California described as follows:

Street Address	City	County

LEGAL DESCRIPTION: *(Exact) If lengthy, attach copy of deed, title report, etc.*

Title to be vested in:

Borrower's Names

If Partnership or Corporation furnish Partnership Agreement or Corporate Resolution to Borrow.
Names of Officers Authorized to Sign Loan Documents

Name	Title	Telephone No.

Name	Title	Telephone No.

Escrow Information: *Legible copy of all Escrow Instructions and Amendments must be attached.*

Escrow Company	Address	

Escrow No.	Escrow Officer	Telephone No.

PURCHASE TRANSACTION: ☐ New Loan ☐ Assumption   Name of Seller _____

Total Consideration	Cash	Other Equity	Association Loan	2nd Trust Deed
$	$	$	$	$

Deposit in Escrow	Cash Outside Escrow	Balance thru Escrow	Describe other Equity, Trade, etc.	
$	$	$		

Holder of 2nd & Address	Telephone No.	Int. Rate on 2nd T.D.	Mo. Payment on 2nd T.D.	
		%	$	

Source of Balance of Cash to Close Escrow:

REFINANCE TRANSACTION: *List all Trust Deeds and Property Improvement Loans; and other Liens:*

	Address	Telephone No.	Loan No.	Original Amount	Mo. Payment	Balance
1st Trust Deed - Lender				$	$	$
2nd Trust Deed						
Other						
Other						

If any of the above are to be subordinated, give details: Prepayment penalties $

If new 2nd Trust Deed to Record: Lender   Approximate amount needed to pay above $

Amount $	Int. Rate %	Mo. Payment $	Due Date	Estimated Closing Costs - By Loan Officer $

If total is LESS than loan requested, the balance will be used for: Total $
If total is MORE than loan requested, the difference will come from:

CONSTRUCTION LOAN ONLY: ☐ Spec.   ☐ Pre-Sale

Contractors Name	Land Value $	Contract $	Completed Value $	Required Deposit $
License No.	Proceeds Available for Construction $		Source of Deposit	

NOTE: All funds are to be advanced according to the Building-Loan Agreement. Signed Plans, Specifications, Cost Breakdown and General Contract will be or have been submitted and considered as a part of this Application.

Upon written acceptance by the undersigned of the loan offered, if this application is approved, the undersigned will agree (1) to pay all costs, charges and fees incidental to the loan including, but not limited to:

Loan Acquisition Fee % $	Loan Set-up Charge $	Tax Lien Service $	Credit Report $	Appraisal $

(2)   to furnish and pay for a policy of title insurance satisfactory in amount, coverage and company to the association showing title to the property subject only to real estate taxes not yet due, covenants, conditions and restrictions of record approved by the association and the Deed of Trust given to secure the loan.

(3)   to authorize the association to pay sums necessary to obtain and record releases of all liens required by the title insurer to enable it to issue the aforementioned policy of title insurance. All sums so paid are to be deducted from the proceeds of the loan. After deducting all costs, charges, fees, expenses and payments incidental to the loan from the loan proceeds, any balance remaining shall be paid to the undersigned. If the proceeds are not sufficient to pay all such sums, the undersigned will furnish the difference upon written demand by the association.

FF-L-13 (REV. 3/76)

Fig. 10–2. Loan application form. (Courtesy of Financial Federation, Inc.)

STATEMENT OF PRIOR SALES

☐ The undersigned has no knowledge of any pending or completed sale, exchange, transfer, or escrow, respecting said real property, during the 24 month period immediately preceding the date of this statement.

☐ The undersigned has knowledge of the following described pending or completed sale, exchange, transfer, or escrow, respecting said real property during the 24 month period immediately preceding the date of this statement. *(Describe each transaction. If none, write "None" in space below.)*

Type	Consideration	Names and Relationship of Parties Involved
	$	
	$	
	$	
	$	

CERTIFICATE OF LOANS TO ONE BORROWER

List all loans made by the Association, including the loan applied for hereby, to the following persons or entities: (1) Any person or entity that is, or that upon the making of a loan will become, obligor on a loan on the security of real estate; (2) Nominees of such obligor; (3) All persons, trusts, partnerships, syndicates, and corporations of which such obligor is a beneficiary, partner, member, or record or beneficial stockholder owning ten (10) per cent or more of the capital stock; or a nominee for any of these persons. (4) If such obligor is a trust, partnership, syndicate, or corporation: all trusts, partnerships, syndicates and corporations of which any beneficiary, partner, member, or record or beneficial stockholder owning ten (10) per cent or more of the capital stock, is also a beneficiary, partner, member or record or beneficial stockholder owning ten (10) per cent or more of the capital stock of the obligor; (5) Members of the immediate family of any borrower.

Other Loans Applied for or Made Borrower's Name	Loan No.	This Loan
		$
		$
		$
		$
		$
	Total	$

STATEMENT OF PURPOSE

I/We, the undersigned, do hereby certify that the property on which I/We have applied to you for a loan in accordance with this application:

I. ☐ Is NOT and is NOT expected to be used as My/Our principal residence.

II. ☐ Is, or is expected to be used as, My/Our principal residence. *If the box on this line was checked, complete the following as applicable:*

     A. ☐ The loan applied for is to be used to pay a portion of the purchase price of the dwelling and/or to construct a residence on the property.

     B. ☐ None of the loan applied for is to be used to purchase the property. Instead, the loan proceeds will be used for:

     C. ☐ The loan applied for is to be used to pay a portion of the purchase price of a lot not improved with a dwelling.

CERTIFICATE OF CHARGES AND FEES

In addition to the charges and fees set forth in this application which the undersigned agrees to pay, the undersigned is also obligated to pay: *(If none, write "None" in the space below.)*

Name of Payee	Purpose	Amount
		$
		$

CERTIFICATE OF OCCUPANCY AND LIENS

☐ The undersigned will occupy the property which is the subject of this application, as My/Our principal residence. There will be no liens affecting title to the property other than the Deed of Trust contemplated by this application.

The undersigned hereby apply for a Borrower's Membership in the association subject to its Charter, By-Laws, Rules and Regulations.

If loan applied for is an FHA insured or VA guaranteed loan, please complete the following section.

What was your total State, Local, and Federal income taxes paid for the latest taxable year? $

What are your annual or monthly life insurance premiums? *Put "X" in box to show if annual or monthly.* ☐ Annual ☐ Monthly $

What are your Social Security or other Retirement payments each month? $

If you own real estate other than the property in which you reside, what are the monthly operating expenses? $

Does it have an FHA or VA loan presently? ☐ Yes ☐ No

If you own any other real estate, is it to be sold? ☐ Yes ☐ No		Sales Price ☐ Yes ☐ No $

Original Loan Amount $	Name of Lendor	Have you sold property the past 2 years which had an FHA loan? ☐ Yes ☐ No

If answer to last question is yes, answer the following:	FHA Case No.	Buyers Name	Property Address

Did buyer intend to occupy? ☐ Yes ☐ No	Date of Transfer	Sales Price $	Original Loan Amount $	Unpaid Balance when Sold $

If dwelling to be covered by loan is to be for rent - is it part of, adjacent or contiguous to any project subdivision or group of rental properties involving eight or more dwelling units in which you have any financial interest? ☐ Yes ☐ No

Do you own four or more dwelling units insured under any title of the National Housing Act? ☐ Yes ☐ No

Fig. 10-2. Continued.

PERSONAL INFORMATION and FINANCIAL STATEMENT   Loan No. _____

Please complete in detail - if space insufficient, attach separate sheet with additional information.

Name of Applicant (1)	Age	Social Security Number	Number of Dependents	
Name of Applicant (2)	Age	Social Security Number	Age of Dependents	
Residence Address - Street	City	State	Phone No.	Zip Code	How Long?
Former Address - Street	City	State		Zip Code	How Long?
Applicant (1) Employed by		How Long?	Salary: $ ☐ Hourly ☐ Weekly ☐ Monthly	
Employer's Address - Street or P.O. Box	City	State	Zip Code Position	Telephone No.
Previous Employer and Address		How Long?	Salary: $ ☐ Hourly ☐ Weekly ☐ Monthly	
Applicant (2) Employed by		How Long?	Salary: $ ☐ Hourly ☐ Weekly ☐ Monthly	
Employer's Address - Street or P.O. Box	City	State	Zip Code Position	Telephone No.
Previous Employer and Address		How Long?	Salary: $ ☐ Hourly ☐ Weekly ☐ Monthly	

This form is not valid without account numbers.   If Corporation, attach an AUDITED Financial Statement   **OR**   If self-employed, furnish most recent balance sheet and profit and loss statement on business for last 12 months - MUST BE dated and signed and not over 90 days old.

Assets

Cash in Savings and Loan Associations and Banks

Check or Saving	Account No.	Name of Association or Bank	Branch	Address	Amount
					$
					$
					$
					$

		Present Value
Furniture and Personal Belongings		$
Stocks and Bonds - *itemize*		$
		$

Mortgages and Trust Deeds owned *(on which you receive payments)*

Location of Property	Interest Rate	Monthly Payment	Due Date on Note	1st, 2nd, 3rd	Unpaid Principal Due
					$
	%				$
	%				$
	%				$

Real Estate - Address or Location	Type of Prop (1)*	Gross Income	Trust Deed Payments	Taxes	Other Expenses	Present Value
						$
						$
						$
						$

Automobiles - *Make, Year*	Present Value
	$
	$
	$

Life Insurance - *Face Value - Name of Insurance Company*	Cash Value
	$

Other Assets - *Itemize*	
$	$
	$
	$
	$
	$
Total Assets	**$**

*(1) Land, Single Family Residence or Number of Units.

Fig. 10—2. Continued.

LIABILITIES

Owed to	Address	Account No.	Mo. Payments	Amount
Real Estate Loans			$	$
			$	$
Automobiles				$
			$	$
Furniture			$	$
			$	$
Other Current Accounts			$	$
			$	$
			$	$
Total Monthly Payments – Liabilities			**$**	**$**

Please answer the following questions.	Yes or No
Have you ever filed bankruptcy?	
Have you ever owned property on which foreclosure was taken?	
Are the payments delinquent with your present lending institution?	
Have you ever been seriously delinquent in your payments on your home?	
Any amount past due on other obligations?	
Are you obligated to pay any alimony or child support?	
Have you ever had any suits, judgements, liens or repossessions?	

If any of the applicants answers "yes" to any of the above questions please attach a separate sheet to this application with explanation of that answer.

Monthly Income	Amount
Salary or wages of Applicant (1)	$
Salary or wages of Applicant (2)	$
Part time or overtime	$
Net Income from Real Estate	$
Interest Income - Savings	$
Interest Income - Trust Deeds	$
Investment Income - Stocks & Bonds	$
Other Income -- itemize on separate sheet. You need not reveal income from alimony, child support, or maintenance payments if you choose not to do so.	$
Total Monthly Income	**$**

Monthly Payments and Housing Expense	
Rent or Mortgage Payments	$
Taxes on Real Estate	$
Automobiles	$
Furniture	$
Personal Loans	$
Other Payments	$
Total Monthly Payments	**$**

Credit References - *Closed Accounts*

Name and Address	Account No.	Date Opened	High Credit	Mo. Payments

The undersigned jointly and severally certify under PENALTY OF PERJURY that all statements made and information given in this loan application are true and correct and that this application was prepared prior to, and submitted for the purpose of obtaining the loan requested herein from the association. The undersigned understand that this loan, if approved, will be made in absolute reliance on the truth of each and every statement and representation herein made and the terms and conditions of this application shall become a part of the loan contract. If the loan is cancelled pursuant to my right of rescission under the Truth in Lending Act I will not be required to pay any costs and any deposit will be returned.

Company Name _____

Signature Applicant (1)	*All applicants must sign*	Date	Officer	Title
Signature Applicant (2)		Date	Officer	Title

FOR ASSOCIATION USE ONLY:

Approved by _____ , Loan Officer

Date credit reviewed and loan approved by Loan Committee _____

By _____   By _____

By _____   By _____

Date _____   Reason Declined _____

Applicant Informed of Decision _____ Date _____

By _____

Terms

Loan Amount	Int. Rate	Term-Years	Principal and Interest Payment	Appraisal	Loan/Value
$	%		$	$	%

Reserve Payments: Taxes $	Payment/Income	Loan Fee Amount	Loan Fee
Insurance $ Replacement $	%	$	%

Fig. 10–2. Continued.

and higher rates of interest so that when the obligations of a second loan are added to those of the first, the borrower may be required to pay as much as 40 to 50 per cent of income just to acquire a home.

Lenders have found that borrowers should be expected to complete the loan application form in all details and to do it accurately. In the past, some lenders have been too casual about reviewing the loan application or requiring its completion. These lenders have learned the hard way that a borrower may deliberately omit unfavorable information or provide inaccurate figures.

There are other protective devices which lenders may use. For example, they may require that the loan payments not exceed an equivalent rental

---

The Property

A single-family home, 2,000 square feet, built in 1957. Three bedrooms and den, 2 baths, kitchen fully equipped with gas appliances installed when the house was built, dining area and living room with fireplace. Detached 2-car garage.

Neglected maintenance would involve approximately $1,500 outlay. In fact, the house reflects minimal care on the part of the present owners.

The Lot

Area is approximately 10,000 square feet of which 5,000 is a flat pad and the remainder a hill with a 45-degree slope. There is landscaping which has been maintained minimally.

The lot is on a hillside with a magnificent view of the coastline. The altitude is approximately 1,200 feet above sea level. Geological surveys indicate the home is on stable soil.

The Neighborhood

The house is part of a tract of 300 homes built between 1957 and 1959. They are all approximately alike in size and architectural styling. The sale prices ranged from $30,000 to $38,000 depending upon the view. Recent sales in the tract have ranged from $75,000 to $85,000.

The area is very hilly. In 1968 heavy rains caused two homes across from the home being considered to slide partially. In 1972 heavy brush fires in the area immediately to the rear of the property threatened the homes in the region but were halted by extraordinary fire-fighting efforts.

There are elementary and senior high schools in the vicinity. Excellent bus service within three blocks. Reasonably complete regional-type shopping centers are located approximately one mile and three miles away and can be reached by bus. A library, two parks (with tennis courts), and a state beach are only two miles from the area and are reachable by bus.

The Borrower

The borrower is married and has one teen-age son. He is a professor at a nearby university, where he has been employed for 15 years. His current university income of $24,000 annually is supplemented through various consulting activities. He is moving from an older area which is beginning to deteriorate. He owns his home which he thinks has a market price of $54,000. His present equity in the home is $18,000. The loan is held by a local savings and loan association and has 15 years remaining. The original loan was for $30,000 with a 9.0 per cent interest rate.

Fig. 10–3. The lending situation.

value of the property being purchased. Or they may place heavy emphasis on the borrower's having sufficient assets to serve as backup in case the family's income is interrupted or declines precipitously. Figure 10–3 contains the kind of information which a lender might collect with respect to a given mortgage loan. Would you, as a lender, consider this to be enough information to make a decision with respect to the loan, or would you want more information? If you want more information, what would it be? Where would you get it? Once you had the information, how would you use it? What efforts would you make with respect to the loan arrangements, to minimize your risk? Remember, there are no hard and fast rules. What you are trying to do is to put together a total package of lending requirements which will enable the borrower to buy a particular home without assuming financial obligations which might cause trouble at a later date.

SUMMARY

A family applying for a mortgage loan must account for its assets and liabilities just as a corporation does on its balance sheet. Personal assets and liabilities are important in indicating an ability and willingness to repay a mortgage loan. An examination of assets and liabilities helps the lender to answer the following questions:

1. What other debt will have to be repaid along with the prospective mortgage?
2. What liquid assets are available to tide the family over in case of sickness, layoff, or other interruptions in the income stream?
3. Considering the family income, how successful has the family been in accumulating assets through saving or repayment of debt?

The lender must also consider the borrower's credit reputation. In the past, how successful has the family been in repaying debt on time?

For repayment of a home mortgage loan, the lender looks primarily to family income. The adequacy of this income depends on its sources and on its size relative to the contemplated payments for the mortgage and other housing expenses. Low income, especially in relation to housing payments, is associated with a relatively high rate of default. Income from self-employment, sales commissions, or unskilled labor is not as stable as other income and is associated with relatively high loan delinquency, as is income from individuals with fewer than five to ten years on the current job. However, each of these factors is just one of many characteristics which the lender must consider. An individual with less than one year on an unskilled job but with little indebtedness, adequate assets, and modest prospective housing costs may be an excellent credit risk.

QUESTIONS

1. Lenders often assume that the borrower's motivation to repay is related to the size of the down payment.
   (a) Do you think that motivation increases or decreases as the size of the down payment increases? Why?
   (b) Lenders have another interest in the size of the down payment. What is it?
2. Lenders often try to keep total housing expenses below 25 per cent of income. What kind of experience justifies this?
3. Ability to repay depends on the quality (i.e., stability) of income as well as the amount of income. Discuss three indicators the lender might review in evaluating the stability of income.
4. What do you think is the most important single entry on the borrower's balance sheet? Why?
5. Take a look at the information in Figure 10–3.
   (a) If you wanted more information about the borrower, what would it be?
   (b) Where would you get it?
   (c) Once you had the information, how would you use it?
   (d) What kind of loan arrangements would you recommend if your goal is to reduce the risk of lending in this situation?

11

PROPERTY ANALYSIS

The lender analyzes the property being offered as security for a loan for the purpose of estimating whether the value remaining in that property during the life of the loan will always equal or exceed the amount not yet paid on the loan. In order to determine this, a market value appraisal is made, to establish loan value. Loan value is usually slightly below the price at which the property will actually sell and, since the loan is always less than the appraised value, loans usually equal between 70 and 90 per cent of market value. The loan-to-value ratio is usually determined by the type of loan being made, legal regulations on the lender, and the lender's general policies. In the case of government-insured or guaranteed loans, borrowers may secure loans which will equal 90 or 95 per cent of the market price. Conventional loans, which are not insured, or guaranteed loans, will usually average 80 to 90 per cent of the market price of the property.

PROPERTY STANDARDS FOR LOAN PURPOSES

Property valuation usually requires a careful look at the site and the improvements as well as the house which has been placed on that site. The process of property value estimation requires consideration of several hundred items. For example, the Federal Housing Administration (FHA) has prepared a volume of over 300 pages, *Minimum Property Standards,* which is supposed to guide appraisers in valuing properties on which FHA loans are to be granted.

FHA Minimum Property Standards. To offer some idea of the number of items must be considered in valuing a property, we shall summarize the minimum property standards for one- and two-dwelling units as established by the FHA. The standards, intended to apply to dwellings containing one or two units on an individual lot, apply to the following kinds of properties:

1. *Proposed construction*, which is supposed to comply with or exceed all the minimum standards that are listed in the volume.
2. *Existing construction*, which includes a review of all repairs, alterations, and additions whether they are underway, not started, or completed; they must meet the general applicable living standards set forth in the volume.
3. *Partially completed construction*, which includes not only partially completed work but all work that is continued or completed through the construction of the property. If work completed does not comply with a specific standard, the appraiser must determine whether the property complies with the stated objectives of the standards.

FHA Appraisal Objectives.   In order to assist appraisers in understanding the intent of its standards, the FHA has created some general statements of objectives which are related to the various items which have to be analyzed. A review of these will give some measure of the extent to which performance as compared to specific standards is used by appraisers in determining the value of the property for lending purposes.

The general objective of lot analysis is to evaluate the provisions for (1) convenient access to and circulation around the dwelling; (2) adequate natural light and ventilation of rooms and spaces; (3) reasonable privacy for each living unit; (4) utilization of the plot for laundry drying, gardening, landscaping, and outdoor living; and (5) where individual water supply and sewage disposal systems are involved, adequate areas to assure a safe and sanitary installation. In every case where there is a general objective, the FHA volume also contains detailed drawings and statements of how to interpret the objective. Since these are rather complex and involved, we shall only mention here that they are available by contacting the FHA. The paragraphs below indicate some of the major items that are of concern to the FHA.

Building Planning.   The general objective of building planning is to provide for a healthful environment and complete living facilities arranged and equipped to assure suitable and desirable living conditions commensurate with the type and quality of the property under consideration.

Space Standards.   Each living unit is to be provided with space necessary to assure suitable living, sleeping, cooking, and dining accommodations, as well as adequate storage, laundry, and sanitary facilities. The space shall be planned to permit placement of furniture and essential equipment.

Light and Ventilation. Light and ventilation shall be productive of a healthful environment within the dwelling and shall be located so as to provide an acceptable degree of comfort. Natural light is to be provided by means of windows, glazed doors, skylights, transparent or translucent panels, or any combination of these items. Artificial light is to be provided and distributed so as to assure healthful, safe, and sanitary conditions in all rooms and spaces.

Natural ventilation is to be provided through openable windows, exterior doors, skylights, and other suitable openings in exterior walls or roofs. The natural ventilation spaces in the building are to be such as will minimize the effect of conditions conducive to decay and the deterioration of structures and will reduce attic heat in the summer. Ventilation or structural spaces are usually required in attics and basements.

Access. The purpose of access is to provide openings adequate in size to admit furniture and equipment to all spaces and to permit inspection for repairs and maintenance.

Privacy. A dwelling unit is to be planned to provide a degree of privacy commensurate with desirable living conditions. This is accomplished by means of the proper location of exterior openings in relation to the exterior conditions and the interior arrangements of rooms, particularly with reference to access to bedrooms and bathrooms.

Stairway Planning. The purpose of stairway planning is to provide safety of ascent and descent and a design and arrangement of stairs which assures adequate headroom and space for the passage of furniture and equipment.

Fire Protection and Safety. The house is to be arranged and constructed so that separate living units will confine and restrict the spread of fire and prevent the passage of flame, smoke, fumes, and hot gases through the concealed spaces within the dwelling.

Materials and Products. Materials installed shall be of such kind and quality to assure that the dwelling will provide adequate structural strength, adequate resistance to weather and moisture, and reasonable durability and economy of maintenance.

FUNCTIONAL QUALITIES OF THE HOUSE

One of the major gaps in the evaluation of property is the failure to attend to the functional qualities of the house as opposed to the physical. The FHA standards do mention functional qualities, but in the minimum property standards a great deal of emphasis is placed on the physical configuration of the property and the kinds of materials used. The following information is useful in evaluating the functional quality of the property:

1. *Durability.* Quality of workmanship and materials, evidences of property deterioration, and the degree to which the property has withstood use and weather.
2. *Structural soundness.* Kinds and present condition of materials used in the property and any evidences of failure in foundations, walls (exterior and interior), doors, ceilings, roof.
3. *Building space.* Do room sizes have sufficient area to permit comfortable use for the intended furnishings of the room? For example, do the rooms avoid traffic patterns which would interfere with the privacy or enjoyment of the space? Is there natural light and ventilation? Are there sufficient electrical fixtures and outlets and are they conveniently located?
4. *Service system.* Is there sufficient capacity and convenience in use and is the general physical condition adequate for all electrical, plumbing, heating, and ventilating systems?
5. *Mechanical and convenience equipment.* Does an examination of the make, the capacity, and the condition of mechanical or convenience equipment indicate that it will provide trouble-free and adequate service? This kind of equipment includes: heating devices, water heaters, air conditioners, stoves, refrigerators, freezers, clothes washers, and clothes dryers.
6. *Architecture and appearance.* Is there evidence of poor or outdated architectural styling, or has the exterior appearance of the property been neglected? Could some amount of architectural redoing make the property more attractive?
7. *Conformance to neighborhood standards.* How does the property compare—in terms of the quality of maintenance, its size, and its style —to typical neighborhood properties?
8. *Assessed value.* Does the assessed value of the house and of the total property show that it is an appropriate improvement in comparison to the neighborhood? Does the assessed value show that the estimated cost or market value of the property is reasonable?
9. *Floor plan of the house.* In thinking about how the family will use the house, how do the use needs compare to the locations and sizes

of the rooms, doorways, windows, closets, electrical outlets, fixtures, and equipment?

VALUATION ESTIMATES

Valuation for lending purposes is usually done through some form of a market comparison approach which may also be checked against a cost approach. The assumption is that in order to acquire the house, the buyer must be willing to pay at least as much as others might bid for the house. On the other hand, no buyer would be willing to pay a price for a used house which would be in excess of the costs of constructing a similar new house, if the buyer can wait until completion of construction.

Most lenders have developed a standardized appraisal form which their appraisers are expected to follow in providing information on property being offered as security for a loan. Figure 11–1 is a Fannie Mae appraisal form, which is used by savings and loan institutions, banks, and other home mortgage lenders. Read the form and the instructions carefully; it will illustrate the tremendous detail which is involved in an appraisal. The numbers on the form are keyed to the instructions that accompany it (pages 198–212).

The final page of the form consists of a rating of the physical security of the property. This is a form which was developed in the early days of the FHA; however, it is still a useful device for providing rating factors which permit the comparison of one property to another. Notice that seven "property factors" are rated in Figure 11–1. The appraiser may decide that any one of the seven is "below standard" and a threat to the potential loan value. A mark in this column calls the attention of the loan committee to the potential danger related to that evaluation.

The appraiser is also required to give rating weights to the visual appeal, livability, resistance to elements, structural qualities, and suitability of mechanical equipment. Weighted ratings are provided for natural light and ventilation and resistance to elements of use. These weights are assigned on the basis of what the appraiser thinks the typical buyer would do. The total of these items is deducted from 100 to give a rating to the property. The meaning of this amount is related to ratings given to comparable properties so that properties can be ranked for loan evaluations. For a full understanding of this procedure, study the "Market Data Analysis" in Figure 11–1 and items 54 through 81 in the instructions.

Financial Appraisals, Inc.

APPRAISAL REPORT   HYPOTHETICAL EXAMPLE

Single Family Residence

FHLMC FORM 70
FNMA FORM 1004
REV. 10-72

To Be Completed By Lender

Borrower/Client ... John Smith ... ①
Property Address ... 1234 Pleasant Avenue ... ②
City ... Harmony ... County ... Los Angeles
State ... California ... Zip Code 90066
Appraiser ... William Brown ... ③
Legal Description ... Lot 29, Tract 22731 ... ⑩

File No. ... C - 3827 ... ④ ... Map Reference 23-A.2 ... ⑤
Lender ... ABC Savings & Loan Association ... ⑥
Lender's Address 5200 Main Street
City Springvale ... State California
Census Tract Number ... 1252 ... ⑦

Insurable Replacement Cost $ ....

Current Sale Price (if Applicable) $33,000 ... ⑨
Date of Sale 7-14-72 ... Percentage of Loan(s) to Sale Price ... 90 ... %
Percentage of Loan Charges paid by Seller ... 0 % ... Property Rights Appraised [X] Fee [ ] Leasehold ... ⑩
Instructions to Appraiser: Contact selling broker, Harold Carson (793-2057), and he will meet appraiser at property. ... ⑪

BUILDING DATA

CONSTRUCTION: [X] Existing ... Year Built 1971 ... [ ] Proposed [ ] Under Construction ... No. of Dwelling Units 1 ... ⑬ ... No. of Stories 1
Est. Remaining Econ. Life 50 yrs ... ⑯ ... Livable Floor Area 1532 ... ⑭ ... Other Buildings None ... ⑮
Total Rooms 4 ... Bedrooms 4 ... Baths 1 3/4 ... ⑫ ⑰

ROOM LIST AND LOCATION	Basement	First Level	Second Level	Third Level
Entry				
Living Room		X		
Dining Room				
Dining Alcove		X		
Kitchen		X		
Family Room				
Den				
Bedroom		X		
Bedroom		X		
Bedroom		X		
Bedroom				
Bedroom				
Bedroom				

EXTERIOR WALLS
[ ] Wood Siding
[ ] Wood Shingle
[X] Stucco
[ ] Brick Veneer
[ ] Brick (Solid)
[ ] Concrete Block
[ ] Stone
[ ] Composition Shingle
[ ] Aluminum

DECORATIVE TRIM
[ ] Wood
[ ] Stone

KITCHEN
[X] Range/Oven
[X] Dishwasher
[X] Fan/Hood
[X] Disposal

ROOF
[ ] Wood Shingle
[X] Wood Shake
[ ] Composition Shingle
[ ] Built Up Gravel
[ ] Rock
[ ] Tile

FOUNDATION
[ ] Concrete Perimeter
[X] Slab
[ ] Stone
[ ] Concrete Block
[ ] Brick

BATHROOM
1 Tubs
2 Toilets
2 Lavatories
1 TubShowers 1 Tiled
[ ] Tub Enclosure

⑭

INTERIOR WALLS
[ ] Plaster
[X] Drywall
[ ] Paneling .... Rooms
[ ] Wall Paper .... Rooms
[ ] Structural Beams
[ ] Decorative Beams

INSULATION
[ ] Walls
[X] Ceiling
[ ] Roof

HEATING
[ ] Gravity
[X] Forced Air
[ ] Floor Furnace
[ ] Wall Furnace
[ ] Radiant

⑱

BASEMENT
[X] None
[ ] Full
[ ] Part
[ ] Floor Drain
[ ] Sump Pump

BASEMENT FLOOR
[ ] Concrete

BASEMENT CEILING
[ ] Finished
[ ] Unfinished

Outside Entrance:
[ ] Yes [ ] No

AIR CONDITIONING
[X] Central
[ ] Wall
[ ] Evaporative Cooler

Bath	☐	[X]	☐	☐	
Bath	☐	☐	☐	☐	
Bath	☐	☐	☐	☐	
¾ Bath	☐	[X]	☐	☐	
¾ Bath	☐	☐	☐	☐	
½ Bath	☐	☐	☐	☐	
¼ Bath	☐	☐	☐	☐	

1 Stall Showers 1 Tiled

BATH FLOOR: ☐ Tile [X] Composition

FUEL: [X] Gas ☐ Electric ☐ Oil ☐ Coal

EXTRAS: 1 Fireplaces Dual; ☐ Patio: ☐ Covered ☐ Enclosed; ☐ Pool

CABINETS: [X] Adequate ☐ Inadequate

ROOM SIZES: [X] Adequate Comment if inadequate.

CAR STORAGE (19)
[X] Garage ☐ Car Port No. of Cars 2
[X] Attached ☐ Detached ☐ Built-in
Adequate: [X] Yes ☐ No

FLOORS: ☐ Hardwood ☐ Pine [X] Composition ☐ Plywood [X] Wall/Wall Carpeting

PROPERTY FACTORS: (20)	Excellent	Standard	Below Standard
Quality of Construction	☐	[X]	☐
Condition of Improvements	[X]	☐	☐
Overall Livability	☐	[X]	☐
Closet Space	☐	[X]	☐
Quality of Plumbing Fixtures	☐	[X]	☐
Adequacy of Electrical Service	☐	[X]	☐
Conformity of Improvements to Neighborhood	[X]	☐	☐

Comment on All Property Factors Rated Below Standard: None (21)

Other Features and Finishes: Luminous kitchen ceiling. Pantry in kitchen. (22)

Comment on Physical and Functional Inadequacies: (If Any) None (23)

MODERNIZATION: (List major items and year completed.) None (24)

REPAIRS: (List repairs, painting, termite treatment, etc. you recommend be made to the improvements to make the property readily marketable.) If none, so state.
(25) None
Estimated Cost $ .... Taxes $ .... ☐ Actual ☐ Estimated

MARKETABILITY OF PROPERTY AT THE FOLLOWING ESTIMATED VALUE: (26) [X] Good If slow Marketability, comment

VALUATION: This appraisal is based upon the definition of market value, the certification, the contingent and limiting conditions, and requirements that are stated on Page 4 of this report. As a result of my investigation and analysis it is my opinion that the estimated Market Value of the subject property as of 8-2-72 (27) is $ 33,000 (28)

PROPERTY RATING A ☐ B ☐ C ☐ D ☐

Appraiser William Brown (29) Date 8-2-72 Review Appraiser George Johnson (30) Date 8-2-72
[X] Did ☐ Did Not Physically Inspect Property

Page 1

Fig. 11–1. Sample of property appraisal form, with accompanying instructions.

NEIGHBORHOOD

(31) Built Up: General Area.. **75** ..% Immediate Area.. **50** ..% If General Area is in a developing stage, indicate the growth rate:

[x] Rapid [ ] Slow Comment if slow

Typical Range in immediate neighborhood excluding extremes: (32) Immediate Neighborhood occupancy: (33)

Price $.. **28,000** .. To $.. **35,000** .. Age (years) **New to 3** Owners **100** ..% Tenants.. **0** ..% Vacant.. **0** ..%

(34) Immediate Neighborhood location: [ ] Urban [x] Suburban [ ] Rural (35)

Describe Immediate Neighborhood: Prime residential area, properties well maintained.

Present immediate Neighborhood uses: Single Family.. **50** ..% Apartments.. ..% Condominiums.. ..% Planned Unit Development.. ..%

(36) Commercial.. ..% Industrial.. ..% (37) Open Green Area.. ..% Vacant.. **50** ..%

Comment if combination of immediate Neighborhood uses affect marketability:

(38) Shopping and Schools: [x] Satisfactory Comment if unsatisfactory

(39) Pride of Ownership: [x] Good [ ] Fair If Fair, indicate percentage of properties not receiving normal maintenance.. ..%

Comments regarding additional favorable or unfavorable immediate neighborhood factors (if any). If older properties prevail, describe upgrading trend. Immediate neighborhood consists of three developing tracts of average quality homes. Very good demand for homes in this neighborhood. (40)

SITE

(41) Dimensions.. **70 x 130** .. Area (Square Feet) **9,100** (42) Topography **Level Pad** (43) Zoning.. **R 1** (44)

If Zoning permits uses other than Single Family, indicate uses permitted **None** (45)

Highest and Best Use: [x] Present Use (46) Other:

Site Improvements: (47) [x] Public Water [ ] Private Well [x] Public Sewer [ ] Septic Tank [x] Sidewalk

[x] Curbs [x] Gutters [x] Street Lights [x] Electricity [x] Gas

Access By: (48) [x] Public Street [ ] Private Road [x] Hard Surface [ ] Gravel [ ] Unpaved

Maintained By: (49) [x] Municipality [ ] Private Association (Attach Association Documents)

Comment on Favorable or Unfavorable Site Factors, if any: (i.e., View, Easements, Nuisances, Adverse Influences, Odors, Drainage, Flood

Conditions, etc.) Good view site. Site is typical of neighborhood. (50)

BUILDING SKETCH

45.5'

25.5'

22.5'

Additive Method:

22.5 x 25.5 =   574.
15 x 45.5 =   682.5
11.5 x 21 =   241.5
2 x 17 =   34.

1,532. Sq. Ft.

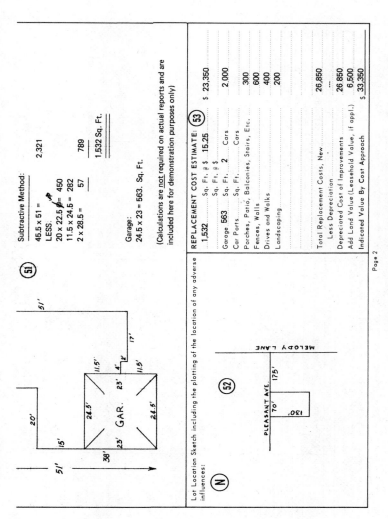

Fig. 11–1. Continued.

Subtractive Method:

45.5 x 51 =   2,321

LESS:

20 x 22.5	=	450
11.5 x 24.5	=	282
2 x 28.5	=	57
		789

        1,532 Sq. Ft.

Garage:
24.5 x 23 = 563. Sq. Ft.

(Calculations are <u>not</u> required on actual reports and are included here for demonstration purposes only)

REPLACEMENT COST ESTIMATE: (53)

1,532 Sq. Ft. @ $ 15.25		$ 23,350
Sq. Ft. @ $		
Garage 563 Sq. Ft. 2 Cars		2,000
Car Ports Sq. Ft. Cars		
Porches, Patio, Balconies, Stairs, Etc.		300
Fences, Walls		600
Drives and Walks		400
Landscaping		200
Total Replacement Costs, New		26,850
Less Depreciation		----
Depreciated Cost of Improvements		26,850
Add Land Value (Leasehold Value, if appl.)		6,500
Indicated Value By Cost Approach		$ 33,350

Lot Location Sketch including the plotting of the location of any adverse influences:

Page 2

MARKET DATA ANALYSIS

This is an analysis of comparable market data showing the relationship of specific items of the comparable data with the subject property. The adjustments are the appraisers estimate of the plus or minus dollar adjustments that the real estate market in the subject area would make for the indicated items. If the item for the comparable property is superior to the subject property, indicate a minus dollar adjustment for the amount it is estimated that the local real estate market would recognize. If the item for the comparable data is inferior to the subject property then indicate the plus dollar adjustment that would be reflected in the local real estate market. Some items have been grouped to allow one adjustment.

Market data selected should be the sales of comparable properties that a buyer of the subject property would have also given consideration to purchasing. In the absence of actual sales of comparable properties, listings of comparable properties may be used but an explanation must be included in the comment section below.

ITEM	SUBJECT PROPERTY	COMPARABLE NO. 1		COMPARABLE NO. 2		COMPARABLE NO. 3	
	DESCRIPTION	DESCRIPTION	+ − ADJUSTMENTS	DESCRIPTION	+ − ADJUSTMENTS	DESCRIPTION	+ − ADJUSTMENTS
Address	1234 Pleasant	780 Meredith		1276 Pleasant		1222 Royal	
	Harmony	Harmony		Harmony		Harmony	
Proximity to Subject		2 blocks west		3 lots west		1 block north	
Classify Exterior Wall Construction	Stucco	Stucco		Stucco		Stucco	
Year Built	1971	1970		1971		1972	
No. of Stories	1	1		1		1	
Room Count Total:Bedrooms:Baths	7 4 1.3/4	7 4 2	−2,000	7 4 1.3/4		7 4 1.3/4	
Livable Area (Sq. Ft.)	1,532	1,700		1,532		1,510	
Livability	Average	Average		Average		Average	
Condition	Excellent	Good		Good		Excellent	
Quality of Construction	Average	Average		Average		Average	
Roof	Shake	Shake		Shake		Shake	
Heating	FAU	FAU		FAU		FAU	
Air Conditioning	Central	None	+1,000	Central		None	+1,000
Fireplace	1	1		1		1	
Kitchen Built-Ins	r/o,d/w,f/h,g/d	r/o,d/w,g/d		r/o,d/w,f/h,g/d		r/o,d/w,f/h,g/d	
Basement	None	None		None		None	
Pool	None	20 x 40	−3,000	None		None	
Other Major Improvements	None	None		None		Covered Patio	−500
Car Storage (No. of Cars)	2	2		2		2	
Lot Size 70 x 130 x 6	70 x 130	60 x 125	+1,000	70 x 130		85 x 145	
Zoning	R 1	R-1		R-1		R-1	
Landscaping	Average	Good	−500	Average		Average	
View	Good	None	+2,000	Good		Average	+1,000

	Subject	Comparable No. 1	Comparable No. 2	Comparable No. 3
Location	Good	Good	Good	Good
Property Appeal	Good	Good	Good	Good
Comments on any other items such as unusual property features, remodeling or any factors pertinent to the sale, for example.			Same model as subject	
Terms of Sale	$3,300 down	10% down	10% down	10% down
Date of Sale (Time Adjustment)	7-14-72	6-20-72	1-6-72 +800	8-11-71 +1,200
Data Source	Lender	S.R.E.A.	S.R.E.A.	Selling broker
Comparison to Subject (Superior / Similar / Inferior)		Similar [x]	Similar [x]	Similar [x]
Price (Sale or List)	$33,000 Sale	[x] Sale List $35,000	[x] Sale List $32,000	[x] Sale List $31,000
Total Net Adjustment (Plus or Minus)		Plus or [x] Minus $2,500	[x] Plus or Minus $800	[x] Plus or Minus $2,700
Indicated Value of Subject		$32,500	$32,800	$33,700
Price per Square Ft. (when applicable)	$21.54	$20.59	$20.89	$20.53

Comments on Market Data including relative weight given to comparables: Heaviest consideration was given to Comparable No. 2 because it was the same model as the subject property and it required the smallest adjustment. The indicated value from Comparable No. 2 was closely supported by the indicated values of Comparables No. 1 and No. 3. The time adjustments reflect appreciation in the subject neighborhood during the past year.

Indicated value of the subject property by the Market Approach $33,000

Page 3

Fig. 11-1. Continued.

GENERAL COMMENTS, IF ANY: _____ Subject property located in one of the most desirable areas of the city. ....

PHOTOGRAPHS

SUBJECT PROPERTY   DATE PHOTOGRAPHS TAKEN _____   STREET SCENE

MARKET VALUE: The highest price estimated in terms of money which a property will bring if exposed for sale in the open market with a reasonable time allowed to find a purchaser, buying with knowledge of all the uses and purposes to which it is adapted and for which it is capable of being used.

CERTIFICATION: The Appraiser certifies and agrees that:

1. The Appraiser has no present or contemplated future interest in the property appraised and that neither the employment to make this appraisal, nor the compensation for it, is contingent upon the appraised value of the property.
2. The Appraiser has no personal interest in or bias with respect to the subject matter of the appraisal report or the parties involved.
3. The Appraiser has personally inspected the property, both inside and out, and has made an exterior inspection of all comparable sales listed herein, and that according to the best of the Appraiser's knowledge and belief, all statements and information in this report are true and correct, and that the Appraiser has not knowingly withheld any information.
4. All contingent and limiting conditions are contained herein (imposed by the terms of the assignment or by the undersigned affecting the analyses, opinions, and conclusions contained in this report.)
5. This appraisal report has been made in conformity with and is subject to the requirements of the Code of Professional Ethics and Standards of Professional Conduct of the appraisal organizations with which the Appraiser is affiliated.

6. All conclusions and opinions concerning the real estate that are set forth in the appraisal report were prepared by the Appraiser whose signature appears on Page 1 of this appraisal report, unless indicated as "Review Appraiser." No change of any item of the appraisal report shall be made by anyone other than the Appraiser, and the Appraiser shall have no responsibility for any such unauthorized change.

CONTINGENT AND LIMITING CONDITIONS: The certification of the Appraiser appearing in this appraisal report is subject to the following conditions and to such other specific and limiting conditions as are set forth by the Appraiser on the report.

1. The Appraiser assumes no responsibility for matters of a legal nature affecting the property appraised or the title thereto, nor does the Appraiser render any opinion as to the title, which is assumed to be marketable. The property is appraised as though under responsible ownership.

2. The sketch in this report is included to assist the reader in visualizing the property, and the Appraiser assumes no responsibility for its accuracy. The Appraiser has made no survey of the property.

3. The Appraiser is not required to give testimony or appear in court because of having made this appraisal, with reference to the property in question, unless arrangements have been previously made therefor.

4. The distribution of the total valuation in this report between land and improvements applies only under the existing program of utilization. The separate valuations for land and building must not be used in conjunction with any other appraisal and are invalid if so used.

5. The Appraiser assumes that there are no hidden or unapparent conditions of the property, subsoil, or structures which would render it more or less valuable. The Appraiser assumes no responsibility for such conditions or for engineering which might be required to discover such factors.

6. Information, estimates, and opinions furnished to the Appraiser and contained in this report were obtained from sources considered reliable and believed to be true and correct. However, no responsibility for accuracy of such items furnished the Appraiser can be assumed by the Appraiser.

7. Disclosure by the Appraiser of the contents of this appraisal report is subject to review in accordance with the by-laws and regulations of the professional appraisal organizations with which the Appraiser is affiliated.

8. Neither all nor part of the contents of this report, or copy thereof (conclusions as to property value, the identity of the Appraiser, professional designations, reference to any professional appraisal organizations, or the firm with which he is connected) shall be used for any purposes by anyone but the client shown on Page 1 of this report, the mortgagee or its assigns and Private Mortgage Insurers, consultants, professional appraisal organizations, any state or federally chartered bank, any department, agency, or instrumentality of the United States or of any State or of the District of Columbia, without the previous written consent of the Appraiser, except upon demand by the Mortgagor; nor shall it be conveyed by anyone to the public through advertising, public relations, news, sales, or other media, without the written consent and approval of the Appraiser.

9. On all appraisals involving proposed construction, the appraisal report and value conclusion are contingent upon completion of the proposed improvements in accordance with the plans and specifications prepared by .... which have been initialed by the Appraiser shown on Page 1 of this

.... with a last revision date of .... appraisal report on the following date ....

REQUIREMENTS:
This report is made subject to the following requirements: ....

....
....　　　　NONE
....

Page 4

Fig. 11–1. Continued.

Appraisal Report—Single-Family Residence

Purpose:	This form is to be used by the appraiser who was previously nominated and recommended by the Seller to FNMA and determined to be acceptable by FNMA. This form is required for appraisals on all single-family mortgages offered to FNMA for purchase.
Prepared by:	Seller and Appraiser (typed and legibly printed). The Seller is to give a copy of these instructions to each appraiser on the Seller's approved list acceptable to FNMA.
Signed by:	Appraiser.
Prepare:	Original and three copies.
Distribution:	Original and one copy (with original photographs) to be forwarded to FNMA with the Seller's Request for Approval (of Credit and Property). Seller should retain third copy and appraiser should retain the fourth copy.

Instructions

A. The Seller must complete the portion of the form entitled "to be completed by lender" prior to giving the form to the designated appraiser.

B. The appraiser may use carbon copies or make machine photocopies of the original report, but, irrespective of the method of duplicating, the appraiser must place an original signature on the original and each copy of the report.

C. The appraisal form may be printed in ink, ball point pen, or pencil, or may be typewritten. When the report is prepared in pencil, the penciled report should be retained as the appraiser's file copy and photocopies should be used for the two copies sent to FNMA and the one copy retained by the Seller.

When the appraisal report is printed in either pen or pencil it must be done in a neat, orderly, and legible manner. Every effort should be made to insure that the completed form is neat and easy to read. An "X" should be used when checking the appropriate boxes on the form.

In addition to being neat, the form should be well documented. Any changes or corrections in the report, particularly the final value estimate, should be crossed out and initialed by the appraiser, rather than erased.

D. The following pages relate to the specific detailed instructions for proper completion of each page on the appraisal report form.

These instructions are numbered and correspond with the [circled] numbers shown on the sample pages of the form.

Appraisal Report Instructions—Page 1

1. Name of borrower or owner of property.

2. Fill in completely the property address (including street, boulevard, drive, place, etc.), city, county (borough), state, and zip code.

3. Name of appraiser.

4. (Optional) Lender's identification number.

5. (Optional) Local map reference.

6. Lender's name and address.

7. (Optional) Lender's use only.

Fig. 11–1. Continued.

8. To be completed by lender or appraiser; if an attachment is used, so state.

9. Give *current sale price (if applicable)* as obtained from real estate broker's sale agreement, escrow, or other sales documentation, and *date of sale* by month,·day, and year corresponding to real estate broker's sales agreement. The *percentage of loan(s) to sale price* is to include first and second mortgages (trust deeds) when applicable. The *percentage of loan charges paid by seller* refers to loan fees paid by the seller of the property.

10. Mark with an "x" whether property rights are leasehold or fee simple estate. (If leasehold, lender is to provide lease information to appraiser).

11. (Optional) Additional instructions to appraiser; for example, "key at _____" or "call owner at _____," etc.

12. Estimated year built (when proposed or under construction, indicate year of completion).

13. Appraiser's verification that subject property is one dwelling unit.

14. For livable floor area, include the square footage of the livable area of all floors of the dwelling only, *excluding* the basement, outside porches, balconies, patios, and garage area. If livable rooms are built in the basement or garage area, give description in Item 22. (For information on calculating livable floor area refer to Item 51.)

15. List guest house, storage shed, horse stable, etc. (if applicable).

16. Include in total room count kitchen and all livable rooms *excluding bathrooms*. A dining alcove, sewing alcove, etc., which is not large enough to be termed a full room may be called a half-room.

17. By marking "x" where appropriate, the appraiser should take an inventory of rooms and bathrooms by floor level, while inspecting the interior of the dwelling. Baths are to be counted as follows:
   (a) Full bath—has a bathtub, lavatory (sink), toilet, and may also have a stall shower.
   (b) 3/4 bath—has a stall shower, lavatory (sink), and toilet.
   (c) 1/2 bath—has a lavatory (sink), and toilet.
   (d) 1/4 bath—has a toilet only.

The room list and location will give the reader of the report an indication of the functional utility of the subject dwelling. For example, a four-bedroom dwelling with all four bedrooms on the second floor with the bathroom facilities on the first floor would warrant a comment by the appraiser concerning the functional acceptability of the dwelling.

18. By marking "x" where appropriate, the appraiser can take inventory of most items pertaining to the building data. Fill in additional information, when applicable, on blank lines. If cabinets are inadequate, explain in Item 23 the effect on the marketability of the subject property. Decorative trim refers to exterior wall trim, such as brick veneer, wood siding, ornamental stone, for example. Under "bathrooms" list the number of bathroom fixtures. Leave items blank if not applicable.

19. Specify if car storage is garage or carport, number of cars, attached, detached, or built-in. If car storage is inadequate, comment on its effect on the marketability of the subject property in Item 23. If only on-site open parking is available (other than driveway) describe this under Item 22.

20. The appraiser is to rate all property factors by marking an "x" in the space identified as "Excellent," "Standard," or "Below Standard," as related to the definition of standard for each item. If an item is superior to standard, mark "Excellent"; if inferior compared to standard, designate "Below Standard." Comments on all property factors rated below standard (refer to Item 21) should include the appraiser's opinion on their effect on the marketability of the subject property.

Fig. 11–1. Continued.

Adjustments for property factors which affect the marketability should also be described and considered by the appraiser in the market data analysis on Page 3.

Quality of construction: "Standard" means the typical quality of construction of dwellings prevalent in the subject neighborhood. If the appraiser were to rate quality of construction as excellent, very good, good, average, fair, or poor, and if the quality of construction prevalent in the neighborhood were rated as good, an average quality dwelling would be rated below standard. If poor quality construction were standard, this should be fully explained in Item 23.

Condition of improvement: By comparing the condition of the subject dwelling to other homes in the neighborhood, the appraiser should estimate whether the condition of the subject is equal, superior, or inferior to standards prevalent in the neighborhood. If subject is in a condition equal to neighboring properties, indicate "Standard." However, if construction is in violation of local building codes and/or condition is inadequate for the security of a mortgage, mark "Below Standard" and include an explanation.

Overall livability: "Standard" refers to what is typically accepted by home buyers in the neighborhood. This item covers the floor plan arrangement, room sizes, style of kitchen cabinets, work counter, built-in equipment, and style of bathroom fixtures.

Closet space: "Standard" means that the closet space is adequate to accommodate a typical size family in subject dwelling. If closet space is rated below standard, also indicate whether the inadequacy can be corrected.

Adequacy of electrical service (includes number of electrical outlets): "Standard" means adequate to serve the typical family's needs in subject dwelling.

Conformity of improvements to neighborhood: "Standard" means subject conforms to neighborhood properties. If subject is an overimprovement or underimprovement, rate "Below Standard." If subject conforms to neighborhood, and is especially desirable compared to most homes in the neighborhood, rate "Excellent."

21. Space reserved for the appraiser's comments, if any, on property factors in Item 20 rated below standard. Here again, the appraiser is reminded that *adjustments for all property factors which affect the marketability of the subject property should be described and considered by the appraiser in the market data analysis.* This includes items related to physical deterioration (condition), functional obsolescence (livability), and economic obsolescence (location) as indicated on Page 3.

22. Space reserved for the appraiser's favorable comments or listing of any additional items not previously shown in the report. For example, (a) dwelling custom designed and quality built by the most reputable builder in town, or (b) architectural appeal makes subject dwelling most desirable in neighborhood, or (c) landscaping and yard maintenance are superior to all other homes in the district.

23. Space reserved for appraiser's comments on physical or functional inadequacy (if any) as in the example given in Item 17 (four bedrooms located on the second floor with the bathroom facilities on the first floor); a comment from the appraiser is necessary.

24. Modernization (includes renovation or remodeling): List major items of modernization since original construction date. Comments regarding remodeling must indicate when the size, shape, or arrangement of the floor plan was changed. The appraiser is not expected to check official records for any of this information. Give approximate date as to year modernization work was completed.

25. This section must contain a response from the appraiser (state *none* if no repairs are recommended). The appraiser should complete this section when making the condition of improvements analysis for Item 20 (property factors rated below standard). Termite treat-

Fig. 11–1.   Continued.

ment should be recommended when, in the appraiser's opinion, a termite report from a professional termite inspector indicates same may be necessary.

26. A rating of good marketability means an allowance for a reasonable time to sell the property, normally from 90 to 120 days. If slow marketability is indicated, comment on the time expectancy required to sell.

27. Date of appraisal should be the same date the appraiser completed an inspection of the interior and exterior of the property.

28. Round off the estimated value to the nearest one hundred dollars.

29. Signature of the appraiser acknowledging Certification on Page 4, and date of signature.

30. (Optional) Signature by a review appraiser is not a requirement unless by special arrangement as may be required by the lender.

Appraisal Report Instructions—Page 2

31. The "immediate area" refers to the area within the boundaries of the subject neighborhood. The "general area" includes other neighborhoods that are *contiguous* to the immediate area. If the general area is less than 100% built-up, indicate whether the developing stage is rapid or slow. If slow, the appraiser should state whether this is a normal or abnormal situation for subject area and why.

32. The appraiser is reminded to exclude extremes when estimating the typical price range or age of the neighborhood. For example, if typical prevailing prices for dwellings in the neighborhood are between $25,000 to $35,000, this should be reported by the appraiser, omitting extremes such as $15,000 and $50,000, which would not be typical prices for the subject neighborhood. As another example, in a neighborhood where most of the dwellings were built between 1950 and 1955 with only two dwellings built in 1972, the typical age range is 17 to 22 years, rather than new to 22 years.

33. The appraiser is reminded when reporting the percentage of owner or tenant occupancy or vacancy in the neighborhood to leave no apparent questions unanswered for the reader of the report; for example, if the appraiser reports in Item 36 that 100% of all dwelling units in the neighborhood are single-family dwellings, and neighborhood occupancy is reported in Item 33 as 60% owners, 30% tenants, 10% vacant, this would warrant a comment from the appraiser as to how this situation affects the marketability of the subject property.

34. Designate subject property as:
    (a) *Urban*—residential district within a town or city; or
    (b) *Suburban*—residential district on the outskirts of a town or city; or
    (c) *Rural*—residential district in the country.

35. Describe neighborhood as:
    (a) *Improving*—home owners generally upgrading and improving their properties; or
    (b) *Stable*—fixed, well-established and well-maintained neighborhood with steady trend; or
    (c) *Declining*—downward trend, properties not receiving required maintenance. If declining, comment on how this trend will affect the subject's marketability.

36. Give approximate percentage of combination of neighborhood uses, if any (total of all uses should equal 100%):
    (a) *Single-family*—detached dwellings on individual sites (includes row houses with no homeowners' association involved).
    (b) *Apartments*—two or more units on individual sites.
    (c) *Condominiums*—multiple-family dwellings with individual unit title ownership.
    (d) *Planned unit developments*—any subdivision with common areas managed by a homeowners' association.

Fig. 11–1. Continued.

(e) *Commercial*—shopping centers, office buildings, etc.

(f) *Industrial*—manufacturing plants, warehouses, etc.

(g) *Open green area*—parks managed by municipality and/or green belt areas controlled by homeowners' associations.

(h) *Vacant*—unlandscaped open fields.

37. When single-family dwellings are 100% of neighborhood uses, no comment is necessary.

38. Comment only when shopping, schools, or transportation facilities are unsatisfactory, and would affect marketability.

39. Pride of ownership relates to how well homeowners in the neighborhood maintain their homes, including yard maintenance.

40. Space reserved for the appraiser's comments of any additional favorable or unfavorable factors which would add to the reader's understanding of the neighborhood. If older properties prevail, the appraiser must give a response as to the upgrading trend.

41. List the frontage, rear line, and then the side line dimensions: for example, 50′ x 100′ or 50′/49′ x 100′/101′. If the lot is too irregular to describe, state "Irregular."

42. Give approximate square-foot area of site. If usable area is less than overall site area, comment in Item 50.

43. Indicate level, slope down, slope up, etc.

44. List actual zoning such as R-1, etc.

45. Include comment if zoning permits boarding of horses, commercial or apartment use, etc.

46. Mark "x" if present use equals highest and best use of site; if not, explain.

47. Indicate by "x" which items apply to subject site.

48. Mak "X" for appropriate public access to property.

49. Specify whether street is maintained by municipality or private association. If by private association or homeowners, comment on how well streets are maintained and what effect this may have on the marketability of the subject property.

50. Space reserved for the appraiser's comments on favorable or unfavorable influences which could affect the salability of subject property.

51. Draw a diagram of the building showing the exterior measurements to the nearest six inches, in order to calculate the gross livable floor area of the dwelling. It is *not* necessary to draw to scale, or show room arrangement, or window or door openings. A single line showing the perimeter of the dwelling is sufficient. Although some aspects of an appraisal report are an estimation by the appraiser, there is no excuse for error in measurement of the building or the appraiser's calculations of the gross livable area. It is suggested that the appraiser double-check these calculations by making sure the dimensions on all four sides of the dwelling are balanced, using the additive and subtractive method of calculation to check for accuracy. For example:

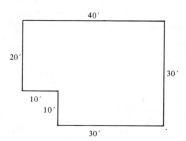

Fig. 11–1. Continued.

In this example, the additive approach would require a calculation of 10' x 30' and 20' x 40' to equal 1,100 square feet, or a subtractive calculation of 30' x 40' equals 1,200 square feet less 10' x 10' or 100 square feet for a total of 1,100 square feet.

52. The appraiser is reminded to include in the lot location sketch the location of any adverse influences near the subject site; for example:

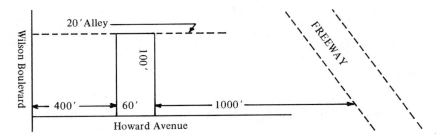

53. The appraiser need not furnish supporting data, such as source of cost estimating data, depreciation, land (leasehold value), etc., for the replacement cost estimate. When subject property is new or nearly new and when the appraiser has placed greater emphasis on the indicated value by the cost approach rather than the market data approach, it is suggested the appraiser have supporting data available upon demand.

Appraisal Report Instructions—Page 3

54. Market data analysis is the appraisal process in which the market value of the subject property is estimated by comparing actual sales of other similar and comparable properties with the subject property and making adjustments for any differences between the comparable property and the subject property.

In the appraisal of a single-family residence, the market data approach is generally given very heavy emphasis in supporting the value conclusion because it reflects the reactions of buyers and sellers on properties similar to the subject property. In processing market data, each comparable property is analyzed and compared with the subject property taking into consideration all of the component factors of the comparable property including the age, quality, condition, size, number of rooms, location, sale price, terms of sale, date of sale, among other items.

The appraiser makes adjustments to the comparable sale property, when required, in an effort to make it similar in all respects with the subject property. The dollar adjustments that the appraiser makes reflect an estimate of the adjustment that typical buyers and sellers in the subject area would make for that item. In essence, what the appraiser is saying in the Market Approach is: "If a property that is generally comparable to the subject property but is newer, slightly larger, and in somewhat better condition and is superior to the subject property sold for $20,000 and the market would make a minus adjustment of approximately $2,000 for these factors, then the comparable price would indicate that the value of the subject property was $18,000." The appraiser then analyzes other comparable sales in a similar manner and reviews the indicated values from those comparable sales giving heaviest weight to the most comparable property in arriving at the final estimated value of the subject property by the Market Approach.

In making the dollar adjustments on the comparable data, cost factors may serve as a guide but the major emphasis should be based on the appraiser's opinion on what the local

Fig. 11–1. Continued.

real estate market would pay for a fireplace or air conditioning unit, for example. When making these market adjustments, the appraiser is attempting to make the comparable property similar to the subject property. If the item for the comparable property is superior to the subject property, indicate a minus dollar adjustment in the amount it is estimated the local real estate market would recognize. If the item for the comparable property is inferior to the subject property, then indicate a plus dollar adjustment that would be reflected in the local real estate market.

For the market data approach to have any real significance in a single-family residential appraisal, the appraiser must have ample sales data, the data must have a sufficient degree of comparability with the subject property to be useful and convincing, and the appraiser's analysis of the market data must be realistic and reflective of the local real estate market.

The key test in selecting comparable market data is: "Would a purchaser of the subject property also have given an alternate consideration to purchasing the comparable property?" It is important that every effort be made to compare properties in similar location with similar utility that would appeal to similar buyers. For example, the sale of a five-bedroom dwelling of 2,800 square feet situated on a two-acre parcel of land would serve as a poor comparison if the subject property were a 1,200-square-foot two-bedroom dwelling on a 60' x 150' lot for the reason that each property would appeal to different types of buyers. If, for example, the subject property is a three-bedroom residence, every effort should be made to obtain the sales prices on other three-bedroom residences in the same subject neighborhood. The fewer adjustments the appraiser is required to make, the better the comparison.

In the absence of actual sales of comparable properties, listings of comparable properties may be used but an explanation must be included in the comment section at the bottom of Page 3.

There are instances where the inclusion of a current listing could be very pertinent to the appraisal because it would tend to set the upper limit of value. For example, if the subject property reportedly sold for $34,000, it would be an important item of market data to indicate that a dwelling similar to the subject property and located across the street had been listed for sale for the past two months at a price of $31,500.

It is required that the appraiser visually inspect all of the comparable market data used in the report to determine the degree of comparability with the subject property. (Refer to Item No. 3 of the certification of Page 4 of the report.)

Page 3 of the appraisal report form is a market data analysis grid designed to assist the appraiser in documenting and analyzing the comparable data in a logical manner.

Following is a detailed discussion of each section of the market data analysis grid:

55. On these lines document the complete address of the subject property and comparable properties so that anyone reviewing the appraisal report in the field would have no trouble finding the comparable properties.

56. The proximity of the comparable data to the subject property is an important item because it makes a difference to know whether the comparable property is located "1/2 block north" of the subject property in contrast to "3 miles west" of the subject property.

On this line indicate in a concise statement the proximity of the comparable property to the subject property. Examples would be "across street," "3 miles south," "1 block west," "1/4 mile north," etc.

57. Certain items have been grouped together in the market data analysis grid to allow for a

Fig. 11–1. Continued.

single adjustment. Included in this first adjustment item are the following factors: exterior wall construction, year built, number of stories, room count, livable area, and livability.

On the line identified as "classify exterior wall construction," indicate the appropriate wall construction for both the subject property and the comparable properties. Examples would be: "stucco," "brick veneer," or "composition shingle."

On the line identified as "year built" indicate the actual year built, if known, or otherwise the appraiser's best estimate of the year built. Put the "year built," such as 1967, for example, rather than the age of the property, such as "10 years," because the year built remains constant and the age continually changes with time, which could confuse the reader at a subsequent date.

On the line "number of stories," indicate the number of stories such as "1," "2," "3" for both the subject property and the comparable properties.

On the line for "room count," indicate, in the appropriate section, the following three numbers for both the subject property and the comparable properties:

Total (total rooms in dwelling *including* bedrooms but *excluding* baths and porches)

Bedrooms (total bedrooms)

Baths (total baths including 1/4, 1/2, and 3/4 baths)

Examples of room counts are:

5-2-1 (5 total rooms, 2 bedrooms, 1 bath)

7-3-2 (7 total rooms, 3 bedrooms, 2 baths)

9-5-3 1/4 (9 total rooms, 5 bedrooms, 3 1/4 baths)

On the line labelled "livable area (square feet)," the livable floor area for both the subject properties and the comparable properties should be shown. This figure should include the livable area on all floors of the dwelling only, excluding the basement, outside porches, balconies, patios, and garage area.

58. The line identified as "livability" refers to the room size and floor arrangement as well as the general livability of the subject improvements on the subject lot. A concise statement such as "excellent," "good," "average," "fair," or "poor" should be made for both the subject property and the comparable properties.

After documenting the above-listed items from "exterior wall construction" to and including "livability," the appraiser should then indicate in the "+− $ adjustment" column the dollar amount that, in the appraiser's opinion, the local buyers and sellers would recognize for these differences between the comparable property and the subject property. The purpose in making these adjustments is to recognize the differences that local buyers and sellers would consider when relating a comparable property to the subject property. In using the market data analysis grid, the appraiser is attempting to make the comparable property similar to the subject property through the process of making minor adjustments so that the adjusted price of the comparable property will offer an indicated value for the subject property.

In making these adjustments, as well as all other adjustments, always compare the comparable property to the subject property. If the comparable property is superior to the subject property, indicate a minus dollar adjustment (−$2,000, for example). If the comparable property is inferior to the subject property, indicate a plus dollar adjustment (+$3,000, for example).

If, in the appraiser's opinion, the local real estate market would recognize a difference in the price paid for a larger, newer house with excellent livability when relating a comparable

Fig. 11−1. Continued.

property to the subject property, then the appraiser should recognize this difference by making the appropriate plus or minus dollar adjustments that local buyers and sellers would recognize.

59. On the "condition" line, indicate the condition of the subject property and the comparable properties by the words "excellent," "good," "average," "fair," or "poor." This factor of condition is not affected by the price range or age of the property. An "excellent" rating could be given to an older building having no deferred maintenance and which has an extremely clean, well kept appearance, for example.

In classifying the subject property or comparable properties on condition, simply compare them to a building in new condition.

As a guide in estimating the "condition" adjustment, consideration could be given to the cost and repair of refurbishing the comparable property to bring it up to the condition of the subject property or vice versa.

Caution should be taken with properties in very bad condition since the market tends to penalize these properties beyond the normal adjustment.

60. On the line "quality of construction," indicate the quality of construction of the subject property and the comparable properties with concise descriptive statements of quality such as "good," "fair," or "poor," for example. This quality rating encompasses both workmanship and materials and relates them to what is ordinarily obtainable and expected at the cost now, regardless of age.

"Condition" and "quality of construction" have been grouped together on the market data analysis grid to permit the appraiser to make a single-dollar adjustment in the amount it is estimated the market would consider for "condition" and "quality" when comparing a comparable sale with the subject property.

If, for example, the subject was considered by the appraiser to be in "average condition" with "good quality of construction" and the first comparable sale was considered to be in "excellent condition" with "excellent quality of construction," the appraiser should estimate the combination of condition and quality of differences that the market would recognize for these items. In this example, it may be the appraiser's judgment that these two factors would warrant a −$2,500 adjustment when relating comparable property to the subject property. This −$2,500 should then be shown in the adjustment column for "condition" and "quality of construction."

61. Individual adjustment lines are shown for the following items:

A. "Roof"—On this line indicate the roof covering for both the subject property and the comparable properties with such descriptive terms as "shake," "rock," or "tile," for example. When making comparison and adjustments for roofs, only recognize those items that the market is willing to pay for. Take into consideration the remaining physical life of the roof and the relationship of the type of roof to the price range of the dwelling. For example, the market may only recognize a small portion in the cost differential between a tile roof and a composition shingle roof in a low-priced residence.

B. "Heating"—On this line, indicate the type of heating for both the subject property and the comparable properties with such descriptive terms as "forced air" or "floor furnace," for example. Comparative cost factors between different types of heating can serve as a guide to the appraiser in making adjustments but the basic criterion is the appraiser's estimate of the adjustment, if any, that the market would make for one type of heating unit as compared with another.

C. "Air conditioning"—On this line indicate the type of air conditioning, if any, for both the subject property and the comparable properties with the terms "central," "wall,"

Fig. 11–1. Continued.

or "cooler" for evaporative cooler and then make the appropriate plus or minus dollar adjustment that in the appraiser's opinion reflects the actions of local buyers and sellers. As with other items in the market data analysis, cost factors can serve as a preliminary guide to the adjustment process but the basic consideration is given to what the market will pay for an air conditioning unit. Consideration should again be given to the price range of the properties and the possibility that a central air conditioning unit could be an overimprovement in a lower-price-range dwelling and the market would give the cost of the air conditioning unit little value in the final consideration of the price paid for the property.

D.   "Fireplace"—On this line, indicate for both the subject property and the comparable properties either "none," "1," "2," or the appropriate number of fireplaces and the appropriate plus or minus dollar adjustments that the local buyers and sellers would make for fireplaces in the subject price range. Cost can again serve as a preliminary guide to the adjustments but the final analysis should be based on the appraiser's estimate of the market recognition for this item.

E.   "Kitchen Built-ins"—On this line, indicate the appropriate kitchen built-ins for both the subject property and the comparable properties with the following code letters: "R/O" (range and oven), "D/W" (dishwasher), "F/H" (fan and hood), "G/D" (garbage disposal), plus any other kitchen built-in items that may exist.

When making the market adjustments for kitchen built-ins, it is important to take into consideration the quality of the units, their remaining useful life and the price range and age of the properties being compared. Normally built-ins are very appealing to the market and are usually considered desirable by a buyer. Built-ins usually aid the marketability of the dwelling. Again, cost factors can serve as a preliminary guide but the heaviest emphasis is placed on the recognition that local buyers and sellers would make for these items.

A lump-sum adjustment should be made for all the kitchen built-ins.

F.   "Basement"—On this line, indicate the following for both the subject property and the comparable properties: "none," if there is no basement; if there is a basement indicate with the word "yes." If the information is available to the appraiser, indicate the square footage in the basement area and whether the space is finished or unfinished. For example, "600 s.f. unf." or "350 s.f. fin."

The plus or minus dollar adjustment is again the appraiser's estimate of the dollar amount that local buyers and sellers would recognize for the basement.

G.   "Pool"—On this line, indicate for both the subject property and the comparable properties whether there is a swimming pool ("yes") or the absence of a swimming pool ("no"). The plus or minus dollar adjustment should reflect the buyers' and sellers' attitude toward the contributory value of a swimming pool. The location of the subject property and the general price range of the subject property and comparable properties are the basic factors to consider when making adjustments for pools. For example, in a luxury home market in certain areas a pool may be an expected item in the property. Properties in this category with particularly well-designed pools can sell at the top of the market range because of the existing pool and the fact that a new buyer would not have to go to the effort of constructing a pool. In contrast, the presence of a pool in a low-priced property may almost have a negative effect on the marketability of a property because the typical buyer in the neighborhood may not be in an income level to handle the added financial burden of the higher property taxes and maintenance costs created by the pool.

Fig. 11–1. Continued.

The adjustment for a pool can be a major dollar adjustment and it is the appraiser's responsibility to recognize the realistic adjustment that the local buyers and sellers would make for a pool.

62. On the lines for "other major improvements," the appraiser should indicate, for both the subject property and the comparable properties, the existence of such major improvements as "covered patio," "barn," "storage building," for example, and then make the appropriate dollar market adjustment for the contributory value on these improvements.

63. On the line for "car storage," indicate for both the subject property and the comparable properties the number of cars and whether the car storage is a garage, carport, or open area and make the appropriate dollar market adjustment. Again the appraiser should go to the local real estate market for an indication of the appropriate adjustment. Consideration should be given to those areas where on-street parking is prohibited or very limited and where car storage facilities are given a premium by the local real estate market. Recognition should also be given to the differences between single and double garages when relating comparable properties to the subject property, especially in those areas where two cars are prevalent in families.

64. On the line for "lot size," indicate for both the subject property and the comparable properties the lot dimensions. Indicate the frontage first, multiplied by the depth on rectangular lots, such as 50' x 150', for example. On irregularly shaped lots, indicate the lot area such as 11,300 s.f. or 1.5 acres, for example.

65. On the line for "zoning," indicate for both the subject property and the comparable properties the zoning classification, such as "R-1," "R-2," "R-3," for example.

In making the market adjustment for "lot size" and "zoning," consideration should be given to the fact that on a single-family residential lot, the market generally thinks in terms of site values and in most instances would not reflect small differences in area between the comparable properties and subject property. If it is the appraiser's opinion that the market would recognize lot size differentials, this plus or minus dollar adjustment must also be recognized by the appraiser.

Regarding the zoning, the appraiser must also give consideration to the highest and best use of the lot. In neighborhoods that are zoned for multiple residential use but predominately improved with single-family residences, the market may show little difference, if any, among lots zoned R-1, R-2, or R-3, for example. It is the appraiser's responsibility to recognize the market conditions and trends that exist in the subject area and acknowledge only the plus or minus dollar adjustment that local buyers and sellers would consider.

66. On the line for "landscaping," indicate for both the subject property and the comparable properties the quality and condition of the landscaping with the descriptive comments of "excellent," "good," "average," "fair," "poor," or "none," and make the appropriate dollar adjustment that local buyers and sellers would consider.

67. On the line for "view," indicate for both the subject property and the comparable properties the desirability of the view. Descriptive comments such as "excellent ocean," "good," or "yes," or "none" may be used and the appraiser should recognize the appropriate plus or minus dollar adjustment that the local buyers and sellers would consider.

In many areas, view factors can account for a sizable dollar adjustment with the local real estate market especially where spectacular ocean or scenic views are involved. It is the appraiser's responsibility to thoroughly research these view premiums and realistically reflect them in the adjustment column.

68. On the line for "location," classify for both the subject property and the comparable properties the location rating for the neighborhood using descriptive comments such as

Fig. 11–1. Continued.

"excellent," "good," "average," "fair," or "poor," for example. The appraiser should then reflect the plus or minus dollar adjustment that local buyers and sellers would recognize for these differences in the neighborhood.

To avoid the difficulties involved in attempting to relate the differences between different neighborhoods, the appraiser should make every attempt to select comparable properties that are in the subject neighborhood.

69. On the line for "property appeal," indicate for both the subject property and the comparable properties the overall property appeal in descriptive terms such as "excellent," "good," "average," "fair," or "poor," for example.

The element of "property appeal" means the related eye-appeal and esthetic attraction of the improvements within the price range, and should be judged from the viewpoint of the typical users. Property appeal takes into consideration such items as architectural design, orientation of the improvements on the lot, and other visual factors not included in any of the above adjustments.

Adjustments for property appeal can often reflect a substantial dollar adjustment in the reactions of buyers and sellers and therefore warrants careful consideration by the appraiser.

70. The next three blank lines are for adjustment items not listed above that the appraiser may wish to write in and recognize in the market data analysis.

71. On the next six lines, space is provided for the appraiser to make any additional pertinent comments about the subject property as well as the comparable properties. Examples of pertinent comments would be "same model as subject," "kitchen and baths completely remodeled in 1970," along with the appropriate dollar adjustment if indicated by the market.

72. On the two lines for "terms of sale," indicate for both the subject property and the comparable properties in concise comments the terms of the sale. Examples would be "10%. cash," "$5,000 cash." If the subject property did not involve a sale, write "N/A" for not applicable under the subject property terms of sale.

On page 4 of the appraisal, the phrase "terms of money" is included in the definition of "market value" and this is intended to mean that the appraisal of the subject property is based upon terms of sale that are typical for the subject market area. If typical single-family transactions in a subject neighborhood are based upon 10 per cent cash down payments by the buyers, the appraiser should make every effort to select comparable properties that reflect similar terms of sale. In a situation such as this, where a 10 per cent cash down payment is prevalent and available market data are lacking, the appraiser is required to select a comparable sale with favorable financing which could have affected the price (no down payment financing, for example). The appraiser should then make an adjustment for the terms of sale on this comparable to bring it into line with the typical financing in the subject area. The minus dollar adjustment in this example would be the loan points included in the no-down-payment sale.

Terms of sale and the effect that they can have on the price of a property are often overlooked by the appraisers. Again, it is the appraiser's responsibility to be knowledgeable on and to reflect realistic market adjustments when required for unusually favorable terms of sale that are not prevalent in the immediate neighborhood.

73. On the line for "date of sale," indicate for both the subject property, when a sale is involved, and for all of the comparable properties the month, day, and year of the sale, such as "3-6-78," for example. When the subject property does not involve a current sale, indicate "N/A" for "not applicable." When a sale is pending but not closed on a comparable property, the words "in escrow" would be appropriate. When the comparable property is a current listing rather than a sale, write the word "current" on the line.

Fig. 11–1. Continued.

The date of sale and the possible time adjustment involved are often overlooked by the appraiser and can be a very sizable dollar adjustment item.

Again one of the tests of comparability of a property is the date of sale. The appraiser should select comparable market data that reflect, as well as possible, the current actions of buyers and sellers in the local real estate market. Often current sales of comparable property are not readily available to the appraiser, who must then use the sale of a comparable property that was sold approximately one year prior to the date of valuation for the subject property. The basic question that the appraiser has to answer here is: "What price adjustment, if any, would be required to reflect what that same property would have sold for in today's market?" Here the appraiser has to have a close familiarity with market trends in the subject neighborhood. In some areas, due to local conditions, there may have been little or no price appreciation in properties during the past year and observation of the market may indicate that there even exists some evidence of depreciation in market prices for real estate comparable to the subject property. On the other hand, there may be neighborhoods where strong evidence exists to support a relatively high rate of appreciation in market prices not only since one year prior to the date of valuation but within the last few months. It is extremely important that the appraiser be aware of these local market changes and that the appraisal report reflects these realistic market adjustments that can be supported by market data.

The best way for the appraiser to observe these market adjustments is to review resales of the same property or similar properties where there have been no physical changes in the property such as remodeling, painting, or the addition of a pool, for example, which would have contributed to the difference between the original price and the resale price. The appraiser should be analyzing resales where the only change that can be attributed to the price difference has been the passage of time. If enough resale data of this type can be obtained, the appraiser can develop some indications of a pattern of appreciation on an annual basis, expressed as a percentage: 3 per cent annual appreciation in a specific area, for example.

Extending this example further, if comparable Sale No. 1 had sold one year prior to the date of valuation for $20,000 and the appraiser could support a 3 per cent annual appreciation in the market, it would be appropriate to indicate a "+$600" on the "date of sale" line to reflect the time adjustment for comparable No. 1.

The time adjustment factor is a very important item in the market data analysis and it must be not only a realistic estimate but also one that could be reasonably supported in the local market.

74. On the line for "data source," indicate in concise terms such as "selling broker," "multiple listing files," "title company records," "S.R.E.A." (for SREA Market Data Center), "owner," or "appraisal files," for example, the source of the comparable data.

75. On the line for "comparison to subject," place an "x" in the appropriate box indicating if on an overall basis the comparable property is "superior," "similar," or "inferior" to the subject property. It is important to remember that in all instances the comparable property is related and compared to the subject property.

76. On the line for "price," place an "x" in the appropriate box to indicate whether each comparable property is either a "sale" or a "listing." As stated in the second paragraph at the top of page 3 of the appraisal form: "Market data selected should be the sales of comparable properties that a buyer of the subject property would have also given consideration to purchasing. In the absence of actual sales of comparable properties, listings of comparable properties may be used but an explanation must be included in the comment section below."

Fig. 11–1. Continued.

When selecting market data, actual sales are generally preferable because they reflect the actions of both buyers and sellers. However, these listings can serve a function in the market data analysis in the absence of sales.

If the subject property has currently sold, indicate the sale price in the appropriate location.

77. On the line for "total net adjustment," place an "x" in the appropriate "plus" or "minus" box.

After tabulating all of the individual plus or minus items listed above on the market data analysis grid, the appraiser should add all the plus adjustments together, if any, and then all of the minus adjustments together, if any. The difference between the total "plus" and total "minus" adjustments is the "total net adjustment" which is to be indicated on this line.

If the total "plus" and "minus" adjustments balance each other out or if the comparable property is so comparable to the subject property that no adjustments are required, indicate "none" for "total net adjustment."

78. On the line for "indicated value of subject," show the results of the "plus," "minus," or "none" adjustment for the sale or list price for each comparable property.

This is a simple mathematical process of either adding or subtracting the total net adjustment from the sale or list price. When no total net adjustment is appropriate, the price will become the indicated value for the subject based on that comparable property.

79. On the line for "price per square foot (when applicable)" indicate the dollar and cents result by dividing the actual sale or list prices before adjustment by the actual square footage of the properties.

This common denominator can be a helpful tool to the appraiser as a check when appraising in subdivisions of similar homes on similar size lots with similar amenities, but caution should be used when such major variables as extreme differences in lot sizes, swimming pools, and view lot situations are encountered. Major variables such as these can greatly invalidate the process of using the price per square foot as a check.

This item is optional and should only be used by the appraiser when it is felt that it contributes something to the report.

80. The lines immediately below the market data analysis grid are for the appraiser to make any additional appropriate comments about the comparables that are pertinent, including the necessity for using listings as market data, when appropriate.

This section is commonly referred to as the "correlation" in the appraisal process and it is here that the appraiser can comment in a concise manner on the relative weight given to the comparables in the final valuation analysis.

81. On the bottom line of the market data analysis page, indicate the correlated value of the subject property that is supported by the above analyzed comparable data. This amount represents the appraiser's opinion of the indicated value of the subject property by the market approach. It may or may not represent the final value conclusion shown on page 1 of the report. This will depend on the appraiser's correlation of this indicated value by the market approach with the indicated value by the cost approach shown on the bottom of page 2 of the report.

Appraisal Report Instructions—Page 4

82. (Optional) Left to the discretion of the appraiser. If the appraiser feels compelled to document the replacement cost estimate or include the income (rent times multiplier) approach, this space and Item 87 may be utilized for this purpose.

Fig. 11–1. Continued.

83. Quality photographs are required (color photographs are optional). The appraiser should identify on the reverse of each photograph the address of the property, date, and appraiser's signature. Attach the photographs of the subject property and street scene in the section provided, and indicate date taken on the line provided. The street scene should include a partial view of the subject property. The appraiser should show favorable and unfavorable influences in the photograph whenever possible.

84. States the purpose of the Appraisal Report—to estimate the Market Value as defined therein (the term "money" refers to U.S. currency).

85. The appraiser should read the Certification prior to signing the Appraisal Report, and is reminded of Item 3 therein, which certifies that the appraiser has personally inspected the property, both inside and out, and has made an exterior inspection of all comparable sales.

86. The appraiser and lender should read the Contingent and Limiting Conditions. Complete Item 9 therein when appraising from plans and specifications.

87. (Optional) Left to the discretion of the appraiser (if there are attachments to the Appraisal Report, the appraiser should so state in this section).

88. The function of this Appraisal Report is to underwrite property as security for a mortgage (trust deed) loan with a maximum balance up to 95 per cent of the appraised value or sales price, whichever is lesser.

Fig. 11–1. Continued.

SUMMARY

The Federal Housing Administration (FHA) has had an enormous impact on standards of property analysis. This is related to the increased loan-to-value ratio which was pioneered by the FHA. With relatively high loan-to-value ratios, the lender must place more confidence in the quality of the property. The quality of the property can be judged by specific standards for materials, workmanship, etc. However, if a property does not meet any specific standards, a difficult judgment must be made: Does the property meet the overall objectives of the appraisal of quality?

A house can be quite functional without meeting any specific physical standard of quality. The FHA standards do not go far enough in defining desirable functional housing characteristics. For example, the size and layout of rooms according to their ability to handle traffic and give light and ventilation may be as important as the physical soundness of the materials used in the construction of the building. A comparison of the house to others in the neighborhood is important in giving an estimate of the degree of conformity. In most areas, nonconformity probably reduces property value.

QUESTIONS

1. What is the role of the appraiser in property analysis?
2. Why has the FHA been particularly interested in developing good standards of property analysis?
3. Looking back to Figure 10–3:
   (a) How would you rate the functional qualities where you have information?
   (b) What additional information do you need to determine all functional qualities?

12

OFFICE BUILDINGS
AND SHOPPING CENTERS

Office buildings and shopping centers differ from other types of real estate because of their large size and long life span. Also, they cater to a very special segment of the real estate market; the investor must be aware of the changing needs of the customers for this type of property. Leasing practices and terms which are unique to these properties often condition the type of financing which is available.

The purpose of this chapter is twofold. First, the major sources of funds—both equity and debt—for shopping centers and office buildings will be outlined. This outline will be supplemented by a discussion of the factors which must be weighed when considering office buildings and shopping centers as opposed to other types of investments. Second, some of the special characteristics of each of these types of property will be examined.

SOURCES OF FUNDS

The amount of the investment in these properties is usually enormous—often tens of millions of dollars and occasionally hundreds of millions. Consequently, large institutions provide almost all of the debt and equity capital. Equity capital may be provided by a large manufacturing corporation, and debt or equity by pension funds, insurance companies, and commercial banks.

As an example, several years ago The Prudential Insurance Company purchased a large shopping center which had been developed about five years earlier by a relatively small syndicate of local investors. Because it was one of the earliest shopping centers, the price of land and construction was within the means of local investors; today, few such syndicates would be large enough to finance a similar venture. The widespread success of shopping centers has increased the price of investment in them to the point where funds sufficient for purchase are available only from a large institution like Prudential.

Prudential's name is not publicly associated with the shopping center. Thus, its value to Prudential is solely as an investment property: Prudential receives an income stream from the property and the possibility of appreciation in land value, nothing more. In contrast, Prudential owns a skyscraper with a surrounding plaza (Prudential Center) in Boston. Since this development is closely identified with Prudential in the public mind, it has advertising value. Along with zoning and planning regulations, this advertising value is one of the forces which has induced developers to build luxury features into office buildings.

SYNDICATION

A limited number of organizations are the size of The Prudential Insurance Company. However, two or more organizations (or individuals) can pool their capital through syndication. The general partners in a syndicate may or may not supply investment funds but their active involvement includes planning the investment and directing its operation. The general partners usually receive a fee for their services and they may receive a percentage of (1) the profits in excess of a certain amount and (2) the appreciation of the property. The limited partners supply capital and receive profits and tax shelter. Their liability is limited to the amount of their investment.

CONTINGENCY LOANS AND LEASEBACK ARRANGEMENTS

Literally hundreds of varieties of financing arrangements can be worked out for office buildings and shopping centers. The large size of these investments makes it economical for the lender and borrower to spend time working out special arrangements. In this respect the financing of office buildings and shopping centers is quite unlike the financing of residential real estate. The latter tends to be standardized whereas the former is usually custom-designed.

Techniques for Custom-Designed Financing. Custom-designed financing packages contain known and tested elements to suit the needs and interests of the parties to the financing. The amount of equity capital to be laid out initially and the amount of the loan servicing costs are particularly important variables. The borrower generally wants to see these variables become as small as possible. The lender may be willing to compromise on them in return for participation in (1) the appreciation in value of the property and (2) better than average rental receipts.

The loan agreement can specify that, if the property is sold, the lender will get a percentage of any increase in value. This type of arrangement is used to compensate the general partners in a syndicate; it also provides them with an incentive to manage the property carefully. For the lender, the participation in appreciation is a sweetener to encourage arrangement of more lenient terms at the front end of the deal.

The percentage-of-rents approach to financing is bound up in the method of drawing leases. This is particularly complex for shopping centers. Many shopping center leases (and a few leases in office buildings) are net of property taxes; i.e., the tenant pays property taxes, prorated for the amount of space occupied. Others are net of maintenance costs, net of repairs, or net of insurance. Leases which are net of all three costs are called triple net leases.

Negotiation of a loan based on rents may seem difficult because of the many forms of leases. However, the ingenuity of lenders and investors intimately involved with these large properties has produced numerous solutions to this problem. Modern shopping center leases (but not office space leases) often have a percentage clause under which the shopping center owners receive a percentage of gross sales above an agreed-upon amount.

Figure 12–1 illustrates how the percentage lease works. The tenant pays a flat amount in rent, perhaps on a net or triple net basis, up to a given gross sales volume. When the sales volume reaches this threshold, additional rents are paid which are a percentage of the sales above the threshold. But the threshold is always related to the percentage, as shown by the curve in Figure 12–1. Thus, the percentage of sales which must be paid in rent declines until the threshold level of sales is reached. At that point, the percentage of sales is at a minimum.

Loans are sometimes arranged so that the lender gets a share of the percentage-of-rent payments; i.e., the total rent paid under the various percentage clauses of the leases is calculated and a percentage of that total is paid to the lender. This gives the lender an opportunity to participate in an above-average sales performance of the shopping center. Another ap-

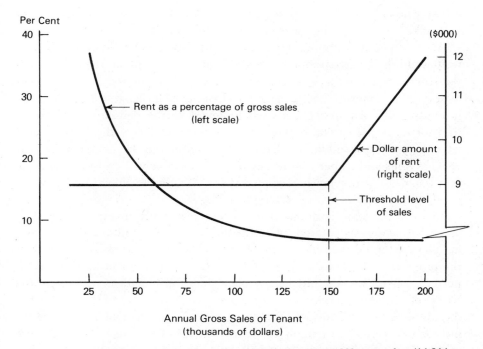

Fig. 12–1. A percentage lease for a shopping center tenant.

NOTE: In this example, the tenant pays a flat $9,000 per year for 1,860 square feet ($4.84/sq. ft.) provided that gross sales are less than $150,000 in any year. When sales exceed $150,000, percentage rents are paid at the rate of 6 cents on each sales dollar.

proach gives the lender a percentage of any increase in rental income which occurs because leases are renegotiated (perhaps under an option-to-renew clause) or because new tenants enter the center.

A lender can negotiate for a percentage of the net income of a shopping center or office building. Under this arrangement, the lender participates in the success (or lack of success) of the project, but only within certain limits. The lender will get fixed loan payments regardless of the percentage clause. Also, there may be a threshold in the percentage clause: when net income falls below a given amount, no extra payments will be made to the lender.

Sale-Leaseback. The sale-leaseback arrangement carries the investor's desire for minimum equity involvement to the logical extreme. The owner of the property sells it outright but takes a very long lease position. With leases of 50 years or more, the holder of the lease is somewhat like an owner who is making mortgage payments. The leaseholder and the owner both take an active, long-term interest in the property.

An example of custom-designed financing arrangements is provided by a well-established, large shopping center which was sold in 1960 to a pension fund on a leaseback arrangement. The seller entered into a 98-year lease of the property, i.e., a lease terminating in 2058, at which time the property with all improvements would revert to the pension fund. In return for an initial capital outlay, the pension fund received a fixed annual lease payment. In addition, the fund is entitled to 15 per cent of percentage rents and 15 per cent of any excess rents received on renewals or on new tenancies of previously occupied space. The basic annual rent payable is scheduled to *decrease* by $500,000 in 1989.

In 1970, the lease position was sold to a real estate investment (REIT) and a sub-lease was entered into with the REIT. The sub-lease terminates in 2055, so the original owner still has a substantial, owner-like interest in the property. The terms of the sub-lease call for a payment of 10 per cent per year of the REIT's initial investment and also includes payment to the REIT of the debt service on mortgages outstanding as of June 1, 1970. As additional rental, the REIT is to receive 50 per cent of the *net* rental income in excess of $3 million per year. The REIT will receive 50 per cent of the decrease of the pension fund's rent; i.e., starting in 1989 the REIT will get additional rental income of $250,000 per year. The rental payable to the REIT decreases by 50 per cent of existing mortgages which are amortized or paid off, and any refinancing benefits are split fifty–fifty between the REIT and the original developer.

The marvelous aspect of these complex financing arrangements is that the original developer still controls the property. A constant upgrading and modernization of buildings and tenant mix, complemented by a continuing expansion program, produces steady increases in the profitability of the property. Careful development and management may enable the original developer to sell the sub-lease position, thus producing capital for further investment.

THE ECONOMICS OF OFFICE BUILDINGS AND SHOPPING CENTERS

Office buildings and shopping centers appeal to large institutions because they provide an investment outlet for millions of dollars. These institutions need large-scale investments: it would be prohibitively expensive for them to search out many investments of a few thousand dollars each. With office buildings and shopping centers, the costs of searching for the investment, analyzing it, and closing the deal are spread over millions of dollars. Thus, these costs, while they will certainly run to tens of thousands of dollars, will be small relative to the total investment.

The large size of these investments gives investors an opportunity to do a thorough and costly analysis of the property (see Chapter 11) and/or the borrower (see Chapter 10). For a proposed development, feasibility studies attempt to account for costs, future demand for the services which will be provided, and government activity which might impinge (positively or negatively) on the value of the property. By using discounting techniques (see Chapter 22), feasibility studies attempt to establish the present value of the proposed project so that the investor can decide which of several alternative projects would be the best investment.

The long life of these investments puts a major stumbling block in the way of feasibility analysis. How can cash flows, competitive conditions, and government regulation be projected 25 to 50 years into the future? Surely investors in high-rise office buildings which were constructed ten years ago would have found it impossible to forecast the glutted market which exists today in New York, Los Angeles, and other major cities. Construction begun within the past year or two (on the basis of plans which are now three to five years old) would not have fared much better. The current situation would have been hard to foresee when the plans were made, and even now the extent or severity of the situation is difficult to determine.

Given the difficulties involved in feasibility studies for an office building or a shopping center, why do investors continue to rely on them? The primary purpose of feasibility studies is to compare one investment with another or to compare several different versions of the same basic investment activity. Even though the studies are subject to large error, they may still have value in determining which of several alternatives is the best course of action. In any event, every investor in long-lived assets must make some projections of distant future events, so a formal approach seems better than a seat-of-the-pants approach.

When investors are considering an existing project, the feasibility study is replaced by an appraisal. The real estate appraiser is assigned the difficult task of determining the value of the property as an ongoing operation.[1] The most important technique which is used for establishing the value of shopping centers and office buildings is based on the discounting of cash flows, as described in Chapter 23. Again, the long life of the investment makes projections of cash flows extremely hazardous.

---

[1] The various techniques used by appraisers are described in publications of the American Institute of Real Estate Appraisers and the Society of Real Estate Appraisers.

Despite the uncertainties inherent in a large, long-term commitment to an office building or shopping center, investors feel that this type of property is usually a very secure investment. There are two reasons for this. One is that population growth tends to make real estate more valuable because land is largely fixed in supply. Although real estate prices have severe cyclical ups and downs, the price is likely to rise substantially over a very long period of time.

Secondly, real estate usually keeps pace with inflation. Inflation is an increase in the price of a market basket of goods and services. Since real estate is part of the market basket, inflation should increase the price of real estate along with other "real" quantities. The losers during inflation are usually the holders of financial instruments such as bonds, savings deposits, and checking accounts. The principal amount of these instruments is fixed in dollar terms, and the dollar depreciates during inflation. Thus, real estate is seen as a good hedge against inflation, especially when viewed in relation to financial instruments.

The dependability of real estate as a long-term investment is valuable to large financial institutions. These institutions have a problem: What should they do with large amounts of money which will not be needed in the foreseeable future? They have a fiduciary responsibility to protect this money in the interests of the ultimate beneficiaries. Real estate is a logical place to store these funds for a long period.

The Value of the Location. If real estate is such a dependable long-term investment, why do institutional investors fret and fuss with expensive, highly unreliable feasibility studies and appraisal reports? The reason is that specific urban locations are subject to extended, severe decline in value. Thus, the real issue in this type of real estate investment is the future of the location; the value of the structures on the location is of lesser importance. A rerouting of a freeway system, for example, could have a major impact on the value of an office building or a shopping center.

These investments are also vulnerable to obsolescence. Standards of good design have changed radically over the years. Relatively narrow and ornate office towers, which may have no air conditioning, are being replaced by unadorned slabs with large floor area and modern facilities. Office buildings constructed in recent years typically use more glass than older buildings, accenting a view, which has been found to have value to tenants. Faster elevators, programmed to respond more efficiently to changing traffic patterns, have been introduced. This is important, since one of the most serious weaknesses of office buildings is the large amount of space (typically 25–30 per cent of gross floor space) which is lost to elevators and hallways.

The design of shopping centers has also changed radically over the years. Early shopping centers were patterned after villages, with interesting winding roadways lined with shops. In the post-World War II period, pedestrian malls came into wide usage but these were not enclosed (or air conditioned). Often they had tunnels through which deliveries could be made into the basement of each store.

In crowded urban settings, multilevel enclosed shopping centers with separate parking structures (or subterranean parking) have been found to use land more efficiently. Since they are air conditioned, the growing cost of energy has raised serious problems for enclosed shopping malls. A currently unanswered question is whether air conditioning will be economical for large mall areas.

Progress has been made recently in the understanding of what makes a particular location valuable. The old idea, which can be found in many recent books on the subject, is that competition from other office buildings or shopping activities is bad for the future of the investment. Undoubtedly, a shopping center which is developed several miles from an existing center will detract from the existing center's business. However, profitable satellite shopping facilities often develop adjacent to a shopping center. These satellites usually benefit the shopping center by enabling potential customers to do a greater variety of shopping in one trip.

For office buildings, proximity to other office functions and to retail activities is very valuable. In the performance of their jobs office workers depend to a greater or lesser degree on face-to-face contact with other office workers (see Appendix C). This is one reason why office buildings are concentrated in places like Wall Street, midtown Manhattan, and the Loop in Chicago. More recently, complexes of office buildings have been designed by developers in order to provide sufficient face-to-face contact to make the space valuable. Century City in Los Angeles is an example of a complex of high-rise buildings with ample parking (subterranean as well as on surrounding land) and connected by pedestrian malls. Century City includes a shopping center, a hotel, condominiums, and theaters. It is essentially a high-density urban center that has been designed to avoid many of the problems which usually accompany high density.

Appendix C presents some new evidence on the value of face-to-face contact for office activities. The striking finding in Appendix C is that the availability of office space nearby has a positive effect on the rent which can be charged for the space in a given building. In other words, tenants are willing to pay for proximity to other office functions. Many investors in office buildings are not yet fully aware of the extent to which the value of their building is enhanced by the presence of nearby "competing" office buildings.

Special Characteristics of Office Buildings. High-rise office buildings have become associated with luxurious design features. The Montauk Block—at 10 stories, Chicago's first skyscraper (built in 1881)—set a pattern which has been followed since. It included central heating and extensive plumbing, astounding innovations for the time. The Rookery, a neighboring building completed in 1888, included a light court (a central courtyard) and a two-story domed lobby decorated with marble and golf leaf. The lobby is one of the early works of Frank Lloyd Wright.

As building heights increased, light courts became impractical, but lavish lobbies have been retained and supplemented by plazas, often with fountains. The inclination of investors to build lavishly has been reinforced by zoning restrictions which require (or provide incentive for) plazas and setbacks. Striking modern examples of luxury in high-rise office buildings include the Chase Manhattan Plaza and the Seagram Building in New York, and the Bank of America Building in San Francisco.

Investors should be aware that luxury features included in office buildings may not be reflected in rental income but may be refracted onto the real estate tax bill. New York appeals courts determined that the Seagram Building is a "prestige" building which has advertising value to the firm. Tax assessors throughout the country have seized the opportunity to tax these prestige buildings on the high value of the luxuries. A building returning the same rental income but without the luxuries (an investment building) is taxed on a lower assessed value. This is important since property taxes are the highest single cost item; at $1.13 per square foot in 1973 they were about 25 per cent of all operating expenses for the average office building.

Table 12–1 indicates that large buildings can charge substantially more per square foot of rented space than small buildings. This is caused partly by the fact that tenants pay more in newer buildings, and large buildings are typically newer than small buildings. The newness is reflected in the vacancy rate, which is less for large buildings. Also, large buildings are more likely to be in large cities, where the general level of rents is higher. The fact that real estate taxes rise dramatically with building size (item 4 in Table 12–1) is probably related to these two factors.

Others factors also cause rental income to rise in relation to building size. Tenants pay more for high floors than for low floors. The thirtieth floor, for example, can command 5–25 per cent more than the fifth floor.

In addition, large buildings facilitate face-to-face contact among tenants. One has merely to take the elevator, a convenient and flexible means of transportation, to another floor. Easy face-to-face contact is certainly valuable to office building tenants (see the discussion above and in Appendix C).

Table 12-1. Charges Per Square Foot of Rented Office Space, Per Year

	Size of Building in Thousands of Square Feet			
	50–100	100–300	300–600	600 and Over
1. Office income	$5.07	$5.50	$6.32	$7.07
2. Operating expense*	2.56	2.74	2.78	2.98
3. Ratio (line 2)/(line 1)	0.505	0.498	0.440	0.422
4. Real estate tax, land, and building	0.63	0.76	1.12	1.58
5. Ratio (line 4)/(line 1)	0.124	0.138	0.177	0.224
6 Average vacancy rate	8.2%	6.3%	5.1%	3.6%

*Out-of-pocket operating expenses (utilities, janitorial, general administration, alterations, and repairs) *exclude* insurance and all property taxes.

Source: 1973 Office Building Experience Exchange Report, (Chicago: Building Owners and Managers Association International), pp. 20–21.

Operating costs (not including insurance or real estate taxes) rise with building size (item 2 in Table 12–1), but not as much as rental income. Thus, the ratio of the costs which can be controlled by management to rental income declines with building size (item 3). This indicates one reason why investors and lenders continue to incur the high costs of constructing tall buildings. While building costs per square foot rise with building height, investors are compensated with a higher net operating income.

Special Characteristics of Shopping Centers.[2] Two characteristics of shopping centers are of special interest to lenders and investors. One is location; the other is internal structure. The location must be appropriate to the type and number of shops which are available and to the customers who have access to the center by major roads (i.e., the "trading area" of the center). The internal structure must place tenants which draw customers—usually large tenants with independent advertising programs—so as to provide customers to the smaller tenants. The benefits of one-stop, multipurpose shopping provide the wellspring of success for shopping centers.

As the shopping center evolved, four distinct types emerged, each definite in its own function: neighborhood, community, regional, and super-regional. Table 12–2 gives an overview of each type of center. In all cases, a shopping center's type is determined by its major tenant classification and the size of the market it serves. Neither the site area nor the building size determines the type of center.

The neighborhood center provides for the sale of convenience goods (foods, drugs, and sundries) and such personal services as laundry and

---

[2] Martin Moskowitz helped in preparing material contained in this section.

Table 12-2. Characteristics of Shopping Centers, By Type

	Type of Center			
	Neighborhood	*Community*	*Regional*	*Superregional*
Leading tenant (basis for definition)	Supermarket or drugstore	Variety, discount, or junior dept. store	One or two full-line dept. stores	Three or more full-line dept. stores
Average gross leasable area (GLA)	40,000 sq. ft.	150,000 sq. ft.	400,000 sq. ft.	1,000,000 sq. ft.
General ranges in GLA	30,000–100,000	100,000–300,000	300,000–1,000,000	Over 1,000,000
Usual minimum site area	4 acres	10 acres	30–50 acres	Over 50 acres
Minimum support	5,000–40,000 people	40,000–150,000	150,000–300,000	300,000 and up

Parking standard = 5.5 parking spaces per 1,000 sq. ft. of GLA or 2.5:1 = ratio of GLA:parking area.

dry cleaning, drive-up banking, hair styling, and shoe repair. It fulfills the day-by-day living needs of an immediate neighborhood. A supermarket is the principal tenant.

The neighborhood center has an average gross leasable area (GLA) close to 50,000 square feet; it may range from 30,000 up to as much as 100,000 square feet. For its site area, the neighborhood center needs from four to 10 acres. It normally serves a trade area population of 5,000 to 40,000 people who live within six minutes' driving time (see Table 12–2). In metropolitan regions, parking facilities may not be available within the center.

The community center is built around a junior department store or variety store and a supermarket as the major tenants. It does not have a full-line department store, though it may have a strong specialty or discount store.

The average GLA of the community center is about 150,000 square feet but the range is between 100,000 and 300,000 square feet. For its site area, the community center needs from 10 to 30 acres or more. It normally serves a trade area population of 40,000 to 150,000 people.

In a metropolitan region, the community center is vulnerable to competition. It is too big to live on its immediate neighborhood trade and too weak to make a strong impact on the whole community. The development of a strong regional center, with the pulling power of its department store, may impinge upon the community center's trade area even though the the two centers are located several miles apart.

In cities of 50,000 to 100,000 population, the community center may actually take on the aspect of a regional center because of its local dominance and pulling power, even though the center's collection of tenants does not include a full-line department store. A popularly priced store (discount) may substitute locally in customer acceptance and may function as a leading tenant.

The regional center provides for general merchandise, apparel, furniture, and home furnishings in full depth and variety. The regional center comes close to reproducing the shopping facilities and customer attractions once available only in central business districts. It is built around one or two full-line department stores as the major drawing powers.

The regional center has an average GLA of 400,000 square feet; the range is from 300,000 up to 1,000,000 square feet. The regional center needs a population of at least 150,000 to draw upon (Table 12–2). Traditionally, site area for a typical regional center averages 50 acres.

The superregional center, a relatively new concept in shopping center development, is the largest type of shopping center. The leading tenants are three or more full-line department stores. The superregional center has a GLA in excess of 1,000,000 square feet and a site area of 50 acres and up. Greater site areas readily accommodate growth without impinging upon site and building area relationships.

The superregional center provides complete comparison shopping goods in depth and variety; its customer drawing power stems from its capacity to offer complete shopping facilities, along with restaurants, fast-food franchises, ample free parking, theaters, and park-like malls. These attractions extend its trade area by 10 to 15 miles or more, modified by such factors as competitive facilities and travel time over access highways.

Site and Architectural Planning. Site planning calls for laying out the basic features which physically distinguish shopping centers. Elements of the site layout are:

> Parking, in adequate amount, arranged for ease in getting from the access highway to the parking stall and for reasonable walking distances from the parking place to the shops.
> Separation of customer movement from visible truck dockage or storage facilities.
> Adequate motor circulation to provide fire lanes at the buildings and to prevent customers' cars from pulling into boundary or access streets when entering or shifting parking places within the center.
> Arrangement of store locations for relative compactness, distribution of pulling power, and elimination of any poor locations.
> Selection of a pattern for the building arrangements which will best achieve the greatest interplay among the stores.
> An agreeable design that creates an atmosphere conducive to shopping in comfort, convenience, and safety; foot traffic separated from vehicle traffic; weather protection in the form of store front canopies or an enclosed air-conditioned mall; landscaping suitably placed for amenity and maintenance; lighting and signing provisions that are unobtrusive.

In the preliminary site planning stage, the project begins its adaptation to the physical conditions of the site and its trade area. Professional site planning and engineering studies proceed toward preliminary architectural plans while tenant negotiations go forward.

The basic layout of the entire shopping center must recognize the traffic-generating capability of the key tenants (e.g., major full-line department stores) and have them suitably positioned with maximum concentration of shopper traffic flowing past as much frontage as possible. Building depths should not exceed 150 feet in order to avoid excessive space not suitable for tenant sales. Malls should not be too wide, probably not greater than 50 feet. The tenant mix (to be discussed later) should include both strong-credit national firms and good local companies, in order to recognize finance credit necessities in subsequent discussions with lenders.

Architectural plans begin when project approval negotiations are concluded. There are accepted patterns for shopping center buildings; each is susceptible to variations fitted to the topographic and other physical conditions of the site. Essentially, the patterns are the strip, the "L," the "U," the "T," the cruciform, and the cluster. A mall, either open-air or covered, describes the building treatment for pedestrian concourses. Strips, L's, and U's are primarily suited to the smaller neighborhood or community center. The following is a brief description of these designs:

> The strip is a straight line of stores tied together by a canopy protecting the pedestrian walk which extends along the entrance fronts to the stores. Care must be taken to avoid elongating the strip beyond a distance that people can comfortably walk.
> The L is an adaptation to shorten the frontage length of a strip. The shape lends itself to variations for tenant locations and for site conditions, particularly for a site located at two important intersecting roads.
> The U creates natural key store locations at its ends and in its center The pattern adapts to rectangular or square sites and to sites having a single-road frontage.
> The cluster is a group of buildings separated by pedestrian ways or courts. The cluster arrangement is most suitable for large regional centers where parking areas surround the buildings; the distances between the farthest parking spaces and the buildings are minimized.

However, it is not the building pattern but the placement of tenants within the structure that is the ultimate key to successful architectural planning. The developer seeks the greatest customer interplay within the center so that the major tenants with their drawing power and customer attraction are placed to benefit smaller tenants and are not concentrated within one segment of the building pattern.

Factors considered by shopping center developers in relation to tenant mix include:

> Total amount of space allocated to each major line of trade, and space allocated to individual merchants in relation to (a) total space allocated to their specific line of trade and (b) closely related lines of trade.

The location of each retail store in relation to every other retail store within a shopping center. This is closely tied to shopper convenience and shopper traffic patterns, and hence to the objective of optimizing sales for all merchants.

The minimum rent and the overage rent, year by year, projected for each merchant.

Financing requirements of the developer based on bankable leases available from various prospective tenants.

Finding the optimum combination of all the elements listed above is most likely to result in a center where the stores will be profitable to the merchants, service will be rendered to the community, and financing will be available on favorable terms to the developer. A center which is carefully located and designed will maintain and improve its sales and profit position in the face of projected competition.

SUMMARY

Financial arrangements for the large, long-lived investments represented by shopping centers and office buildings give full scope to human ingenuity. The amount of money involved restricts equity or debt participation to large institutions or syndicates of smaller investors. The cost to these institutions of working out intricate arrangements, custom-designed for the property and for the principals in the deal, is small relative to the amount of money involved. The key elements in the financing of shopping centers and office buildings are:

1. The amount of money put in by the equity investors: i.e., the debt-to-equity ratio. In some cases the developer puts in nothing; the property is leased on a long-term basis (over 50 years).

2. The amount of the periodic payment to the lender, or the amount of the lease payment. This can be made variable over time, unlike residential mortgages.

3. The way in which the lender participates in capital appreciation of the property. The lender may get a percentage of appreciation; the purchaser who gives back a long lease gets everything at the end of the lease, but improvements in rental income which occur meanwhile will benefit the leaseholder.

4. The way in which the lender participates in above-average performance of the project. Various arrangements give the lender a percentage of rents or net operating income, provided that a threshold level of performance has been achieved.

The long life of an investment in a shopping center or office building presents certain difficulties and opportunities. The major difficulty is in planning for the future of the investment. Feasibility studies for proposed projects and appraisals of the value of existing projects are extremely difficult. They are attempted in order to give investors and lenders some basis for comparing alternative investments.

Real estate has a good record for generally improved value over a long period of time. Population growth makes land more valuable, and inflation typically increases the dollar value of real estate. Institutions with large amounts of funds which will not be needed for the foreseeable future find that real estate is a dependable investment. But specific locations and property types can suffer declines; hence the need for feasibility and valuation studies.

The investor should be careful to involve experts in the planning, design, and management of office buildings and shopping centers. A large, multi-tenant office building will have operating characteristics which differ greatly from a small or special-purpose building. Design and marketing require sensitivity to the needs of the different tenants involved. For example, the high value which tenants place on face-to-face contact with other office functions is important in negotiating an appropriate lease. Appendix C contains some recent research findings on this point.

The size of a shopping center must be suited to the type of customers who have access to the center by major roads. The type of leading tenant, i.e., the one which best attracts customers, is also a function of access by different population segments. The internal structure of the shopping center, both design and tenant mix, is another area requiring extensive specialized expertise. The negotiation of a lease requires knowledge of the various lease arrangements and of competitive market conditions affecting lease terms.

QUESTIONS

1. In real estate circles, a triple net lease is sometimes called a "net lease." What is a net lease?
2. In an inflationary environment, landlords are more and more interested in the terms of percentage leases.
   (a) What are the most important terms in those leases?
   (b) Why are they particularly important during inflation?
3. Discuss two characteristics of investments in shopping centers and office buildings which make them particularly attractive to insurance companies and similar investors seeking preservation of capital over long periods.

4. If you had unlimited capital to invest in an office building, would you look for one of 600,000 square feet or one of 100,000 square feet? Why?

5. For shopping centers:
   (a) What is the difference between a neighborhood center and a community center?
   (b) A community center and a regional center?
   (c) A regional center and a superregional center?

6. The developer of a shopping center must make difficult decisions about the appropriate tenant mix. What, in your opinion, are the two key factors in the decision?

13

APARTMENT BUILDINGS

Individuals often get involved in the ownership and rental of apartments, with the extent of involvement ranging from renting a converted attic to owning and renting structures housing 50 or more families. Even individuals who start with little capital can hope to save enough to acquire small income-producing properties; by reinvesting earnings they can build up a substantial capital investment which provides a comfortable living. Historically, immigrants to the United States have found that apartment ownership provides an opportunity to acquire a stake in the economy, to establish an independent business, and to secure an adequate income stream.

Individuals investing in apartments are competing against a variety of professional investors. Most formidably, the investors include governments (federal, state, and local) which can use tax money to subsidize the public housing tenant. Insurance companies also own and operate apartments, usually through an agent such as a real estate broker or developer. The broker or developer has an experienced full-time staff devoted to improving the performance of the apartment buildings. These professionals may have an ownership interest in some of the buildings they manage. For example, they may have formed syndicates, selling shares in the project to other investors and retaining some shares for their own account. We will discuss the role of syndication from the point of view of the individuals who participate in apartment buildings through ownership of shares in the syndicate.

Individuals who hope to compete directly against professional investors need to assess their strengths and weaknesses. They may have an advantage if they confine their investment to a neighborhood where years of residence have provided intimate personal knowledge of the rental market. The extent of this advantage will depend on the individuals' ability to put aside emotional attachments and realistically appraise the future prospects of an investment in apartments.

For most individuals, the greatest weakness will be inability to do financial analysis. To be successful, the individual must acquire some of the sophistication which is possessed by most professionals. This chapter studies sources of financing for apartment buildings in relation to cycles in business activity, a relationship which is studied by the most sophisticated professionals. The chapter turns then to an analysis of the cash flows produced by an apartment building. A technique will be suggested for making an investment decision (deciding how much to pay and what property to invest in) with no outside help from professional appraisers, real estate lawyers, or tax accountants.

Investment in an apartment building shares much in common with investment in any other income-producing property. Therefore, the detailed decision rules discussed here can be applied, with some modification, to other types of property. This chapter is intended to provide an example of how the methods developed in other chapters on property analysis, borrower analysis, and the cost of real estate capital can be realistically applied.

THE AVAILABILITY OF FINANCING

Figure 13–1 demonstrates that mortgages on apartment buildings grew substantially over the decade ended in 1975. In the first quarter of 1975, multifamily mortgage holdings stood at $93 billion, 173 per cent above the level 10 years earlier. This represents an annual growth rate of 10.6 per cent. During the same period, the holdings of other mortgages, not on multifamily property, grew at an average annual rate of only 7.6 per cent. Therefore, mortgages on apartment buildings grew from 14.5 to 18.2 per cent of all mortgages outstanding. Appendix Table A–5 gives more detail on the data used to plot Figure 13–1.

Demographic changes account for the rapid growth in multifamily mortgages during this decade. This was the decade when the bumper crop of postwar babies became young adults, in an age when apartment living offers a number of advantages. Young adults have not yet had a chance to accumulate the capital needed to purchase a single-family home, and typically they have not settled on a permanent place of residence. Thus, even if the capital were available for a house, the young adult may prefer to be free to move at fairly short notice.

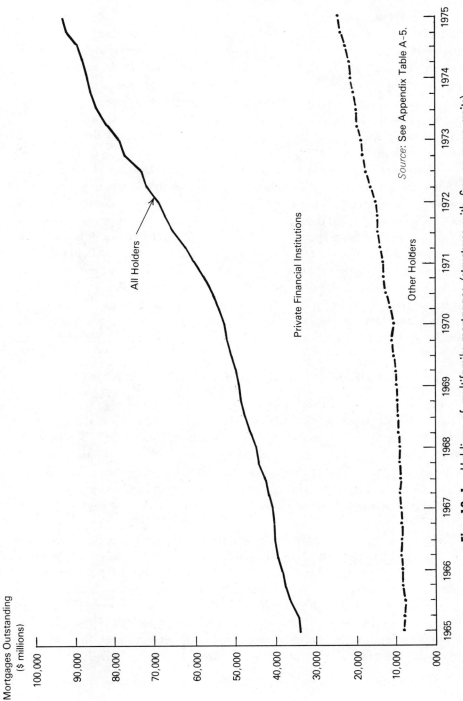

Mortgages Outstanding
($ millions)

All Holders

Private Financial Institutions

Other Holders

Source: See Appendix Table A-5.

Fig. 13–1. Holdings of multifamily mortgages (structures with five or more units).

The continuing trend toward urbanization also contributed to the growth of multifamily mortgages. Urbanization is measured by the percentage of the total population residing in urban areas. This percentage grew from 70 per cent in 1960 to 73.5 per cent in 1970.[1] Since 1970, the urbanized population has remained around 74 per cent. In urban areas, where land is scarce, apartment living is necessary for a large percentage of the population. Tenants of urban apartments are likely to live in buildings with five or more units, whereas nonurban renters are more likely to be in a converted house.

Where would an investor in apartment buildings go to find a mortgage? Figure 13–1 indicates that most of the growth in multifamily mortgages was provided by private financial institutions, not by other holders. The bulk of the lending during the period (loan extensions less repayments) came from savings and loan associations and from life insurance companies, while commercial banks and mutual savings banks provided only 24 per cent of the net lending on apartments. For savings and loans, the aggressive acquisition of mortgages on multifamily properties came about as a result of their location in areas experiencing rapid population growth. This enabled savings and loans to replace mutual savings banks as the most important holder of multifamily mortgages (see Appendix Tables A–1 through A–3).

MULTIFAMILY HOUSING STARTS AND LENDING

Figure 13–2 shows that multifamily mortgage lending closely parallels multifamily housing starts. In this respect the financing of apartments is very similar to the financing of single-family housing (see Chapter 21). When the market for housing (multifamily or single-family) declines, the suppliers of funds reduce their lending. The important point here is that declines in multifamily housing starts, which represent only new apartments, are paralleled by declines in lending on both new and old apartments.

Mortgage lending and housing starts are both related to cycles in business activity and interest rates (see Chapter 21). The relationship to the business cycle is confirmed by Figure 13–2. During periods of recovery in the general level of economic activity, all sectors of the economy begin competing to borrow money. Eventually this drives interest rates up. But the cost of housing is heavily dependent on the cost of mortgage money. Furthermore, high interest rates cause the disintermediation of mortgage lenders, as detailed in Chapter 9. Therefore, relatively high interest rates

[1] James Heilbrun, *Urban Economics and Public Policy* (St. Martin's Press, 1974), p. 27.

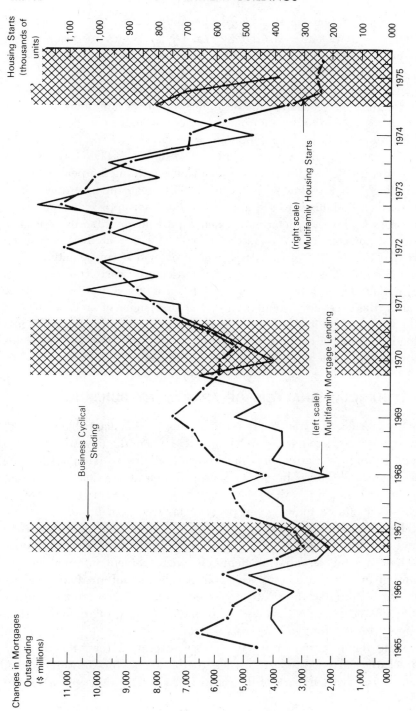

Source: See Appendix Table A–5.

Fig. 13–2. Multifamily mortgage lending and multifamily housing starts.

cause lending and housing starts to decline long before the general level of economic activity (as measured by real GNP) begins to decline.

The multifamily sector of the housing market, like the single-family sector, is frequently subjected to long periods of declining activity. This declining volume of trading activity, including trading of existing multifamily structures, is reflected in the declining volume of mortgages in Figure 13–2. It is reasonable to assume that the prices of apartment buildings are not rising rapidly during these periods of decline; indeed, they may be declining relative to the prices of other investments. Therefore, the investor in apartment buildings should avoid purchases at the peak in mortgage lending. An investment at the peak will mean an investment in a building which is difficult to sell and which does not appreciate rapidly.

How does an investor determine when a peak in multifamily mortgage lending and housing starts has been reached? A crude method is to keep a chart like Figure 13–2 up to date. The peak will occur sometime after a recession ends. The investor should be particularly wary if an expansion in the market for multifamily structures has continued for two years or more after the recession trough. Also, the first signs of a downturn in starts or lending activity should make an investor cautious. It may signal an extended period of decline, and a purchase just after the decline begins is almost as bad as a purchase just before the peak.

FINANCIAL ANALYSIS OF APARTMENT BUILDINGS

The investor needs a framework for analyzing the financial characteristics of properties considered for purchase. Even when the investment is to be made through a partnership or syndication, the individual investors should protect themselves by taking a critical look at the financial characteristics of the property. Many investors have regretted a plunge into a syndicate that offered glowing prospects of tax-free cash flows.

The keys to sound financial analysis are (1) to collect the appropriate data and (2) to arrange and manipulate the data to give useful information. These are the essential elements of a management information system through which the investor can collect relevant information to allow comparison of alternate investment projects. Many realty groups provide formats for data gathering, analysis, and manipulation. Figure 13–3 offers a composite format for the most useful data.

Since the rental income is derived from several sources, the investor should ask the current property owner, or the agent, for the information outlined in the bottom part of Figure 13–3(a). The description of the apartment should include number of square feet, number of rooms, number of bedrooms, type of drapes and carpeting, number of baths, the presence of a dishwasher, furniture, or fireplace, etc. The prospective investor should then visit tenants to ask how much it costs to rent and to get a first-hand impression of the number and ages of the renting families. Finally, the investor can determine from gas and electric meters whether the vacancy estimate is realistic. The seller will want to exaggerate the value of the building, which can be done without outright falsification of information. The market for apartment buildings (or any income-producing property) is tricky, so the investor must follow the basic rule of *caveat emptor:* Let the buyer beware.

The information at the bottom of Figure 13–3(a) launches the investor into an analysis of the financial characteristics of the property. Large variations in rental per square foot may signal that something is wrong. Some units may be badly located. Others may be occupied by friends or relatives of the present owner. Some tenants may be willing to pay unusually high rent for a few months because they plan to move. However, the analysis of square-foot rental must be tempered by reference to the description of the apartment. Renters pay for balconies, high floors, and other characteristics of apartments, so there may well be some variation in square-foot rental.

The number and ages of occupants tell the investor something about the future rental and operating cost situation. Children cause high maintenance expenses, whereas the elderly place little stress on a building. On the other hand, families with children may be willing and able to pay high rents whereas the elderly may not. The dates of lease expiration indicate how quickly the tenant mix is likely to change.

The data required by Figure 13–3(b) must be obtained from the seller of the building, but most information is surprisingly easy to verify. Revenues from laundry machines can't be very large and the cleaning fee is usually standard, with the total amount collected depending only on the turnover of the apartments.[2] The operating expenses can be verified by examination of ledgers and cancelled checks. In addition, the ratio of operating expenses to income is usually fairly predictable. In Figure 13–3(b), item 17 should usually be 45 to 55 per cent of item 6. Finally, the investor should be aware of possible omissions in the operating ex-

---

[2] By asking the amount of cleaning fees collected, the purchaser gets valuable information on the number of new leases signed in a year. This may indicate (1) unusually high turnover (transient tenants), or (2) recent difficulty in leasing apartments (low turnover and high vacancy).

(a) Description of Property and Rental Income

Date:

Address:

Asking price:

Number of units: Age of structure:

Number of square feet of rentable space:

Zoning in immediate area: In adjacent area:

Type of financing: Amount which can be borrowed:

                                     Loan-to-value ratio:

                                     Interest rate:

                                     Month and year of loan maturity:

                                     Monthly payment:

Description of building amenities (lobby, elevator, pool, brick facing, yard, etc.)

Description of neighborhood (types of buildings, income level, age composition, occupations, trends in income level, access to transportation, noise from freeway or airport, cleanliness of streets, access to shopping, amount of vandalism, other types of crime, etc.)

Derivation of rental income:

Apartment Number	Description of Apartment (include no. of sq. feet)	Monthly Rent $ $ per sq. ft.	Occupant Description (Number and Ages)	Lease Expiration

Total rental income: Monthly _____ Annual _____ Vacancy Loss _____

Fig. 13–3. Suggested format for financial analysis of a multifamily property.

(b) Schedule of Financial Characteristics of the Property

| | Properties Compared | | | |
Date:	A	B	C	Comments

1. Asking price

Cash Inflow (Revenue)

2. Apt. rental [(a) for each prop.]
3. Laundry machines
4. Cleaning fee
5. Less: Vacancy and collection losses
6. Total operating income
7. Gross income multiplier (1 ÷ 6)

Operating Expenses

8. Property taxes
9. Management
10. Payroll
11. Utilities
12. Replacement reserve
13. Insurance
14. Trash removal
15. Pest control
16. Other (list)
17. Total operating expenses
Line 17 as a percentage of income, line 6

Federal Tax Analysis

18. Depreciation
19. Interest expense (first year)
20. All deductible expenses
    (lines 17 + 18 + 19)
21. Federal taxable income (est.)
    (6 − 20)
22. Estimated taxes (shelter)

Investment Decision Information

23. Net cash flow before financing
    (line 6 − 17 − 22)
24. Return on investment (23 ÷ 1)
25. Debt service (principal and interest)
26. Spendable cash flow (23 − 25)
27. Equity investment (first year)
28. Return on equity (26 ÷ 27)
    (Spendable return to investor)

Fig. 13–3. Continued.

penses as provided by the seller. The omission of replacement reserves, trash removal, and pest control could result in a reduction of five percentage points in the ratio of operating expenses to income.

Depreciation and interest expenses (items 18 and 19) are determined by the buyer and the buyer's tax accountant and banker. Note that the calculation of federal income tax is a crude approximation for the purposes of making an investment decision. It is no substitute for consultation with a tax accountant, who may be able to suggest numerous deductions and credits which are not shown in the illustration.

To arrive at an investment decision, the investor should calculate two tables similar to the one shown in Figure 13–3(b). One table would have actual figures on revenues and expenses; the other would have scheduled (i.e., anticipated) figures. The goal would be to try to turn a building around by lowering expenses or raising rental income. The investor would then have a chance of getting good capital gains. When acquired, the building was doing poorly; by improving its return on investment, the investor raises the future sales price.

When dealing with anticipated revenues and expenses, investors must be aware that they are on uncertain ground. It may take years to turn a building around, and the task may prove to be impossible. Therefore, the investor should look for reasonably good current performance (the actual revenues and expenses) as well as future opportunities.

The first step toward an investment decision comes from looking at item 7 in Figure 13–3(b), the gross income multiplier (GIM). A low multiplier is desirable, although one which is extremely low may indicate a property with serious problems. In a given local market for apartment buildings, the typical multiplier becomes widely known, so buildings which have a slightly lower multiplier are eagerly sought by investors. Typical multipliers in most parts of the United States used to run between 6 and 10; with inflation and competition for investment opportunities, multipliers of 10 to 15 were not uncommon in the early 1970's.

The gross income multiplier is a useful guide to investment decisions, provided that expenses, including income tax, are a constant percentage of gross income. However, the expense ratio for buildings will differ because of building age, tenant mix, or many other factors. Therefore, a more thorough investment decision focuses on items 24 and 26.

In the industry, item 24 is called the "cap rate," although the usual cap rate omits federal income tax considerations. A property which has a high after-tax return on the total investment (equity plus mortgage loan) is desirable. Therefore, the investor should lean heavily toward purchase of the property with the highest rate of return on investment (item 24). However, this should be qualified by several considerations, including the size of the numbers in item 26, overall cash flow. If the overall cash flow is negative (or only slightly positive), the investor may have to put additional cash into the property in future years. If so, the investor must try to determine whether the cash will be available and whether the additional investment will yield a reasonable return. In general, a property which will carry itself (in terms of cash flow) is highly desirable, even if this means lower tax shelter. Many syndicates have invested in properties which offer a sound tax shelter but no margin of safety on cash flows. In this situation, increases in expenses or declines in income result in negative cash flows. This, in turn, results in mortgage foreclosure or calls to the investors for additional cash.

The return on equity (item 28) should be compared with the return on investment (item 24).[3] If item 28 is lower than item 24, it means that the return to the equity investor is less than the return to the mortgagee; i.e., the bank is earning a higher rate of interest on its investment than is being earned on the owner's investment. This situation is called "negative leverage," since the rate of return to the owner could be increased by reducing the amount of the mortgage. In other words, the usual advantage of carrying debt (the rate of return to the investor increases as the amount of debt increases) is not available when negative leverage is present. In most cases, negative leverage should be avoided.

Negative leverage is usually caused by high levels of long-term interest rates associated with an expansion in the general level of business activity. For an apartment building, it is not unusual for interest expense to be 30 to 50 per cent of gross income. (For other types of real estate investments, interest expense may be even higher as a percentage of income.) Thus, small increases in mortgage interest rates have a dramatic effect on the cash which flows into the investor's pocket (item 26). In fact, negative leverage will usually coincide with peaks in the activity in the market for multifamily structures. Thus, negative leverage—or a small amount of positive leverage, as evidenced by a cap rate (item 24) which is only a little greater than the interest rate on the mortgage—is a signal that a difficult period is ahead for apartment buildings.

USING CAUTION IN FINANCIAL ANALYSIS

The financial analysis which we have suggested in our discussion of Figure 13–3 does not automatically give correct answers. It is simplified in a number of respects so that an investor who is aware of the basic

[3] The spendable return on equity for apartment buildings typically runs between 8 and 14 per cent for reasonably successful investments. In deteriorating neighborhoods, returns can drop toward zero, perhaps leading to the abandonment of the property.

principles can avoid serious mistakes. Two important factors have not entered into our analysis: the age of the structure and the future of the neighborhood. When actual data are used in Figure 13–3(a), the analysis centers on the performance of the building in the first year after purchase. It may well be asked, "What happens after the first year?"

When an old apartment building is involved, the outlook for rents may not be as promising as for a newer building. In an inflationary economy, few prices decline, but rents on an older building may not rise as fast as those on a newer building. Therefore, net income may be squeezed. Or, major repairs may be required in heating, plumbing, electrical wiring, and roofing. These costly repairs to the older building would definitely depress the investors' net return.

The future of the neighborhood can have an even greater impact on the value of an apartment building. Actual declines in property values, a catastrophe in an inflationary economy, frequently occur at the neighborhood level. This is the reason for including a detailed description of the neighborhood in Figure 13–3(a). The investor who is aware of potential problems will construct a table of scheduled (i.e., anticipated) future income and expenditure which reflects neighborhood factors. Thus, a building which looks good in terms of current revenues and expenses may show up as a bad investment when the future of the neighborhood is considered.

The financial analysis suggested by Figure 13–3(b) does not substitute for a professional valuation of the property. An appraiser should do a complete analysis of the net present value of the property after considering the future prospects of the neighborhood, the age of the building, and projections beyond the first year for net cash flow (item 23). Furthermore, net present value analysis allows for the investor's equity build-up (beyond the first year) as the mortgage is paid off. With the equity build-up and changes in cash flow, the overall rate of return on equity investment (item 28) will be changed.

On the other hand, an appraisal does not substitute for the financial analysis suggested by Figure 13–3(b). For most investors, appraisals would be too expensive to conduct for all buildings which are possible investments. Also, the appraiser may not tell the investor about potential cash flow problems. The appraiser is skilled in estimating market value, not in considering all of the ramifications of an investment from the individual investor's point of view.

A professional appraiser usually does not consider the possibility of turning a building around. The appraiser has to consider the facts, not speculation about what a skilled manager can do with the apartment building. Therefore, the potential investor should develop scheduled (i.e., anticipated) financial characteristics along the lines suggested in Figure 13–3(b). This is the best way to look into the future of the property under the assumption that the investor has control of the property.

SYNDICATION OF INVESTMENTS IN APARTMENT BUILDINGS

A syndicate is formed when two or more people share in an unincorporated investment. A syndicate may begin when a broker, lawyer, accountant, or other professional involved with real estate sees an attractive deal in an apartment building.[4] If the professional does not have enough cash to make the purchase, participations can be offered to clients. The real estate professional will be the active party to the syndicate, planning and operating the investment. Usually, the clients will be passive participants, i.e., they will put up capital but they will not participate directly in the operation of the project. The professional is the general partner; the clients are limited partners. The general partner may put some cash into the project; full share may be received in return for a partial payment.

Syndicates offer passive investors the advantages of "flow-through accounting." In terms of Figure 13–3(b), the syndicate need not pay federal income taxes; item 22 is avoided, whereas a corporation would have to pay any taxes due (item 22). Any taxable income or tax shelter from item 21 is passed directly to investors by the syndicate. Thus, each investor pays income taxes (or receives shelter) on his or her portion of the total shown as item 21. (This assumes a non-recourse mortgage; i.e., the lender relies entirely on the property.) The double taxation applied to corporations (profits are taxed before dividends are paid, then dividends are taxed as income to each recipient) is avoided.

The syndicate offers many other advantages to investors. Foremost is the spendable cash flow (item 26), which is distributed regularly to investors. It is possible that the investor will receive spendable cash, perhaps 6 to 15 per cent of the investment, and still owe little income tax. The major tax shield is accelerated depreciation, but this only delays taxation and converts the tax into a capital gains tax. (See Chapter 7.) When the property is sold, the investors pay tax on the difference between the sale price and the original cost less depreciation, and some of the tax is at the rate for capital gains. This is a valuable tax shield, despite the ability of the IRS to recapture depreciation in excess of straight-line (i.e., tax it at ordinary income rates).

---

[4] Since syndicates take many forms, it is oversimplified to think only in terms of a professional and clients. For example, REITs and joint tenancies are forms of syndicates.

Investors in a syndicate receive two other advantages. One is the ability to combine their capital with that of others to invest in a larger property than would otherwise be available. The other is professional management. The cost of legal services, accounting, and management will be a smaller percentage of the revenues from the large syndicated investment than for the smaller investment that the individual investor could afford.

Unscrupulous operators (active or general partners) are the principal danger involved in joining a syndicate. In fact, the syndicate may not begin with a good investment as described above. It may begin with a salesperson who seeks out contacts with people who will listen to tales of large tax shelters and heavy cash flows. The syndicators may not be motivated to find a good investment, since they have little or no capital invested in the project and they are compensated by a fee. Their fees are already collected by the time the syndicate turns its belly up.

Investors should protect themselves by dealing only with professionals with whom a bona fide client relationship has been established. Also, it is wise to see that the syndicate is formed so that (1) the active partner cannot get personal loans from the syndicate, (2) the passive partners can vote on sale of assets, replacement of the active partner, and other important matters, and (3) the active partner has "a piece of the action" as an incentive to make careful, prudent business decisions. The active partner should have some cash in the project and any compensation arrangements should be tied directly to the long-term performance of the project.

The best way to keep the active partner interested in the performance of the property is to tie compensation to capital appreciation. Thus, it is wise to get involved in deals where the active partner gets a relatively small fee and a relatively small portion of the spendable return but a relatively large portion of the appreciation of the property when it is sold. This gives the active partner an interest in buying a property which is a good investment. For example, a property which can be made to produce larger cash flows and larger return on investment would be attractive to a general partner whose compensation depends to a large extent on capital appreciation. In contrast, an active partner whose compensation depends largely on fees will have few regrets if foreclosure is the eventual outcome.

SUMMARY

The investor considering an income-producing property such as an apartment building should be keenly aware of changes in long-term interest rates and in the general level of economic activity. A purchase at the wrong time, when interest rates are high, can lead to an investment which performs poorly. The wrong time is signaled by high and rising levels of multifamily mortgage lending and multifamily housing starts, as well as high interest rates.

The investor should perform a financial analysis on each property which is a prospective purchase. An appropriate format for the analysis is suggested in the chapter. It is important to investigate prospective future earnings and expenses as well as current earnings and expenses. This forces the investor to consider: (1) the age of the property, (2) the possibility of turning the property around by increasing income or decreasing expenses, and (3) the future of the neighborhood. It may also indicate unusually high interest rates, since negative leverage may show up. Negative leverage indicates that the purchase is being considered at the wrong point in the business cycle or that the building is overpriced relative to other investments.

The investor seeking opportunities in apartment buildings may consider participating in a syndicate. This offers tax advantages, enables the investor to participate in a large project, and provides professional legal, managerial, and accounting services. However, the investor should deal only with trusted professionals and should retain substantial voting rights. It is a good idea to have the compensation of the active partner depend heavily on the capital appreciation realized when the project is eventually sold. This makes the active partner anxious to avoid foreclosure.

QUESTIONS

1. Mortgage lending on multifamily structures was a growing business during the 1965–1975 decade.
   (a) What factors contributed to this?
   (b) Would you expect this to continue in the future?
2. How would a forecast of real GNP help to make a decision whether to lend on or invest in multifamily structures?
3. Suppose that you have just purchased an apartment building which has been losing money under its previous owner.
   (a) What parts of Figure 13–3(b) would you concentrate on as you try to turn the building around?
   (b) How would Figure 13–3(b) help you to make a decision about the best thing to do?
   (c) Would it be desirable to contact outside specialists?
4. What are the principal advantages which syndication offers to investors?

14

INDUSTRIAL AND SPECIAL-PURPOSE PROPERTY

The risk associated with a mortgage secured by special-purpose property can be very high. Land which has been adapted to a special-purpose use may be difficult to convert to another use, so the lender must be keenly aware of the many factors which bear on the success or failure of the special-purpose activity. This difficult task may involve technical expertise not possessed by most lending institutions.

Not all industrial property is adapted to special purposes. Light manufacturing, for example, may require little more than a large expanse of floor area furnished with workbenches and small machines. In this case, the building could be adapted to a number of manufacturing activities. Transfer and warehousing operations often have similar characteristics, since the property usually consists of little more than a loading dock, some space for office workers, and storage space. With this type of general-purpose property, the lender has the security of knowing that a fairly broad market exists for the property. If the borrower's business turns sour, causing a default in the mortgage, there may be another line of business for which the property will be useful. The lender has a chance to recover an investment through sale of the property; it offers real security for the loan.

Special-purpose property does not offer the lender the same type of security; if the borrower's business turns sour, it is unlikely that another business will pay much for the property. Thus, the property has little value as security for a loan. This is why mortgage loans often are not made on special-purpose properties. Instead, loans (but probably not mortgage loans) are based on the credit worthiness of the borrower. Borrower analysis becomes more important than property analysis.

How does the lender evaluate the borrower? By drawing upon principles of marketing, accounting, and corporate finance. If a product is going to be manufactured on the property, the market for that product should be analyzed. The financial strength of the company as reflected in available financial statements should also be scrutinized. Finally, specific investment plans are important, even when the investment is to be financed by an issue of stocks or bonds. Purchasers of stocks and bonds participate in the success or failure of the entire operation, but that can depend heavily on major investment plans. Certainly an unsecured bank loan to finance investment in special-purpose property would depend on careful review of the investment plans.

To deal knowledgeably with special-purpose properties, courses in marketing, accounting, and corporate finance are required. This is not the place to try to summarize those large subjects. However, we will contrast corporate finance to real estate finance so that the reader who knows some corporate finance can see the relationships between them. We will also discuss some principles which are useful in evaluating a location and property for industrial or special-purpose use.

INDUSTRIAL BORROWER ANALYSIS: CORPORATE FINANCE vs. REAL ESTATE FINANCE [1]

The theory of corporate finance includes a number of techniques for evaluating a corporation as an ongoing business. All of the activities of the corporation are grouped together so that they can be analyzed in terms of their impact on the financial health of the business. Real estate finance, on the other hand, focuses much more narrowly on the analysis of the individual borrower and the specific piece of property.

In practice, the application of corporate finance overlaps and interacts with the application of real estate finance. A corporation considering an investment in real estate—e.g., an insurance company which holds real estate as well as stocks and bonds—should have experts in real estate finance. These experts can put together an analysis of the location and property and an appraisal of the property value. If a mortgage were

[1] Readers with limited background in corporate finance should consult a basic text for definition and discussion of terms in this section. See, for example, Elvin F. Donaldson, John K. Pfahl, and Peter L. Mullins, *Corporate Finance* (4th ed.; New York: The Ronald Press Co., 1975).

desired, they can go to the appropriate sources of mortgage funds.

In real estate finance, the area of borrower analysis overlaps with corporate finance. When the borrower is a corporation, the techniques of borrower analysis include ratio analysis and cash flow analysis, which are methods of evaluating a corporation as an ongoing business. These techniques should be employed for industrial borrower analysis. The full and proper use of techniques from corporate finance is important because the industrial borrower is much more important than the industrial property, especially when a special-purpose property is involved.

The techniques of industrial borrower analysis will include the calculation of balance sheet and income statement ratios. Current assets to current liabilities, debt to total assets, sales divided by inventories, and profits divided by sales are some of the most important ratios. In analyzing the ratios, allowances must be made for peculiarities in the firm's accounting system. Furthermore, the ratios for the individual firm should be compared to industry averages. When used in this way—augmented, perhaps, by analysis of past and projected future trends in the ratios—ratio analysis can provide a powerful tool for indicating potential sources of trouble in the operations or financing of the company.

Ratio analysis can be supplemented with various financial forecasts for the company. The anticipated sources and uses of funds follow from projected balance sheets and income statements. Attempts to project the cash flows from all of the company's operations can indicate whether cash shortages will develop. A lender is vitally concerned with receiving advance warning of such shortages, since inability to meet debt payments may result.

Other techniques from corporate finance, such as breakeven and net present value analysis, are important in the evaluation of specific investment projects. We turn, therefore, to a detailed comparison of corporate finance and real estate finance in the context of a decision on alternative investment projects.

An Investment in Machines vs. an Investment in Plant. A typical problem in corporate finance is to evaluate an investment in machine A against an investment in machine B. The machines do the same job (the investments are said to be "mutually exclusive") but the operating costs and productivity of the two are different. An approved technique for making the investment decision is to compare the net present value of cash flows (cash inflows produced by the machine less after-tax cash outlays, including initial outlays) for the two investments. The cash flows should be discounted at the cost of capital, a weighted average of the after-tax rates of return which must be offered to holders of equity and debt.

Similar techniques can be used to evaluate alternate investments in industrial property; two different locations or different types of plants on a given location can be evaluated with net present value techniques. However, there are some important modifications of the usual net present value techniques when a real estate investment is being considered. One difference is that the investment in plant requires knowledge of the location. The factors which contribute to a good industrial location will be discussed in a separate section below.

Since the plant is permanently attached to land, both must be valued. This makes the analysis of the investment in industrial real property more difficult than the analysis of an investment in machines. The land does not physically depreciate, whereas the building is a wasting asset. Thus, the two parts of the investment may be handled separately, through land residual or building residual techniques.

Another important difference is that the terms of a mortgage loan may be tied to the property and its location. The quality of the property, as perceived by lenders, has an influence on the cost of borrowing for that particular property. This is presumably a major influence, especially in the case of nonindustrial and general-purpose industrial property. Therefore, real estate appraisers substitute bands of investment calculations for the cost of capital when discounting cash flows.

Bands of Investment vs. Cost of Capital.   In the bands of investment technique, the interest rate on the mortgage is multiplied by the loan-to-value ratio and added to the required rate of return on equity multiplied by the equity-to-value ratio. The sum of these two terms becomes the capitalization rate for discounting cash flows. This capitalization rate is critically dependent on the interest rate and on the loan-to-value ratio for the specific mortgage on the property.

The cost of capital, on the other hand, does not depend on any specific issue of stocks or bonds. It is established by the long-run prospects for future debt and equity issues, combined so as to minimize the cost of capital. These future prospects are determined by the overall operations of the firm as a going concern; they are influenced by current investment plans, but they do not depend wholly on investment plans.

Why do real estate appraisers rely on the bands of investment technique whereas financial analysts use the more general concept of cost of capital? No satisfactory answer can be found in the literature of either finance or

appraisal. There is little communication between the two bodies of literature, even though they deal with similar problems. Perhaps both sides
should take a closer look at their methods.

There are cases where the cost of capital is obviously superior to the
bands of investment.[2] Suppose that an appraiser is valuing a shopping
center for an insurance company. The shopping center is currently mort-
gaged, but the insurance company wants to acquire it free and clear.
Clearly, the cash flows should be discounted at the cost of capital to the
insurance company. The cost of the mortgage, which is held by another
investor, is irrelevant to the insurance company. The insurance company
is interested only in how much it must pay to raise the funds which will
be invested in the shopping center.

It is more difficult to give an example where the bands of investment
technique is superior to the cost of capital. Such an example would require lenders (as a group) to be influenced exclusively (or nearly exclusively) by the characteristics of the property, not by the characteristics of
the borrower. In this case, that particular property would be associated
with a borrowing cost substantially different from the borrowing cost associated with the mortgagor in the mortgagor's other business (or personal)
pursuits. Thus, the cost of capital associated with that particular property
would be different from the cost of capital associated with other investments being considered by the borrower. The bands of investment technique capitalizes cash flows at the cost of capital for the particular property,
so it would be the correct technique in this case.

The problem with this example is that lenders are *not* influenced exclusively by the property. Lenders don't relish the prospect of having a
mortgage in default; default interrupts their cash flow and makes government regulators nervous (see Chapter 6). Therefore, lenders are very
much concerned about the creditworthiness of the borrower. In the case
of industrial property, particularly special-purpose industrial property, the
concern with borrower analysis is paramount.

In the usual situation where borrower analysis is important, the cost of
capital appears superior to the bands of investment technique.[3] We realize that this is contrary to accepted appraisal practice, but we think that
appraisers should take a hard look at the finance literature on the cost of
capital.

---

[2] We are considering a "simple" cost of capital, i.e., one which is *not* derived from
the capital asset pricing model.

[3] The cost of capital approach also has a superior method of treating taxes. Interest
on debt (e.g., mortgage debt) is tax-deductible, so the cost of capital approach takes
the after-tax cost of debt. The bands of investment method ignores the tax treatment
of interest payments.

PORTFOLIO THEORY

Investors in stocks and bonds have long been familiar with the value of diversification. The literature on corporate finance has developed the theory and measurement of diversified portfolios to a high degree of sophistication. Regression analysis is currently being used by large institutional investors to define portfolios which have desirable risk characteristics. We cannot summarize the vast literature on this subject, but we do want to suggest that some of the basic concepts could be applied profitably by investors in real estate.

Real estate values and rental returns from real estate respond to two forces: (1) systematic changes in general economic conditions (e.g., cycles in business activity and interest rates); and (2) purely local, random, unsystematic factors. A well-diversified portfolio of real estate holdings seeks to eliminate risk which is associated with the unsystematic factors.[4] If real estate holdings are located in different neighborhoods and represent different types of property, the unsystematic movements in real estate values should largely cancel out. If the value of one property decreases because of random factors, it is likely that the value of another property will increase by roughly the same amount over the same period of time. Therefore, the investor with a diversified portfolio is protected against losses from random or local-market changes.

The investor with well-diversified holdings of real estate will receive an average rate of return, and this return will not be as unpredictable as the return on a poorly diversified portfolio. Thus, diversification is an important and powerful tool for reducing the risk associated with real estate. The only risk which a diversified investor has to incur is the risk associated with changes in general economic conditions.

Another basic concept in portfolio theory is the risk–return trade-off. Suppose that an investor plans to hold a well-diversified portfolio. The investor still has a choice as to how much systematic (or undiversifiable) risk to incur.[5] An investor who accepts a high amount of systematic risk holds property which responds strongly (in terms of value) to changes in

[4] Theoretically, the best portfolio is the "market portfolio," a combination of all assets. But, in a world of information costs, different investment opportunities, limited borrowing ability, and nonmarketable assets, each individual or corporation will want to choose its own best portfolio.

[5] This concept comes from the capital asset pricing model (CAPM) from the theory of finance. Statistical work with CAPM has attempted to define an appropriate trade-off between risk and return. This trade-off gives the increase in the rate of return which investors should demand in return for accepting larger systematic (undiversifiable) risk. See J. Fred Weston and Eugene F. Brigham, *Managerial Finance* (5th ed.; Hinsdale, Ill.: The Dryden Press, 1975), pp. 657–81.

the general level of economic activity. A low amount of systematic risk is associated with property values which do not fluctuate as much as the general level of economic activity.

An important concept in portfolio theory is that the rational investor should be compensated for accepting higher systematic risk: a higher rate of return is necessary on a portfolio consisting of more speculative properties. However, the investor should not be compensated for unsystematic risk. That kind of risk can be virtually eliminated through diversification, so there is no reason to be compensated for it.

These concepts from portfolio theory have limited value to the homeowner or the small investor in real estate, since these investors do not have enough money to hold diversified portfolios, although they can diversify through investment in syndicates or REITs. But large institutions may be able to improve the diversification of their real estate holdings and, in addition, to invest in the statistical work necessary to measure the systematic risk associated with a piece of property and define the most profitable trade-off between risk and return.

ANALYSIS OF INDUSTRIAL LOCATION AND PROPERTY

The analysis of location and property will be valuable to a lender when a mortgage loan is to be made on the property. As we indicated at the beginning of this chapter, only general-purpose property has much value as security for a mortgage, so mortgage loans probably will not be made on special-purpose property. However, analysis of the location will be valuable to the investor. Naturally, the investor will want to choose the location and design the buildings so as to maximize profit.[6]

Industry can be viewed as an input–output process in which raw materials, labor, and the activity of machines are transformed into finished goods. The cost of transporting labor, raw materials, and finished goods is important in choosing the maximum-profit location. Often, a location close to sources of raw materials will not be a location close to the market for finished goods. Thus, the industry must decide whether it is better to be near raw materials or markets.

Petroleum refining is usually located near large urban centers which demand gasoline, jet fuel, and other petroleum products even though this involves the shipment of crude petroleum over long distances at enormous expense. Why is the crude oil shipped rather than the refined products? The reason is that the crude can be shipped in bulk in tankers and pipe-

---

[6] Since analysis of the industrial location and property is peripheral to the financing problem, we discuss it briefly.

lines, whereas the numerous products of refinement must be kept separate. They are usually shipped by truck or rail. The shipment of relatively small quantities of refined products to the market is more expensive than the bulk shipment of crude oil, so the refineries locate near markets.

At the end of the nineteenth century and during the early part of the twentieth century, refineries were located near the wells, not near the markets, because markets did not exist for many petroleum products. Kerosene could be sold along with a small amount of grease and lubricating oil, but much of the petroleum was discarded after refinement. Thus, weight was lost during petroleum refining. It would have been too expensive to ship crude petroleum to the market only to discard large amounts of liquid after refinement.

Supplies of power are needed by most industrial activities and some need large amounts of water. Also, no matter where an industrial activity locates, it must be near a labor market that offers an ample supply of workers at various levels of skill. The workers must have access to the plant through a good system of roads connecting the industrial location with residential locations. The property should contain ample parking, with provision for traffic and parking problems associated with a change in shift.

The desire for proximity to labor, power, raw materials, and markets for output must be tempered by the cost of the land. Most industrial activities require a large amount of land for machines and assembly lines. Therefore, they cannot compete for land with activities such as shopping centers and office buildings; industrial activities must accept locations on the periphery of cities. Oil refineries, for example, have located in New Jersey, as near as possible to New York City. If they could disregard land values, they would certainly prefer to be in the city.

Since industrial activities have large amounts of money invested in land and buildings, they are sensitive to local property taxes. The locating firm is interested in the tax bill which it must pay, not in the tax rate which is levied on assessed valuation. It is difficult to estimate the tax bill in advance because the practices of local tax assessors vary from one area to another. Furthermore, the locating industry has to worry about future inflation in the tax bill; this inflation often occurs through increases in assessed valuation rather than through the more overt method of increased tax rates.

The design of industrial property is best left to experts in industrial design. However, it is important to keep the firm's engineers in touch with the industrial designers. If the engineers are planning changes in the methods of production, the designers may have to revise their standard plans. Designers often develop a habit of recommending standard layouts that have worked in the past, and it may be difficult to make them think in terms of a new idea. The problem may be compounded by the communication barriers that exist between designers and engineers. The intervention of a manager who speaks the language of neither designer nor engineer, but who should have an appreciation for the thinking of both, may be required.

SUMMARY

Some industrial property is general-purpose. If one business should fail at the location, another may find the property valuable. This property has value as collateral for a loan, since the lender who receives the property through default may be able to sell it to another business. Special-purpose property, on the other hand, does not have much value as collateral for a loan. Therefore, analysis of the creditworthiness of the borrower is much more important than property analysis where special-purpose property is concerned.

When the borrower is a corporation, the analysis of the creditworthiness of the borrower involves a number of techniques derived from corporate finance and, to a lesser extent, accounting and marketing. These techniques include ratio analysis, cash flow projections, and projections on financial statements.

Corporate finance differs from real estate finance in several respects. Real estate finance has developed special techniques for valuing the two elements of property—land, which does not physically depreciate, and the building, which is a wasting asset. Beyond that, real estate finance deals with the institutions, public and private, which are involved in supplying debt and equity funds for the purchase of real property.

Corporate finance capitalizes cash flows with the cost of capital, a weighted average of the long-run optimal mixture of debt and equity. Real estate finance, on the other hand, capitalizes cash flows with a rate which depends on the specific terms of the mortgage associated with the particular piece of property. It is difficult to tell whether this is the correct approach. Real estate appraisers should take a hard look at their methods of choosing capitalization rates.

Corporate finance has developed sophisticated theoretical and statistical techniques for choosing the best portfolio of stocks and bonds.[7] It is unrealistic to expect that these techniques will be adopted in the near future by professionals involved with real estate finance. However, the general concepts can be useful. Investors in real estate should attempt to diversify

---

[7] We reiterate that real-world considerations imply that the composition of the optimal portfolio differs from one individual (or corporation) to another.

their holdings so that (1) unsystematic, random changes in value will cancel out, and (2) the amount of systematic risk remaining is adequately compensated by the yield on the portfolio, with higher systematic risk demanding a higher yield. These concepts can guide real estate investors toward controlling the amount of risk associated with their investments.

Location and property analysis is important primarily for investments in general-purpose industrial property. A number of factors should be considered, including access to raw materials and labor, access to markets, availability of power or water, land values, and property taxes. The main objective of locational analysis is to choose the location which will maximize the profits of the firm.

QUESTIONS

1. In Chapters 10 and 11 we discussed the analysis of the borrower and the property for the purposes of mortgage lending. The problem to be solved by the mortgage lender is similar to the problem faced by the commercial banker making a secured loan (e.g., secured by inventory) to a corporation. The commercial banker might use cash flow and ratio analysis.
   (a) In what ways are the elements of cash flow and ratio analysis reflected in Chapters 10 and 11?
   (b) Do the corporate finance techniques of cash flow and ratio analysis suggest improvements which might be made in borrower and property analysis?
   (c) Is it necessary for borrower and property analysis to differ from corporate finance techniques in specific ways? Enumerate and discuss some necessary differences.
2. Discuss two ways in which the bands of investment approach differs from the cost of capital.
3. The concepts of portfolio theory may be applied to real estate investment decision making.
   (a) What are some possible applications which do not require any statistical work to calculate betas or other values?
   (b) Would it be possible to use existing data and charts to implement the concepts of portfolio theory at small cost?
   (c) What is your prognosis for a full-scale statistical study to measure betas for different types of property?
4. Evaluation of an existing or potential location can be an important part of real estate investment decision making. List several important factors which have a bearing on the typical location decision.
5. Do you think that Coca-Cola should locate its bottling plants near markets, raw materials, or labor? Why? Where should manufacturers of steel locate their plants?

15

CONSTRUCTION FINANCING

A construction loan is made for the purpose of constructing improvements on real property. The proceeds of the loan are dispersed during the period of construction, and at the end of the construction period the loan is either converted to a long-term mortgage loan or a new loan is created which provides for long-term financing. The lender must evaluate the quality of the proposed construction, see that payments are made to the builder only as the work is completed, and be sure that the amounts do not exceed the actual values of the materials, labor, and land which are existent in the property.

SOURCES OF CONSTRUCTION LOANS

Since a construction loan is outstanding for a short period of time, the institutions which make construction loans are typically different from the institutions which make loans to the permanent investor or occupant. The pie chart in Figure 15–1 indicates the primary sources of construction financing. The thrift institutions are much less important in construction financing (26 per cent of the total) than they are in permanent financing (47 per cent of the total). On the other hand, commercial banks are more important in construction financing (37 per cent of the total) than in permanent financing (19 per cent of the total).

The different degrees of specialization in construction financing are related to the asset and liability structure of lenders. As we pointed out in Chapter 4, commercial banks have a large percentage of their liabilities in demand deposits which can be withdrawn without notice. Furthermore, commercial banks have long specialized in short-term loans for business purposes. Therefore, by structure and tradition, commercial banks are well suited to the short-term construction loan.

Figure 15–1 indicates the importance of real estate investment trusts (REITs) and mortgage banks in construction loans. REITs have 38 per cent of their assets in construction loans, much more than other financial institutions. Thus, they are really the specialists in this type of loan. Construction loans are well suited to their liabilities, which consist largely of commercial paper and commercial bank loans, both with typical maturities of less than one year.

Mortgage banks, like REITs, depend on commercial bank loans for most of their loanable funds. In Chapter 5 we explained how they make permanent loans to sell rather than to hold. But mortgage banks can hold construction loans since their short maturity does not tie up money. Thus, mortgage banks, which are insignificant as holders of permanent mortgages, hold almost 13 per cent of construction loans (Figure 15–1).

The picture is a little different for residential versus nonresidential construction financing. REITs specialize more in commercial construction (25 per cent of the total) than in residential construction (17 per cent of the total). This is consistent with the general emphasis which REITs give to nonresidential property. Similarly, the residential emphasis of the mortgage banking business is reflected in their construction loans: they have 16 per cent of the construction loans made for residential purposes but only 6 per cent of the loans made for nonresidential purposes. For commercial banks (non-residential emphasis) the corresponding figures are 32 per cent and 50 per cent, whereas for savings and loans (residential emphasis) the figures are 27 per cent and 14 per cent.

Lenders emphasizing residential construction have a much larger market within which to work. About 56 per cent of all private construction is for residential purposes, but a much larger part of all construction lending, about 73 per cent, is for residential purposes. There are two reasons for this. First, there is a broad market for residential property, so it makes good collateral for construction loans. This would not be true of special-purpose industrial property (see Chapter 14). Second, residential construction is usually undertaken by small developers or contractors. They cannot rely on unsecured loans, such as commercial lines of credit or commercial paper, for much of their funding. The larger builders which are more prevalent in nonresidential construction—for example, Diesel, Fuller, Tishman, Uris, Ajax and McShane—can use a certain amount of unsecured credit.

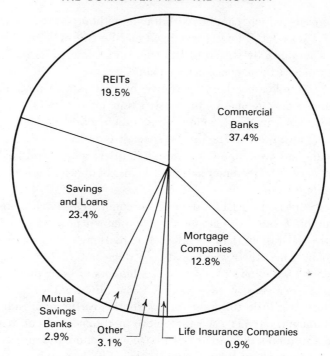

Total dollar amount outstanding = $45,725 million

Source: *The REIT Fact Book 1974* (Washington, D.C.: National Association of Real Estate Investment Trusts), p. 35.

Fig. 15–1. Construction loans outstanding at year end 1973.

ELEMENTS OF CONSTRUCTION LENDING

Since the lender must agree to make a loan before there are any improvements on the vacant land, a set of plans and specifications will be required, to show exactly what is to be placed on the land. If the lender is prepared to exercise firm controls and careful checking of progress and construction, a construction loan can be a source of a good amount of income. The major hazard which the lender faces is the inability of the contractor to complete the building for any of a number of reasons—excessive costs, delays caused by bad weather, materials shortages, labor strikes, etc. For self-protection, the lender must also consider whether the resources to complete the project are available, in case of foreclosure.

Another hazard for the lender is the potential for either mechanics' liens or material liens to be placed on the property. Under the lien law in most states, persons who supply labor or material to a project can record a lien against it and have first financial recovery rights against the property in case the builder fails to pay for the labor or the materials. In other words, if a construction loan is made and labor and materials have been supplied to the site, and if the builder then fails to make a payment to the workers or to the material suppliers, they can file liens against the property and their liens would have priority over the lender's loan lien. If the lender wished to protect the loan, the entire costs associated with the material liens or mechanics' liens would have to be paid before the mortgage lien would gain precedence.

In construction lending two loans are frequently involved. The first loan is made for the purpose of paying for the construction. This loan is usually short-term and equal in amount only to the value of the improvements to be placed on the land. The second loan is a long-term loan which is usually made to the buyer of the completed property. In some cases, the lender may convert the short-term construction loan to a long-term loan or may even agree from the beginning that the loan will be a permanent single loan. Usually the construction loan is referred to as interim financing and the final loan as a takeout loan.

CONSTRUCTION LOAN PROCEDURES

The person applying for a construction loan must submit a rather complete file. If the application is only for an interim loan, the file usually must include a statement from a lender indicating that a takeout or long-term loan will be made once the property construction is completed.

Documents. An application for a construction loan should include a complete and detailed set of plans and specifications and a builder's contract which indicates that the builder will furnish all materials and labor and will, for a designated amount, complete the building according to the plans and specifications submitted. Usually lenders prefer that the builder's statement be accompanied by a detailed cost breakdown sheet which shows precisely the kinds of materials to be supplied and the manner in which they are to be used in the building.

Lenders usually require that the builder complete an application form which indicates the amount of loan requested, the length of time for which the loan is to continue, and the repayment schedule proposed. The builder must also submit a financial statement showing assets, liabilities, and financial capacities to undertake the work and to meet the financial obligations in connection with the particular property. Sometimes the lender will ask that the builder provide a commercial credit report—a statement from the creditors of the builder showing what the firm owes and owns, and the terms and conditions of its existing loans or obligations.

Payment of Construction Loan Proceeds. There are a number of ways in which a lender can make money available to a builder. The most common of these is a *voucher system* under which the contractor is reimbursed for bills which have been paid and receipted. The receipted bills are submitted to the lender, who makes immediate reimbursement. The lender should, of course, make sure that the materials and labor itemized on the voucher have actually been applied to the job.

A second system is the *warrant system*. As bills come due, they are presented to the lender and paid by the lender directly to the supplier of materials or labor.

A third system involves the use of a *fixed disbursement schedule*. The lender, the builder, and the contractor agree on the number of payments which will be made during the span of the construction loan and at which stages these payments will be made. For example, a disbursement schedule may provide that portions of the loan (assuming 100% represents the total loan) would be disbursed as certain phases are completed:

1. Excavations and foundations	15%
2. Framing partitions, rough floors, exterior walls sheathed and covered	35
3. Wiring, plumbing, and heating roughed in, utilities in place, walls plastered	25
4. Completion of the property, owner's certification of satisfaction, builder's certification that all the bills are paid. At this point there is a final accounting of finances and a Certificate of Occupancy is secured.	15
5. After the period for filing of liens has passed and there is no potential that there are any outstanding obligations, the final amount is paid.	10
	100%

No matter what the method, the lender must always be sure that the amount disbursed is no greater than the cost of improvements constructed to that point. It is also important for the lender to hold back some of the funds after completion of the work in expectation that problems may arise which will require that the builder make alterations, repairs, or adjustments to put the property in a satisfactory condition. Since material and labor suppliers can place liens on the property for a period of 30 to 60 days after the completion of their work, the lender will usually hold back this lien amount for a period of up to 90 days. When the property has been completely finished and all the work has been terminated, the owner of the property usually files a Notice of Completion which states the name of the contractor, the date and amount of the contract, and the location of the property on which the building has been constructed. This document is then recorded and serves as public notice for all persons who may be contemplating placing any liens or other requirements against the building.

The Takeout Commitment. The developer (or builder) and the construction lender are both interested in the availability of permanent financing. Before the project is completed, and sometimes before the ground has been broken, the developer can pay a fee for a commitment on the part of a construction lender to make permanent financing available on prearranged terms. This gives the developer the ability to plan future expenses and rental strategy, since the costs of the permanent financing are a large part of the costs of running the completed project. For the construction lender, the takeout commitment offers greater certainty that involvement in the deal can be terminated once the construction is completed.

The value of the takeout commitment is limited by the terms and conditions which the construction lender imposes in the interest of protecting the loan. If one of these conditions is violated (the project ends up with slightly less square footage than specified, for example), the construction lender need not carry through on the commitment. Consequently, it is possible to arrange a construction loan without a takeout commitment.

Several kinds of takeout commitments are available: we have been discussing the standard takeout commitment. The standby commitment is the same as the standard commitment except that it is written at substantially higher interest rates. Consequently, neither lender nor developer expects to carry through with the commitment. The commitment is made, for a fee, for the security of the interim (construction) lender. If the market for the completed project is poor, the construction lender knows that permanent funds will be available as an exit from the deal.

Another kind of takeout commitment is the split-level commitment.

The terms of these takeouts are such that when the finished construction has achieved a certain percentage of the planned rent role or occupancy, the permanent lender will issue a permanent mortgage for dollars. If the designated rent role is not achieved, then the permanent lender will only issue a permanent mortgage for Y dollars, where Y is usually about 15 per cent less than X.

Some lenders are willing to issue "gap financing" commitments in consideration of a fee. These commitments essentially offer the borrower the difference between X and Y in the event that he is unable to achieve the rent role necessary to qualify for the upper-tier of the two-tiered takeout commitment. The gap financing, if it is made, is made at second mortgage rates for it is secured by a second mortgage, the takeout lender having the first mortgage.[1]

[1] *The REIT Fact Book 1974* (Washington, D.C.: National Association of Real Estate Investment Trusts, 1974), p. 45.

THE CONSTRUCTION LOAN FILE

Prior to disbursing any funds for a construction loan, lenders make sure that the files include the following documents:

1. An application for a loan and an agreement for repayment;
2. If a takeout loan is required, a firm written commitment from the lending agency which will make the final loan;
3. A completion bond or other guarantee to the lender that if the builder is unable to complete the project according to contract someone else will take up responsibilities for it, with no cost to the lender;
4. A copy of the loan agreement which shows: the legal responsibility for the lender to make payments to a given individual as the construction is completed; the number of inspections that are to be made; the number of payments that will be made and when they will be made; an agreement by the lending agency to set aside funds for the construction; and an agreement on the part of the builder or borrower to provide the lending agency with any funds, over and above the amount provided in the loan, that are necessary for the completion of the entire project;
5. A title insurance policy which assures the lender that the builder has clear title to the property and that there are no taxes due or other liens against the property;
6. Appropriate property, fire, or other risk insurance;
7. An authorization for the borrower to disperse the funds according to the loan agreement.

SUMMARY

To this point, the discussion has emphasized the lender's viewpoint. Let us summarize the entire process from the viewpoint of someone who is planning to undertake construction. The steps involved are:

1. Builder decides to build. The builder confers with architects on problems of design, with contractors on costs and methods of construction, with bonding companies on methods of controlling construction costs and time budgets, with appraisers to determine the market value of the property, and with lenders to determine whether construction loans are available and the terms on which loans might be made available.
2. Builder selects the site. The selection of the site may or may not precede the decision to build. Sometimes the availability of a site helps the builder decide the kind of structures to be placed on that site. On the other hand, a builder may specialize in a certain kind

of property and look for sites which fit that specialty. A builder who is firmly decided to build will purchase the land at once; if the builder is not yet ready to begin construction or wishes to determine whether financing is available, an option can be paid to acquire the land.

3. Builder approaches the lender. Once the land has been secured and plans for building have been firmed up, the builder will probably approach several lenders to determine in a general way what funds are available and the terms on which these funds will be made available. In this process, the builder may ask more than one lender to provide a description of the loan that would be made. This approach helps the builder to estimate the amount of cash needed, what it will cost to use borrowed funds, and the most likely source of borrowed funding. At this point, interest shown by a lender does not constitute an actual commitment to furnish funds for the project, so the builder still has a great deal more to do before the necessary funds are secured.

4. Builder prepares detailed plans, specifications, and estimates. An indication that funds can be obtained is usually the signal for the beginning of the more complex aspects of the building process. The builder will usually contact an architect, an engineer, and others who will assist in developing plans and specifications, including the kinds of labor and materials needed to complete the planned building. Since the builder will probably be using a number of contractors to help construct the property, general requests for bids will be issued and contractors will be selected on the basis of their bids. Usually the selection is based on the lowest bid, the kind of work that the bidder has done previously, capacity to do the present work, recommendations of former clients, and reputation among material suppliers, labor unions, and creditors. The builder usually selects contractors from among those who have the tools, equipment, and labor sufficient to undertake the job; a reputation for doing good work according to the contract; experience in the kind of construction to be undertaken; and a financial capacity to complete according to contract. After the plans and specifications have been completed, they are submitted to the proper authorities for approval and review in order that building permits and other approvals can be secured.

5. Builder seeks a loan. The detailed plans, specifications, and bid estimates of the contractors are submitted to lenders who have indicated an interest in the project. Each of the lenders can agree to make either the short-term interim loan or the long-term final loan.

6. Lender makes the funds available. The funds are made available according to the way in which the lender and the contractor or builder have originally agreed. The lender, for example, can open

an account in the builder's name and permit withdrawal of the needed funds. The lender may make the funds available only as the builder presents certified statements on bills that have already been paid, or the funds may be provided in a lump sum but with the builder required to furnish a bond guaranteeing completion of the work.

7. Lender disperses loan funds. Usually funds are made available only as the work progresses and according to schedules which have been agreed upon beforehand. Ninety per cent of the funds is typically made available on the completion of the work and the acceptance of the property by the owner; 10 per cent is withheld until all creditors have been satisfied.

8. Owner accepts the finished product. After the owner has accepted the building and signed the necessary legal documents, the builder still has to provide some service to the property. Usually for a period of six months to a year after the property has been constructed, the builder must agree to come back and make any necessary minor adjustments. For example, plumbing may need adjusting, plaster may crack, doors may stick—any of a number of things can happen. The lender usually expects the builder to provide some kind of a warranty that the materials and labor will meet specifications and that the builder will replace any defective material or make any adjustments because of poor labor. The entire process from the time the builder decides to build until completion of the project may take as much as 36 months for large-scale projects and as little as 12 months for a single-family home.

QUESTIONS

1. When examining the disbursement of funds under a construction loan, the lender has to be particularly careful that the remaining loan funds are sufficient to complete the project. Why?

2. What factors give commercial banks an edge over savings and loans in competition for the best construction loans?

3. There are three methods for the disbursement of funds.
   (a) Briefly describe them in your own words.
   (b) Which do you think gives the lender the most protection against false billing? Against shoddy workmanship?
   (c) Under each system, how does the lender attempt to assure retention of some equity in the property?

4. Construction lending is often called "interim financing."
   (a) What does the term mean? What does the term "permanent financing" mean?
   (b) What role does permanent financing play in the lender's decision about a construction loan?

5. What is gap financing and how is it used in construction lending?

IV

The Legal Aspects
of Real Estate Finance

16

BASIC FINANCE LAW

The value of a piece of real estate is directly related to the quantity and quality of rights possessed by the owner of the property. The process of establishing the quantity and quality of these rights is complex and involves the interpretation and preparation of many kinds of documents. The responsibility of a lender is to know in a general way how to analyze the rights involved in order to determine that there is sufficient security for the loan being negotiated. The lender must also recommend the documents required to establish rights related to the financing transaction and should seek expert legal advice on matters relating to any of the rights or documents. The processes, instruments, and rights which a lender should understand are summarized in Figure 16–1.

THE MEANING OF PRIVATE PROPERTY

Private property is the exclusive right of one or more persons to possess, control, enjoy, and dispose of an economic good. Private property is the exclusive right of a private person to own the economic good, whereas public property is the right of ownership of a political unit, and common property is the ownership of undivided rights by a number of persons. In order that private property may exist there must be an owner, a good of economic value, and a government organized to protect and enforce the property rights.

Real Property. There are two principal classes of private property—real and personal. In the majority of cases the differences between the two

The Process	Legal Instruments and Rights
1. Acquiring ownership rights	Contract—purchase Wills—inheritance Natural forces Forcible occupation Government assistance—homesteading Others
2. Determining the amount of ownership	Deeds of title, contracts Fee simple Life estates Dower, common property, homesteading
3. Determining when ownership or use rights occur	Leases and contracts Lease rights, future estates Immediate estates

4. Allocating ownership shares	Contracts, deeds of title, leases
	Tenancies:
	    In common
	    Joint
	    By the entirety
	    By legal entity

5. Determining the rights of those other than the owner	Court records, public records Contracts, leases Adverse possession Easements Temporary lease or renting Liens—mortgage, tax, judgment, mechanics'

6. Proving ownership	Deeds of title:
	    Warranty or grant
	    Quitclaim

7. Public notice of ownership	Public records:
	    Recording
	    Acknowledgment

8. Proving ownership rights and protecting against the claims of others	Title reports and documents:
	    Abstract and title
	    Title insurance
	    Certificate or title

9. Transferring part or all of ownership rights (permanently)	Contracts Land and sales contracts

10. Yielding to superior governmental rights	Tax bills, legal notices:
	    Tax liens
	    Special assessments
	    Condemnation
	    Dedication

Fig. 16–1. Legal processes in financing real estate investments.

are clearly evident; however, questions may arise as to whether a particular piece of property is real or personal. For example, in describing the property which is to be the security for a mortgage, are the pieces of mechanical equipment such as a dishwasher, refrigerator, stove, and air conditioning real or personal property? Are they or are they not security for the loan? Legally, real property consists of the land and all things permanently attached to the land. Personal property is all other types of property. Unfortunately in practice this distinction is not always very clear. It is important therefore for the lender to be sure that all property which is to serve as security for the loan is adequately described.

Distinguishing between real and personal property is particularly difficult when a property item once classified as personal is attached to a piece of real property. Articles of this kind include rugs, carpeting, mirrors, venetian blinds, electrical fixtures, stoves, refrigerators, and many similar kinds of goods. Problems have arisen over classification of furnaces, bay windows, and other bulky types of property.

There are three criteria for deciding whether a piece of property is legally real property:

1. Was it the intent of the parties concerned to make the property real property?
2. Was the property attached to the real property in such a manner as to indicate that it was to be a permanent attachment?
3. What was the relationship between the parties? Were there, for example, any agreements relating to the ownership of the property involved?

The land on which real improvements are placed must be clearly defined in all contracts relating to the transfer of rights. Under the law, land consists of everything on the surface of the earth, under the earth, and above the surface of the earth to a given height. In areas where oil, coal, and minerals are known to exist, a purchaser may acquire only rights to the surface use. In desert areas, land may have little value unless it carries water rights. The rights to the space above the land have not been established conclusively; however, ownership of land usually gives rights to the space above the land to a lesser height in congested areas than in open areas. In large metropolitan areas the air rights above land can be as valuable as the land itself.

Personal Property. Personal property is all property other than real property. Typically personal property is portable or movable rather than fixed. Of course some of it may be moved with great difficulty. Nevertheless, if it is clearly something which can be moved and is lacking some form of permanent attachment, it should be considered personal property.

Limitations on Private Property. The system of private property provides maximum expression of individual preferences in the use of property rights. However, there are these limitations:

1. Taxation and other payments such as special assessments for the maintenance of government.
2. Eminent domain or the right of a sovereign government to compel sale of private property in the public interest, in return for the payment of compensation to the private owner.
3. Police power or all regulations necessary to protect public health, welfare, safety, and morals.
4. Escheat or the return of private property to the state when there is no known private owner.
5. Private contractual obligations.

ACQUIRING AND PROVING OWNERSHIP

The degree, quantity, nature, and extent of interest in a piece of real estate is determined by the kind of estate possessed by the person involved. The lender is interested in the estate only because the estate determines the extent to which the property has economic value and serves as an adequate security for the loan being negotiated.

Acquiring Ownership. The method of acquiring real estate is of minimum concern to a lender, but the quantity and quality of rights conveyed by means of the process are of the utmost importance. In early history the ownership of property was frequently established by occupation, conquest, or forcible takeover, but today in the United States both governments and individuals must use peaceful means of acquisition to obtain the highest quality of title. Title to property may be acquired through:

1. The purchase of rights, either all rights or a portion of them
2. Receipt of the property as a gift
3. Inheritance of the property by means of a will or by descent or by court decree
4. Action of natural forces in which additional land is created by accretion or other means, or in which land is removed because of erosion
5. Actual occupation and denial of another's rights
6. The assistance of the government by means of occupation as in homesteading or by court ruling in case of controversy.

Kinds of Ownership. The legal terminology relating to the kinds of ownership or estates or rights is complicated and obscure. The lender should become acquainted with the legal terminology and procedures in order to advise clients when they need assistance. There are three general questions relating to the quality and quantity of rights which a real estate lender must answer before the economic quality of an estate can be measured: (1) how much of an estate is owned? (2) when is the estate to be owned? and (3) who shares in the ownership?

How Much of an Estate Is Owned? Fee simple ownership is the most complete form of ownership available to private persons because it permits the use of the property in any way which will not interfere with the rights of others and is within the limits established by government. There is no limit of time during which fee simple rights may be or must be exercised.

Life estates give use rights only during the user's life or for a period of time beyond the user's control. Usually the life tenant may occupy or lease the estate and use it in any manner which does not injure the interests of those who succeed him or her. Life estates are usually created by wills for the benefit of a surviving spouse, with the estate to be distributed among children or relatives upon the death of the survivor.

Interests in real estate may be created through marriage. Property acquired prior to and during marriage may or may not become the property of both parties to the marriage. State laws vary on this point; however, there are two principal types of state rulings. In some states the wife is given a dower or automatic interest in her husband's property acquired prior to and during marriage with the amount of interest defined by specific state statutes. This interest cannot be alienated by the husband. In those states the signature of the husband is often required in the sale of the property by the wife even though the husband has no legal interest in the property.

In community property states, the wife owns an undivided one-half of all property defined by state statute as community property. In such states both partners in the marriage must be very careful to differentiate property which they have acquired prior to marriage from property which they have acquired without using the assets of the marriage, otherwise all property can be ruled as community property.

Many states protect a portion of the family home from the claims of all creditors. For example, in California a form of right called homesteading protects the family home. Homesteading is easily exercised since the property owner need only file a card with the public recorder indicating an intention to homestead. When this is done, a given portion of the value of the home cannot be taken by the creditors, except for those creditors who may have filed prior liens against the home.

A lender dealing with married persons or persons living together must determine the exact interests of the couple and require that both sign any documents relating to transfer or change of ownership rights.

WHEN IS THE REAL ESTATE TO BE OWNED? In the majority of cases a transfer of ownership conveys immediate occupancy and use rights; however, there are exceptions to this rule. Tenants occupying property under the terms of a valid long-term lease often may not be removed when the ownership changes hands. For this reason agreements effecting changes of ownership should include statements which identify the rights of tenants.

A real property may have value even though some of the rights of ownership must be deferred. For example, a person occupying a property under the terms of a lease has a temporary estate which terminates with the expiration of the lease. The amount of estate returned to the fee simple owner is known as a reversionary estate. The rights of a tenant are known as a leasehold estate. Both the leasehold and reversionary estates have value; however, the full value of the fee simple owner cannot be realized until the lease rights expire.

A fee simple owner may wish to provide for a future sharing in the estate by two or more persons. This can be done by giving one or some of these persons an immediate estate and the other(s) a remainder interest. Those obtaining immediate rights have all of the rights of ownership except disposition but they must not abuse the estate so that the remainder interests are damaged. Both the immediate estate and the remainder are of value.

An immediate fee simple estate has the most value. A remainder interest coming due upon the happening of an unpredictable future event must have lesser value.

WHO SHARES IN THE OWNERSHIP? One or many persons may share in the ownership of an estate without exercising visible or readily ascertainable control over the estate. These persons may be real persons or they may be legal persons such as corporations or business entities.

A wife may be separated from her husband and yet have an interest in his estate. A widow may have an interest in the estate of her recently deceased husband or her interest may exist in the real property owned by the business of the husband. Two persons may own an estate but only one of them may control the use of the estate. One group of persons may actually possess the estate but others may have the right to cross over it or to use it in any way which they see fit.

Multiple ownership in real property may include:

1. Tenancies in common—an estate held by two or more persons with each person having a distinct interest which can be sold or transmitted as desired. Although the shares may be distinguished legally, they are in actual fact undivided and not necessarily equal. Tenancies in common occur in California, for example, in connection with community property.

2. Joint tenancies—an estate of two or more persons who hold ownership in the same degree. The ownership shares are not separate and upon the death of one party the survivor or survivors take all of the estate. Each party in the estate has an equal right to occupy and share in the rights. An interest in a joint tenancy may be conveyed but this action usually creates a tenancy in common. Joint estates are a convenience for married persons because of the ease with which an interest in the estate may be transferred in the event of the death of either spouse. But the conditions under which such a transfer is possible vary from state to state.

3. Tenancy by a legal entity—a partnership or corporation or other type of business organization may own a property for the benefit of the owners of the business. Property rights held in this manner cannot be transferred unless the procedure meets both organizational and legal requirements. For example, all of the partners would be required to participate in the sale of partnership property. The approval of the board of directors and other principal officers of a corporation as provided in the charter would be required for transfer of corporation property.

This array of estates in which two or more persons may participate underlines the necessity for a lender to seek legal assistance when determining how many persons may share in the ownership of a parcel of real property. The person in apparent control may have no legal interest in the property, and persons who might logically be expected to have legal rights in the estate may have no rights in the eyes of the law.

Rights Less Than Fee Simple. Rights less than fee simple, or noncorporeal rights, may ripen into important and valuable fee simple rights. Reversion and remainder rights, previously mentioned, and adverse possession are noncorporeal rights of this nature.

Adverse Possession. Adverse possession occurs when two or more persons claim title to a property. The terms under which one of the parties may secure the dominant or fee interest vary from state to state but usually the following terms must be met:

1. The property must be actually occupied so that any person can observe the occupancy
2. The occupancy must be accomplished against the apparent owner's interest and must deny that person's title
3. The occupancy must continue without interruption for the period of years specified by the state law
4. The person in possession must claim the title; usually this is accomplished through the payment of taxes on the property
5. The person in possession must remain in exclusive possession.

EASEMENTS.   Easements give permission to persons other than the owner to cross over the property. Utility companies often reserve the right to cross over the rear of lots in order to service poles and wires. Cities may reserve the right to take a portion of a lot in order to widen streets or provide public thoroughfares. Owners of lots with no direct access to public roads may receive permission from other landowners to build access roads on the intervening private land. In some cases the easement must be recognized and maintained by all succeeding owners. Other easements are extinguished with a change of ownership.

Easements may be created by specific written or oral agreement or they may be implied by the manner in which the owner permits others to use the land. Whenever land uses under the terms of an easement terminate, the land reverts to the original owner.

LEASING.   Leasing or renting by means of an agreement gives temporary use of occupancy in return for a payment. Since the rights of a tenant may be paramount as the result of a carefully drawn lease, lenders must exercise particular care in evaluating the security for a property in which a lease right is involved. Perhaps the only security lies in the value of the lease.

LIENS.   Liens are created whenever property is pledged as security for a debt or other obligation. There are four principal types of liens: (1) mortgage, (2) tax, (3) judgment, and (4) mechanics' liens. The existence of a lien is usually a matter of public record. If the debt connected with the lien is not satisfied, the property on which the lien has been placed may be sold by the lien holder or his or her agent. The owner of the property receives nothing from the sale unless the proceeds of the sale are more than sufficient to pay the costs of the sale and the debt owed.

JUDGMENT LIENS.   Judgment liens arise from lawsuits in which damages have been awarded and the courts use the property as a guarantee that the damages will be paid.

MECHANICS' LIENS. Mechanics' liens are created whenever materials or labor have been furnished for the construction or repair of real property and the amounts due have not been paid. (See Chapter 15.) The circumstances under which these liens are created and satisfied vary according to state law. Typically all of the suppliers of materials and labor have an equal priority of lien so that none may be paid before the others if the lien is satisfied through legal processes. In addition, mechanics' liens must be recorded within a specific period of time, must be accompanied by proof that the materials and labor were supplied, and must show that the property owner ordered the work or was aware that it was being done. Some states give mechanics' liens priority over all other kinds of liens except tax liens.

LIEN SEARCH. A lender must determine—usually through a search of public records—whether liens exist upon a particular property. Serious investigation should be made as to whether liens exist, especially if it is apparent that someone other than the owner has some form of right in the property being financed.

Proving Ownership. Ownership in property is established by means of a deed, which is a written instrument used in transferring interests in real property. Of the three principal types of ownership deeds—warranty, grant, and quitclaim—the most common are warranty and quitclaim. There are also gift, sheriff, tax, executor, and many other kinds of deeds, but these are only special forms of the three principal types of deeds.

WARRANTY DEED. A warranty deed conveys the most complete rights and warranties and is used in all states. The warranty deed conveys the rights of:

1. Enjoyment of the use of the property
2. Conveyance of the property rights to others
3. Freedom from the existence of encumbrances at the time the property is acquired
4. An assurance that no future rights will be created by others

In a few states the conveyance of any additional future rights is also acquired by the seller.

GRANT DEED. A grant deed receives considerable use in California but is also found in some other states. The deed must contain the word *grant* in mentioning the conveyance of rights, and it conveys these warranties:

1. The grantor or seller has not already conveyed the property to another

2. The estate conveyed is free of encumbrances except as indicated
3. No rights of way across the property or building restrictions exist except as provided in the deed
4. The seller conveys any rights conveyed after the title passes

The warranties can be expressed in the deed or simply implied.

QUITCLAIM DEED. A quitclaim is used whenever the warranties of the warranty deed or grant deed cannot be certified. The quitclaim deed passes on only the interest presently held by the current owner and warrants nothing with respect to the quantity or the quality of the estate rights conveyed.

MINIMUM REQUIREMENTS FOR TITLE DEEDS. Regardless of the type of deed, minimum requirements for creating such a document include:

1. There must be a grantor, usually a seller, and a grantee, or buyer, and consideration.
2. The property must be legally described.
3. The instrument must be physically delivered by the grantor or his or her agent.
4. The instrument must contain words indicating that the property is being conveyed or transferred.
5. The instrument must be signed by the grantor.
6. The instrument probably should be acknowledged although this is not always required. Acknowledgment is simply the formal declaration by a designated public official or a public notary that the deed is the act of the person or persons who signed the instrument.

Conditions, Covenants, and Restrictions. Deeds often include statements which restrict the rights of the property owner. These are private contractual agreements and can cover a variety of items such as limiting the size or the price of the house to be built, location of the house on the lot, limits on the number of families in the house, landscaping, and many other kinds of restrictions. These restrictions may be enforced legally by persons having residual interests in the property or by any owner whose property interest may be affected adversely by the violation of these restrictions. Restrictions not in the public interest will not be enforced. For example, the Supreme Court has ruled that any restriction which relates to limitation of ownership because of race, creed, or color is not enforceable.

Public Notice of Ownership. Public recording of instruments relating to property rights is used to notify third parties of the existence of these rights and to establish priority of rights or claims to a given property. Public recording is not always required but it is conclusive proof of ownership rights in case of a dispute. Recording consists merely of depositing the instrument to be recorded with the appropriate public official. The entire instrument is copied or photostated together with a notation as to the time and date of recording. The instrument must be recorded in the county in which the property is located. The time and date of recording establish the priority of rights in the property. However, if a person recording an instrument has personal knowledge of the existence of a prior claim which has not been publicly recorded, the act of recording does not therefore convey a priority.

Acknowledgment may or may not be required but it is a process by which those who are signing the documents establish their identity. In effect, it means that a public official has certified that the person mentioned in the documents is the same person signing the documents.

Proving Ownership Rights. A number of means have been developed for establishing the quantity and quality of rights being transferred. The most common include: an abstract and opinion, certificate of title, and title insurance. The kinds of systems used vary among the states; however, all kinds may be used in a given area.

ABSTRACT AND OPINION. An abstract is a legal history of the claim of ownership, prepared by a lawyer, public official, or abstract company. The value of an abstract is related directly to the ability of the person preparing it. Accompanying the abstract is an opinion, usually rendered by a lawyer after examination of the abstract, as to the quantity and quality of title transferred. The abstractor is financially liable for any errors committed in the preparation of the abstract, but the abstractor does not render an opinion about the title. The lawyer is responsible only for rendering a qualified and expert opinion.

CERTIFICATE OF TITLE. Attorneys are sometimes asked to examine public records and then render an opinion about the title of a given property. This opinion is a certificate of title and may be used in place of an abstract and an opinion.

TITLE INSURANCE. The limited facilities and financial responsibility of abstract companies and lawyers has encouraged the development of title insurance companies. These companies will provide insurance against losses occasioned by defects in or encumbrances on title to a property. Such defects may arise because of changes in marital status, insanity on the part of a grantor, a lack of ability to execute a legal contract, public actions which have impaired the title, or similar types of defects not apparent from an examination of public records. The title insurance company agrees either to defend the owner of the policy in court against any challenges to the owner's rights or to give compensation for any loss of rights that may be suffered.

Any amount of insurance can be purchased but the company will not pay for losses in excess of the value of the property. The insurance policy states the amount of the liability assumed, liens and encumbrances and other matters which affect the title, items covered by the policy, and exceptions not covered by the policy. Because of these limitations it is very difficult to collect from a title insurance company. Indeed, the value of title insurance is doubtful, but state law usually requires it. In almost every case where title insurance is available, lenders will buy a policy of an amount equal to the amount owed to them and require that the borrower pay the insurance proceeds.

SUPERIOR GOVERNMENTAL RIGHTS

Governmental agencies have some very important powers which affect the quality and quantity of private rights. These include taxation, condemnation, and dedication.

Taxes. Taxes are payments made by property owners for the support of general or special governmental functions; they include not only the normal property taxes but special tax assessments. Failure to make these payments gives the government the power to seize property and to sell it in order to recover the amounts due. When taxes have not been paid and sale of the property does not produce a private owner, the land reverts to the government, which may do with it as it sees fit.

General property taxes usually pay for police and fire protection, schools, and the general costs of operating the government. Special assessments arise when some special type of government service or facility is being created for the benefit of a limited number of property holders. These assessments may cover improved lighting, paving of sidewalks, or the building of schools, sewers, or recreation facilities.

Condemnation. The power of condemnation, derived from the power of eminent domain, permits governments to take private property for the general good. In order to condemn the land the governmental agency must prove that the land is needed for public use. Once this fact is established the agency sets a price on the land which the owner can accept or reject. If the offer is rejected the suit is tried in court and the award is set by court action. Private owners must always be compensated for any land taken under the rights of condemnation.

Dedication. A private owner may set aside land for public use. If this offer is accepted, the land becomes the property of the public and may not be used for any purposes except those provided in the dedication. Under common-law dedication the owner offers the land and, when public officials accept the offer, the public secures an easement for the use of the land. Under statutory dedication the owner presents the land and conforms with statutory requirements. When public officials accept the land, the public acquires a fee simple title to the land and may use it in accordance with the dedication.

SUMMARY

The value of a property lies entirely within the bundle of rights associated with that property. These rights should be in writing in legally acceptable format. However, a prudent lender or investor will not only ask for an expert legal opinion on the quantity and quality of rights which exist in a particular property but will also inspect the property to determine whether there are any other infringements on the rights which have not been listed in the legal documents. Anyone with a financial interest in a property will always try to obtain the maximum number of rights available to a private person while recognizing that public agencies may have better rights because of taxation, zoning, building codes, eminent domain, and many other kinds of rights. The lender or investor will want to make sure that any contracts relating to the property do not impair the total bundle of rights, or, if the impairment is deliberate, that all possible financial compensation is received for the lessening of any rights. Financial interests in real property are protected best by using expert legal advice in acquiring and proving ownership.

Unfortunately, legal processes are complex and involved, and legal documents contain special words and phrases that may seem esoteric and confusing. A lender or investor may be tempted to avoid the expense of legal advice or assistance. The innumerable litigations over problems of ownership are ample evidence that such practices are "penny wise and dollar foolish." A wise lender or investor, no matter how experienced, will not attempt to act as his or her own lawyer.

QUESTIONS

1. Indicate whether each of the following would be real (R) or personal (P) property for lending purposes and indicate the basic criteria you would use in making the decisions:

   ___ Rugs

   ___ Carpeting

   ___ Built-in stoves and refrigerators

   ___ Furnace

   ___ Custom-built and fitted venetian blinds

   ___ Rose bushes

   ___ Potted plants placed outside as decoration

   ___ Kitchen ventilating fan

   ___ Air conditioning

   ___ Wall-hung mirrors

2. Land consists of more than ownership of the surface of the earth. Why is this of concern to a lender who plans to provide financing?

3. Fee simple is presumably the highest bundle of rights that an individual may own, yet there are restrictions even on these rights. What are the possible major restrictions?

4. What three ownership questions should a lender always ask about any property on which a loan is to be made?

5. If a lender suspects that others besides the represented owner may hold an interest in land, which persons would be the most likely holders of interest and how would this problem be treated in lending?

6. Would it be legal for you to transfer title to the Brooklyn Bridge to another person?

17

MORTGAGES AND TRUST DEEDS: BASICS AND VARIATIONS

Mortgages and trust deeds become liens on property when the owner of the property wishes to borrow money and pledges the property as security for the repayment of the debt. In order for a mortgage or trust deed to exist there must first be a debt, which is usually recognized by means of a note or similar written legal instrument. In order to assure the lender that the note will be repaid the borrower pledges property as security for the repayment of the debt. This pledge can be a mortgage or trust deed instrument. Lenders normally look first to the prospective borrower's credit and ability to repay the debt from sources other than through the sale of the property. Some lenders see the property as the last defense to which they will turn in seeking recovery of the money owed.

Some lenders may simply accept the note and rely on the general security or other assets of the borrower as guarantee for its repayment. This form of unsecured credit requires that the lender proceed against the debtor personally for the collection of the monies owed.

Real estate lenders do not want to and legally cannot be placed in the position of unsecured creditors. Institutional lenders such as savings and loan associations, commercial banks, and life insurance companies are required by law to secure a pledge of real estate as security for real estate loans which are being made. The mortgage type of security agreement is found primarily in the eastern and midwestern states while the deed of trust predominates in the western states. Both accomplish the same end—a pledge of property as security for a debt—but each is somewhat different in terms of the security and the manner in which the lender can recover upon default of the note. Both have these common characteristics:

1. The borrower has an equity in the purchase.
2. The period of repaying the debt extends over a relatively long period of time, varying usually from 15 to 30 years.
3. The annual rates of interest can be relatively low but the total interest during the life of the loan may equal or exceed the principal amount of the loan.
4. The loan is repaid in equal installments which include repayment of the principal with interest.
5. The terms of the mortgage lending agreement sometimes influence, to some degree, the price paid for the property.

A number of factors are responsible for the use of the mortgage or trust deed type of financing agreement. Mortgage financing allows the buyer to acquire title with a relatively small down payment. Also, the buyer enjoys exclusively any increase in equity which occurs in the property as the result of growth or inflationary changes. Thirdly, the borrower's obligation remains fixed so that the total obligations under the loan agreement can always be anticipated accurately. Finally, any costs in connection with the creation of the loan can usually be amortized over a given portion of the life of the loan so that the borrower is not faced with a large loan payment at one time.

Lenders have become somewhat disenchanted with the traditional type of mortgage loan agreement, primarily because of inflation. They are faced with increasing costs of acquiring money to make mortgage loans, and their costs of operation are constantly going up. Thus, they consider it unfair that they should not be allowed to pass on some portion of these increased costs to borrowers. As a result there has been an increasing movement to introduce variable payment mortgages which would allow lenders to pass on to borrowers some of the increased costs of acquiring money and doing business, by varying the monthly payments of the borrowers.

THE MORTGAGE AGREEMENT

There are only two parties in a mortgage agreement: the borrower or mortgagor and the lender or mortgagee. If the loan is repaid according to agreement, the borrower can ask for and the lender must provide a certificate which indicates that all the terms of the mortgage have been met; the full fee simple title is then returned to the borrower. If default occurs, the lender must give the borrower full notice of default. If after the period of time specified by law—and this differs from state to state—the borrower has not made up the amounts which are owed, the mortgagee can proceed with foreclosure. The mortgagee must then commence a lawsuit in the courts asking for the sale of the mortgage property and the application of the proceeds of that sale to the amounts owed. If the court is satisfied as a result of the documents which are submitted that the mortgagee has an unfulfilled obligation, the announcement of a foreclosure or sale by a court-appointed officer is made. The foreclosure notice must include a description of the property, the time and place where the sale is going to be held—it must always be in a public place—and the date on which the sale is to be held. This notice must be published in appropriate public papers for a given period of time. When the public auction is held, the sale must be to the highest bidder.

The mortgagor or borrower typically has a 12-month period in which to redeem all interests in the property which is sold, by paying up all the amounts due and the costs of conducting the sale. If the borrower fails to exercise this right of redemption, the purchaser at the foreclosure sale has a title to the property equivalent to that held by the debtor.

If the sale is held and the mortgagee does not recover a sufficient amount to pay for the debt owed and the costs of the sale, the mortgagee may secure a deficiency judgment—the right to proceed against other assets of the borrower to satisfy the amounts still unpaid.

Proceedings under foreclosure on a mortgage can extend over 12 to 18 months.

THE TRUST DEED

A trust deed involves three parties: the borrower, the lender, and the trustee. The borrower/trustor acknowledges a debt by means of a note. The borrower receives some conveyance of the property title and receives the proceeds from the loan. The lender/beneficiary extends the credit to the trustee, receives the note and a pledge of property as security for the debt, and conveys to the trustee sufficient rights to carry out the terms of the note. The third party, the trustee, holds sufficient title to the property to permit foreclosure on the property if the terms of the note are not being met. Legally the trustee may take title to the property in case of a default on the part of the borrower and may sell the property in order to recover amounts which are still owed.

In the case of a default under a trust deed, the lender/beneficiary must notify the trustee in writing of the borrower's failure to meet agreed-upon obligations. The beneficiary can then ask the trustee to exercise the power to sell the property and delivers to the trustee the promissory note and the trust deed or the pledge. The trustee records the notice of default and publishes public announcements of the default and intention to sell. For a period defined by the law of each state—usually 90 days—the borrower has the right to cure the default by paying all the sums due on the obligation; the entire amount of the mortgage does not have to be repaid. If the borrower fails to reinstate the terms of the agreement, the sale can proceed. The notice of sale is published and if the 90-day period in which the borrower can perform has expired, the sale is offered at public auction at a specified place. The trustee is under obligation to obtain the highest possible bid from a qualified bidder. At the end of the sale the highest bidder receives a trustee's deed to the property which conveys to the purchaser the title of the property which had been formerly held by the borrower. The important difference between the trust deed and the mortgage is that the lender cannot receive a deficiency judgment and the borrower cannot exercise any form of redemption after the 90-day period has expired.

VARIATIONS IN THE USE OF THE MORTGAGE

The mortgage instrument has evolved more through tradition and experimentation than through a deliberate effort to create a satisfactory real estate financing instrument. Because of the weight of history and legal precedent, efforts to change the instrument have not met with much success. However, with the changes that have occurred in the money markets and the impact of inflation, serious questions are now being raised about the value of the instrument as it is now found and more and more ideas are being advanced as to how it might be changed. Even within the limits imposed by present legal and historical precedent, lenders are finding new ways to use the instrument more effectively or to couple it with other forms of investment instruments to produce the funding they need at prices they can afford. The need to find a new form of instrument can perhaps be dramatized by what has been happening in recent years. Lenders have been making home mortgage loans at rates which have varied between 7 and 10 per cent. This of course means that the borrower is paying the interest rate based on a percentage of the value of the loan so that if a borrower were financing a home with an 80 per cent loan and paying a 10 per cent rate on the mortgage, the borrower would in effect be paying 8 per cent on the original value of the home. If inflation were increasing the value of that home at a rate of approximately 8 per cent, the borrower is in effect using cost-free money while the lender is taking all the risks of nonrepayment. On the other hand, the borrower is committed to a fixed payment which does not change no matter what the borrower's economic condition may be and which requires substantial penalties to be paid if the borrower attempts to be rid of the instrument or to change to something more effective.

Direct Reduction. The present direct reduction mortgage instrument came into wide use as a result of the experiences of lenders during the depression of the 1930's and early 1940's. Prior to that time money could be borrowed for a short term at a substantial rate of interest with only interest payments required until the loan reached maturity. At maturity the entire principal amount was due in a "balloon" payment. As the depression deepened, an increasing number of borrowers were unable to repay the entire amount of the loan at maturity. Therefore, the direct reduction loan was used to "pop" the balloon payment. This loan was considered better because it required the borrower to repay on a periodic basis not only the interest but a portion of the loan itself; at maturity the entire loan had been paid off, so the borrower was not faced with a balloon. Lenders liked the direct reduction loan because it helped them to plan on a more systematic basis for the amount of funds that they could anticipate receiving from their various investments and the amount that they would earn on those funds.

The direct reduction loan did not originate with the Great Depression, but it did become much more widely used afterward. Today, it has virtually replaced the balloon payment mortgage loan. In Chapter 9 we discussed the role of the Federal Housing Administration in encouraging the widespread use of direct reduction loans.

The direct reduction loan has two other names which are frequently used: it is called a "self-amortizing" loan and a "level payment" loan. Amortization is the gradual repayment of debt by making relatively small periodic repayments. With the direct reduction loan, the borrower makes constant ("level") payments on the loan but a part of each payment goes to principal and a part to interest. After a certain number of periodic payments, each of equal size, the borrower has repaid the entire loan with interest.

An interesting aspect of the self-amortizing (or level payment or direct reduction) loan is the way in which the level payment is split between interest and principal. Suppose that a homebuyer makes payments of $350 per month on a mortgage. During the first year, a small amount, e.g., $25 per month, goes to principal. The rest is payment of interest. Thus, the homebuyer repays only $300 of principal in the first year. But, in the second year interest payments are less since the amount of the loan has been reduced by $300. This means that a slightly larger part of the $350 monthly payment goes to repayment of principal. After many years, as the mortgage approaches maturity, a large part of each monthly payment goes to repay principal; a small part goes to interest. The remaining balance of the loan has become small so the interest payment on this balance is also small.

The level payment mortgage solved many of the problems associated with balloon payment mortgages, but some problems remain. For example, when inflation accelerated in the 1960's and 1970's, lenders found themselves committed to long-term, low-interest, level payment mortgages while facing higher costs of operation. This led to experimentation with alternatives to the direct reduction loan.

Traditional Variations. Since a mortgage or trust deed involves the creation of a contract in which money is borrowed and property is pledged as security, variations in the contract terms can result in special forms of the mortgage or trust deed agreement. Among these are the following:

JUNIOR MORTGAGE OR TRUST DEED. This is a mortgage or trust deed instrument in which the rights of the lender are subordinate to the rights of another lender who has already made a loan on the property. The determination of whether a mortgage is a primary or a junior instrument relates to the time when the agreements are completed and recorded. In other words, if a borrower were able to make two mortgage loans at the same time, there is a possibility that the borrower with the superior or primary interest would be the one whose interests were entered first in the public records.

PURCHASE MONEY. Sometimes the seller of a property will take back a mortgage or trust deed as partial payment for the sale of the property. In such cases, particularly when a mortgage is involved, the seller has no rights beyond that of taking back the property. In other words, it is not possible for the seller to obtain a deficiency judgment of any kind.

WRAPAROUND MORTGAGE. A variation of what is also called a blanket mortgage, this means simply that a number of properties or property rights are offered as security for a single debt. In the wraparound mortgage, for example, a borrower who already has a first and second mortgage or trust deed on a property and is seeking additional funding may use a single lending agreement to include all of these borrowing obligations. A blanket mortgage may include as security more than one type of property, e.g., real and personal property.

PACKAGE MORTGAGE. Both real and personal property are included in a package mortgage. Lenders who use such an instrument usually require that all property which may be thought of normally as personal property be fully described in the lending agreement. This means that mechanical equipment would be identified by make, style, and model number, and perhaps even by identification number.

CONSTRUCTION LOAN. A construction loan is the same as a mortgage loan except that it is for a much shorter period. Typically a borrower may go to one lender and use a short-term mortgage or trust deed to secure sufficient funds to construct a property. However, the borrower will probably be obligated to find some other lender who will provide a take-out or long-term mortgage which the purchaser can use in acquiring the property.

BLANKET MORTGAGE. Under a blanket mortgage a borrower can assemble several different pieces of property and use them as security for a single loan. As the loan is repaid, various pieces of property can be taken out from under the blanket. Such a mortgage allows a borrower to secure more money than might be available if only a single piece of property were pledged. The blanket mortgage gives the lender the added security of all the various kinds of property which are being pledged.

OPEN-END MORTGAGE. A borrower may want to guarantee that a given amount of money will be available at a given rate of interest even though the entire amount is not needed at the time the mortgage is created. In order to accomplish this, an open-end mortgage may be created. This is really a form of line of credit which permits the borrower to secure additional amounts up to the total principal mentioned in the original mortgage instrument.

An open-end mortgage may be used when a developer wants to deal with only one lender through the entire duration of the project. The developer will therefore ask for advances of funds as the construction proceeds and for a final advancement of funds when it is necessary to finance the long-term use of the property.

This instrument creates problems in trying to determine what the date of lien is for the lender. A question revolves around whether the additional advances which are made under the terms of the agreement have the same priority as the original amount which was advanced or whether the priorities are changed as these advances are made. Most state laws provide that any future optional advances have the same priority of rights as the original advance so long as certain conditions are met. The major condition is that the amounts advanced cannot exceed the total obligation which is mentioned in the original document. This type of priority is frequently limited to loans which have been made for the construction of improvements on the property. The intent is to prevent other liens, which may arise as the property is improved, from taking a priority.

The attraction of this type of loan to lenders is that they need not provide funds until they are satisfied that the funds already advanced have been used properly and that the new funds are necessary to move forward with the program of improvement or construction as outlined in the original agreement.

LEASE AND MORTGAGE. Sometimes a lender wants to make a loan to a borrower who has a good credit reputation and a good prospect for repayment but who has no real property to offer as security for the loan. For example, a developer may have an agreement from a triple-A-rated business firm to lease property to be constructed but the builder has no funds with which to buy the land or to begin construction. The solution may be to have the business firm sign an airtight lease and offer the lease to the lender as security for the repayment of the loan. Leases are valuable means of financing properties and will be discussed in more detail later.

TWO LENDERS. Lenders are always searching for ways in which to increase the amount of funds which can be made available to borrowers without increased risk to the lenders. Sometimes institutional lenders join with private lenders in providing a mortgage loan in which the institutional lender covers the normal loan-to-value ratio. In other words, the institutional lender's loan is equal to 75 or 80 per cent of the value. The private lender then provides additional funds so that the borrower may have to pay only 5 per cent down for the property designated for purchase. The institutional lender has the senior rights and retains all of the privileges necessary for self-protection. The private lender may secure mortgage insurance as a measure of protection. Variations in this kind of loan may require the borrower to offer other forms of collateral to secure the amount desired from the private lender. The principal requirement in this arrangement is that the institutional lender be kept fully informed of all such arrangements and be protected legally for the amount of funds which it advances, particularly since the borrower is courting disaster because of the thin equity held in the property.

USURY

Some states place definite restrictions on the amount of interest which a lender can charge. Any contract which charges a rate higher than the stated rate involves a condition of usury. Usury can sometimes be defined to include not only the interest being charged but various loan costs connected with the completion of the lending agreement. Where this is not the case, the usury ceiling is ineffective: by increasing loan costs, the interest on the loan can be raised to any level (see Chapter 23). Since usury is a matter of state law, few general statements can be made about it.

TRUTH IN LENDING

The Real Estate Settlement Procedures Act of 1974 (Public Law 93–533) was tried and found to be too costly for all parties involved in the transfer of property rights. Undoubtedly, efforts by some consumer groups will produce regulations similar to this Act. However, a review of the purposes of the Act gives some measure of the complications related to closing a real property transaction. The purpose of the Act was to warn borrowers of the kinds of charges they may face and to permit them to obtain information ahead of time which would tell them accurately what their total obligations would be. Over 31 items were to be reported in the disclosure statement. Almost all of them have been discussed to this point. They include:

1. Contract sale price
2. Personal property
3. Settlement charges
4. Adjustments
5. Gross amount due from the borrower
6. Deposit or earnest money
7. Principal amount of loan or loans
8. Existing loan or loans being taken subject to
9. Prorations (e.g., of property taxes)
10. Total amounts paid by or on behalf of the borrower
11. Cash required from the borrower or payable to the borrower
12. Real estate broker's sales compensation
13. Loan origination fee
14. Loan discount points
15. Appraisal fee
16. Credit report
17. Lender's inspection fee
18. Mortgage insurance application fee
19. Assumption fee
20. Prepaid interest
21. Prepaid mortgage insurance premium
22. Prepaid hazard insurance premium
23. Reserves deposited with the lender
24. Settlement closing or escrow fees

25. Title charges
26. Notary fees
27. Attorney fees
28. Title insurance
29. Government transfer taxes and charges
30. Surveys relating to legal descriptions
31. Inspections

Since this law is rather recent, it is still in the process of being tested and improved.

SUMMARY

The mortgage lending instrument is merely a specialized form of business contract in which a lender seeks additional security for the repayment of a loan. However, because the security is real property, varieties of special laws and customs have been developed which make the lending process cumbersome, slow, and costly. The process is further complicated because each state can pass laws affecting the mortgage instrument. The trust deed is becoming more popular because it simplifies the process of lending, repaying, and foreclosing; but it too has defects. Experienced lenders and borrowers are learning how to develop special forms of trust deeds and mortgages which help overcome problems associated with fixed interest rates, long-term payments, and other costs associated with both mortgages and trust deeds. When money is difficult to obtain because of tight money markets, variations of the mortgage—blanket, open-end, wraparound, package, purchase—become more popular. However, lenders must exercise great care to insure that these variations are developed legally. A lender should never try to "practice law" when implementing a new variation of the more acceptable lending instruments.

QUESTIONS

1. A borrower wants to borrow additional amounts on property that has already been financed with two mortgages. What may be the reason, and could you as a lender offer any help?
2. Would a rate of 15 per cent charged on a home mortgage loan be usurious?
3. What are some of the most apparent advantages to a lender of a fixed payment and a variable rate mortgage?
4. What are the major differences among the following types of loans: direct reduction loan, amortizing loan, level payment loan?
5. Suppose a seller wanted to sell but could not find an institutional or third-party lender to provide sufficient loan funds. What might the seller do?

18

CREATIVE FINANCING

Investors who have unusual investment opportunities to offer or who, for other reasons, find they are unable to use normal sources of funds and normal financing instruments turn to a variety of means for securing their ends. These means involve encouraging others to provide equity or investment funds in return for somewhat higher rates of return. On the other hand, lenders have been seeking unusual ways of increasing their loan funds and are turning to such things as mortgage-backed bonds and mortgage futures. This chapter discusses some of the ways for using equity funding of real estate investments.

EQUITY FUNDING

Equity funding means that funds are secured by finding persons who are interested in participating in an investment and sharing in the profits or income which the investment produces. They become owners of a part of the investment and, as a result, have the obligations and opportunities of ownership. This is in contrast to a borrower's exchange of some ownership rights for money to finance real estate investments. In the latter case, those providing funds are creditors with liens against the property if the borrower fails to meet the terms of the lending agreement.

Partnerships. A partnership is an agreement between two or more persons to conduct business according to the terms of the partnership. In real estate investment situations, the use of partners makes it possible to raise more money than would be available if there were only a single investor.

The partners can be recognized as either general or limited partners. In a general partnership, the partners share equally in the management and profits of the business operation. In a limited partnership, one of the partners is responsible for all of the debts and obligations of the partnership while the others, who are limited in their responsibility or financial obligations, share with the general partner in the proceeds of the partnership. For example, an experienced builder who wishes to raise funds to erect a large office building may create a limited partnership: the builder would organize and operate the entire investment, while the other partners simply provided the funding and shared in the profits.

The value of a partnership arrangement is that there can be a pooling of capital and talents of many kinds of investors, thus permitting a larger scale of investment and greater stability for management of the investment. A partnership also has some federal tax advantages, the principal one being that all tax liabilities are owed by individuals and no part of the partnership funding has to be paid for taxes.

Partnerships succeed primarily because the partners are able to work well together. However, the ease of dissolution of a partnership gives a tenuousness to the life of the investment which makes it difficult for the investors to secure funding from other sources. When funding is secured, the property—rather than the borrowers—is considered the chief protection for the lenders.

An important disadvantage in a general partnership is that the personal assets of each partner are subject to the interests of the creditors to the partnership, and either partner can bind the partnership for performance on contracts. In such cases, an unscrupulous or inept partner could be a distinct threat to the real estate investment.

Corporations. In order to avoid some of the liabilities of a partnership, the investors may form a corporation whose principal asset will be the building or property to be purchased. The corporate form of ownership permits investors to become a part of the investment opportunity with only a small purchase of stock. The corporate form also gives limited liability to all those who invest, because the assets of the corporation are the only thing which can be pledged for repayment of the debts of the corporation. For this reason, the principal attraction of a corporation is the limited liability of the incorporators or the owners of the stock.

There are some tax-saving advantages in the corporate form of investment. However, a corporation must pay corporation taxes, which run as much as 48 per cent of the net income produced by the corporation. This means that stockholders receive their returns only after corporate taxes have been paid.

Corporations also must operate according to a charter which outlines in rather specific terms what they can or cannot do. Corporations are subject to review usually by both state and national officials. If the corporation issues bonds, a written agreement called an indenture further limits the corporation.

The corporate form is not used very often for real estate investment because of the complexities and costs involved in organizing the corporation and in submitting the required reports. Only the larger, more complex type of investment undertaking requires the use of corporations. It is extremely difficult for a small corporation to borrow money because the creditors know that they can take action only against the assets of the corporation. This severely limits the growth of small corporations.

Syndicates. Syndicates are usually partnership forms of organization, but they are organized for a single purpose; when that purpose is accomplished, the syndicate is dissolved. For example, a group of individuals may form a partnership for the purpose of buying, renovating, and selling a property. They could use a syndicate form of ownership.

The syndicate form is attractive because it allows a number of people to share both the risks and the opportunities of a specialized form of real estate investment. If the syndicate fails, the syndicators lose nothing but their investment and usually have no additional liabilities.

Traditionally there have been few laws governing syndicates, but disastrous experiences on the part of syndicates organized by inexperienced people have led to an increasing number of rules and regulations. Because the primary responsibility for regulating syndicates has fallen on state governments, the rules vary considerably among the states.

The syndicate always suffers under the disadvantages that it is usually small in size and has been organized by a group of people, very few of whom are fully acquainted with real estate markets or real estate investment operations. On the other hand, syndicates organized under Securities and Exchange Commission regulations have sold stock and engaged in some important and large-scale real estate investment activities.

Real Estate Investment Trusts. Real estate investment trusts (REITs) came into prominence after 1960 legislation and subsequent Internal Revenue Service regulations. A REIT has the characteristics of a corporation in that the assets of the corporation are owned by stockholders. But special rules apply to REITs which distinguish them from corporations.

A REIT is organized either to hold or invest in property or real estate instruments. The creation of a REIT requires that there be at least 100 investors, with no five persons owning more than 50 per cent of the trust.

Ownership is evidenced by a transferable certificate and each certificate carries an equal right to vote. At least 90 per cent of the net income must be distributed to investors, at least 75 per cent of the gross income must come from real estate investments, and less than 30 per cent of the income of the trust can come from short-term gain on the sale of stock or securities or from the sale of real estate held for less than four years.

The trust is managed by a group of trustees who must use property managers, appraisers, and others to conduct the work of the trust with respect to its investment property. A major problem facing the trust is that at least 90 per cent of its earnings must be passed through to its shareholders, thus preventing the trust from building up a fund of capital reserve in case it runs into trouble with its investments. In fact, in 1973 REITs began to have the problem of lack of capital reserves, and by 1975 many of them were in extreme difficulty because they were unable to raise additional funds or to save anything from their income to apply against mounting capital deficit.

In a REIT, each stockholder can take full advantage of Internal Revenue Service regulations with respect to depreciation and capital gains so that the shareholder receives all the advantages of income tax law with respect to real estate investments.

Real estate investment trusts are regulated not only by local state governments: many are regulated by the Securities and Exchange Commission because they are viewed as corporate organizations engaged in the selling of stock. This means that the process of organizing a REIT is somewhat complicated and can be expensive. Sometimes the organizers can recoup some of their investment by becoming the trustees of the organization, but in order to be trustees they must be elected by the stockholders of the REIT.

Joint Ventures. Joint ventures are another form of the partnership arrangement: a group of investors pool their funds for the purpose of undertaking a particular real estate investment activity. In discussing various kinds of funding opportunities for real estate investments, partnerships, syndicates, or joint ventures should not be spoken of indiscriminately; each has particular characteristics which make it a distinctive kind of investment fund-raising activity.

UNCOMMON USE OF COMMON INSTRUMENTS

When experienced investors are unable to secure funds through their usual chanels, they use considerable ingenuity in creative financing. However, they exercise this ingenuity by using well-accepted legal instruments in unusual ways.

Personal Notes. If a borrower has an established financial reputation or is the owner of a sizable business or other investment, personal credit can sometimes be the basis for securing funding. In other words, in order to get an investment financed, the borrower may be able to persuade others to accept personal notes for the amount to be borrowed. In effect, the notes are unsecured but the lenders realize that, if necessary, they can proceed by putting liens or attachments on other assets which the borrower owns.

In the case of personal notes, the only protection that the borrower may have against the actions of the lender in foreclosing would be to declare bankruptcy through either Chapter 11 or Chapter 12 of federal bankruptcy law. Chapter 12 is an unusual bankruptcy law which is not known by most borrowers and lenders. In effect, under the Chapter 12 provisions, the borrower does not lose rights to a real estate investment if the creditors can be persuaded to accept some form of refinancing which will help to pay off what is owed. The decision as to whether the agreement is acceptable will rest with the bankruptcy judge. However, experience would suggest that if a borrower offers any kind of a reasonable program for repaying creditors without substantial loss on their part, the courts would accept such an arrangement.

Short-Term Credit. Sometimes an experienced real estate investor can join forces with an efficient builder or contractor and plan for a new kind of investment which can be completed in a reasonably short period of time. An investor with a good credit reputation may be able to buy materials and secure labor under an agreement that no payment be made for 45, 90, or 180 days. For example, if a builder with unusually good credit could persuade the suppliers of materials and labor to allow postponement of any payments on purchases for 180 days, it may be possible to create a substantial real property and secure other financing in the six-month period. The builder is said to buy materials and labor on accounts payable, since the transaction is entered in the books as an obligation to pay at some definite future time.

The builder buys materials and labor on accounts payable with the understanding that payments will be made on those accounts according to some agreed upon formula. For example, the formula may be 1/10 net 30, which means that a one per cent discount is allowed if payment is made within ten days. No discount is allowed after ten days, and full payment is required within 30 days. This is called borrowing on trade credit.

In this example, the builder is paying one per cent to borrow money for 20 days; i.e., the annual rate of interest is about 18 per cent. Clearly, it can be expensive to borrow through trade credit, but the builder can search for easier terms of credit. Another supplier may offer terms of 1/30 net 60. In this case, the builder can borrow money for 30 days without paying any interest and for an additional 30 days at about 12 per cent per year.

Accounts Receivable. Accounts payable is a liability; accounts receivable is the corresponding asset. For example, the builder may have done some work on contract for a large developer. The builder has already performed according to the terms of the contract, but the developer has not paid for the services. The builder is extending a form of trade credit to the developer.

In this example, the builder can secure funds by pressing for payments on the contract. Or, future contracts can be written so as to require prompt payment, or even advance payment, for services performed. Thus, the builder attempts to tighten the terms of the trade credit offered, while seeking suppliers who offer easy credit terms. The builder will be limited in the ability to do this by competition from other builders. Furthermore, it may be difficult to find reliable suppliers who offer easy credit terms *and* competitive prices for the products sold.

Hypothecation. A borrower can pledge assets which could serve as security for the loan or which could be sold, without relinquishing the rights to the earnings on the securities. In other words, the borrower retains the right to receive the earnings from investments but pledges the investments themselves as security for any funds advanced. This is known as hypothecation: the process of pledging assets as security for a loan but retaining the rights to all earnings on those assets.

Lease-Backed Financing. Lease-backed financing, another form of financing which has been very popular for some time, involves the use of a lease as a primary financing device. It would work something like this: A builder buys an empty piece of land on which a business property could be constructed. The builder finds a business firm which would like to have a particular kind of property built on the land, but the business firm does not wish to tie up its funds in such construction. Instead, it will give the builder a lease which guarantees fixed or variable rental payments for the building over a stipulated period of time. Using this lease, the builder then secures construction financing. The builder may further provide that a given portion of the lease will be credited to the business firm's account as a down payment whenever the business firm wants to purchase the property and secure other financing. Lease-backed arrangements thus provide security for the lender, the builder, and the business firm, and allow them to time their financing arrangements to fit their capital flows.

Options. Options are another form of non-mortgage financing which is used very effectively by developers. The developer makes a small payment to a property owner in return for which the property owner gives the developer the right to buy that property at a stipulated price within a given period of time. This means that the builder is protected against further increases in the value or the price of the property while investors or sources of funding are found which will permit completion of the project as planned. An option is typically a rather inexpensive instrument, equal to perhaps less than 5 per cent of the value of the property which is being purchased. Since the amount paid for the option is credited to the purchase price of the property when the transaction is completed, the person using the option runs a rather small risk of loss.

No Interest. Inflation has produced large incomes for business firms and private individuals and equally large income taxes. In an effort to avoid income taxes, particularly on earned income, investors will frequently advance large sums of money without interest but with the stipulation that they share in the capital gains of the property. Or, they may require that the interest be paid in a lump sum at some given date which fits with their income tax planning. Since interest is deductible as a tax expense to the borrower, property investors frequently find this form of financing most advantageous. They can, for example, buy a piece of property and make either no payments on the property or only minimal interest payments for a short period of years. At the end of that time, increases in the market may permit them to sell the property, taking capital gains sufficient to cover interest and provide a profit.

LENDER PARTICIPATION

Lenders may participate directly in providing funding for a real estate investment which they feel has a good promise of success. We have already mentioned a pooling of lenders' interests under some form of a joint venture agreement in which the lenders share net income or receive a guaranteed rate of return on the monies which they advance.

Sometimes an investment can be financed by selling shares of stock in the ownership of that investment. Lenders therefore can buy shares of stock which will provide them with either a guaranteed yield on each share of stock or the right to share in a given proportion of the net profits from the investment. The net profits would include not only some payment of interest on the investment but a share in capital proceeds on the sale of the investment.

STOCKS

When a property to be financed requires rather large amounts of funds, a corporation will sometimes be created with the proposed property as its principal asset. Shares will then be sold in the corporation with the stockholders having the opportunity to receive profit from the operations of the property and a capital gain if the assets of the corporation are disposed of through the sale of the property. If there is to be widespread ownership of the stock, the corporation which is formed will be subject to regulation by both state and national regulatory authorities. In fact, it is possible that the stock and the corporation would have to be registered with the Securities and Exchange Commission and be subject to all its rules and regulations.

Corporations formed for this purpose may have some difficulty in securing financing from institutional lenders, since the liability of the corporation is limited to the assets of the corporation. Since lenders like to use the borrower as well as the property as a basis for making a loan, the ability of the corporation to escape with limited liability in case of foreclosure make this form of ownership less attractive to institutional lenders. On the other hand, selling stock can be the least expensive means of acquiring funding without all the limitations inherent in using a large mortgage and dealing with a large institutional lender.

Since the stockholders are the owners of the corporation, they are in effect engaging in a form of equity financing. The corporate form simply provides them some additional legal protection and an opportunity to obtain complete disclosure and reasonably accurate reporting on the manner in which their investment is being handled.

BONDS

Bonds are used for financing by pledging the value of the real estate and the earnings from it for payment of the interest and repayment of the principal amount. Bonds have some attraction since the amount of interest which will have to be paid is fixed. In an inflationary condition in which the costs of money are rising, a fixed rate of interest will be attractive to the borrower but may make the bonds less attractive to the potential future investors. Since the security of the bonds may be less well known or less understood by the typical investor, those seeking to secure financing by the selling of bonds may find that they have to promise a higher rate of interest on the bonds than the rate they could obtain through equity financing.

The attraction of the bonds, as with stocks, is that large amounts of money can be obtained without the usual restrictions which would be imposed by an institutional lender. There are, however, regulations which must be faced. Since these regulations are in a constant process of review and change, it is important to secure good legal advice during the planning phase of bond and stock financing.

CONTRACTS AND FINANCING

Property frequently consists of a bundle of rights, for example, the right to use the land, the right to use the improvements, the right to use of the improvements for advertising purposes. Sometimes these rights can be broken down into separate packages and identified so that each package is salable to a different investor. The value of these separate packages frequently adds up to more than the market value of the property. A lender who takes an equity position in the property will want to consider a number of factors. We shall list them at this point, and discuss them in other chapters in more detail with respect to particular types of properties. These factors include:

1. Loan-to-value ratio. If loans are to be placed on the property, what percentage of the total investment will be represented by such a loan, and how much of a threat does this provide to the equity position? What is the length of the loan and what are the interest rates to be paid?
2. What is the period of time required to recover the equity in the property through the net income earnings of the property?
3. What is the period of time over which the entire purchase price could be recovered either through net income or capital gains?
4. What income tax advantages can be obtained?
5. What are the loan's servicing costs and what can be done with respect to extending the loan, getting additional advances, or refinancing or repaying the loan?
6. What are the costs of closing out the loan? What would happen in case of delinquency or foreclosure?
7. What are the following investment ratios?
   a. Purchase price to gross income

b. Total expenses as a percentage of gross income
c. Mortgage payments as a percentage of gross income
d. Mortgage payments as a percentage of net spendable income
e. Net spendable income before and after mortgage payments as a percentage of the purchase price
f. Gross income as a percentage of equity
g. Net spendable income as a percentage of equity
h. Rate of increase in the equity position either because of capital gains or through loan payments

There are no particular dollar amounts or numbers against which to measure these ratios. Lenders who are participating simply compare these ratios with earnings on other real estate and non-real estate investments. It is useful to make a list of all investments under consideration, then rank them from best to worst on each ratio. The investments which rank consistently high in terms of the ratio analysis are candidates for further investigation.

TRANSFERRING RIGHTS

Rights to property are transferred by three principal documents: (1) contracts for buying and selling, (2) contracts for leasing, and (3) contracts for financing the change of ownership. Standard forms are available in most communities and can be used if no changes are made in their contents. However, as a matter of professional practice, lenders should secure competent legal advice with respect to the contracts which they use and any changes which have to be made in such contracts. In dealing with contracts, lenders should secure a simple statement of the facts involved in the agreement and an indication that the parties to the agreement are legally competent and willing to contract. Specifically, contracts should include the following:

1. The names of the parties legally competent and willing to complete the transaction
2. The amount of consideration and an indication from all parties that the terms offered have been accepted
3. A complete description of all consideration when other than money is involved
4. Terms other than consideration on which the transaction is to be completed
5. A description of the property

Such a contractual agreement must also meet all the minimum elements of a legal contract such as legality of object. Usually, all contracts which relate to real property must be in writing.

Escrow. The escrow process is used in some states to facilitate the preparation of the documents involved in any kind of transaction. In the escrow process all contracts relating to the sale and the financing of the property are deposited with a third person, the escrow agent. Each party in the escrow tells the agent the terms on which the escrow is to be closed. Once a party has performed, withdrawal from the escrow is not possible until the other party either performs or does not perform according to agreement. The only function of an escrow agent is to carry out the terms of the transaction.

Lease Contracts. A well-drawn lease involving strong tenants can provide ample security for a loan. In fact, leases are often integral parts of multimillion-dollar financing agreements. Although their contents may vary, lease terms which lenders should study carefully include:

1. An agreement in writing
2. The exact dates of occupancy
3. Complete and accurate description of all properties
4. Limitations on use and occupancy
5. The amount of rent and method of payment
6. Liability for repairs, modernization, injuries to tenants, injuries to third parties, and payment of operating employees
7. Responsibility for payment of taxes, insurance, damage or destruction of the premises, fixtures, subleasing cancellation

As tenants are able to secure increasing numbers of rights, the lender must take great care in making sure that the tenants' rights are well defined. For example, if there is no written agreement and the rent is paid from month to month, a month-to-month tenancy is created and continues until notice is given by either the owner or the tenant that the lease is to be terminated. A year-to-year tenancy is created whenever an agreement is made from year to year and renewed automatically each year. In resort areas, tenancies for a variety of periods may be created, depending upon the customs of the area.

A tenancy at will is created whenever there is an agreement between the landlord and the tenant that the occupancy may be terminated whenever either party wishes to do so.

A tenancy at sufferance is created whenever the tenant has been in legal possession of the property under an agreement which has expired.

Although the tenant may continue to occupy the property, liability for rent remains during the occupancy and the tenant may be moved at any time without notice.

Although the rights of a tenant may be outlined fully in a lease agreement, the increasing militancy of tenants has complicated the processes of eviction. Eviction is surrounded by a body of custom and tradition, as well as statute, so lenders will want to avoid getting tied up in such processes.

Land Contracts.   A land contract is a contract which relates to the sale of a piece of property, usually unimproved land. However, the terms of a land contract and a sales contract are sometimes used interchangeably so that it is difficult to determine whether improved or unimproved property is involved.

A land or sales contract is sometimes used for improved property when the purchaser does not have enough money to secure financing using the normal mortgage lending processes. The contract usually provides that the buyer must periodically pay a given amount on the purchase price with some portion of the amount being credited to the buyer's equity. Whenever the equity reaches a given amount, theoretically the buyer has the right to transfer the financing to a mortgage or other type of lending agreement.

The courts sometimes view such agreements with suspicion because they may be used by sellers to avoid some of the restrictions found in mortgage contracts which are designed to protect buyers. Contracts are often created, however, when unusual lending terms are required and the mortgage agreement cannot be prepared to meet these terms. For these reasons, contracts for the sale of land or property should be drawn by competent lawyers who can protect the interests of both parties and still create an agreement acceptable to both. No general form has been developed for these contracts because of variations in state laws and local customs with respect to these agreements.

SUMMARY

When opportunities for real estate investing are numerous, money to finance these opportunities is usually in short supply. Investors and lenders must learn how to find new sources of funding by using methods common in other fields of finance. Special forms of business organizations—corporations, syndicates, partnerships, REITs—are becoming more widespread as lenders and investors learn how to work with legislators and lawyers to adapt these organizations to the special needs of real estate financing. Lenders may find more opportunities for increasing their earnings by actually participating with investors in well-planned real estate projects. Whatever devices are used to finance real estate projects, all rest on the use of appropriate instruments to transfer rights, among which sales contracts, leases, and financing contracts are the most common. However, even though these are special kinds of legal instruments, they are still basically contracts, and contract law is the legal foundation on which much of real estate financing rests.

QUESTIONS

1. Explain the similarities and differences among partnerships, syndicates, and joint ventures.
2. How would a corporation form be used to finance a real estate project?
3. What are some advantages to investors of owning a share of a REIT?
4. When and how can a personal note be used to finance a real estate transaction?
5. Under what conditions might the use of an option be desirable as a part of a real estate financing project?

19

ALTERNATIVES TO DIRECT REDUCTION LOANS

Lenders have been seeking to recover more of their costs of operation through some kind of change in the mortgage payment. Several variations have been discussed.

PROPOSED CHANGES IN MORTGAGE PAYMENTS

Variable Rate Mortgage. A variable rate mortgage (VRM) has all the characteristics of the normal mortgage or trust deed except that the lender may at specified times change the rate of interest. The rate change is usually related to a change in some form of index which reflects the cost of money to the lender. The theory is that the lender should be allowed to receive interest which includes the cost of the money plus a margin of 1½ to 2 per cent to permit the lender to make a profit and to continue business operations. There are many arguments as to the advantages and disadvantages of this type of mortgage so that its use is not yet as widespread as might be anticipated.

Various laws have been introduced in the states and in Congress and it will probably be some time before a uniform type of variable rate mortgage is developed. In the meantime, in some states, the state-chartered savings and loan associations have always had the right to use the VRM. Some are using it now but most feel that there is still sufficient borrower resistance that it should not be used. Many lenders also feel that the VRM should be one of several types of mortgages which they could offer to borrowers depending upon the borrowers' capacities and interests.

Variable Payment Mortgage. A variation of the VRM is the variable payment mortgage. In this mortgage the borrower pays a different monthly payment which reflects the changing market rate of interest on mortgages or changing ability to pay for the mortgage.

Under one form of the variable payment mortgage, the same amount is credited to the recovery of the mortgage every month but the amount which is credited to interest changes, depending upon what the lenders have been able to charge for interest during that period. In other words, the periodic amount repaid changes as the lender is allowed to change the charges for use of the money. Under another form, the amount paid to principal changes with the ability of the borrower to repay.

Minimum Payment Mortgage. Another form of mortgage repayment would require a minimum payment which would be related to the amortization of the loan over a predetermined period of time. The periodic payment in addition to the minimum could be based on a variable interest payment, a variable payment loan, or the normal loan. However, whenever the borrower wished, extra payments could be made which would be credited to a savings account from which the borrower would earn the contract rate of the mortgage. Whenever the borrower wished, payments could be made on the loan from this account. The borrower could also use this account to pay off the mortgage ahead of time without a penalty payment.

Fixed Interest, Variable Payment. A variation of the direct reduction loan requires a fixed interest rate but a variable payment. However, during the early years of the loan the borrower would have a lower periodic payment to make on the principal. As the borrower's capacity to pay increased or as the property gained more value, increasingly larger amounts would be paid on the principal. This, of course, could be combined with a variable interest rate; in any case, it is again an effort to accommodate to the borrower who in early years may be in a lower-paying job or may be just starting in a business career and unable to afford a very substantial mortgage payment. The borrower may be able to pay a larger amount in later years. In effect, both the borrower and the lender anticipate increasingly higher income for the borrower under conditions which reduce the risk of anticipating this for both the borrower and the lender.

Interest Only. Other alternatives to the direct reduction loan have been developed to aid borrowers who are having difficulty making payments on both principal and interest. In this case, lenders find themselves in a situation of dealing with a borrower who is unable to make the periodic payments as required. These borrowers are typically low-income or minority families trying to buy a home which is important to them and which they need, but which frequently they are unable to finance because of the requirements of the direct reduction loan. For these borrowers variations of the mortgage loan that have been discussed include requiring a borrower who is in difficulty to pay only on the principal or only on the interest. Lenders prefer that the payment be on the interest since this guarantees them some earning on their investment and the property is always there to permit them to recover the capital which they have in the mortgage loan. Variations of interest-only payments were tried during the Great Depression and are still tried when the lender has a borrower who is considered credit worthy but who is faced with a temporary incapacity to repay the loan according to schedule.

The interest-only loan is also used when the person providing the funds wants to receive a form of income which is tax-sheltered. The loan agreement provides that a given amount will be loaned for a definite number of years at a given rate of interest. Usually the term of the loan is rather short. During that period the borrower has an obligation to pay the interest only as it comes due or may even be allowed to pay interest ahead of time. The principal amount of the debt comes due at the end of the loan period.

Renewal is usually not allowed under such a loan. If the borrower is unable to pay, the property may have to be foreclosed or a new form of lending agreement may have to be arranged under which both the principal and interest would be repaid periodically.

MORTGAGE-BACKED SECURITIES

Lenders often have opportunities to make more mortgage loans than they have the funds to support. Savings and loan associations can obtain additional funds from the Federal Home Loan Bank or from commercial borrowing, but these activities create debt situations which the associations prefer to avoid. Commercial banks often have opportunities to make mortgage loans but are reluctant to keep them in their investment portfolios. For both of these types of lenders particularly, and for others who want to make mortgage loans but lack the capital to do so, mortgage-backed securities seem to be an ideal means of raising additional loan funds.

A mortgage-backed security is one which is issued by a lender with repayment of the security protected by a package of mortgage loans. The buyers of the securities receive the interest from the loans, with a small charge deducted by the original lender for servicing the mortgages. The lender who creates the security has no obligation since the buyers of the securities own a portion of the mortgage loans used as a guarantee for repayment of the investors' monies.

Mortgage-backed securities, sometimes called pass-through certificates, are particularly attractive to pension funds, bank trust departments, and individuals with reasonably large sums to invest who want higher fixed earnings but with well established guarantees as to the quality of the securities they are buying. For example, the GNMA (Government National Mortgage Association) has packaged 3,000 home mortgage loans that have an average unpaid principal of $55,000 and pay an interest rate of 8.75 per cent (compared to a prime rate of about 7.0 per cent, or to certificates of deposit that pay between 7.0 and 7.75 per cent). Certificates were offered, backed by these loans, in denominations of $25,000. The annual yield to investors, because the payments are monthly, will be between 8.55 and 8.65 per cent. None of the loans has any kind of government loan guarantee or insurance, but the loans are partially covered by private mortgage guarantee insurance.

The Government National Mortgage Association (GNMA) also puts together packages of Federal Housing Administration and Veterans Administration guaranteed and insured loans with a pool having a life of approximately 30 years. Investors are then encouraged to buy the securities which have these FHA and VA mortgages as the basic guarantee of repayment of the funds borrowed. The full faith and credit of the U. S. Government stands behind the GNMA-issued mortgage.

The Federal Home Loan Mortgage Corporation, the major instrument for savings and loan associations, creates mortgage-backed bonds which are secured by pools of conventional loans. The Federal Home Loan Mortgage Corporation guarantees the quality of the loans to a given point. However, in some cases some form of private mortgage insurance is associated with the investment so that the investor knows the insurance will pay at least 20 per cent of the value of the loan which is serving as security for the entire investment.

Savings and loan associations and commercial banks may also put together packages of conventional, FHA, or VA loans and then issue mortgages with the loans as security for the payment of the principal and interest. If the bonds are not paid and the security fails, the holders of the bonds become general creditors of the savings and loan association.

Bank of America has used these certificates and reports that its losses have been as little as 2¢ per $1,000 invested. Since inflation causes the prices of homes to rise while the debt is being lowered monthly, the certificates are considered to be unusually good investments, especially because of their very good yield. An equally attractive feature is that although the mortgages are usually for terms of 20 to 30 years, actual repayment experience suggests that the actual life will be about 12 years. This means that buyers of the certificates get the equivalent of a long-term yield for a medium-term investment. Ultimately a secondary market for buying and selling these securities is expected to develop, according to financial analysts who are working in this market.

MORTGAGE FUTURES

One of the problems which lenders have always faced is the cyclical character of the real estate market and the mortgage-lending market. Frequently lenders have made long-term lending commitments at rates which subsequent market changes have made unprofitable. The first organized trading in mortgage futures began in New York in November 1975.

The mortgage futures market is like any other futures market. Assume that a savings and loan association (S&L) is creating a pool of mortgages which it plans to resell at some future time in order to secure additional funding for more lending. The S&L can hedge against changes in interest rates by agreeing now to sell the entire pool at a fixed rate of interest sometime in the future. If speculators believe that mortgage rates will go down, causing a rise in the price at which the pool is offered, they will buy the futures contract. If the S&L feels that interest rates may be increasing, it can anticipate some amount of profit by creating mortgage instruments at higher rates of interest sometime in the future. Most important, the S&L eliminates uncertainty. Mortgage loans can be made with the confidence that they can be packaged for future sale at a known rate of interest.

So far, trading in mortgage futures has been met with mixed feelings. In most cases, the savings and loan associations are waiting to see how the market develops. On the other hand, mortgage bankers see this as another opportunity for gaining additional funding for the secondary mortgage market.

MORTGAGE INSURANCE

In an effort to increase the attractiveness of mortgage loans for secondary markets and in view of the success which the Federal Housing Administration has had in insuring mortgage loans, more and more lenders are turning to private mortgage insurance companies. A mortgage insurance company guarantees to the lender that in return for a modest premium (usually paid by the borrower) the lender can be sure of recovering the unpaid balance of a loan if the borrower defaults at any time. Theoretically, this form of insurance should permit the lender to make loans at a lower rate and increase the number of lenders who would be willing to make mortgage loans during difficult economic conditions.

Mortgage insurance has been growing and has been of real assistance to the mortgage markets—so much so that variations of it are now being discussed. One variation of mortgage insurance was introduced by the Federal Home Loan Mortgage Corporation (FHLMC) which puts individual loans together in packages equal to about a million dollars per package and then sells the entire package to other investors with the guarantee that the loans will be repaid as provided; or if a loan goes into default, the investor may select another loan of equivalent value for its replacement. The FHLMC accomplishes its goal through the sale of guaranteed mortgage certificates (GMC). A GMC is an ownership in a large pool of mortgages which are administered by the FHLMC. Interest is paid semiannually and the principal is returned annually. Moreover, the FHLMC agrees to purchase unrepaid principal amounts of mortgages at the end of 15 years or at the investor's option instead of letting the mortgages run their entire 30-year term. The instrument is fully guaranteed by FHLMC as to the payment of interest, minimum annual passthrough of principal, and overall safety of principal. Investors can participate in the GMC in minimum amounts of $100,000. The mortgage loans which are being sold are those made by investment banking firms, commercial banks, and savings and loan associations. The investors in GMC include pension funds, investment and trust funds, and institutional investors of various types.

MORTGAGE EXCHANGES

From time to time, the suggestion has been made that a market should be created where mortgage instruments could be bought and sold. Early efforts at this were disastrous primarily because of the unprincipled or illegal activities of some of those who formed these trust exchanges.

An even greater barrier to a free market in mortgages has been the lack of uniformity in the legal format of the pledge which creates a trust or a conventional mortgage. The Federal Home Loan Bank and other federal agencies have been taking steps to create a uniform package which would consist of a promissory note, a pledge of property as security for the repayment of the note, and an appraisal form. Good progress is being made in this regard. The fact that this can be done is reflected in the extent to which FHA and VA mortgages can be exchanged across the country. However, with the decreasing importance of FHA and VA loans in mortgage markets more and more attention is being paid to creating some form of a private exchange which would be made possible by uniform instruments.

SUMMARY

Inflation has caused problems for the direct reduction (or level payment or self-amortizing) loan, since lenders find that inflation increases interest on deposits without increasing the interest on most of their mortgage loans. Furthermore, other costs of operation may rise beyond the ability to pay as determined by long-term, low-interest direct reduction loans. The direct reduction loan was a great improvement over the balloon payment, a form of mortgage loan widely used before the Depression, but changing economic conditions now require the search for other instruments.

One alternative is the variable rate mortgage (VRM) where the interest rate would vary according to interest rates paid on deposits or other financial instruments. The variation in interest would mean variable payments for the borrower unless the maturity of the mortgage were also variable. With the variable maturity mortgage, an increase in interest rates means that less of the level payment is credited to principal repayment. The reduction in principal repayment means that the maturity of the mortgage has lengthened, although a reduction in interest rates would allow the maturity to shorten again.

Another alternative to the level payment mortgage would make the payment variable, but the variations would depend partly on the ability of the borrower to repay. Thus, an increase in earning power because of inflation or because of promotion would result in larger payments and shorter loan maturity. A decrease in earning power would lead to a reduction of monthly payments, but, under one proposal, there would be a minimum payment which would not be flexible.

Alternative financial arrangements include long-term lease of the property or mortgages which give the lender participation in the income-producing aspect of a property. A logical extension of participation in income is to give the lender an equity position. In corporate finance this is done through bonds convertible into stock or bonds with warrants for the purchase of stock. In the real estate field, the lender might take an equity position as part of a package which includes some financing with the direct reduction mortgage.

QUESTIONS

1. What do lenders hope to achieve in developing alternative forms of mortgage payments to replace the direct reduction loan?

2. Under what circumstances would an interest-only loan be attractive to both the borrower and the lender?
3. Explain why mortgage futures financing may be attractive and how it would be used.
4. How can private insurance companies undertake mortgage loan insurance and make a profit?
5. How would a mortgage exchange operate, and why would it be needed?

V

Advanced Topics

20

PROPOSALS FOR CHANGE IN THE STRUCTURE OF THRIFT INSTITUTIONS

In 1970, the Nixon Administration appointed a group of experts to conduct a comprehensive study of the structure and regulation of financial institutions. This Presidential Commission on Financial Structure and Regulation, which has since become known as the Hunt Commission (see Chapter 7), made numerous proposals for change. Some of these proposals are still untested, but others are being tried on an experimental basis. A pending federal legislation, the Financial Institutions Act (FIA) of 1975, embodies many of the most important Hunt Commission recommendations. If that legislation passes, practices which are currently experimental and on a small scale will undoubtedly be rapidly expanded. Therefore, a professional working with real estate financial institutions should be fully aware of proposed changes which may become law very shortly.

The Hunt Commission dealt with all sorts of financial institutions. In this chapter, special attention will be given to the proposals which affect the structure, regulation, and taxation of mutual savings banks and savings and loan associations. The discussion of proposals for change will be organized around proposals which influence (1) the asset side of the balance sheet, (2) the liability side, (3) taxation of thrift institutions, and (4) minor matters such as chartering and FHA–VA interest ceilings.

Before discussing these four categories of proposed changes and their implications for the housing sector, let us review the fundamental economic

315

forces which have created pressure for changes in the structure of thrift institutions ("thrifts").

THE AGENTS OF CHANGE

In Chapter 21 we discuss the severe and extended recessions which plague the real estate industry. Changes in interest rates are an important cause of declines in housing market activity. Like housing, all real estate investment is very sensitive to changes in the general level of interest rates; the large role played by financing costs explains this sensitivity.

Interest rates are related to cycles in the general level of economic activity (see Chapter 21). In the past 20 to 25 years, these cycles have been closely monitored by the executive branch of the federal government, with an eye to moderating the size of the cyclical swings. But, these countercyclical government policies may increase the swings in interest rates. Monetary policy, which is implemented largely by purchases and sales of financial instruments, is notorious for its tendency to increase interest rates in an attempt to reduce inflationary pressure. One of the most controversial aspects of monetary policy is its effect, through interest rates, on real estate markets.

The structure of mutual savings banks and savings and loan associations accounts for some of the sensitivity of real estate lending to changes in interest rates. There are basically two problems: (1) high leverage (small amounts of equity compared to the large volume of loans made) and (2) borrowing short-term liabilities in order to acquire long-term assets.

The leverage problem is related to the fact that thrift institutions get most of their loanable funds from deposits, not from capital stock. Since the position of stockholders is very small, the earnings of thrifts can be squeezed by changes in the rate of interest paid to depositors.

Leverage.   Leverage can be measured by the ratio of debt to total assets (i.e., one minus the ratio of equity to total assets). Public utilities, which are considered highly leveraged corporations, have a debt–total asset ratio of about 65 per cent. Manufacturing companies have a ratio of about 45 per cent. Contrast to this the position of savings and loan associations: At the end of 1974, their debt–assets ratio was 94 per cent! The reason is the large size of deposits: 82 per cent of total liabilities was provided by deposits.

The highly leveraged position of the thrift institutions is clearly related to their role as financial intermediaries. If a manufacturing corporation had a leverage ratio of 94 per cent, it would reflect excessive risk taking; but this is not the case with thrift institutions. Interest payments on thrift deposits need not meet legally fixed levels; interest on corporate bonds does have to meet predetermined levels. The payment of interest on thrift deposits is not required. Thus, proposals to change the structure of thrift institutions do not include proposals to reduce leverage.

Asset–Liability Structure.　The maturity structure of assets and liabilities exacerbates the leverage problem. The assets of thrift institutions, principally mortgage loans, have very long maturities. Therefore, when interest rates rise, these assets do not roll over fast enough to produce a corresponding rise in the earnings of thrift institutions. (A loan is said to roll over when it is paid off and the proceeds are reinvested in another loan. The new loan will earn a higher interest rate when rates are rising.) Commercial banks do not have this problem to nearly the same degree, because the assets of commercial banks include large amounts of short-term business and consumer loans. These loans roll over frequently, causing bank earnings to rise with interest rate increases.

The long life of their assets prevents the thrifts from bidding for more deposits when interest rates rise. They are also prevented by law: the Interest Rate Adjustment Act of 1966 granted the Federal Home Loan Bank Board the power to fix maximum rates payable on deposits at S&L's. Similar authority is exercised over mutual savings banks by the FDIC. Therefore, a rise in market interest rates means an outflow of deposits. Depositors can invest directly in Treasury bills or notes or in federal agency issues. When depositors withdraw funds in order to invest them in such securities, it is called "disintermediation": the financial intermediaries are bypassed.

The most important proposals for change in the structure of thrift institutions follow a common logic:

1. It is difficult and probably undesirable to change countercyclical monetary policy. Cycles in interest rates caused by the business cycle and by monetary policy can be expected to continue.
2. The high ratio of debt to total assets is inherent in the nature of financial intermediaries. It is undesirable to try to change this.
3. The asset structure and regulation of interest rates paid on deposits can be changed to reduce the length and severity of recessions in mortgage lending. It is also possible to improve the ability of thrifts to attract deposits by allowing them to issue interest-paying demand deposits.

PROPOSED CHANGES IN THE STRUCTURE OF ASSETS

As noted above, the long life of most mortgage loans is responsible for part of the structural problem faced by thrift institutions. Therefore, it is logical that some of the proposals for change focus on allowing thrift institutions to accept short-term assets. The proposed shortening of the maturity structure of assets should make the thrift institutions less sensitive to an increase in interest which must be paid on deposits: interest on short-term assets will increase correspondingly as these assets mature and are replaced by higher yielding loans and investments. It is argued that the changes will enable thrifts to compete more easily for deposits during periods of rising interest rates.

If it is desirable for thrift institutions to shorten the maturity of their assets, why haven't they done so? The reason is that legal restrictions prevent them from making most short-term loans and investments which are currently available to commercial banks. Actually, it is difficult to generalize about these restrictions; some thrifts (including most mutual savings banks) are state-chartered while others are federally chartered. Generally, the assets of thrifts are largely limited to loans related to housing and real estate. However, mutual savings banks often have the power to invest in a wider variety of assets than savings and loans.

It is easier to generalize about federally chartered savings and loans and the forty-odd mutual savings banks which are federally chartered. The restrictions on their lending and investing power may be summarized as follows:

1. Like commercial banks, these thrift institutions cannot hold equity securities. However, they can own corporations exclusively providing related services such as data processing.[1]
2. They may make "passbook loans" to account holders, secured by their deposits and limited by the amount of funds in the accounts.
3. They may make loans to individuals to pay for college, university, or vocational expenses.[2]
4. They may make construction loans, but only by using mortgage instruments. This is cumbersome, since legal formalities such as recording of the instrument must be followed.
5. Cash and liquid assets must be held to meet withdrawals; currently they amount to about 8 per cent of assets. But liquid private debt instruments, such as commercial paper, cannot be held by federally chartered thrifts.

One of the proposed changes would allow federally chartered thrift institutions to invest in consumer loans. This means that they would be able

[1] *The Financial Institutions Act of 1975, A Bill* (Washington, D. C.: Dept. of the Treasury, March 19, 1975), p. 21.
[2] *Ibid.*

to make auto loans, vacation loans, and other unsecured personal loans. But the thrifts would be restricted in one way in which commercial banks are not: they could invest no more than 10 per cent of assets in consumer loans.

Consumer Loans. Consumer loans have much shorter maturities than mortgage loans, so allowing 10 per cent of assets in consumer loans will do much to produce desirable changes in the structure of the balance sheet at the typical thrift institution. These loans could be rolled over frequently during periods of rising interest rates. Therefore, earnings on consumer loans would keep pace with the market, allowing thrifts to pay more interest to depositors.

If consumer loans are desirable, why are they being limited to 10 per cent of assets? The reason is that it would be undesirable for thrifts to shift too much of their assets out of mortgage loans. Thus, the regulators are trying to walk a narrow line between more diversification in asset structure and too little investment in mortgages. (The final section of this chapter has a further discussion of the pros and cons of the proposed changes with respect to the housing sector.)

Commercial Loans. Another change would allow thrift institutions to hold commercial paper, bankers' acceptances, and investment grade corporate debt to 10 per cent of total assets. The arguments for this change are similar to those advanced for allowing investment in consumer loans.

Asset Diversification. Finally, the thrift institutions would be allowed two other types of assets: (1) community rehabilitation and development loans up to 3 per cent of total assets; and (2) unsecured lines of credit for the purpose of constructing improvements on real property.[3] The first of these provisions will allow thrifts to participate in federal programs such as those authorized by the Housing and Community Development Act of 1974. The second will make investment in construction loans less costly and less time-consuming.

PROPOSED CHANGES AFFECTING LIABILITIES

One of the provisions of the Financial Institutions Act (FIA) of 1975 would phase out the ceilings on interest which can be paid on deposits. About 5½ years after enactment of the legislation, interest paid by thrifts and by commercial banks would be free to fluctuate with competitive

---

[3] *Ibid.*

forces. The significance of this should not be overemphasized: the differential between ceilings for commercial banks and thrift institutions is currently only about ¼ per cent.[4]

Removal of Limits on Deposits. As the FIA is now written, the phasing-out of interest rate ceilings is implied but not required. Regulatory authorities would presumably take their cue from earlier versions of the legislation which called for a phased elimination. The authorities could do this by making the interest regulations less restrictive over time; e.g., the limits for deposits of a specific maturity or size could be raised substantially above the market level. Repeating this process for different types of deposits would eventually eliminate the restrictions.

It is expected that the removal of rate ceilings on deposits will benefit depositors by giving them a more competitive return on their savings. During periods of rising interest rates it should no longer be necessary for large depositors to withdraw money in order to invest directly in money market instruments: i.e., "disintermediation" should pose a lesser problem.

Q: If interest rates on savings eventually increase, won't this mean higher rates on mortgages and bank loans?

A: Not necessarily. First of all, there is no reason to assume that removal of the regulatory ceilings will automatically lead to higher deposit rates. The goal is for competitive rates that respond to changing market conditions.

To the extent that interest rates do increase, the supply of funds available for lending should also increase, since financial institutions will be better able to compete with other forms of investment. The increased supply for lendable funds will tend to keep loan interest rates down.

Q: Why not remove Regulation Q immediately?

A: Savings and loan associations, due to their portfolios of long-term mortgages paying fixed interest, do not have the ability to immediately start paying freely competitive rates. They must be given a period of time to adjust their portfolios so as to improve the composition of their assets and increase their ability to compete in the market for consumer savings.

While banks could probably pay increased rates now, allowing them to do so could drain deposits from thrift institutions, severely damaging the mortgage market, and thus the housing industry.

Q: If Regulation Q and its companion regulations are removed, will all savings and loan associations, mutual savings banks, and banks pay the same rate?

A: The amount of interest which deposit institutions will pay for funds will depend on local supply and demand conditions, costs of operations, and the uses to which the institutions expect to put the funds.

Institutions will be free to "tailor-make" savings deposit services in terms

---

[4] Kent W. Colton, speech given at the Alumni Consumer Credit Management Conference, Columbia University, New York, January 26, 1975.

of minimum amounts, maturity, liquidity and the like. Each service can be expected to carry its own rate of return.[5]

Free competition for deposits requires more than the removal of ceilings on interest rates. Commercial banks currently have several advantages in this competition. They have the same advantage over thrift institutions as supermarkets have over the corner grocery: they offer a full range of services, including demand deposits, consumer loans, and commercial loans (many of which require compensating deposit balances). These advantages have led to advertising slogans such as "your full-service bank," "one-stop banking," and "the only bank your family ever needs."

We have seen that the restructuring of the assets of thrift institutions will do much to make them more competitive with commercial banks. We turn now to a discussion of new deposit-related services which are developing at savings and loans and mutual savings banks.

Improved Savings and Loan Association Services [6]

The Federal Home Loan Bank Board (FHLBB), which regulates Federally chartered savings and loan associations (S&L's), has encouraged greater competition between S&L's and commercial banks by allowing Federal S&L's to offer a number of new services to their customers. In January 1974, the FHLBB adopted a temporary regulation which permits Federal S&L's to operate experimental place-of-business funds transfer systems. These systems allow customers to conduct financial transactions through the use of electronic signals generated by on-line computer terminals as well as off-line automated teller machines.[7] The terminals, which are called remote service units, allow depositors to conduct transactions with their S&L's at places of business other than the associations' offices. The remote service units, which may be shared with other Federally insured financial institutions, are not treated as branch or satellite offices of the S&L's by the FHLBB.

Also, in January 1974 the funds transfer system initiated by the First Federal Savings and Loan Association, Lincoln, Nebraska was approved under the new regulation.[8] This place-of-business system allows depositors of First Federal to make deposits to or withdrawals from their interest-bearing savings accounts at two Hinky Dinky supermarkets in Lincoln. Transactions are made with the use

---

[5] *The Financial Institutions Act of 1975, op. cit.,* p. 18.

[6] Extracted material to p. 324 is from Jean M. Lovati, "The Changing Competition Between Commercial Banks and Thrift Institutions for Deposits," *The Monthly Review* of the Federal Reserve Bank of St. Louis, July 1975, pp. 2–5.

[7] Transactions initiated through the use of on-line computer terminals are instantly communicated to and verified by the S&L's central computer. Off-line facilities generally are not connected directly to the computer of the S&L; transactions initiated at these terminals are recorded on magnetic tape or a like medium which is subsequently delivered to and read by the S&L's computer.

[8] "Nebraska S&L Begins Point-of-Sale EFTS," *American Banker,* January 16, 1974.

of plastic cards on which account information is encoded on magnetic stripes. At the supermarket, Hinky Dinky employees transmit transaction data to First Federal's central computer which records the actions. Settlement is accomplished electronically by entries to the accounts of depositors and Hinky Dinky at First Federal. At the supermarket, money is accepted from or disbursed to the customer-depositor by the employees through cash drawers maintained by Hinky Dinky for completion of the physical part of the transactions.

Within two months after the installation of the system, legal action interrupted this service. The state of Nebraska first brought suit against Hinky Dinky on the grounds that the supermarket was offering banking services without a license. The Nebraska Banking Association also brought suit, charging that First Federal was violating the state's anti-branching laws. With litigation still pending, the savings and loan services in the two Hinky Dinky stores resumed operation in September of last year. Since resumption of the service, First Federal has installed its funds transfer units in three additional Hinky Dinky stores in Lincoln and has received FHLBB approval to expand the service to 19 of the supermarket chain's stores in eastern Nebraska.

In April [1974], the state of Washington enacted legislation which allows state-chartered commercial banks, mutual savings banks, and S&L's to establish any number of unmanned facilities throughout the state, provided that those operating the facilities share the costs and operation of the terminals when asked to do so by the state authorities. Commercial banks are required to share facilities with other commercial banks and have the option of sharing with thrift institutions. Thrifts are permitted, but not required, to share facilities. These facilities are not considered branches under Washington law.

An electronic facility began operation in July 1974 on a 24-hour basis in Bellevue, Washington.[9] In this case, the unit is shared by four mutual savings banks, ten Federal savings and loan associations, and two state-chartered S&L's. Unlike the Hinky Dinky terminal, this automated teller machine is unmanned and is operated by the depositor, independent of any business. Cash disbursements are made through the use of automatic cash dispensers which are activated by the depositor's magnetic card. Deposits are handled in a manner similar to that used for night depositories.

Other S&L's across the country have also initiated funds transfer systems, implementing place-of-business terminals and automated teller machines similiar to those just described. Because of the rapid development and implementation of these systems in many states, only two have been described here in detail.

In addition to these electronic innovations, other changes have taken place which permit savings and loan associations to compete more effectively for deposits. One such change involves the bill payment services which S&L's are able to offer. At the depositor's request, Federal S&L's may honor nontransferable orders to transfer funds, periodically or otherwise, from the depositor's savings account to third parties. In the past, such payments were limited to housing-related items and loans on these items, such as payments on mortgages, rent, taxes, utilities, and home improvements. The FHLBB recently removed the housing-related restriction, thus allowing Federal savings and loan associations to offer a full range of bill payment services.

---

[9] "15 Washington State Thrifts to Test Electronic Teller," *American Banker*, February 21, 1974.

In December [1974], the FHLBB also adopted a regulation which gives depositors traveling more than 50 miles from their home access to their savings account balances through any other Federally-insured savings and loan association by means of a Travelers Convenience Withdrawal. The S&L at which a customer has requested such a withdrawal notifies, by wire or telephone, the S&L at which the customer has a deposit account to deduct the amount of the withdrawal from that account. Funds are then disbursed by the cooperating savings and loan association, and the S&L's which have chosen to offer this service make settlements among themselves.

Making Mutual Savings Banks More Competitive

Financial institutions in New England have attracted widespread attention by offering Negotiable Order of Withdrawal (NOW) accounts. Unlike conventional savings accounts, NOW accounts permit depositors to make check-like withdrawals from their interest-bearing savings accounts for making payments to third parties. The withdrawal orders are cleared through the Federal Reserve System's check clearing facilities by means of special routing numbers which are assigned to the thrift institutions.

This type of account was first offered in 1972 by the Consumers Savings Bank of Worcester, Massachusetts, and was rapidly initiated at other savings banks in Massachusetts and New Hampshire.[10] At the time, commercial banks in those states opposed the use of NOWs and urged a ban on them by Congress. Legislation was subsequently enacted which limits the use of NOW accounts to these two states, but allows not only mutual savings banks but also commercial banks and savings and loan associations within these states to offer such accounts.

This legislation, which permitted an additional 427 depository financial institutions to offer NOW accounts, affected the competitive balance among institutions in the two states. Of these newly eligible institutions, commercial banks introduced the majority of the new NOW accounts. The 200 mutual savings banks in Massachusetts and New Hampshire, which were previously the only financial institutions permitted to offer NOW accounts, experienced a decline in their NOW account deposits during the initial implementation of the legislation. As more financial institutions began to offer NOW accounts, service charges on drafts from the accounts were reduced or eliminated by many institutions and, in addition, some commercial banks began to offer free checking accounts.

Thrift institutions have also been involved in a new system for making payments, called "pay-by-phone," which was initiated last fall by a savings bank in Connecticut and one in Minnesota. Under this system, depositors at these savings banks who open special interest-bearing accounts may make payments to third parties without writing checks or negotiable orders of withdrawal. Depositors use their telephones to make payments to utilities, merchants, and other organizations which participate in the system.

Approval by state banking authorities is necessary before such a system can be put into effect. Although the pay-by-phone system was judged to be illegal under Connecticut's existing statutes, the People's Savings Bank, Bridgeport, has been permitted to continue its pay-by-phone operations on a test basis until the

[10] "Early History and Initial Impact of NOW Accounts," *New England Economic Review* (January/February 1975), pp. 17–26.

end of 1975. At the same time, it was ruled that under the current provisions no other Connecticut mutual savings bank should be permitted to initiate such a system.

At the People's Savings Bank, depositors who open a special account are given a personal identification code number in addition to an account number. The customer can then dial a special telephone number and give these numbers to the operator who is told which companies and what amounts to pay. This information is transcribed by the operator, who tallies the total amount paid and informs the customer of the balance left in the account.

Minnesota is the only other state in which regulatory authorities have approved a pay-by-phone plan on a test basis. At the Farmers and Mechanics Savings Bank, Minneapolis, the pay-by-phone system operates either through an operator, as above, or by computer for those depositors with push-button telephones. With a push-button phone, the depositor indicates the amounts to be paid by depressing the corresponding telephone digits. The companies which participate in the Minnesota system, as well as those using the Connecticut system, receive daily printouts listing the name, account number, and amount paid by every customer, along with a cashier's check issued by the savings bank for the total amount of payments.

The Financial Institutions Act (FIA) of 1975, currently pending before Congress, will drastically alter the development of new deposit services. All of the thrift institutions, regardless of charter, *and* all commercial banks will be permitted to offer NOW accounts to individuals and corporations. Furthermore, the thrift institutions will be allowed to issue demand deposits to individuals and corporations on the same basis as commercial banks.

PROPOSED CHANGES IN TAXATION

In Chapter 7 we discussed the complicated tax deductions which are currently available to the thrift institutions. We noted that the deduction for funds transferred to loan loss reserve reduces the risk associated with mortgages, as well as subsidizing the thrift institutions. We also noted changes currently underway which would reduce that tax subsidy and change its character.

Another proposed tax change which is incorporated into the FIA would eliminate the loan loss deduction altogether. It would substitute a tax credit, available to all individuals and corporations, for investment in residential mortgages. The amount of the tax credit would be a percentage of the dollar amount of interest received from a mortgage loan. For all individuals, and for corporations holding exactly 10 per cent of assets in residential mortgage loans, the credit would be 1.5 per cent. For corporations with 70 per cent of assets in residential mortgage loans, 3.5 per cent of the interest received could be credited against their tax liability. A sliding scale would operate between the 10 per cent and 70 per cent limits: the percentage of the tax credit would increase by $\frac{1}{30}$ of one per cent as the percentage of mortgage loans held increased by one per cent.[11]

The proposed tax provision lacks the risk reduction feature which characterizes the loan loss deduction. However, it does encourage investment in residential real estate. The sliding scale encourages financial institutions to hold a large percentage of their assets in residential mortgages. Furthermore, all financial institutions are treated equally for the same kind of investment in real estate.

OTHER PROPOSED CHANGES

The pending FIA would increase competition among regulatory authorities as well as among financial institutions. This unique feature would make it easy for thrift institutions to change from one regulatory authority to another.

State-chartered institutions could opt for federal charters and federal institutions could convert to state chartering. Mutual (i.e., depositor-owned) institutions could convert to a stock form and vice versa. Finally, the current statutory prohibition against federal charters for stock associations would be removed. Thus, a stock association will be able to change to federal regulatory authority without changing to the mutual form.[12]

These changes, if implemented, will no doubt make regulatory authorities more aware of the needs of the thrift institutions and it may make the regulators more innovative. However, it is also possible that the regulators will begin to relax strict regulatory requirements. For example, states may lower or abolish reserve requirements in order to attract institutions. Similarly, supervision of operations might be relaxed. If this occurs, regulation may be subverted; it may serve only the industry, not the national interest.

By law, the FHA and the VA set administrative ceilings on the interest which can be charged on insured loans. When the market interest rate rises above these ceilings, lenders charge points to bring the effective interest rate up to the market rate. The same practice is often followed when the market rate exceeds state usury ceilings. Thus, these ceilings are not generally enforceable. The FHA and VA ceilings would be abolished by the FIA of 1975.

Variable interest rate mortgages have been authorized by the FHLBB

---

[11] *The Financial Institutions Act of 1975, op. cit.*, p. 29. Note that the tax credit is available for property improvement loans, loans for construction of public use facilities in residential areas, and loans on mobile homes when secured by a first mortgage.

[12] *Ibid.*, p. 22.

for federal savings and loan associations. The authorized variable-rate mortgages subject borrowers to small changes in the amount of their monthly payments. The interest rate can change by steps of ¼ per cent, but no more frequently than once every six months. A change is triggered by a rise in the rate on newly issued mortgages.

The cumulative effect of these changes could get large if interest rates were to rise or fall steadily for a few years at a time. Is it politically feasible to subject individuals to substantial increases in their monthly mortgage payments? For some families, these substantial increases would result in the loss of their home, an anathema to American traditions and values. (Renters can easily be turned out by rent increases, but a similar situation for homeowners is hard to visualize.) This may be the reason that these variable-rate mortgages have met a cool reception by bankers and public alike.

A level payment mortgage which varies in rate and maturity has also been proposed. The interest rate would fluctuate with the market rate of interest on new mortgages, but increases in the interest rate would be offset by extensions in the maturity of the mortgage. Thus, the amount of the monthly payment would remain constant. There are two drawbacks to this proposal:

1. Financial institutions do not want to deal with the possibility of a very long mortgage life (e.g., 50 years).
2. Relatively small increases in the market interest rate would result in large changes in the maturity; on a new mortgage at 8 per cent for 30 years, a 1 per cent increase in the rate would make the life of the mortgage infinite. Further increases could not be accommodated with a fixed monthly payment. Therefore, variable maturities provide only part of the answer.

The advantage of the variable-rate and the variable-maturity mortgages is that they reduce the sensitivity of thrift institutions to increases in interest rates. As rates increase, so do the earnings of thrifts.

The variable-rate (or variable payment) mortgage has the advantage of protecting thrift institutions from increases in the general level of interest rates. With rates variable, the rate of return on earning assets would tend to rise along with increases in the rate paid on deposits. (However, restrictions on the amount and frequency of rate increases would make interest earned rise more slowly than interest paid.) The variable-maturity mortgage, on the other hand, would not change the cash flow to the thrift institution. Instead, it would change the amount of the payment credited to repayment of principal. In a cash-short situation this would not be effective in alleviating the basic problem, which is inability to pay higher interest on deposits.

Under one proposal, the variable payment mortgage would make payments a function of the borrower's income; e.g., the mortgage payment would be 20 per cent of income, but there would be some minimum payment required. This may be acceptable to borrowers, but it suffers from two drawbacks:

1. It involves the difficult process of verifying income. This could be quite costly.
2. It does nothing to solve the thrift institutions' sensitivity to rising interest rates. Interest and cash flow from existing mortgages would not increase along with the market rate of interest—and the rate of interest paid on deposits.

IMPLICATIONS FOR HOUSING FINANCE

Many changes with different effects on the housing market have been proposed. The FIA of 1975 is interesting, even if it does not become law, because it represents a package of proposed changes. Assuming that this package were implemented, what would be the implications for the housing market and for financial institutions?

Clearly the thrust of the legislation is toward structural convergence of financial institutions by allowing diversification in the assets of thrifts. The legislation would also promote the NOW accounts; all types of financial institutions would be allowed to issue them. Commercial banks would be distinguished from thrift institutions primarily through various types of commercial loans which would still be denied to the thrifts.

Structural convergence of financial institutions is consistent with a long history of structural change. All of the institutions began as highly specialized intermediaries. For example, commercial banks made short-term loans to finance trade or agriculture, and savings and loans made residential mortgage loans to a limited group of members. Gradually, they have diversified their menu of deposit and lending services.

The most significant proposed change for the housing market is the tax credit for residential mortgage interest. Will that be sufficient to attract mortgage funds from individuals and institutions? Will the permission granted to thrifts to invest in consumer loans and commercial paper drain funds away from the housing market?

Full answers to these questions will not be available until the package of proposed changes is actually implemented. However, the FIA of 1975 is based on extensive study by qualified bodies such as the Hunt Com-

Savings and Loan Associations and Mutual Savings Banks

Before	After

Deposit Powers

1. Payment of interest: ceilings on deposit rates set by FHLBB or FDIC.

Payment of interest: ceilings eliminated after five and one-half years. Secretary of the Treasury to report findings and recommendations to Congress on competitive strength of all financial institutions five years after enactment of the FIA.

2. Savings accounts: full powers; individual and corporate.

Savings accounts: full powers; individual and corporate (no change).

3. Demand accounts: not permitted.

Demand accounts: full powers; individual and corporate.

4. NOW accounts: not permitted.

NOW accounts: full powers; individual and corporate.

Lending and Investment Powers

5. Loans for housing and closely related areas.

Loans for housing and closely related areas; real estate loans under same conditions as commercial banks; plus (on a limited basis) consumer loans (up to 10 per cent of assets); construction loans not tied to permanent financing; community rehabilitation loans under a 3 per cent leeway authority.

6. Equities: no acquisition of private sector issues.

Equities: no acquisition of private sector issues (no change).

7. Securities: no acquisition of private debt securities.

Securities: limited acquisition of commercial paper, bankers' acceptances, and high-grade corporate debt (up to 10 per cent of assets).

Taxes

8. Loan loss deductions: preferential treatment compared to banks.

Loan loss deductions: will move to same treatment as banks by 1979, or earlier, at their option.

9. Tax credits: none.

Tax credits: special tax credits for investment in residential mortgages; significant incentive to retain high percentage of portfolio in residential mortgages.

Chartering Alternatives

10. Federal: mutual associations only.

Federal: mutual and stock associations.

11. State: mutual and stock associations.

State: mutual and stock associations (no change).

Fig. 20—1. Impact of the proposed Financial Institutions Act.

Savings and Loan Associations and Mutual Savings Banks

Before	After

Branching

12. Federally chartered: governed by FHLBB.	Federally chartered: governed by FHLBB (no change).
13. State-chartered: governed by state law.	State chartered: governed by state law (no change).
	Provides freedom of conversion from state to federal, federal to state, mutual to stock and stock to mutual.

Summary

Consumer interests penalized owing to prohibitions against service competition and forced specialization among financial institutions.	Consumer interest strengthened by availability of new sources of supply of both deposit services and lending services and the promise of direct price competition between thrift institutions and banks.
Opportunities to compete for funds limited and little ability to withstand tight-money pressures without substantial government support.	Virtually unlimited opportunities to compete for funds. Ability to withstand tight-money pressures strengthened, minimizing need for government rescue operations.

Source: The Financial Institutions Act of 1975, A Bill, March 19, 1975, Department of the Treasury.

Fig. 20–1. Continued.

mission. These studies tend to indicate that the proposed changes will reduce the cyclical sensitivity of the housing industry while continuing an adequate supply of residential mortgage funds.

Figure 20–1, prepared by the U.S. Treasury, presents a before-and-after picture of the thrift institutions, assuming the FIA of 1975 passes. It is well worth careful study, since it contains information about the current situation as well as the proposed changes. Aside from the pending legislation, Figure 20–1 gives an overview of some of the most important issues in real estate finance.

Some of the changes are currently underway, and they will be implemented, albeit more slowly, even if the legislation does not pass. Most notably, new types of deposit services are being implemented by thrift institutions as well as commercial banks. Banking at the place of business through checkless electronic funds transfer systems (EFTS) is developing rapidly. The payment of interest on deposits which are very similar to demand deposits, the NOW accounts, is spreading to more and more institutions and regions.

SUMMARY

The proposed changes in thrift institutions have developed from the long, severe recessions in the housing industry. The extreme cyclical sensitivity of real estate finance is related partly to the fact that interest constitutes a large part of the cost of an investment in real estate. This fundamental truth will not be changed by any of the proposals to restructure financial institutions.

The proposals for structural change affect one part of the problem: the imbalances which occur because of the long maturity of the assets of thrifts and because of their limited ability to compete for deposits. If the proposals are successful in shortening asset maturity, and if they provide for continuation in the supply of funds to residential mortgage lending, they should at least partially dampen the cycles in the housing industry.

QUESTIONS

1. Why can thrift institutions live with much higher leverage than manufacturing firms?
2. The structural problems of thrifts have been described as a mismatch in the maturities of assets and liabilities. This mismatch is said to contribute to instability in the flow of mortgage money to borrowers.
    (a) Describe this mismatch and explain why it causes instability.
    (b) How would variable-rate mortgages help solve the problem?
    (c) How would allowing thrifts to hold consumer loans help solve the problem?
3. The NOW accounts have been defended as a means of increasing the volume of funds available for mortgage lending.
    (a) How do NOW accounts differ from checking accounts?
    (b) How do they differ from the bill payments authorized by the FHLBB?
    (c) If they increase the flow of money to the mortgage markets, where would the extra money come from?
4. The removal of interest rate ceilings has been hotly debated. One side says that removal would increase the rates charged for mortgages and/or reduce the money available for mortgages.
    (a) How could removal reduce money available for mortgages?
    (b) Would the introduction of NOW accounts and other approved services change the argument in (a)?
    (c) How would you evaluate the claim that interest rates charged for mortgages would increase?
5. Variable-rate mortgages might have fixed payments or variable payments. How would the two work? How would they differ?
6. Regulators try to keep the interest rate on savings accounts at S&L's above those on accounts at commercial banks. Why?

21

FORECASTING
REAL ESTATE MARKETS

The unknown future presents such important problems to investors in real estate that every investor should form some idea as to what the future will hold. The builder of residential units—and the builder's lender—must make some estimate of the level of interest rates and sales activity which will prevail at the time the units are scheduled to be sold. The builder of income-producing commercial property is similarly interested in vacancies and rental levels at the time the property will be ready for occupancy.

Nothing is more distressing to an investor than to develop a property only to find that it cannot be sold or rented at reasonable prices. Nevertheless, experienced investors sometimes find themselves in this difficult situation. These investors have not built a bad product or even one which is unwanted. They have built a desirable product which is temporarily unsalable. They have failed to give adequate forethought to the general level of business activity and financial conditions.

FORECASTING TO REDUCE RISKS

Up to this point, we have discussed many aspects of the riskiness of real estate lending and investing. In the approach to risk reduction developed in this chapter, risk is greatly reduced to the extent that some forecast of real estate markets can be obtained, even if it is a very crude forecast. For example, suppose it is known that residential mortgage interest rates will rise sharply within the next year. A builder armed with this information might: (1) build fewer units; (2) build smaller units; (3) build cheaper units; (4) build nonresidential structures. Depending on the situation, any or all of these activities could substantially reduce the risk associated with the real estate investment. A lender could benefit from the same kind of planning for changes in general economic activity and financial markets.

This chapter will not present a step-by-step guide to obtaining precise forecasts of real estate markets. Forecasting is still an art, not a science. The goal of this chapter is to help in developing some judgment as to:

1. The flow of mortgage funds. An introduction to money market rates and securities is included.
2. The direction of future change in interest rates, housing starts, and construction activity.
3. The extent of the future change. Will future change be fast or slow, large or small?
4. The possibility that there will be a turning point in the near future. A turning point occurs when a trend reverses direction, e.g., when interest rates which were going up reverse and begin going down.

Real estate markets function as part of national and local economies; in Chapter 3 we developed some important ways in which real estate is influenced by general economic activity. This chapter explores the relationships between real estate markets—as measured by housing starts, construction spending, and mortgage interest rates—and the general level of economic activity and interest rates. Knowledge of these relationships is the raw material needed to form judgments about the future of real estate markets. Such knowledge is currently used by many specialists planning their lending and investing in real estate. The future will bring ever greater use of rational planning and forecasting techniques.

INFLUENCES ON MORTGAGE MONEY FLOWS

There are three major influences upon the amount of mortgage money available and the terms on which it is available. The Federal Reserve influences money markets by determining the amount of money which is available and by setting the terms on which it can be borrowed. The Congress influences money markets by its decision on how to finance government operations. Expenditures can be financed through higher taxes, through reducing the money available for savings and mortgage lending, or through borrowing from banks and others, which also reduces the flow of mortgage capital. The federal government influences the general level of the economy and the flow of savings by its various subsidy programs. The federal government competes with private institutions by offering unemployment insurance, health insurance, social security, medical insurance, and similar programs. By the extent to which families are assured of an economic future they are influenced against putting savings into institutional lenders; this reduces the normal flow of mortgage funds.

Forecasting the flow of mortgage funds therefore requires anticipating or interpreting the actions of the Federal Reserve Board and of the government as represented by the President and the Congress. We will examine here the ways in which their actions influence the money markets in the United States. The next section deals with the broader problems of forecasting mortgage flows and housing construction.

The Supply of Money. There is a divergence of opinion as to what data should be used to evaluate changes in money markets. One group of economists believes that changes should be measured by the actions of interest rates, on the assumption that interest rates reflect adjustments between the demand for and the supply of money. They follow interest rates, believing that as rates go up the decision to borrow money will be strongly influenced and that high rates tend to discourage investments. On the other hand, low rates encourage people to think of new forms of business adventures and to invest in things that they want to buy; as a result, low rates forecast an expansion of economic activity.

Although basic economic theory suggests that interest rates would be determined by the relationships between the supply of. and the demand for money, other economists believe it is the actions of the Federal Reserve Board in controlling the supply of money which determines what happens to rates. In their view, the Federal Reserve follows a deliberate policy of withholding funds when it wants rates to go up and making ample funds available when it wants rates to go down. However, this position is not as strong as it might be, since a review of the literature indicates that variations in money market rates are influenced more by the uses to which the money can be put than by the actual rate demanded. For example, if a business firm found that it could start a new business, borrow money, pay for the money and its expenses of operation, and still make an attractive profit, it would not be concerned about small variations in the interest rate. Furthermore, those who believe in interest rates as an important indicator of money markets have not yet dealt with the problem of inflation in an adequate way. Suppose a business firm expects inflation to continue and prices to increase steadily, and realizes that it will have to construct a building sometime in the near future. Machinery or equipment will have to be purchased or other investments will be involved. From watching the price trends the firm anticipates that purchase of these items at a later date will be rather costly. Given current interest rates and prices and the levels to which they may rise, the firm decides that it would be better to borrow now with cheaper money and invest at less expense. Inflation alone would provide an increase in price which would permit the repayment of any borrowings on a fixed interest rate without any difficulty.

Money Definitions. An increasing number of economists are coming to believe that it is the supply of money which is available that determines interest rates and the general conditions of money markets. In support of this they have developed various measures of the supply of money which include the following:

M_1 = currency and demand deposits (checking accounts) in the hands of individuals and corporations (excluding banks and government)

M_2 = time deposits of commercial banks, exclusive of large certificates of deposit, plus M_1

M_3 = time deposits in thrift institutions plus M_2

Additional definitions are sometimes given; economists may speak of M_4, M_5, and M_6. The body of the literature and a survey of the market support the idea that the most important measure of money market conditions is M_1. Currency and demand deposits in the hands of the non-bank public (M_1) provide the base on which credit can be expanded and, therefore, are a major influence on the rates at which money is made available. Following changes in M_1 is, therefore, an important way of anticipating what is happening in money markets. However, there is good reason to believe that a change in the supply of money will not cause a change in general economic activity or money markets until at least three months later. Many analysts follow changes from day to day and try to read into them something of what is happening over the long run. This is not as useful as taking a longer look. Compounding or averaging of weekly or monthly changes to produce a six-month moving average is probably the best measure of what is happening.

The actions of the Federal Reserve, the President, and Congress are in large measure determined by larger financial and economic goals including a number of qualitative goals which are difficult to measure. Their efforts to meet these goals are probably dominant over any efforts which might be made to influence the price of money. In other words, changes in money markets are an outgrowth of other economic programs, policies, or goals. Therefore, in the forecast of money market conditions and ultimately of mortgage conditions, one has to look at certain fundamentals which we will be discussing in this chapter.

MONEY MARKET ANALYSIS

Although there is a large body of literature on various ideas about what causes changes in money market conditions, for our purposes these arguments will be simplified to an analysis of a limited number of money market indicators. We are interested primarily in mortgage markets, not in financial analysis or proficiency in monetary economics. We shall give a few rules of thumb for using readily available data to anticipate what might happen in money markets.[1]

Monetary Base. The monetary base consists of the member bank reserves at the Federal Reserve banks and the currency which is in circulation, adjusted for certain Reserve requirements and other factors which limit the availability of the total money supply. Changes in the monetary base are a rough indicator of the ease (large changes) or strictness (small changes) of Federal Reserve policy. An increase in the monetary base suggests that more money will be available in the near future.

FEDERAL RESERVE CREDIT AND THE MULTIPLIER

Recall that the basic money stock (M_1) is measured by demand deposits plus currency held by the non-bank public. This, of course, is affected by the monetary base, so a ratio derived from dividing the money stock by the monetary base gives some indication of the extent to which the total money supply might be increased. In 1975, for example, the multiplier was running at around 2½.

Whenever the Federal Reserve buys securities from the public it is said to extend credit. The check which the Federal Reserve uses to pay for its purchase is drawn on itself; i.e., it is new money. It is also "high-powered money" since it functions as reserves for commercial banks. Since Federal Reserve credit provides reserves, it is the most important part of the monetary base. When Federal Reserve credit increases (and the multiplier remains the same) money supply increases proportionately.

---

[1] All of the data mentioned are reported weekly by the Federal Reserve Bank of St. Louis in a newsletter titled "U. S. Financial Data." This can be received without charge by writing to the bank. These same data are also available in other Federal Reserve publications and from Federal Reserve Banks in local areas.

Money Stock. Money stock is simply M_1. An increase in currency and demand deposits provides a base for additional credit. The increase in M_1 tends to fluctuate rather widely over short periods of time. For example, at the end of April 1975, the money stock consisted of less than $281 billion, but at the end of July, about two months later, it equalled almost $294 billion. This represented a 27 per cent annual rate of increase. To determine what impact the money stock might have eventually on mortgage credit it would be necessary to trace this trend over a period of six months. Clearly the Federal Reserve Board would attempt to adjust money stock not on a week-by-week or month-by-month basis in any significant manner, but through major changes over periods of six months or more.

Money Stock Plus Net Time Deposits. Time deposits are long-term savings put aside for future expenses or guaranteed financial return. Time accounts can serve as a base for increased lending by institutional lenders. They represent a reasonably stable source of funds, and lenders can make loans with some confidence that the funds in the time account will not be withdrawn. For that reason money stock (M_1) when added to net time deposits gives a clear picture of the increased potential for credit which might be available. In the latter part of 1975, money stock plus net time deposits had increased dramatically over the amount in 1974, which meant that the commercial banks had the potential for providing a sharp increase in long-term loans if they wished. We will see whether they did by looking at other data.

Yields on Selected Securities. The first and most important short-term measure of the cost of money is the prime bank loan rate. This is the interest rate on money which a bank makes available to its best business borrowers. If that rate is going down it could mean either that businesses are not borrowing as much as the banks would like to have them borrow or that the supply of funds is increasing faster than the demand for them. For example, economic conditions may be getting worse. The prime rate gives some clue to the future of prime mortgage rates. Since mortgage rates are long-term, lenders demand more money for a prime mortgage rate; adding approximately two hundred basis points (2 per cent) to the prime bank loan rate usually gives an indication of the earning rate for mortgage lenders.

Short-term rates are reflected in the charges for commercial paper (usually due in 30, 60, or 90 days) and the amount being paid on 90-day certificates of deposit. Presumably, decreasing rates in these categories indicate that there is ample money available or that there is less demand for it in the commercial or non-mortgage sector; more money should therefore be available to mortgage borrowers.

An increasingly important competitor for long-term funds has been municipal bonds. Municipal bonds are normally long-term tax-exempt bonds. Because of the tax-exempt feature, mortgages can compete for investors' money only by paying a higher rate. Prior to New York City's credit problems, the rate on municipal bonds usually had to be increased by approximately 3 per cent to estimate what the prime mortgage rate might be.

The inability of New York City to repay its bonds according to schedule increased the costs of borrowing on all municipal bonds by much more than 3 per cent.

Three other short-term interest rates are pertinent:

1. The federal funds rate—the rate which commercial banks pay to each other for deposits at the Federal Reserve
2. The discount rate—the interest which the Federal Reserve charges commercial banks for borrowing from the Fed
3. The three-month Treasury bill yield—a measure of what the Treasury has to pay in order to get the money to keep the government operating.

The important thing to remember in watching the costs or the rates at which the federal government has to borrow money is that these are usually the risk-free rates; mortgage rates will have to be higher, probably anywhere from 25 to 50 per cent, depending upon which government rates are observed. For example, if short-term government securities are yielding 6 or 7 per cent, long-term prime mortgage rates will probably have to earn 50 per cent more than this, or 9 to 10 per cent as a very minimum.

COMMERCIAL BANKS

Although commercial banks emphasize consumer and commercial lending, they do compete for the savings which form the base for mortgage lending. Forecasting the activities of commercial banks is therefore vital to anticipating the availability of mortgage money.

Net Time Deposits.   Although time deposits in savings and loan associations are an important measure of the availability of money for mortgage lending, we do not have a way of tracking them from week to week. Net time deposits in commercial banks serve as a reasonable substitute on a short-term basis. If they are increasing, we can expect deposits in commercial banks to be increasing. Although time deposits do not pay high rates, families use them as a final liquidity reserve against future needs. Therefore, net time deposits tend to increase as population and income increase, suggesting that there will be a gradual increase in the amount of money available for mortgage lending.

Demand Deposits. Demand deposits held by individuals or families measure confidence in general economic conditions. If families are confident about the future, they will not keep much in their demand deposit accounts. If they feel that things are uncertain and that they would like to wait but do not want to tie up their money in long-term deposits, demand deposits will tend to increase. Demand deposits do not have any direct relationship to the volume of mortgage money available but they are useful as a means of anticipating what is likely to happen in terms of housing investment by families.

Certificates of Deposit. Certificates of deposit are monetary notes which banks sell in large denominations for short periods of time at high interest rates. There is some disagreement as to whether certificates of deposit affect mortgage money availability. However, when mortgage rates are higher than rates paid on certificates of deposit, typically money which would have been in certificates of deposit flows to the mortgage markets. Since this is short-term money it does not provide much of a base for a large volume of increased mortgage money. Savings and loans keep close track of this "hot money"; it is "hot" because it is large in amount and it moves with changes in short-term interest rates. As a competitive measure, some savings and loan associations now offer the equivalent of a certificate of deposit or a high interest rate guarantee for the deposit of a large sum for a fixed period of time—perhaps up to six or seven years. In any case, if money is not going into certificates of deposit it can be expected to go into other places where it may be more readily available to mortgage money borrowers.

FORECASTING MONEY MARKET RATES

By way of illustration let us consider part of the St. Louis newsletter [2] for the week ending July 30, 1975 (Figures 21–1 and 21–2). This was a period in which housing starts were down and there was some general concern as to whether the housing industry could recover. Apparently savings were

---

[2] See footnote 1.

flowing in large amounts to savings and loan associations but mortgage rates were still high. What could be expected to happen during the last five months of 1975, given the following happenings in the money markets between June 25, 1974 and July 30, 1975? (1) The monetary base had increased from $108 billion to almost $117 billion; (2) the multiplier was at 2.5, down from 2.6; (3) the availability of Federal Reserve credit had increased from about $94 billion to about $102 billion with various short-term fluctuations of plus or minus 1 to 5 per cent. All of this together indicated that an ample supply of money was available on July 30, 1975, as compared with June 25, 1974.

The monetary stock plus net time deposits had increased from $595 billion in June 1974 to more than $650 billion in July 1975. The money stock itself had increased from $280 to $295 billion, 5.4 per cent. This suggested that not only was there a monetary base on which short-term money could be available, but also a base on which long-term money could be made available. Because of the recession in real economic activity over the same period—the overall rate of unemployment went from less than 5.5 to 8.5 per cent—there was no corresponding increase in the demand for funds. Therefore, we would expect interest rates to go down.

There was a precipitous drop in yields on selected securities during this thirteen-month period (Figure 21–2). For example, the prime loan rate had gone down from 12 per cent to 7 per cent. Ninety-day certificates of deposit had gone from about 12 per cent to the neighborhood of 6 per cent. On the other hand, corporate AAA bonds and municipal bonds were showing a slight upward movement. These trends suggested that perhaps business and industry had a wait-and-see attitude, that consumers were not buying as much as might be expected, and that as a result the need for short-term funds was declining. On the other hand, the need for long-term funds was still strong. With the search by investors for longer-term, higher-yielding investments this meant that any long-term investment with reasonable security could command an interest rate of not less than 7 per cent and probably as much as 9 per cent.

There is no convincing mathematical way in which these data could be manipulated to develop an accurate forecast. Together they say that the supply of funds available for long-term investment, while increasing was attracted to corporate and municipal bonds as well as mortgages. Unless there was an even more substantial increase in net time deposits and accounts in savings and loan associations, the long-term mortgage interest rate was not likely to go below about 7 or 8 per cent nor was it likely to get higher than around 11 per cent.

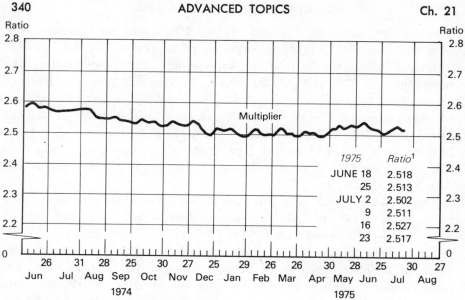

1975	Ratio[1]
JUNE 18	2.518
25	2.513
JULY 2	2.502
9	2.511
16	2.527
23	2.517

Latest data plotted week ending July 23, 1975.

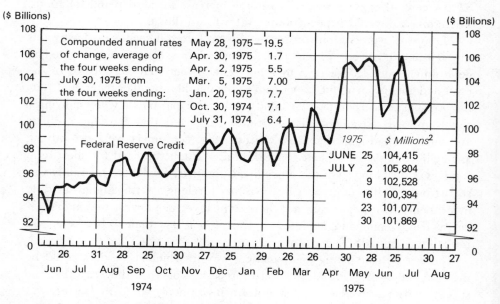

Compounded annual rates of change, average of the four weeks ending July 30, 1975 from the four weeks ending:

May 28, 1975	19.5
Apr. 30, 1975	1.7
Apr. 2, 1975	5.5
Mar. 5, 1975	7.00
Jan. 20, 1975	7.7
Oct. 30, 1974	7.1
July 31, 1974	6.4

1975	$ Millions[2]
JUNE 25	104,415
JULY 2	105,804
9	102,528
16	100,394
23	101,077
30	101,869

Latest data plotted week ending July 30, 1975
[1]Ratio of money stock (M1)/monetary base.
[2]Defined to include holdings of securities, loans, float and "other" assets, adjusted for reserve requirement ratio changes and shifts in the same type of deposits between banks where different reserve requirement ratios apply. Data are seasonally adjusted by this bank.

Source: Federal Reserve Bank of St. Louis, *Weekly Financial Data*, July 30, 1975, p. 3.

Fig. 21–1. Multiplier, Federal Reserve credit; averages of daily figures seasonally adjusted.

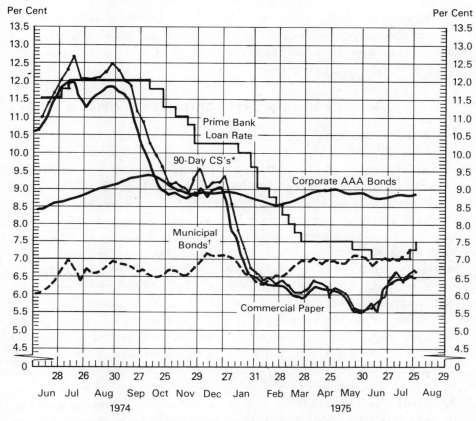

Latest data plotted are averages of rates available for the week ending August 1, 1975.

1975	90-day CD's*	Prime Commercial Paper 4-6 Month	Prime Bankers' Acceptances	Corporate AAA Bonds	Municipal Bonds†
June 6	5.58	5.60	5.50	8.85	7.05
13	5.71	5.63	5.55	8.76	6.80
20	5.55	5.65	5.58	8.73	6.93
27	5.93	6.18	6.03	8.75	7.00
July 4	6.46	6.34	6.19	8.82	6.96
11	6.61	6.45	6.38	8.85	6.98
18	6.43	6.43	6.34	8.82	7.09
25	6.51	6.48	6.52	8.85	7.22
Aug. 1**	6.66	6.40	6.51	8.84	N.A.

*Seven-day averages of secondary market rates for the week ending Wednesday, two days earlier than dates shown. Current data appear in the Board of Governors' release.

†Bond buyer's average index of 20 municipal bonds, Thursday data.

**Averages of rates available.

N.A. = not available

Source: Same as Figure 21-1.

Fig. 21–2. Yields on selected securities; averages of daily rates ended Friday.

Obviously, there is a complex of interrelationships here which could be misinterpreted. Any forecasts of the kind which we have just made must be done with great care and must be backed up by other studies which are done on a more scientific basis.

FORECASTING MORTGAGE FUNDS FLOWS

The maximum period over which we can forecast with any kind of accuracy at all is five years. In most cases the five-year forecasts are revised annually so that in effect a long-term mortgage market forecast consists of anticipating what will happen for the year ahead. Even then, a review of the forecasts which are being made suggests that there is plenty of room for error and these forecasts must be used with great care. Perhaps the best way to use a mortgage market forecast is to look at the various assumptions about the factors which will influence the ultimate conclusions. The weekly monetary letters can be used to see how well the assumptions are being realized. Adjustments can be made to the long-term forecast to reflect discrepancies between the assumptions and actual market events.

A statement of sources and uses of funds provides a basis for forecasting what will happen to mortgage capital markets. The best of the forecasts which are done this way is that provided by the Bankers Trust Company of New York which each year publishes a report of credit and capital markets. Let us take a look at some of the elements in that report. Since the report contains more than 20 pages of tables we have reproduced only two of them (Tables 21–1 and 21–2) to illustrate how these reports, if studied carefully, can become an important means of forecasting what will happen to mortgages. Table 21–2 summarizes financing requirements for all forms of credit. For example, the forecast was for a need for about $190 billion in financing for 1975 of which $115 billion was to be longer-term investment-type funding. Where was this money going to come from? We find that $37.3 billion was expected to come from thrift institutions, with savings and loan associations providing $26.3 billion. Since thrift institutions are the source of mortgage lending, it is important to notice that in 1968, when housing markets were in a depressed condition, thrift institutions provided only $16 billion in funds. Now they were expected to provide more than twice that amount, which suggests that ample funds were to be available for a housing recovery in 1975.

Table 21–2 shows that of the money to be made available to mortgage lenders or for mortgage lending purposes, about $59 billion would be needed for real estate mortgages. Of the total funds to be raised for investment-type activities ($115 billion) approximately one-half would be needed for real estate mortgages. Since thrift institutions were expected to

supply only about $30 billion, life insurance companies, investment com-
panies, commercial banks, and others were expected to provide the remainder. One of the most important changes anticipated in the supplying
of funds is that commercial banks, life insurance companies, and pension
funds are seen as playing an increasingly large role in providing these
funds. We therefore expect that some of the money needed to make up the
difference between the $30 billion provided by thrift institutions and the
$59 billion needed for real estate mortgages would come from commercial
banks, life insurance companies, and pension fund investors.

We notice that, of the $59 billion which was anticipated to be needed
for mortgages, $34 billion was for homes and $7.5 billion for multifamily
structures. About $41.5 of the $59 billion was needed for residential financing. The bulk of it ($29.7 billion) was expected to come from thrift
institutions: $13.5 billion from commercial banks, $6 billion from insurance
companies and pension funds, and $9.3 billion from the federal government.

Let us examine the role of the federal government in providing money
for mortgages (bottom of Table 21–2). In 1968, when housing markets
were depressed and mortgage money was not available, federal agencies
provided about 4 per cent of all the mortgage money available. If we add
what are called non-budget agencies, such as FNMA and FHLMC (but
not GNMA), the government provided slightly more than 10 per cent of
all the funding. In 1972, when housing markets were particularly depressed, the government did not provide funding. In fact, it was taking
some money out of the markets: there is a negative $.2 billion reported in
the financing of the mortgage market. However, the non-budget agencies
did pick up some of the slack and provided $4 billion of the $68.8 billion
that was needed in mortgages or about 6 per cent of the total mortgage
funds available. On the other hand, in 1975, when housing markets were
expected to be reasonably strong, the government was expected to provide
about 6 per cent of the mortgage funds available; together with the non-
budget agencies about 13 per cent of all the mortgage money was to come
from federally related agencies. We can say that the mortgage markets
were depressed by the extent to which the federal government failed to
provide at least 13 per cent of the mortgage money. In early 1975 the
federal government was still not clear on what it was going to do about
housing, so it was apparently going to let housing be a residual actitivity.
This jeopardized even the 1.275 million new housing starts and the $59
billion in mortgage money that was forecasted for 1975. Clearly, it was the
actions of the federal government in the latter part of 1975 that maintained
a reasonable level of housing market activity.

The data in Table 21–2 show what kinds of funds were raised and who
provided the financing of homes as compared to non-residential, commer-

Table 21-1. Summary of Financing Requirements—Total Funds (Billions of Dollars)

	1968	1969	1970	1971	1972	1973	1974	197
Uses (Funds Raised)								
Investment funds	54.3	60.2	66.4	101.1	114.7	113.3	111.5	115.
Short-term funds	26.2	35.7	19.0	20.5	42.5	65.5	66.9	29.
U. S. Government and budget agency securities, privately held	8.7	− 8.8	6.9	16.7	20.5	− .4	9.0	45.
Total uses	89.2	87.0	92.3	138.3	177.8	178.3	187.4	189.
Sources (Funds Supplied)								
Insurance companies and pension funds:								
Life insurance companies	8.7	8.7	9.0	11.9	13.4	15.9	16.3	17.
Private noninsured pension funds	7.0	6.4	7.8	8.6	9.3	9.2	10.0	11.
State and local retirement funds	4.7	5.6	6.1	6.2	7.8	9.2	10.3	11.
Fire and casualty insurance companies	2.5	2.3	4.0	6.2	6.8	5.8	3.3	5.
Total	23.0	23.0	26.9	32.9	37.3	40.1	39.9	45.
Thrift institutions:								
Savings and loan associations	10.2	9.5	12.5	28.9	35.8	25.4	20.8	26.
Mutual savings banks	4.4	2.8	4.2	9.8	10.2	4.7	3.0	8.
Credit unions	1.6	2.0	1.6	2.5	3.0	3.7	3.1	3.
Total	16.1	14.4	18.3	41.2	49.0	33.8	26.9	37.
Investment companies	2.4	3.5	1.7	.4	− .2	−	1.1	.
Other financial intermediaries:								
Finance companies	5.1	8.1	.7	3.4	7.9	10.2	5.8	3.
Real estate investment trusts	.2	.9	2.1	2.5	4.9	4.5	1.4	− .
Total	5.3	9.0	2.8	5.9	12.8	14.7	7.2	3.
Commercial banks	40.0	17.1	36.5	49.7	74.6	78.2	62.5	67.
Business:								
Business corporations	7.0	3.9	1.9	7.1	6.6	10.0	11.4	9.
Noncorporate business	.5	.6	.6	.7	1.1	1.3	1.0	.
Total	7.5	4.5	2.5	7.8	7.7	11.3	12.4	9.
Government:								
U. S. Government	1.4	1.4	.4	.4	.1	− .3	2.0	3.
Nonbudget agencies	2.3	4.7	8.4	3.0	4.5	9.9	10.7	6.
State and local general funds	.8	3.3	2.1	− 1.7	6.9	3.5	3.7	1.
Total	4.5	9.4	10.9	1.8	11.4	13.1	16.4	11.
Foreign investors	1.5	.1	11.0	27.1	10.6	3.4	7.0	14.7
Residual: individuals and others	.1	30.2	− 6.7	− 18.3	.7	16.2	37.4	12.
Total gross sources	100.5	111.2	103.9	148.4	203.8	210.8	210.8	202.
Less: Funds raised by financial intermediaries:								
Investment funds	1.7	3.4	4.1	6.5	9.2	5.4	5.4	5.
Short-term funds	6.4	10.3	− .8	3.0	13.9	11.1	5.2	.
Nonbudget agency securities, privately held	3.1	10.4	8.3	.6	2.9	16.0	12.8	6.5
Total	11.2	24.1	11.6	10.1	26.0	32.5	23.4	12.6
Total net sources	89.2	87.0	92.3	138.3	177.8	178.3	187.4	189.7

Source: Bankers Trust Company, *Credit and Capital Markets*, 1975.

Table 21–2. Financing Mortgages (Billions of Dollars)

	1968	1969	1970	1971	1972	1973	1974	1975
Uses (Funds Raised)								
Residential mortgages:								
Home	15.3	15.6	13.4	28.0	40.7	41.7	32.0	34.0
Multifamily	3.4	4.9	5.8	8.8	10.4	8.5	6.8	7.5
Total	18.7	20.5	19.2	36.8	51.2	50.3	38.8	41.5
Commercial mortgages	6.6	5.4	5.5	10.1	15.1	17.3	13.2	12.5
Farm mortgages	2.0	2.0	2.0	2.0	2.6	4.4	4.5	5.0
Total	27.4	27.8	26.7	48.9	68.8	71.9	56.5	59.0
Sources (Funds Supplied)								
Insurance companies and pension funds:								
Life insurance companies	2.5	2.1	2.3	1.3	1.8	4.5	5.1	5.4
Private noninsured pension funds	–	.2	.1	– .6	– .6	.4	1.5	1.0
State and local retirement funds	.4	.6	.8	.3	– .3	– .1	.2	.3
Total	2.8	2.8	3.2	1.0	1.0	4.8	6.8	6.7
Thrift institutions:								
Savings and loan associations	9.4	9.6	10.5	25.4	32.9	26.0	18.6	24.0
Mutual savings banks	2.8	2.5	2.0	4.8	6.2	6.1	2.8	5.0
Credit unions	.1	– .1	.2	.5	.5	.5	.5	.7
Total	12.3	12.0	12.7	30.7	39.6	32.6	21.9	29.7
Other financial intermediaries:								
Finance companies	.6	.3	.1	.8	.8	1.4	.4	.3
Real estate investment trusts	.2	.9	2.1	2.5	4.9	4.5	1.4	– .5
Total	.8	1.2	2.2	3.3	5.7	5.9	1.8	– .2
Commercial banks	6.7	5.4	2.5	9.9	16.8	20.0	11.7	13.5
Government:								
U. S. Government	1.1	.7	.3	–	– .2	– .6	1.8	3.5
Nonbudget agencies	2.2	4.4	5.4	3.6	4.0	7.2	9.7	4.3
State and local general funds	.3	.1	1.0	1.0	3.1	1.9	2.1	1.5
Total	3.6	5.2	6.7	4.7	6.9	8.5	13.6	9.3
Residual: Individuals and others	1.2	1.2	– .6	– .7	– 1.1	.1	.7	–
Total	27.4	27.8	26.7	48.9	68.8	71.9	56.5	59.0
Memoranda:								
Private housing starts (in thousands of units)	1,508	1,467	1,434	2,052	2,357	2,045	1,336	1,275
Private residential construction put in place:								
New housing units	24.0	25.9	24.3	35.1	44.9	47.8	35.8	33.5
Other	6.5	7.3	7.6	8.2	9.4	9.8	10.6	11.5
Total	30.6	33.2	31.9	43.3	54.3	57.6	46.4	45.0

Source: Same as Table 21–1.

cial, farm, and multifamily properties. For example, in 1968, multifamily, commercial, and farm mortgages equaled about 44 per cent of the financing provided for all mortgages, but in the recovering markets of 1975 they were expected to equal about the same percentage of the funds available for mortgages. A revival was expected not only in the home market but in a variety of other real estate markets and some competition for funds was anticipated. In fact it was forecasted that housing starts would not change very much over 1968, 1969, 1970, and 1974, but that private multifamily housing units would decline somewhat compared to the historical trend for these years. Commercial construction was expected to pick up and reach one of its all-time highs of $16 billion.

Since we have emphasized that savings and loan associations are important to mortgage markets, let us take a closer look at Table 21–3, which shows the sources and uses of funds for savings and loan associations.

Table 21–3. Sources and Uses of Funds—Savings and Loan Associations (Billions of Dollars)

	1968	1969	1970	1971	1972	1973	1974	1975
Sources of Funds								
Savings capital	7.5	4.1	11.0	28.0	32.7	20.2	16.0	29.
Net worth*	.8	.9	.8	1.2	1.6	1.8	1.5	1.
Federal home loan bank advances	.9	4.0	1.3	− 2.6	.1	7.0	6.6	− 3.
Bank loans	.1	.1	− .1	.7	.7	.3	1.3	− .
Total	9.2	9.0	13.0	27.3	35.1	29.4	25.4	27.
Uses of Funds								
Mortgages:								
Home mortgages	7.2	7.8	7.5	18.8	25.7	21.5	16.3	19.
Multifamily, commercial, and farm mortgages	2.1	1.7	3.0	6.6	7.2	4.5	2.3	4.
Total	9.4	9.6	10.5	25.4	32.9	26.0	18.6	24.
Short-term funds:								
Open market paper	–	–	.4	.8	1.3	− .9	.3	–
Consumer credit	.1	.2	.3	.1	.2	.2	.2	.
Total	.1	.2	.7	.9	1.5	− .7	.5	.
U. S. Government and agency securities:								
U. S. Government securities	.4	− 1.9	− .2	1.4	.6	− 1.0	2.0	2.
Federal agency securities	.3	1.7	1.5	1.2	.8	1.0	− .3	–
Total	.7	− .2	1.3	2.6	1.4	–	1.7	2.
Total funds	10.2	9.5	12.5	28.9	35.8	25.4	20.8	26.
Cash	− .5	− .5	1.4	− .2	− .2	–	.1	.
Other—net†	− .5	–	− .9	− 1.5	− .4	4.0	4.5	1.
Total	9.2	9.0	13.0	27.3	35.1	29.4	25.4	27.

*Surplus and reserves prior to 1972.
†Other assets less loans in process and other liabilities.

Sources: Federal Savings and Loan Insurance Corporation, Federal Home Loan Bank Board, Federal Reserve, Flow of Funds Accounts, and Government National Mortgage Association; see also source for Table 21–1.

The important thing to notice is that the increase in mortgage funds by savings and loan associations was expected to relate directly to their increases in savings capital. Between 1968 and 1975 the flow of savings capital was expected to increase by 395 per cent. Notice that of the total of $27.5 billion which savings and loan associations were expected to raise, $19.2 or 70 per cent was to be used for home mortgages and 17 per cent for multifamily, commercial, and farm mortgages. A small amount of the money was to be put into government securities, reflecting the need for savings and loan associations to maintain a certain liquid reserve against the savings capital which they were acquiring. A recovery of housing in 1975 was expected to depend upon the flow of savings capital and the ability of savings and loan associations to increase their lending activities. This happened in the remainder of 1975.

FORECASTING DECLINING HOUSING CONSTRUCTION

Figure 21–3 illustrates the type of risk faced by investors and lenders in the market for residential real estate. The right-hand scale measures millions of housing units started each year. The shading coincides with periods of declining housing starts. In the past 25 years there have been violent swings in housing starts, and there is no sign that the ups and downs are any less severe now than they were in the 1950's. In fact, the very large up-and-down cycle which began in 1970 suggests the housing market is even more volatile now.

Figure 21–3 gives the relationship between declines in housing starts and declines in the general level of economic activity. Declines in real GNP (GNP adjusted for inflation) are represented by the area labeled "business cycle shading." Two important relationships should be noted:

1. Declines in housing starts usually last much longer than declines in real GNP. On average, declines in real GNP have lasted less than one year, whereas declines in housing starts average almost two years in duration. Consequently, periods of increasing starts are shorter by about one year than periods of increasing real economic activity.
2. Periods of declining housing starts usually precede periods of declining real economic activity. However, the length of time between the beginning of a decline in housing starts and the beginning of a decline in real GNP is quite variable. Housing starts, taken by themselves, are not a reliable "leading indicator" of economic activity. On the other hand, a decline in housing starts does signal a decline in real GNP at some indefinite future time.

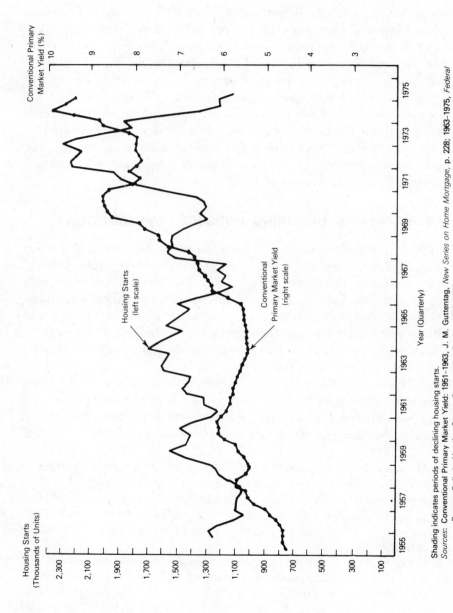

Shading indicates periods of declining housing starts.
Sources: Conventional Primary Market Yield: 1951–1963, J. M. Guttentag, *New Series on Home Mortgage*, p. 228; 1963–1975, *Federal Reserve Bulletin*. Housing Starts: *Construction Review*, 1955–1976.

Fig. 21–3.   Conventional primary market yield vs. housing starts, 1955–1975.

How can these relationships be used for forecasting by an investor or lender in residential real estate? There are a number of ways, including the following:

1. Signals from real economic activity; changes in economic activity are widely forecast by many experts.
2. Signals from the general level of lending activity.
3. Signals from interest rates.

Each of these is discussed below; the discussion will cover some fundamental causes of the dismal cycle in housing starts.

Signals from General Economic Activity. When a recession in the economy comes to an end, real estate activity is virtually certain to swing up (Figure 21–3). A lender or investor who thinks that a recession is ending would do well to make plans based on a strong market for real estate. But there is a problem with this signal: the end of a recession often occurs after housing starts have already begun to improve. Thus, the lender or investor who waits until a recession is over will probably make a late entry into the improving housing market.

Expert forecasts of general economic activity can be useful to real estate lenders and investors. These forecasts predict the end of a recession by two to six months. An investor who receives a reasonably reliable forecast should act immediately, since the housing slump will probably be over soon.

How does one determine what is a reasonably reliable forecast of economic activity? Expert forecasters are often wrong. However, their errors are usually confined to the rate of inflation or the extent of a change in GNP. The real estate investor is primarily interested in the *direction of change;* i.e., the investor wants to know whether the economy will be on an up-track or a down-track. By listening carefully to a consensus of forecasters, the investor will usually get reliable information on this point.

A major problem with signals from real economic activity is that they do not help the lender or investor to forecast the beginning of a decline in housing starts. Figure 21–3 indicates that declines in housing starts always begin well before declines in real GNP. On average, a decline in housing starts begins more than 18 months before a decline in the general level of business activity. Thus, while forecasts of business activity may be useful in predicting an increase in housing starts, they would be useless in predicting a decline in housing starts. In order to predict a decline, it is necessary to get more deeply into the relationship between housing construction activity and mortgage lending.

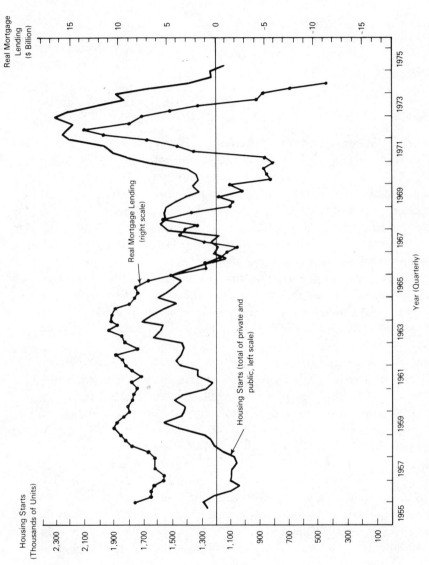

Shading represents periods of declining housing starts.

Sources: Real Mortgage Lending: *Federal Reserve Bulletin*, 1955-1976. Original data (mortgage debt outstanding) are translated into real mortgage lending at seasonally adjusted annual rates (i.e., taking the changes of mortgage debt outstanding divided by "construction cost index," and converting into seasonally adjusted figures; same process is used in housing starts figures).
Housing Starts: *Construction Review*, 1955-1976.

Fig. 21-4. Real mortgage lending vs. housing starts, 1955-1975.

Signals from Lending Activity. Figure 21–4 indicates a strong relationship between housing starts (measured on the right scale) and the dollar value of residential mortgage lending (measured in real terms on the left scale). This relationship is not as obvious as it might appear: residential mortgage lending, although net of repayments, includes lending on existing structures which are changing hands. While a decline in housing starts clearly entails a decline in borrowing for new construction, it does not necessarily entail a decline in total net residential mortgage lending.

Figure 21–4 is evidence of a strong causal connection between financial conditions in the mortgage market and residential construction activity. Figure 21–5 gives additional evidence on this point. In Figure 21–5, the dollar value of residential construction is plotted with the dollar value of mortgage lending. Both are on the same axis and neither is adjusted for price level changes. Clearly, there is a strong relationship between construction expenditures and mortgage lending.

The reason for the strong causal connection between the financial markets and construction activity is not hard to find. Interest costs constitute a large part of total housing costs. A homeowner with a 9 per cent mortgage covering 70 to 80 per cent of the home value has interest payments totalling 65 to 75 per cent of the total cost of homeownership before income tax considerations. A one per cent increase in the interest rate increases the cost of homeownership by about 7.5 per cent. Similar estimates hold for renters in new structures, since landlords must charge enough to cover interest costs.

Money and Economic Activity. Mortgage interest rates are part of a complex mechanism which links general economic activity—and national fiscal and monetary policies which influence economic activity—to expenditures in the real estate market. Housing must compete with other sectors of the economy for funds, but the other sectors such as business investment and government borrowing are not as sensitive to interest rate changes. Thus, housing tends to be the first sector which is squeezed as interest rates rise. Housing is also the last sector to benefit when interest rates begin to fall. This is why declines in housing starts are so much longer than declines in real GNP.

In Figure 21–3, during the periods immediately following the end of a decline in real GNP (i.e., the periods just to the right of the business cycle shading), housing starts are rising and mortgage interest rates are usually stable or declining. The general level of business activity is rising at the same time. As business activity rises, the competition for loanable

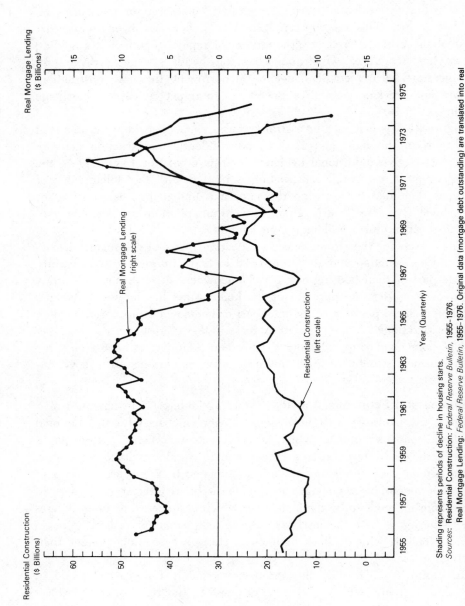

Shading represents periods of decline in housing starts.
Sources: **Residential Construction:** *Federal Reserve Bulletin,* 1955–1976.
　　　Real Mortgage Lending: *Federal Reserve Bulletin,* 1955–1976. Original data (mortgage debt outstanding) are translated into real
　　　mortgage lending at seasonally adjusted annual rate.

Fig. 21–5.　Real mortgage lending vs. residential construction, 1955–1975.

funds becomes keener. Business investment in plant and equipment is booming, so companies issue debt to finance the expansion. Consumers are taking on debt to buy durables (autos, appliances, etc.) and all levels of government are issuing debt to finance their expenditures. Eventually, the competition for loanable funds drives interest rates up, making borrowing more costly.

A rise in interest rates associated with recovery in business activity has a large effect on the cost of investment in real estate. The associated rise in mortgage lending and construction activity is quickly snuffed out by increasing interest rates. This is why construction activity as measured by housing starts or residential construction expenditures turns down long before real GNP turns down (Figure 21–3).

Early Warning. The investor seeking early warning of poor housing market conditions can get a clue from the level of mortgage lending (Figure 21–5). Mortgage lending usually turns down one quarter before construction expenditures. A one- or two-quarter downturn in mortgage lending is clearly important when construction expenditures also turn down. An investor watching movements in mortgage lending would have gotten false signals in 1962 and again in early 1963; i.e., the investor would have seen a decline in lending which was not followed by a decline in construction. But, by the end of 1964, declines in both lending and construction should have clearly signaled a long period of poor housing market conditions.

Investors and lenders who follow these statistics—local as well as national statistics—can get forecasts of the direction of change in real estate market activity. The statistics help them to distinguish a general pattern of real estate market activity from temporary or purely local movements. Thus, they can act in a more decisive and timely fashion than those who rely on intuition or seat-of-the-pants judgment.

The statistics to be used in forming a forecast on real estate activity are widely available. The Department of Housing and Urban Development has helpful publications, and the *Federal Reserve Bulletin* is an important source for national data. Local data can be obtained from banks, research firms, and the nearest branch of the Federal Reserve System.

Signals from Interest Rates. The sophisticated real estate lender or investor used to get an early-warning signal from long-term corporate bond yields or yields on long-term government bonds. These long-term interest rates usually turned before mortgage interest rates. Furthermore, they exhibited stronger movements (larger up and down movements) than mortgage yields.

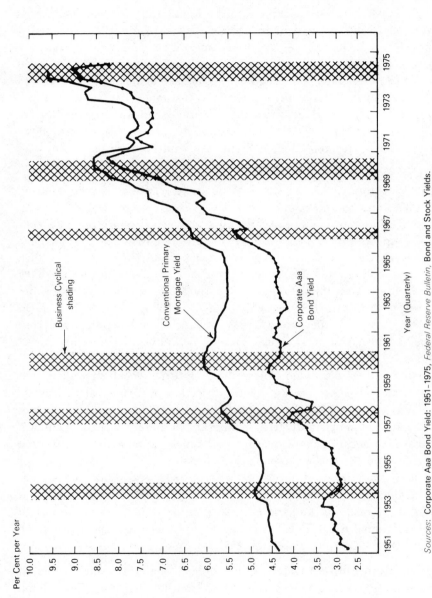

Sources: Corporate Aaa Bond Yield: 1951–1975, *Federal Reserve Bulletin*, Bond and Stock Yields. Conventional Primary Mortgage Yield: 1951–1963, J. M. Guttentag, *New Series on Home Mortgage*, p. 228; 1963–1975, *Federal Reserve Bulletin*.

Fig. 21–6. Conventional primary market vs. corporate Aaa bond yields (per cent).

In Figure 21–6, corporate bond yields are compared to conventional mortgage yields. Prior to 1970, the relationships noted above appear to hold. The Aaa bond yield foreshadowed movements in the mortgage yield; the Aaa bond yield would have provided good forecasting signals. However, since 1969 the Aaa corporate bond yield has moved at about the same time and by about the same extent as mortgage yields. Therefore, it is necessary to look in more detail at the reasons for the pre-1970 experience.

MORTGAGE YIELDS. Three reasons have been advanced to explain the narrow and laggard movement of mortgage yields prior to 1970. All of these reasons focus on the difference between the mortgage market and the market for corporate bonds, since it is the movement of mortgage yields *relative* to bond yields which must be explained.

The first explanation focuses on the difference between the effective yield and the yield unadjusted for fees and charges. This explanation was advanced in 1961 by Saul Klaman, before good series were available on the effective yield. The argument was that lenders would be more willing to change fees than interest rates, because fees are less visible. Furthermore, fees can be changed in small incremental steps, whereas interest rates are usually changed by at least ⅛ per cent. While the arguments are intuitively appealing, later data have tended to disprove them. The mortgage yields plotted in Figure 21–6 include an adjustment for fees and charges, yet a different pattern for mortgage yields relative to the Aaa bond yield is still observed.

The second explanation focuses on the high costs of servicing mortgage loans. Part of the mortgage yield goes to cover these costs of billing, collecting payments, handling delinquencies, etc. This part of the mortgage yield does not change over the business cycle, so only a portion of the mortgage yield is free to fluctuate. This is not the case with bonds: the servicing of bonds (interest payment, transfers, and redemptions) is paid by the issuing corporation, not out of the interest rate.

This explanation might account for the somewhat narrower movement in mortgage yields, since the servicing costs dampen the size of cyclical swings. But it does not account for the fact that mortgage yields turned later than Aaa bond yields prior to 1970. The timing of the turning points should not be affected by the constant servicing costs. Furthermore, the servicing costs were not large enough to account for the small swings in mortgage yields. After accounting for fees and charges, most of which are related to the servicing and origination functions, the servicing costs cannot be much higher than ¾ per cent. Before 1970, the gap between mortgage rates and Aaa bond rates (Figure 21–6) was usually larger than ¾ per cent.

The third explanation focuses on the fact that bonds are sold in an impersonal dealer market whereas mortgages are presumably negotiated on a personal basis. A mortgage lender who has a personal relationship with a customer may be reluctant to quickly and fully pass along changes in interest rates. The lender may be interested in obtaining deposits from the customer or in making further loans. This would not be the case on the market for corporate bonds, where many buyers and sellers trade the financial instruments on an impersonal basis.

This explanation is generally preferred by observers of the mortgage market, but it is not free of problems. One problem is that the explanation remains untested since adequate data would be hard to find. Casual observation would suggest that mortgage borrowers do not negotiate with lenders, and they often keep their deposits and other borrowing at other banks. It is difficult to believe that mortgage borrowers go out of their way to accommodate their lenders: they are paying for the lending service through the interest rate, fees, and other charges. Furthermore, it is unusual for the lender to pressure the borrower into keeping other banking business with the lender. Often, the lender never meets the borrower face-to-face; i.e., the loan application and approval can be an impersonal process.

Why has the relationship between mortgage yields and Aaa bond yields changed since 1969? One possibility is that no fundamental change has occurred. The apparent change which is documented by two cyclical peaks and one cyclical trough since 1969 may be a temporary exception to the general pattern. Or, the mortgage market may have become more impersonal in recent years.

If the mortgage market has become more impersonal, the fundamental cause of the different behavior of mortgage and bond markets may have been removed. However, there is doubt that the "personality" of the mortgage market was ever much different from the bond market, and it would be virtually impossible to get reliable data on a *change* in market structure.

RISK PREMIUMS. The most convincing explanation of the changed behavior of mortgage rates focuses on the risk premium which is present in any interest rate. The risk premium associated with mortgages has probably declined substantially over the 25 years ended with 1975. If so—*and if the risk premium does not change appreciably over the business cycle*—this could account for the post-1969 increase in the size of the up and down movements of the mortgage yield (Figure 21–6). With a decreased risk premium, less of the mortgage rate would be fixed over the business cycle; more would be free to move up and down.

There is some evidence that the risk premium on mortgage rates has declined. In Figure 21–6, it can be seen that the gap between the mortgage yield and the Aaa bond yield declined steadily over the period through 1969. The gap can be attributed to two factors: liquidity and risk. In the early 1950's investors considered mortgages much more risky than Aaa bonds (the least risky corporate bonds). During the Great Depression, many mortgages went into default; investors of the 1950's were probably still reacting to that experience. But the default rate on mortgages was very low during the 1950's and 1960's (it has recently been around .2 per cent per year), prompting investors to reduce their estimate of risk.

An objection can be raised to this argument: If the risk premium on mortgages has been reduced, why haven't mortgage rates fallen? Instead, the gap between mortgage rates and corporate Aaa bond rates has been reduced by a relative increase in bond rates (Figure 21–6). The reason is that inflation affected all interest rates during this period, especially during the last half of the 1960's.

Expectations of inflation must be incorporated in interest rates. No lender can afford to loan money at 3 to 4 per cent (the Aaa bond yield before 1955) if the rate of inflation is expected to be more than 4 per cent. Furthermore, borrowers can afford to pay higher interest rates when high rates of inflation are anticipated. Borrowers expect to repay the loan with dollars which have shrunk in terms of real purchasing power.

INFLATIONARY EXPECTATIONS. The surge in inflationary expectations was particularly strong in the period 1966 through 1970. It drove long-term interest rates up so fast that it tended to disguise the cyclical movement in interest rates during the mini-recession of 1966–1967. The risk premium on mortgages, which had been reduced prior to 1965, was replaced by inflationary expectations during the 1965–1970 period.

Inflationary expectations, unlike the risk premium, are sensitive to the business cycle. Inflation is likely to decline when real business activity declines because there is less competition for scarce goods and services. Similarly, inflationary expectations rise when business activity rises. Thus, it is reasonable to expect mortgage rates to be more sensitive to the business cycle in the post–1969 period, when the risk premium had been largely replaced by inflationary expectations. The timing of cyclical turns and the size of swings would both be influenced by growing inflationary expectations.

Conventional mortgages became increasingly liquid during the 25 years ended with 1975. The reason was the further development of the secondary mortgage market, as helped by the growing activity of Fannie Mae, and the development of other governmental organizations to assist the mortgage market (see Chapter 8). Since liquidity is valuable to investors, increased liquidity enables them to accept a smaller return on mortgages relative to Aaa bonds.

The improved liquidity of mortgages may help to explain the changed timing of cycles in mortgage yields; i.e., it may explain why turns in Aaa bond yields no longer lead turns in mortgage yields. Mortgage yields which are more closely tied to secondary market activity would be expected to reflect market changes more quickly. As a national capital market develops for mortgages, the latest information on the supply and demand for loanable funds should be incorporated in the market transactions. This greater informational content would seem to be reflected in the timing of mortgage yields after 1969 (Figure 21–6).

Knowledge of these relationships can be useful to real estate lenders and investors. For one thing, forecasts on long-term government bond rates or corporate bond rates are usually available. Forecasts are also available on inflation. Anticipation of an increase in inflation may enable the investor to get a loan before the mortgage interest rate rises to fully reflect the inflation. Or, the sophisticated lender may be able to avoid making loans at unusually low market interest rates.

SUMMARY

The risk associated with debt or equity investment in real estate can be reduced with forecasts on construction, sales, lending, and interest rates. These forecasts enable investors and lenders to react quickly to the changing market situation. Projects can be cancelled or modified to meet anticipated future conditions.

Fortunately, the real estate investor or lender does not need a detailed forecast which is accurate to the fourth decimal point. The forecasting effort should concentrate on anticipating the *direction of change* in the market. Changes in the direction of the market ("turning points") should also be forecasted. The point of this chapter is that forecasts of this type can be done with a few readily available numbers on trends in national and local business conditions. The investor or lender can use these numbers—

e.g., long-term Aaa bond rates, government bond rates, real GNP, mortgage lending, and yields on mortgages—to form a judgment as to the direction of change and the timing of turning points. Or, forecasts by experts on national and local economic conditions can be used.

The end of a recession gives a reliable signal of improved conditions for housing construction. For downturns in housing construction, it is well to watch mortgage lending. When it turns down at the same time as housing starts, a long period (usually two years) of poor market conditions is probably in store.

The complex causal mechanism linking the housing market to the national economy is centered on mortgage interest rates. Mortgage interest rates are such a large part of the cost of housing that small changes in the interest rate can produce large changes in housing construction and lending. Forecasts on inflation can aid in forecasting the interest rate, and so can forecasts on real economic activity and other interest rates. For example, Figure 21–6 makes it clear that interest rates usually peak during a recession. This is a good sign for real estate investment: the subsequent decline in mortgage interest rates makes it much easier to finance real estate.

QUESTIONS

1. Suppose that you were a mortgage lending officer in August, 1975. From the information in Figure 21–2, you were trying to decide whether to encourage additional applications from mortgagors.
   (a) Which interest rate would you expect to most closely parallel mortgage rates? Why?
   (b) How would you use the information on other rates to help you make the lending decision?
2. Again, as a mortgage lending officer considering the problem stated in question 1, you pick up the summaries of investment funds illustrated in Tables 21–1 and 21–2.
   (a) Would this information help you to forecast inflows of deposit funds? How?
   (b) Does it help you in determining your major competitors for mortgage business?
   (c) How would you use this information to decide whether the market for mortgages will be good over the next year?
3. What is the typical relationship over the business cycle between:
   (a) Declines in real GNP and declines in housing starts?
   (b) Declines in mortgage interest rates and rises in housing starts?
4. Discuss some reasons for the relationships you found in response to question 3.
5. What are some changes in the economy which might disrupt the typical business cycle pattern of mortgage rates and mortgage lending?

22

THE MATHEMATICS OF
REAL ESTATE FINANCE

Financial markets are involved in the process of translating cash in hand now to cash in hand at some future date or vice versa. For example, developers of industrial property lay out cash now for land acquisition, clearance, and construction because they expect to get more money later; i.e., they expect to increase their wealth by engaging in land development. Some of the cash invested now may be borrowed from a bank at a given interest rate. The bank is willing to invest in the venture because it expects to recover its investment and earn interest as time passes.

The bank and the borrower are both interested in the mathematics of real estate finance because both want to translate between dollars which are firmly in hand now and dollars which will be received (they hope) at some future time. They use the interest rate—or a special form of the interest rate, the capitalization rate—to perform the translation over time.

The mathematics of real estate finance are not difficult; no special training is required beyond high-school algebra. Once the basic concept is understood, it is important to keep the time frame firmly in mind. What time or times are you translating from and what time or times are you translating to? It is useful to draw a time line like the one in Figure 22–1, with the expected time of cash expenditures and cash receipts clearly labeled. Once this is accomplished, the mathematics of real estate finance reduce to the simple problem of multiplying or dividing repeatedly by the interest rate until the cash expenditures and receipts are translated to the desired time period.

This concept will be developed fully below, in conjunction with the tables and formulas which make the translation process quicker and easier.

INTEREST AS THE PRICE OF TIME

In Figure 22–1, the concept developed above is applied to the situation where a borrower takes out a mortgage loan. The borrower receives a capital sum now, labeled P in Figure 22–1, and promises to repay equal installments, labeled R, over time. The concept can be formalized as follows:

The borrower sells an income stream by promising to provide a fixed stream of payments over time. In return, the borrower gets a capital sum now. Thus, the borrower is translating income which is expected in the future into cash in hand now.

The lender buys an income stream. The price of that income stream is the capital sum which must be paid in cash now.

What determines the price which the lender must pay to buy an income stream? This is where the interest rate comes into play:

The interest rate is the price of time. A dollar in hand now can be translated into a dollar one year from now as long as the price of time is paid. If I spend $3 on the movies now I pay the price of time, since the $3 could be put into a savings bank to yield $3.20 one year from now; i.e., the same money could be used to buy a movie and an ice cream cone if I were only willing to wait one year. On this reasoning, the interest rate is sometimes called "the cost of impatience."

The ice cream cone example brings up the problem of inflation. The best way to adjust for inflation is to increase the interest rate. Thus, if the price of a movie is going to increase by 10 per cent to $3.30, it is clearly not worthwhile to wait for one year unless the interest rate is greater than 10 per cent. In the above example, with a 10 per cent inflation rate, the return to a savings deposit would have to be 16 per cent in order to have a 6 per cent real increase in the value of the money deposited.

There is strong evidence to suggest that market interest rates do increase in response to inflation. Corporate bond rates have increased from 3.5 per cent in the early 1950's to 9 per cent in the early 1970's; almost all of the increase can be attributed to inflation. But the adjustment of interest rates to inflation is sluggish. Over the past 20 years, investors have been continually surprised by the extent of inflation. They have lost ground repeatedly in the sense that the sums repaid to them have been worth less in terms of real purchasing power than the sums they lent.

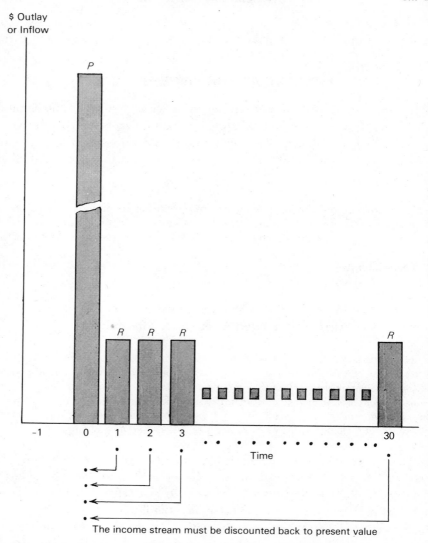

The income stream must be discounted back to present value

Note: P = principal amount borrowed at some time labelled "time 0."
        R = periodic payments of principal and interest.

Fig. 22–1. Time frame for cash expenditures and cash receipts in a real estate transaction. Borrowing is selling an income stream of $R per period for $P cash-in-hand now.

FEES AND CHARGES

Periodic interest charges are not the only costs of real estate capital. Borrowers typically incur substantial "closing costs" at the time the loan is negotiated. These are one-shot costs which are difficult to compare with interest costs. A technique for evaluating the relative importance of closing costs and interest costs is suggested in this section.

There are three important actors in any real estate deal: the buyer (who is also the borrower), the lender, and the seller.[1] Each may pay different fees and charges, but we are primarily concerned with the cost of the real estate capital invested by the buyer. Thus, the fees paid by the seller— e.g., a builder pays "points" to the lender or a seller pays for an alteration, appraisal, or termite inspection—are not important. These fees paid by the seller are simply a reduction of the net revenue received; they are not part of the cost of the capital invested by the buyer.

Some of the fees paid by the borrower are not part of the cost of capital. For example, the buyer may want insurance (liability, title, and fire), or the buyer may have to pay to have the deed recorded. The buyer has to pay property taxes and certain tax stamps must be purchased for the deed. All of these costs would be incurred even if there were no loan, so these costs are part of property ownership or property transfer. They are not part of the costs of debt capital, even though some tax and insurance costs are usually paid at the time the deal is closed.

Many of the fees paid by the borrower should be considered part of the cost of debt capital. These include legal fees, appraisal fees, and such title and insurance fees as are required for the protection of the lender.[2] Title insurance on a new home, for example, may be required by the lender even though the borrower does not consider it necessary. In this case, title insurance is part of the cost of capital, whereas title insurance for the borrower's protection is not part of the cost of capital.

The borrower using an FHA or VA loan will be charged fees specifically related to the federal insurance. The lender has incurred clerical costs associated with making the arrangements with the Federal Housing Administration and the Veterans Administration. The fee which covers these costs should be considered part of the borrower's cost of debt capital.

A borrower often pays fees which are not associated with any particular service. These fees may include "points": a given percentage of the face amount of the loan (e.g., 1 to 3 per cent) which is a one-shot payment

---

[1] If the seller is offering a purchase money mortgage, the lender and seller are one. Here we consider the typical case where they are separate.

[2] The borrower sometimes pays a fee to the broker for help in obtaining the loan.

at the time the loan is closed. Or, the borrower may pay a flat dollar amount (e.g., $100) or some combination of points and flat fees (e.g., 2 points plus $100). These fees should be assigned to the general overhead involved in mortgage lending—although it is difficult to see why the large borrower should pay more of the overhead than the small borrower—so they are included in the cost of capital.

We now turn to the difficult question of how to include fees and charges in the cost of debt capital to the borrower.. To begin with, the costs associated with property ownership and property transfer (discussed above) should not be included as costs associated with the loan. Only a part of closing costs, albeit the largest part, should be considered.

These loan-related closing costs can be considered as a discount from the face value of the loan. The borrower does not receive the full amount of the loan since the fees and charges must be paid "up front." Suppose, for example, that the borrower gets a $40,000 loan for 30 years at 9½ per cent, but with loan-related fees and charges amounting to 2½ per cent. At the time that the loan closes, $40,000 is remitted to the seller on behalf of the borrower: The borrower has bought the property and incurred a mortgage debt of $40,000. At the same time, the borrower must present a check for $1,000 to the lender. This payment is not part of the down payment; it is a one-shot payment to the lender. In effect, the lender has provided only $39,000 to the borrower.

The $1,000 in fees and charges are a discount from the loan because the borrower has incurred a debt of $40,000 in exchange for a loan which has a cash value to the borrower of only $39,000. When fees and charges are viewed as a discount, it is possible to convert them to an annual percentage rate by using a mathematical formula.[3] These formulas have been developed for other financial instruments, such as Treasury bills, which are offered on a discounted basis.

The conversion of fees and charges to an annual percentage rate is difficult because the life of the loan is usually unknown. Few residential mortgage loans are held to maturity; most are prepaid before 10 or 12 years have elapsed.[4] The length of the loan's life clearly makes a big difference to the annual percentage rate. Consider the example given above and sup-

----

[3] The formula is:

$$d = 1 - \frac{i - i\,(1 + i_e)^{-n}}{i_e - i_e\,(1 + i)^{-n}},$$

where n is the length of life of the loan, i is the annual percentage rate (e.g., .095), and d is the percentage discount (e.g., .025). This formula must be solved for the effective interest rate, i_e.

[4] There are also fees associated with prepayment, unless the new owner of the home gets a mortgage from the same bank. This is often the case.

pose that the loan were held only one year. The annual percentage cost (12.31 per cent) of that loan is calculated in two steps: first, 9½ plus 2½ equals 12 per cent. Second, the 12 per cent must be divided by .975 (= 12.31 per cent) to adjust for the fact that interest is paid on 2.5 per cent less than the face amount of the loan. But, if the loan were held for two years, the annual percentage rate would be approximately 9½ plus 1¼ equals 10¾ per cent which, divided by .975, equals approximately 11 per cent.

Figure 22-2 gives the pre-tax interest cost of borrowed capital as a function of the time of prepayment. The top line gives the "effective interest rate," i.e., the interest rate adjusted for fees, while the shaded area gives the fees and charges in terms of annual percentage rate. Thus, for any given prepayment date on the X axis it is possible to read off the effective interest rate. An annual interest charge of 9½ per cent is assumed and tax effects are ignored since the effective interest rate is stated on a pretax basis.

THE PRESENT VALUE OF ONE DOLLAR

Suppose that $P is deposited into a savings account at 6 per cent interest. Each year the $P earns $.06P. But the interest need not be withdrawn. It can be left to accumulate more interest. The process by which interest earns more interest (i.e., the compounding process) can be illustrated with Figure 22-3. The sums shown in column (4) are all equivalent after the price of time is taken into account.

What is the present value of $1 received in 3 years if the price of time is r? Inspection of Figure 22-3 should make it clear that the answer is $1 × 1/(1 + r)^3. The third power is used because of the compounding process. Suppose that there were no compounding process: the first two columns of Figure 22-3 indicate that the present value of $1 received in 3 years would be $1/(1 + 3r)$; i.e., the third power would not appear.

What is the present value of $1 received in n years if the interest rate is r? After taking compounding into account, it is $1 × 1/(1 + r)^n. The present value of $1 depends on only two values: the interest rate, r, and the time when the $1 is received, n. Thus, it can be tabulated with different values of r across the top of the table and different values of n down the side. Appendix A contains part of a table of the present value of $1 (Table A-1).

Suppose that a developer of real estate plans to invest in a property and sell it for $100,000 at the end of three years. In order to determine whether the property is a good investment, the investor wants to know the present value of the $100,000. The investor must decide on an appropriate interest

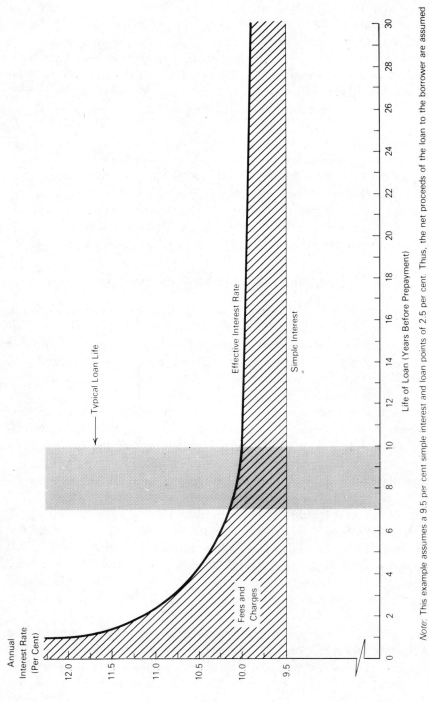

Note: This example assumes a 9.5 per cent simple interest and loan points of 2.5 per cent. Thus, the net proceeds of the loan to the borrower are assumed to be $P \times .975$ where P is the principal amount which must be repaid.

Fig. 22-2. Fees converted to an addition to the simple interest rate.

(a)

End of Year	(1) Principal Amount on Deposit	(2) Interest on Principal	(3) Interest on Interest	(4) Total Amount on Deposit (1) + (2) + (3)
0	P	0	0	P
1	P	rP	0	$P + rP$
2	P	$2rP$	$r(rP)$	$P + 2rP + r(rP)$
3	P	$3rP$	$3r(rP) +$	$P + 3rP + 3r(rP)$
			$r[r(rP)]$	$+ r[r(rP)]$

The arrows between column (4) entries are labeled $+(1+r)$.

(b)

End of Year	Total Amount on Deposit	Mathematical Expression for Total Amount on Deposit*
0	P	$P(1 + r)^0$
1	$P + rP$	$P(1 + r)^1$
2	$P + 2rP + r(rP)$	$P(1 + r)^2$
3	$P + 3rP + 3r(rP)$ $+ r[r(rp)]$	$P(1 + r)^3$

*Obtained by factoring the expression for the total amount on deposit.
Note: The principal amount is represented by P and the interest rate by r.

Fig. 22–3. Interest compounding, assuming interest is left on deposit.

rate, e.g., 10 per cent. From Table A–1, the present value of $1 received in three years is $.751 if the interest rate is 10 per cent. Therefore, the present value of the $100,000 is $75,100. The investor should not pay any more than that to develop the property.

THE PRESENT VALUE OF ONE PER PERIOD

The problem faced by the borrower and the lender, represented by Figure 22–1, is somewhat more difficult. The lender is exchanging a principal sum, P, for a stream of future payments. Each payment is a constant amount, R. What is the value at time zero of the stream of payments? At this point, the value of locating each dollar of inflow and outlay on a time line should be clear. The first payment of R should be discounted for one year at interest rate r, the second payment should be discounted for two years, etc.

The present value of $R per period can be obtained by repeatedly applying the present value of $1 for each of the years in which the $R will be received:

Present value of $R per period for 3 years =

$$= \$R[1/(1+r)^1 + 1/(1+r)^2 + 1(1+r)^3]$$

Thus, there is really no more mathematics involved than has already been encountered in understanding the present value of $1.

The process of repeatedly applying the present value of $1 would be too time-consuming for practical applications. It is possible to tabulate the present value of $1 per period in the same kind of table used for the present value of $1. Appendix A tabulates the present value of $1 per period. Table A–2 is called an "annuity table," since a constant dollar amount received at regular intervals is an annuity. An annuity without a maturity date is called a perpetuity, since it will presumably be paid forever.

The numbers presented in Table A–2 depend on only two variables: the maturity of the annuity, N, and the interest rate, r. This is because the present value of an annuity of $1 is the sum of numbers from Table A–1 (the present value of $1). In the above discussion, we saw that the present value of a three-year annuity was calculated by taking the sum of the present values of three different payments of $R each. Thus, each of the values in Table A–2 is the sum of N values from Table A–1.

The student should be able to verify the relationship between Tables A–1 and A–2. Suppose that you have an annuity of $1 each year for five years at an interest rate of 10 per cent. What is the present value of the annuity? You can calculate this from Table A–1 by adding up the first five values in the column headed by 10 per cent: .909 + .826 + .751 + .683 + .621 = 3.79. Table A–2 enables you to get the same number with much less difficulty: it is the number at the intersection of $N = 5$ and $r = 10$ per cent.

A special mathematical symbol is used to represent the numbers in Table A–2: a_{Nr}. This symbol tells us that each number in Table A–2 is uniquely identified by the two values, N and r. Armed with this symbol, we can write a precise mathematical sentence for the borrower–lender relationship shown in Figure 22–1:

$$P = R(a_{Nr}) \tag{1}$$

This formula is very useful to real estate lenders. It says that the annual loan payment, R, must be set so that the total amount lent, P, is repaid at the end of N years. Meanwhile, the compounding implicit in equation 1 assures that the balance of the loan is always paying interest at the rate r.

To see how the lender uses equation 1, we can outline the most important steps in calculating the annual loan payment, R:

1. Determine the principal amount which can be loaned, P. (This depends on borrower and property analysis discussed in Chapters 10 and 11.)
2. Determine the maximum maturity of the loan, N. For home mortgage loans, the maturity is highly standardized.
3. Determine the competitive market interest rate, r, for the type of property and borrower.
4. Using equation 1, calculate $R = P/a_{Nr}$.

THE USE OF A CONSTANT CARD

This process of calculating the annual loan payment is made easier by tables which give the amount of the loan payment per $1,000 borrowed. An example of such a table is given in Table A–3. The values in Table A–3, like those in Table A–1 and A–2, depend on the maturity of the loan and on the interest rate. The reason for this should be apparent from step 4 (above) in the lending process: *The numbers in Table A–3 are simply the reciprocals of the numbers in Table A–2.*

In the real estate trade, the numbers in Table A–3 are called constants. Similar tables are reduced to wallet-sized cards known as "constant cards." Investors use these constant cards extensively to calculate cash flows and return on investment. The steps involved in the use of a constant card are as follows:

1. Talk to lenders and other borrowers to determine how much can be borrowed on a given type of property, P, the prevailing interest rate, r, and the maturity, N.
2. Use the constant card with the values N and r to look up the annual loan payment per $1,000 borrowed.
3. Multiply the constant by the total amount borrowed, P, to get the total annual mortgage payment.
4. Subtract the estimated mortgage payment from the gross income from the property. This gives the amount of income left over to meet other expenses and to provide a return on investment.

COMPOUNDING MONTHLY FOR MONTHLY LOAN PAYMENTS

The above discussion is simplified to the extent that mortgage loan payments are usually made monthly. This means that the compounding process takes place monthly, so it is inaccurate to simply divide the annual loan payment by twelve. Instead, *it is necessary to work with a monthly interest rate and a maturity in months.*

This can be illustrated with Table A–2, although more detailed tables are needed in practice. Suppose that the annual interest rate is 60 per cent and the loan maturity is 1½ years. This means that the monthly interest rate is 5 per cent and the loan matures in 18 months. Looking at the intersection of $r = 5$ per cent and $N = 18$, we see that the present value of the annuity is 11.69. Thus, the borrower would be paying $1,000 monthly for 18 months for borrowing an amount equal to $11,690.

The general principles used in compounding monthly for monthly loan payments are:

1. Always divide the annual interest rate by 12. Go into the present value tables with the monthly interest rate.
2. Convert the maturity of the loan (or life of the investment) into months by multiplying the number of years by 12.

SUMMARY

The mathematics of real estate finance deals with the problem of translating between dollars held now and dollars to be received or paid at some future time. The interest rate—or its relative, the cost of capital—is the price of time. To carry money held now into the future, one multiplies repeatedly by the cost of capital. The technique is explained in Figure 22–4.

Figure 22–4 introduces interest compounding: interest earns interest if left on deposit. In real estate finance, it is customary to work with tables which take monthly compounding into account. The idea is that money invested in real estate could be invested in a savings account where it would compound monthly, if not more frequently. Tables giving the present value of $1 received N periods in the future (available in Appendix A) take compounding into account.

When working with real estate loans, we are dealing with annuities—periodic payments (usually monthly) of a constant dollar amount. The present value of an annuity can be calculated by repeated multiplications with different values for the present value of $1. But it is more convenient to work with an annuity table—i.e., the present value of $1 per period—such as the one in Appendix A. The values in the annuity table are the sum of values from the table for the present value of $1.

Real estate investors and lenders use "constant cards." A simple example of a constant card in Appendix A gives the amount of periodic loan payments for each $1,000 borrowed. The amount depends on the maturity of the loan as well as the interest rate. For monthly compounding, a more detailed table of constants is needed so that the interest rate and maturity can both be converted to a monthly basis. For example, a 12 per cent, 30-year loan requires a table which gives an interest rate of 1 per cent (12 per cent divided by 12 months in a year) and a maturity of 360 months (30 years times 12 months per year).

Fees and charges on mortgage debt are an important part of the total cost of debt. To estimate these costs as an annual percentage rate, it is necessary to estimate the expected life of the loan, i.e., the years before the loan will be prepaid. (Few residential real estate loans are held to maturity). The life of the loan has a large impact on the effective interest rate (including fees) on the loan. The tax effects of a mortgage should also be taken into account. Since mortgage interest is deductible, the after-tax cost of a mortgage is reduced.

Financing can make an impact on the investor in terms of cash flow as well as in terms of net present value. The constant card is widely used by investors to estimate these effects. The constant card gives the periodic mortgage payments per dollar borrowed for any combination of interest rate and maturity date. This constant is multiplied by the principal amount of the loan to determine how much cash must be turned over to the lender each year. The remaining cash flow from the investment, if any, accrues to the equity investment.

QUESTIONS

1. What is the value 10 years from now of $8 if it is compounded annually at 8 per cent? If it is compounded monthly?
2. In question 1, what is the interest on interest earned during the third year? During the first three years?
3. What is the present value of $8 per year (i.e., an annuity of $8) for the next 10 years if the discount rate is 8 per cent (compounded annually)?
4. A property is purchased for $100,000. The after-tax net cash flow from the property is $10,000 next year, $15,000 in the second year, and $20,000 in the third year. At the end of the third year the property is sold for $120,000. Your cost of capital is 10 per cent.
   (a) Graph the net cash outflows and inflows on a time line.

(b) What is the present value of the cash inflows (the R's)?

(c) What is the net present value of the investment?

5. Why is it important to graph cash inflows and outflows (see Figure 22–1) before attempting to find their present value?

6. What is the difference between simple interest and effective interest?

7. Why must a risk premium be included in the cost of equity capital?

8. If loan points increase and everything else stays the same, will simple interest increase, stay the same, or decrease? Will effective interest increase, stay the same, or decrease?

Appendixes

A

STATISTICS ON
THE OWNERSHIP OF
MORTGAGE DEBT

Table A-1. Ownership of Mortgage Debt by Type of Property and Mortgage, 1964
(Millions of Dollars)

Type of Property and Mortgage	All Types	Financial Institutions					All Other Holders		
		Savings and Loan Associations	Life Insurance Companies	Commercial Banks	Mutual Savings Bank	Total	Federal Agencies	Other Holders	Total
1. Total	%100.0 $311,617	32.5 101,333	17.7 55,152	14.1 43,976	13.0 40,556	77.3 241,017	3.7 11,400	19.0 59,200	22.7 70,600
2. Nonfarm	%100.0 $292,622	34.6 101,333	17.4 50,848	14.1 41,338	13.8 40,503	80.0 234,022			20.0 58,600
3. Residential	%100.0 $231,200	40.8 94,300	15.4 35,700	12.4 28,700	15.8 36,500	84.5 195,400	3.1 7,100	12.3 28,400	15.5 35,800
4. 1-4 Family	%100.0 $197,600	44.1 87,200	14.4 28,500	13.7 27,000	13.9 27,400	86.2 170,300	3.0 6,000	10.8 21,300	13.8 27,300
5. FHA	%100.0 $ 44,029	12.4 5,470	28.1 12,384	19.8 8,711	25.3 11,121	85.6 37,686	6.1 2,685	8.3 3,649	14.4 6,334
6. VA	%100.0 $ 29,852	22.2 6,683	21.5 6,403	9.2 2,742	37.3 11,121	90.1 26,904			9.9 2,948
7. Conventional	%100.0 $123,500	60.7 75,000	7.9 9,700	12.6 15,600	4.2 5,200	85.4 104,900			14.6 18,000
8. Multifamily	%100.0 $ 33,600	21.1 7,100	21.4 7,200	5.1 1,700	27.1 9,100	74.7 25,100	3.3 1,100	22.0 7,400	25.3 8,500

9.	FHA	%100.0 $ 8,814	0.6 54	21.7 1,908	16.1 1,422	24.6 2,166	63.0 5,550	8.0 711	29.0 2,553	37.0 3,264
10.	Conventional	%100.0 $ 24,800	28.3 7,050	21.2 5,300	1.2 300	28.1 7,000	78.8 19,500	1.6 400	19.6 4,900	21.2 5,300
11.	Commercial	%100.0 $ 61,500	11.5 7,033	24.3 14,900	20.3 12,405	6.6 4,016	62.7 38,500			37.3 22,900
12.	Farm	%100.0 $ 18,900	0.0 0	22.8 4,304	14.0 2,638	0.3 53	37.0 7,000			63.0 11,900

Sources:

1. Total: Total financial institutions and totals for commercial banks, mutual savings banks, savings and loan associations, and life insurance companies from *Federal Reserve Bulletin*, December, 1966, pp. 1820–22. Other totals are by addition.
2. Nonfarm: For life insurance companies, commercial banks, mutual savings banks, and "other holders" total, *Federal Reserve Bulletin*, December, 1966, pp. 1820–22. For savings and loan associations, *1966 Fact Book*, p. 78. For life insurance companies, sum of lines 4, 8, and 10 is 50,600, not 50,848 as reported in *Federal Reserve Bulletin*.
3. Residential: By addition of lines 4 and 8.
4. 1–4 Family: Dept. of Housing and Urban Development, *FHA Trends*, May, 1970, p. 51; except subtotals, derived by addition.
5. FHA: *FHA Annual Report 1964*. All Types total ($44,029) differs from $38,330 given in *Federal Reserve Bulletin*, December, 1966, p. 1822.
6. VA: *Federal Reserve Bulletin*, December, 1966, pp. 1820–22. "Other holders" total is by addition.
7. Conventional: Same as for line 5.
8. Multifamily: Same as for line 4.
9. FHA: Same as for line 5.
10. Conventional: By subtraction of lines 8 and 9.
11. Commercial: For commercial banks and mutual savings banks, same as for line 6. For other categories, line 2 minus line 4 minus line 8.
12. Farm: For life insurance companies, commercial banks, mutual savings banks, and total, same as for line 5. For financial institutions, "other holders," and savings and loan associations, by subtracting three institutions from total.

Table A-2. Ownership of Mortgage Debt by Type of Property and Mortgage, 1974
(Millions of Dollars)

Type of Property and Mortgage	All Types	Financial Institutions					All Other Holders		
		Savings and Loan Associations	Life Insurance Companies	Commercial Banks	Mutual Savings Banks	Total	Federal Agencies	Other Holders	Total
1. Total	%100.0 $687,484	36.3 249,306	12.6 86,258	19.1 131,043	10.9 74,890	78.8 541,497	10.5 72,267	10.7 73,720	21.2 145,987
2. Nonfarm	%100.0 $643,214	38.8 249,306	12.4 79,937	19.4 125,015	11.6 74,830	82.3 529,088	8.9 57,538	8.8 56,588	17.7 114,126
3. Residential	%100.0 $506,237	44.5 225,248	8.4 42,366	16.1 81,640	12.2 61,874	81.2 411,128	11.4 57,538	7.4 37,571	18.8 95,109
4. 1–4 Family	%100.0 $414,344	48.6 201,564	5.4 22,382	17.9 74,039	10.8 44,649	82.7 342,757	11.0 45,748	6.2 25,839	17.3 71,587
5. Multifamily	%100.0 $91,884	25.8 23,684	21.8 19,984	8.1 7,572	18.8 17,225	74.4 68,371	12.8 11,790	12.8 11,732	25.6 23,513
6. Commercial	%100.0 $136,977	17.6 24,058	27.4 37,571	31.7 43,375	9.4 12,956	86.1 117,960	0.0 0,000	13.9 19,017	13.9 19,017
7. Farm	%100.0 $44,270	0.0 0,000	14.3 6,321	13.6 6,028	0.1 60	28.0 12,409	33.3 14,729	38.7 17,132	72.0 31,861

Sources: Lines 1, 2, and 3 are by addition. Lines 4, 6, and 7 are from *Federal Reserve Bulletin,* June, 1975, p. A42.

Table A-3. Changes of Ownership of Mortgage Debt by Type of Property and Mortgage, 1974-1964
(Thousands of Dollars)

Type of Property and Mortgage	All Types	Financial Institutions					All Other Holders		
		Savings and Loan Associations	Life Insurance Companies	Commercial Banks	Mutual Savings Bank	Total	Federal Agencies	Other Holders	Total
1. Total	%100.0	39.4	8.3	23.2	9.1	79.9	16.2	3.9	20.1
	$375,867	147,973	31,106	87,067	34,334	300,480	60,867	14,520	75,387
2. Nonfarm	%100.0	42.2	8.3	23.9	9.8	84.2			15.8
	$350,592	147,973	29,089	83,677	34,327	295,066			55,526
3. Residential	%100.0	47.5	2.4	19.2	9.2	78.4	18.3	3.3	21.6
	$275,037	130,948	6,666	52,940	25,374	215,928	50,438	9,171	59,609
4. 1-4 Family	%100.0	52.70	− 2.8	21.7	8.0	79.6	18.3	2.1	20.4
	$216,944	114,364	− 6,118	47,126	17,249	172,657	39,748	4,539	44,287
5. FHA*	%100.0								
	$ 31,230								
6. VA*	%100.0								
	$ 26,348								
7. Conventional*	%100.0								
	$398,884								
8. Multifamily	%100.0	28.5	21.9	9.9	13.9	74.2	18.3	7.4	25.8
	$ 58,284	16,584	12,784	5,778	8,125	43,271	10,690	4,332	15,013
9. FHA	%								
	$								
10. Conventional	%								
	$								
11. Commercial	%100.0	22.5	30.0	40.9	11.8	105.1			−5.1
	$ 75,723	17,025	22,671	30,970	8,940	79,606			−3,883
12. Farm	$100.0	0.0	7.9	13.3	0.3	21.5			78.5
	$ 25,438	0	2,017	3,390	7	5,477			19,961

*Changes of total mortgage debt.

Sources: By subtraction of 1964 ownership of mortgage debt by type of property and mortgage from 1974 figures.

Table A-4. Percentage Distribution: Ownership of Mortgage Debt, by Type of Property and Mortgage, 1964 and 1974

Type of Property and Mortgage	All Types		Financial Institutions										All Other Holders					
			Savings and Loan Associations		Life Insurance Companies		Commercial Banks		Mutual Savings Banks		Total		Federal Agencies		Other Holders		Total	
	1964	1974	1964	1974	1964	1974	1964	1974	1964	1974	1964	1974	1964	1974	1964	1974	1964	1974
Total	100.0	100.0	100.0	100.0	100.0	100.0	100.0	100.0	100.0	100.0	100.0	100.0	100.0	100.0	100.0	100.0	100.0	100.0
Nonfarm	93.9	93.6	100.0	100.0	92.2	92.7	94.0	95.4	99.9	99.9	97.1	97.7		79.6		76.8	83.1	78.2
Residential	74.2	73.7	93.1	90.4	64.8	49.1	65.4	62.3	90.0	82.6	81.1	75.9	62.3	79.6	48.0	51.0	50.7	65.2
1–4 Family	63.4	60.3	86.1	80.9	51.7	26.0	61.5	56.6	67.6	59.6	70.7	63.3	52.6	63.3	36.0	35.1	38.7	49.0
FHA	14.1		5.4		22.5		19.8		27.4		15.6		23.6		6.2		9.0	
VA	9.6		6.6		11.6		6.2		27.4		11.2						4.2	
Conventional	39.7		74.0		17.6		35.5		12.8		43.5						25.5	
Multi-family	10.8	13.4	7.0	9.5	13.1	23.1	3.9	5.7	22.4	23.0	10.4	12.6	9.7	16.3	12.5	15.9	12.0	16.1
FHA	2.8		0.1		3.5		3.2		5.2		2.3		6.2		4.3		4.6	
Conventional	8.0		7.0		9.6		0.7		17.2		80.9		3.5		8.3		7.5	
Commercial	19.7	19.9	6.9	9.7	27.0	43.6	28.2	33.1	9.9	17.3	16.0	21.8		0.0		25.8	32.4	13.0
Farm	6.1	6.4	0.0	0.0	7.8	7.3	6.0	4.6	0.1	0.1	2.9	2.3		20.4		23.2	16.9	21.8

Sources: Derived from Tables A-1 and A-2.

Table A–5. Residential Mortgages Outstanding (Millions of Dollars) and Housing Starts (Thousands of Units), 1965–1975

Quarters of Years	All Holders*		Private Financial Inst.†		Other Holders†		Housing Starts†	
	Total	Multifamily (5 or More Families)	Total	Multifamily (5 or More Families)	Total	Multifamily (5 or More Families)	Total	Multifamily (2 or More Families)
1975 II	511,693	93,016 (3,892)	415,212	69,122 (16.65)	96,484	23,894 (24.76)	1,066	223 (20.93)
I							995	246 (24.70)
1974 IV	507,004	92,043 (7,092)	411,895	68,521 (16.64)	95,109	23,522 (24.73)	1,001	242 (24.14)
III	500,454	90,270 (8,048)	408,701	67,844 (16.60)	91,753	22,426 (24.44)	1,209	345 (28.56)
II	490,395	88,258 (6,704)	401,997	66,583 (16.56)	88,398	21,675 (24.52)	1,545	569 (36.86)
I	478,333	86,582 (4,725)	392,221	65,377 (16.66)	86,112	21,205 (24.62)	1,628	691 (42.46)
1973 IV	471,883	85,394 (7,492)	387,019	64,723 (16.72)	84,864	20,671 (24.36)	1,584	700 (44.21)
III	461,903	83,521 (9,564)	380,320	63,566 (16.71)	81,583	19,955 (24.46)	2,009	898 (44.72)
II	447,332	81,130 (8,520)	369,852	62,429 (16.88)	77,480	18,701 (24.14)	2,210	1,013 (45.84)
I	432,800	79,000 (10,400)	357,400	61,100 (17.10)	75,500	17,900 (23.71)	2,404	1,049 (43.62)
1972 IV	422,500	76,400 (11,600)	347,900	59,100 (16.99)	74,600	17,300 (23.19)	2,403	1,121 (46.66)
III	409,300	73,500 (8,800)	336,100	56,900 (16.93)	73,200	16,600 (22.68)	2,365	1,004 (42.46)
II	395,800	71,300 (10,000)	342,100	55,300 (17.06)	71,700	16,000 (22.32)	2,022	1,064 (52.61)
I	382,900	68,800 (8,000)	312,900	53,300 (17.03)	70,000	15,400 (22.00)	2,500	1,163 (46.53)
1971 IV	374,700	66,800 (10,000)	306,100	52,000 (16.99)	68,500	14,900 (21.75)	2,241	992 (44.28)
III	364,000	64,300 (8,000)	298,400	50,400 (16.89)	65,600	13,900 (21.19)	2,113	936 (44.28)
II	353,100	62,300 (10,400)	290,100	49,400 (17.03)	63,000	12,900 (20.48)	2,002	860 (42.98)
I	343,300	59,700 (7,200)	281,600	47,200 (16.76)	61,700	12,500 (20.26)	1,789	805 (45.00)
1970 IV	337,600	57,900 (7,200)	277,300	45,700 (16.48)	60,300	12,200 (20.23)	1,777	755 (42.51)
III	331,800	56,100 (6,400)	272,800	44,200 (16.20)	59,000	11,900 (20.17)	1,512	664 (43.88)
II	326,300	54,500 (5,200)	268,900	43,200 (16.07)	57,400	11,300 (19.69)	1,284	533 (41.51)
I	321,700	53,200 (4,000)	265,900	42,900 (16.13)	55,800	10,300 (18.46)	1,251	582 (46.50)
1969 IV	319,000	52,200 (6,400)	265,000	41,300 (15.58)	54,000	10,900 (20.19)	1,357	589 (43.42)
III	314,100	50,600 (4,800)	262,700	40,200 (15.30)	51,400	10,400 (20.23)	1,429	634 (44.40)
II	308,900	49,400 (4,400)	259,300	39,300 (15.16)	49,900	10,100 (20.24)	1,515	682 (45.00)
I	303,000	48,300 (5,200)	254,400	38,400 (15.09)	48,600	9,900 (20.37)	1,697	742 (43.71)

(continued)

Table A-5. (continued)

Quarters of Years	All Holders*		Private Financial Inst.†		Other Holders†		Housing Starts†	
	Total	Multifamily (5 or More Families)	Total	Multifamily (5 or More Families)	Total	Multifamily (5 or More Families)	Total	Multifamily (2 or More Families)
IV	298,500	47,000 (3,600)	251,200	37,600 (14.97)	47,800	9,600 (20.08)	1,604	673 (41.94)
III	293,300	46,100 (3,600)	246,600	36,700 (14.88)	46,700	9,500 (20.34)	1,547	642 (41.50)
1968 II	288,500	45,200 (4,000)	242,800	36,000 (14.82)	45,800	9,400 (20.52)	1,440	590 (40.97)
I	283,500	44,200 (2,000)	239,000	35,100 (14.69)	44,700	9,300 (20.80)	1,156	428 (37.02)
IV	279,800	43,700 (4,400)	236,600	34,700 (14.67)	43,400	9,200 (21.20)	1,332	544 (40.84)
1967 III	274,600	42,600 (3,600)	232,500	33,800 (14.54)	42,300	9,000 (21.28)	1,496	520 (34.76)
II	269,500	41,700 (3,600)	228,300	32,900 (14.41)	41,400	8,900 (21.50)	1,484	472 (31.81)
I	265,700	40,800 (2,800)	225,000	32,200 (14.31)	40,700	8,800 (21.62)	896	316 (35.27)
IV	263,800	40,100 (2,000)	223,700	31,500 (14.08)	40,100	8,700 (21.70)	876	292 (33.33)
III	261,500	39,600 (2,400)	222,100	31,000 (13.96)	39,400	8,700 (22.08)	1,204	388 (32.23)
1966 II	258,600	39,000 (4,800)	220,100	30,500 (13.86)	38,500	8,700 (22.60)	1,640	572 (34.88)
I	254,700	37,800 (3,200)	217,100	29,200 (13.45)	37,600	8,600 (22.87)	1,148	448 (39.02)
IV	250,700	37,000 (4,000)	213,700	28,500 (13.34)	37,000	8,500 (22.97)	1,408	536 (38.07)
1965 III	245,500	36,000 (4,000)	209,100	27,600 (13.20)	36,400	8,400 (23.08)	1,600	556 (34.75)
II	240,100	35,000 (3,600)	204,000	26,600 (13.04)	36,100	8,400 (23.27)	1,864	656 (35.19)
I	234,800	34,100	199,000	25,700 (12.91)	35,800	8,400 (23.46)	1,148	448 (39.02)

*Figures in parentheses are changes in mortgage lending in millions of dollars.
†Figures in parentheses are ratios (multifamily/total) in percentages.

Note: Figures from 1973 I to 1965 I are accurate to three digits.

Sources: Federal Reserve Bulletins: August, 1975, pp. A42, A51; August, 1974, pp. A44, A53; August, 1973, pp. A49, A63; August, 1972, pp. A51, A65; August, 1971, pp. A52, A65; August, 1970, pp. A52, A63; August, 1969, pp. A52, A63; August, 1968, pp. A50, A61; August, 1967, pp. 1410, 1421; August, 1966, pp. 1218, 1231; August, 1965, pp. 1149, 1161.

B

PRESENT VALUE TABLES USED IN REAL ESTATE FINANCE

Table B-1. The Present Value of \$1
$$(1/(1+r)^N)$$

Maturity (N)	Interest Rate (r)											
	5%	6%	7%	8%	9%	10%	12%	14%	15%	16%	18%	20%
1	.952	.943	.935	.926	.917	.909	.893	.877	.870	.862	.847	.833
2	.907	.890	.873	.857	.842	.826	.797	.769	.756	.743	.718	.694
3	.864	.840	.816	.794	.772	.751	.712	.675	.658	.641	.609	.579
4	.823	.792	.763	.735	.708	.683	.636	.592	.572	.552	.516	.482
5	.784	.747	.713	.681	.650	.621	.567	.519	.497	.476	.437	.402
6	.746	.705	.666	.630	.596	.564	.507	.456	.432	.410	.370	.335
7	.711	.665	.623	.583	.547	.513	.452	.400	.376	.354	.314	.279
8	.677	.627	.582	.540	.502	.467	.404	.351	.327	.305	.266	.233
9	.645	.592	.544	.500	.460	.424	.361	.308	.284	.263	.226	.194
10	.614	.558	.508	.463	.422	.386	.322	.270	.247	.227	.191	.162
11	.585	.527	.475	.429	.388	.350	.287	.237	.215	.195	.162	.135
12	.557	.497	.444	.397	.356	.319	.257	.208	.187	.168	.137	.112
13	.530	.469	.415	.368	.326	.290	.229	.182	.163	.145	.116	.093
14	.505	.442	.388	.340	.299	.263	.205	.160	.141	.125	.099	.078
15	.481	.417	.362	.315	.275	.239	.183	.140	.123	.108	.084	.065
16	.458	.394	.339	.292	.252	.218	.163	.123	.107	.093	.071	.054
17	.436	.371	.317	.270	.231	.198	.146	.108	.093	.080	.060	.045
18	.416	.350	.296	.250	.212	.180	.130	.095	.081	.089	.051	.038
19	.396	.331	.276	.232	.194	.164	.116	.083	.070	.060	.043	.031
20	.377	.312	.258	.215	.178	.149	.104	.073	.061	.051	.037	.026
25	.295	.233	.184	.146	.116	.092	.059	.038	.030	.024	.016	.010
30	.231	.174	.131	.099	.075	.057	.033	.020	.015	.012	.007	.004

Table B-2. The Present Value of $1 Per Period

$$(a_{N/r})$$

Maturity (N)	Interest Rate (r)										
	5%	6%	7%	8%	9%	10%	12%	14%	16%	18%	20%
1	0.952	0.943	0.935	0.926	0.917	0.909	0.893	0.877	0.862	0.847	0.833
2	1.859	1.833	1.808	1.783	1.759	1.736	1.690	1.647	1.605	1.566	1.528
3	2.723	2.673	2.624	2.577	2.531	2.487	2.402	2.322	2.246	2.174	2.106
4	3.546	3.465	3.387	3.312	3.240	3.170	3.037	2.914	2.798	2.690	2.589
5	4.329	4.212	4.100	3.993	3.890	3.791	3.605	3.433	3.274	3.127	2.991
6	5.076	4.917	4.766	4.623	4.486	4.355	4.111	3.889	3.685	3.498	3.326
7	5.786	5.582	5.389	5.206	5.033	4.868	4.564	4.288	4.039	3.812	3.605
8	6.463	6.210	5.971	5.747	5.535	5.335	4.968	4.639	4.344	4.078	3.837
9	7.108	6.802	6.515	6.247	5.995	5.759	5.328	4.946	4.607	4.303	4.031
10	7.722	7.360	7.024	6.710	6.418	6.145	5.650	5.216	4.833	4.494	4.193
11	8.306	7.887	7.499	7.139	6.805	6.495	5.938	5.453	5.029	4.656	4.327
12	8.863	8.384	7.943	7.536	7.161	6.814	6.194	5.660	5.197	4.793	4.439
13	9.394	8.853	8.358	7.904	7.487	7.103	6.424	5.842	5.342	4.910	4.533
14	9.899	9.295	8.745	8.244	7.786	7.367	6.628	6.002	5.468	5.008	4.611
15	10.838	9.712	9.108	8.559	8.060	7.606	6.811	6.142	5.575	5.092	4.675
16	10.838	10.106	9.447	8.851	8.312	7.824	6.974	6.265	5.669	5.162	4.730
17	11.274	10.477	9.763	9.122	8.544	8.022	7.120	5.373	5.749	4.222	4.775
18	11.690	10.828	10.059	9.372	8.756	8.201	7.250	6.467	5.818	5.273	4.812
19	12.015	11.158	10.336	9.604	8.950	8.365	7.366	6.550	5.877	5.316	4.844
20	12.462	11.470	10.594	9.818	9.128	8.514	7.469	6.623	5.929	5.353	4.870
25	15.094	12.783	11.654	10.675	9.823	9.077	7.843	6.873	6.097	5.467	4.948
30	15.373	13.765	12.409	11.258	10.274	9.427	8.055	7.003	6.177	5.517	4.979

Table B-3. The Constant Card: The Annual Payment
Required per $1,000 Mortgage Loan
$(1{,}000 \times 1/a_{N/r})$

Maturity (N)	Interest Rate (r)										
	5%	6%	7%	8%	9%	10%	12%	14%	16%	18%	20%
1	1050	1060	1070	1080	1091	1100	1120	1140	1160	1181	1200
2	538	546	553	561	569	576	592	607	623	639	654
3	367	374	381	388	395	402	616	431	445	460	475
4	282	287	295	302	309	315	329	343	357	372	386
5	231	237	244	250	257	264	277	291	305	320	334
6	197	203	210	216	223	230	243	257	271	286	301
7	173	179	186	192	199	205	219 ·	233	248	262	277
8	155	161	167	174	181	187	201	216	230	245	261
9	141	147	153	160	167	174	188	202	217	232	248
10	130	136	142	149	156	163	177	192	207	223	238
11	120	127	133	140	147	154	168	183	199	215	231
12	113	119	126	133	140	147	161	177	192	209	225
13	106	113	120	127	134	141	156	171	187	204	221
14	101	108	114	121	128	136	151	167	183	200	217
15	96	103	110	117	124	131	147	163	179	196	214
16	92	99	106	113	120	128	143	160	176	194	211
17	89	95	102	110	117	125	140	186	174	237	209
18	86	92	99	107	114	122	138	155	172	190	208
19	83	90	97	104	112	120	136	153	170	188	206
20	80	87	94	102	110	117	134	151	167	187	205
25	71	78	86	94	102	110	128	145	164	183	202
30	65	73	81	89	97	106	124	143	162	181	201

C

ELEMENTS OF VALUE IN THE RENTAL OF OFFICE SPACE AND SHOPPING CENTERS

PROXIMITY IN THE RENTAL OF OFFICE SPACE

The nature of office buildings is to concentrate office employees in a small space. The tenants of office buildings find this concentration valuable—up to a point. If it were not valuable, office employees could be scattered across the countryside in low-rise buildings. Certainly the rentals in low-rise buildings are less than those in high-rise buildings; urban land is more expensive than suburban land and high-rise construction is both less efficient (because elevators consume valuable floor space) and more expensive (because building materials must be lifted and expensive structural steel must be used).

Why are tenants willing to pay more for space in high-rise office buildings, especially space which is located "downtown"? Two considerations would appear to be relevant when considering a downtown location as opposed to a suburban location:

1. Access to employees. A central location makes it easier for a large number of employees, equipped with different skills, to reach the office.

2. Face-to-face contact. During working hours, office activity requires access to other office functions. Within a large firm, which may occupy multiple floors in a high-rise building, employees in one section of the firm may require personal contact with those in another section. Or, a firm may require services—e.g., legal, accounting, advertising, reproducing, etc.—which are provided most efficiently by other firms. Face-to-face contact is an important aspect of most of these services.

Clearing functions, e.g., the exchange of checks or common stock, provide an example of the need for face-to-face contact. Commercial banks receive deposited checks during the course of a workday. In a large urban center these checks are worth billions of dollars daily. The banks receiving deposits want to return the checks quickly so that the money will become available for investment. (The value of $2 billion invested overnight at a 10 per cent annual rate is $530,000 per night.)

The first step in the clearing function is to bring all the checks to a central location, the clearinghouse. At the clearinghouse, the local banks exchange checks which are written on each other. Checks written on out-of-town banks are sent to the Federal Reserve branch for collection. All of the transportation is accomplished by a bonded messenger.

This clearing process requires proximity of the branches to each other *and* to the clerical labor which processes the checks. The processing is a difficult, labor-intensive job that requires totaling batches of checks, sorting of checks by hand, and entry into high-speed computers. Thus, some of the labor hired by the banks must be centrally located. The supervisors of the clerks and the people with whom the supervisors communicate must also be centrally located. A similar location pattern is inherent in the process of clearing transactions in stocks, bonds, mortgages, or commodities.

It is generally true that some clerical and secretarial labor must be located with executives, even though the clerks do not have to see each other face-to-face. Many executives who require face-to-face contact also require immediate response from clerical and secretarial labor. Thus, the location pattern for general management activities is similar to the pattern for clearing operations: important, high-value communications require large numbers of centrally located office workers.

Different types of office activities have different requirements for access to employees and face-to-face contact. The clearing of checks, which we have described in some detail, is particularly important to commercial banks, so they can afford to pay high rents for centrally located office space. The commercial banks rely on accounting, legal, advertising, and other business services which must be centrally located also. The administrative offices of insurance companies, on the other hand, usually do not need to pay for a location near the commercial banks. The insurance company may do better to choose a more peripheral location which is available at lower rental rates.

The spatial pattern of rents available on commercial property is not well understood, but it is important to investors. Lenders and developers conduct feasibility studies and appraisals to determine the value of commercial properties. These studies must make some assumption about the future earning potential of the property. These assumptions are often little better than wild guesses, since many persons who deal daily in real estate do not understand the need for access to employees and for face-to-face contact.

The purpose of this section is to offer recent research on factors which influence office building rents. For the sample of between 95 and 113 high-rise office buildings in the Los Angeles area, annual rental rates were measured on a per-square-foot basis (Table C–1). The other variables defined in Table C–1 influence rents through the supply and demand for office services. Technically, the regression equations presented in Table C–2 are "reduced form" equations: they are the result of solving the two equations, supply and demand, under the assumption that the market for office services is in equilibrium. This solution of the supply and demand equations gives a single equation for the rental rate (on the left-hand side) as a function of the various factors which enter the calculations of landlords and tenants.

In equations 1 to 3 in Table C–2, access to employees is measured by the number of minutes from the building to the nearest freeway exit (AVGFRWY). This variable has the expected negative sign: an increase of one minute in time from the freeway reduces the rent which can be charged by 7 to 8¢ per square foot per year. This reduction, about 1 per cent of total gross revenues collected, is substantial, and the coefficient of AVGFRWY is significantly different from zero.

It might be objected that AVGFRWY measures access to major transportation routes, not access to employees who have a long drive on the freeway. However, a variable was tried for total commuting time from home to the office. It was found not to be significantly different from zero. Thus, the statistics suggest the surprising conclusion that commuters are not much concerned with the total length of the commutation; they are concerned only with the difficulty of negotiating city streets. While this is

Table C-1. Definitions of Variables with Means and Standard Deviations
(Cross-section of Los Angeles Office Building, 1975)

		Mean (Std. Dev.)
RENTLRATE	Quoted rental rate ($/sq. ft./yr.) for part of a middle floor. Full services are included. Source: Interviews with rental agents.	7.708 (1.090)
BHZONING	A dummy variable (1 in Beverly Hills, 0 otherwise) for strict height limitations in Beverly Hills.	0.1400 (0.3487)
AVGFRWY	Average number of minutes from the nearest freeway exit to the building. Source: Interviews with tenants. Interviews taken in elevators from 8:00 a.m. to 9:30 a.m., 12 noon to 2 p.m. and 4:30 p.m. to 5:30 p.m.	9.116 (3.095)
SQFT2BLK	Number of square feet of high-rise office space within a two-block radius of the building (000,000 omitted).	1.701 (2.134)
NETSQFT	Net (rentable) square feet of office space (000,000 omitted).	0.2518 (0.2068)
PKGDUMY	3-no parking; 2-external parking on ground or structure; 1-mixed external and internal; 0-all parking internal.	1.0100 (0.8586)
YROPEN	Year the building was ready for occupancy.	1967 (6.512)
OFCFLRS	Number of floors for office use.	13.82 (8.022)
SMOGCO	Carbon monoxide (parts per million) in the area, 1974 average. Source: Los Angeles Air Pollution Control District.	4.101 (0.9681)
FRWYDIST	Distance by the best available roads from the building to the nearest freeway off-ramp.	

an interesting hypothesis, it cannot be accepted on the basis of a sample of 95 office buildings in the Los Angeles area. Further statistical work is needed.

In equations 4 to 7 in Table C–2, time from the freeway was replaced by the distance from the freeway (FRWYDIST). This allowed an increase from 95 to 113 office buildings in the sample, with a corresponding improvement in the R^2. An increase of one mile in the distance from the nearest freeway exit leads to a reduction in rent of about 42¢ per year per square foot of floor space.

The amount of available face-to-face contact is measured by two variables. One is SQFT2BLK, the amount of office space within two blocks of the building, and the other is NETSQFT, the amount of office space in the building itself. The idea is that tenants will pay for access to other

Table C-2. Relationship of Building and Neighborhood Characteristics to Annual Rental Rate per Square Foot (Dependent Variable)

EQ#	R^2/Obs.	CONST	BHZONING	AVGFRWY	SQFT2BLK	NETSQFT	PKGDUMY	YROPEN	OFCFLRS	SMOGCO	FRWYDIST
1	0.6353 95	-45.80 (-1.96)	1.256 (5.45)	-0.07482 (-2.87)	0.2667 (6.46)	1.571 (3.88)	-0.4397 (-4.96)	0.0272 (2.30)			
2	0.6490 95	-43.42 (-1.90)	1.361 (5.90)	-0.0722 (-2.83)	0.2570 (6.32)		-0.4037 (-4.68)	0.0259 (2.23)	0.0455 (4.36)		
3	0.6417 95	-51.32 (-2.17)	1.448 (5.29)	-0.0816 (-3.08)	0.2766 (6.60)	1.503 (3.69)	-0.4814 (-5.10)	0.0298 (2.49)		0.1220 (1.25)	
4	0.6866 113	-86.30 (-3.57)	1.371 (5.23)		0.2822 (7.39)	1.769 (4.99)	-0.4530 (-4.73)	0.0478 (3.89)			-0.4246 (-4.15)
5	0.6940 113	-85.59 (-3.57)	1.414 (5.41)		0.2718 (7.07)	0.8327 (1.21)	-0.4354 (-4.55)	0.0474 (3.89)	0.0268 (1.59)		-0.4183 (-4.12)
6	0.6897 113	-88.58 (-3.70)	1.436 (5.49)		0.2743 (7.13)		-0.4195 (-4.41)	0.6488 (4.02)	0.0444 (5.13)		-0.4192 (-4.12)
7	0.6928 113	-91.89 (-3.77)	1.55 (5.37)		0.2871 (7.53)	1.716 (4.85)	-0.4911 (-4.97)	0.0503 (4.08)		0.1411 (1.46)	-0.4208 (-4.14)

Note: t values are in parentheses. The number of observations in a cross-section of Los Angeles office buildings, 1975, is below the unadjusted R^2.

office functions, especially if those functions can be reached by an elevator ride or by an elevator ride and a short walk. Both variables are significant with the expected positive sign (Table C–2). It is especially interesting that SQFT2BLK has a high t statistic, suggesting that increases in the square footage within two blocks are closely associated with increases in rental rates.

When the amount of office space within two blocks increases by one million square feet—an enormous increase—rental rate per square foot increases by 25 to 30¢. This increase of about 3.5 per cent in rental income is a disappointing return for a location which is so central that it is located near an extra one million square feet of office space. However, there seems to be much more return to building a large structure: the rental rate increases by $1.50 to $1.75 for adding one million square feet to a structure. This is true despite equation 5, which gives a coefficient of only .8327 for NETSQFT; the coefficient is insignificant because the number of office floors (OFCFLRS) is too closely related to square footage in the building. The two variables do not act independently, so they rob each other of a significant relationship with the rental rate. The R squares in equations 2 and 6, compared to those in equations 1 and 4, suggest that OFCFLRS is a stronger variable than NETSQFT.

A multistoried office building offers tenants something beyond rich opportunities for face-to-face contact within the building; height is associated with a desirable view and with prestige. Tenants will pay more for higher floors. Typically, the rental rate increases by 10 cents per floor in tall buildings. In small buildings, there may be no variation from one part of the building to another.

Access to employees and face-to-face contact are not the only determinants of the rental rate. There may also be a prestige factor, which is poorly represented in the equations reported in Table C–2. Tenants may pay in order to be associated with large banks, law firms, and accounting firms. This association may not lead to face-to-face contact, but it may increase the revenues of the smaller firm. The smaller firm may benefit from traffic to the larger, nationally known firm (although it is hard to see how that traffic can be diverted to a particular floor in the high-rise building).[1] Or, some customers may come to the smaller firm simply because it is in an area which is associated with solid, nationally known firms.

---

[1] It is possible that employees of the large firm might direct customers to a lawyer, CPA, or other business which is located in the same building. Or, customers in search of these services might consult the building directory or the directories of nearby buildings, especially if they want to close a deal quickly.

Thus, it is possible that the SQFT2BLK and NETSQFT variables capture factors other than face-to-face contact.

Beverly Hills has zoning restrictions which limit the heights of buildings to 11 or 12 stories. Since this reduces the supply of office space in the area, one would expect rental rates to be higher than in areas which can supply more office space within a given geographical radius. The coefficients of BHZONING in Table C–2 suggest that rents in Beverly Hills are between $1.25 and $1.50 higher than in the rest of Los Angeles. This may reflect a prestige factor as well as the limitations on supply.

No significant relationship was found when an estimate of the number of parking spaces associated with a building was regressed on rental rate. However, a dummy variable for the type of parking available, PKGDUMY, was strongly significant in the regressions. More desirable parking (internal) commands more rent than parking which is adjacent to the building. Buildings with no parking get rents per square foot which are 40 to 50¢ less than those with adjacent parking.

Office buildings tend to become obsolete as new design features are developed, so newer office buildings command more rent. Table C–2 suggests that each year adds 3 to 5¢ per square foot to rental value.

The statistics presented here suggest the kinds of factors which lenders, investors, and managers ought to consider when dealing with office buildings. However, more research is needed on other cities, other samples of buildings, and other ways of quantifying access, prestige, face-to-face contact, and other factors. Over time, the weights attached to the different variables (the coefficients in Table C–2) may change, even for the sample of Los Angeles buildings which were used in this study. Meanwhile, the coefficients are certainly interesting, since they suggest the value associated with various characteristics of high-rise buildings and their locations.

TENANT MIX AT A SHOPPING CENTER [2]

One of the important decisions in the management of a shopping center is where to locate a prospective tenant. Are there any principles which can be followed in determining where a particular tenant will prosper? Where will the business of the prospective tenant best reinforce the business of neighboring tenants, maximizing the overall sales and rentals of the shopping center?

In determining tenant mix, it is important to decide which tenants will draw customers to the center because of purchases which must be made

[2] Martin Moskowitz helped in preparing the material contained in this section.

at a particular store. Tenants of this type will usually have an advertising campaign and an established reputation. In some cases the tenants may have an unusual product which is not generally available in the area (e.g., a special type of imports).

This principle explains a lot about tenant placement. For example, the mall will contain lunch counters, but important restaurants serving dinner will usually be located on the periphery or in a free-standing building. They develop a clientele which comes during evening hours, and it would be a waste to have them occupying a mall location during the day.

As explained in Chapter 12, the key tenants in a shopping center depend on the type of center. The key tenants should be dispersed through the center so that the pedestrian traffic attracted to them will get maximum exposure to other stores. These other tenants—small clothing and shoe stores, stores for gifts, books, cards, gourmet food, etc.—depend on the pedestrian traffic since they can not draw customers from long distances. Basically, the number of pedestrians walking by their doors determines how large their sales will be. Since rental rates are usually linked to sales, the profits of the owner of the shopping center depend on clever placement of tenants.

The statement that traffic determines sales which, in turn, determines rental payments is too simple. Another important factor is the appropriate size of the store. The shopping center management has an incentive to keep each store small. In this way, the variety of services offered by the center can be maximized. On the other hand, a store with a good location and some drawing power of its own may feel that it could do even better with more space. Similarly, it is important to put space between competitive activities. Lunch counters, for example, should be dispersed, preferably on different streams of pedestrian traffic.

Another important factor in tenant location is the amount of window-display space. Some boutiques (especially shoes) require a lot of window space, whereas a candy store needs just enough window area to suggest that some candy should be purchased. The location of window displays so as to catch the attention of passing pedestrian traffic can depend partly on window design. An irregularly shaped window can provide just enough variety to greatly increase sales.

Figure C–1 is designed to provide a crude test of the hypothesis that small shops on a shopping center mall benefit from proximity to one of the key tenants. The vertical axis is the square-foot rent paid by 45 mall tenants at Lakewood, a successful shopping center in southern California. The horizontal axis gives the distance of each tenant from the key tenant (May Company) which is located in the center of the mall. Thus, the top

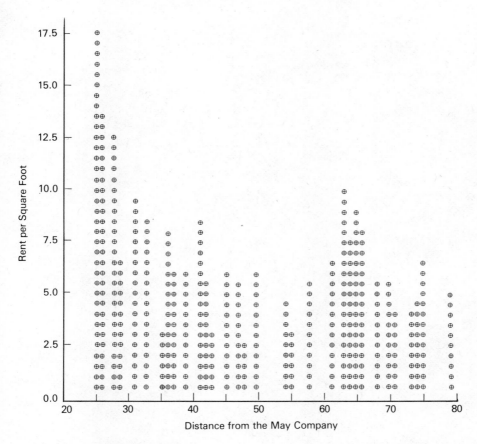

Source: Martin Moskowitz.

Fig. C–1. Rents of small mall tenants as a function of distance from a key tenant.

of each bar gives the coordinates in terms of rent and distance for each mall tenant.

Figure C–1 tends to confirm that tenants close to the May Company benefit from the proximity: their higher sales enable them to pay higher rents. Statistical tests on the data also confirm the existence of a significant negative relationship between square-foot rent and distance from the key tenant. However, many important variables are left out of the relationship shown in Figure C–1. In addition to competition, amount of display space, and size of store, it must be recognized that there are several key tenants at Lakewood. Thus, a much more sophisticated statistical study of the determinants of shopping center rents is needed.[3]

[3] The authors are currently undertaking such research.

D

SERIAL AND PERIODICAL REFERENCE MATERIALS

The materials and exhibits in the text can be updated by using the following references, almost all of which can be obtained with minimal or no cost:

National Trends

GNP, money market changes, construction housing starts, sources and uses of funds (including mortgage funds):

Construction Review (monthly)
Supt. of Documents
U. S. Government Printing Office
Washington, D. C.   20402

Credit and Capital Markets 1976
Bankers Trust Co.
P.O. Box 318
Church Street Station
New York, New York   10015

Economic Report of the President
Supt. of Documents
U. S. Government Printing Office
Washington, D. C.   20402

Federal Reserve Bulletin (monthly)
Division of Administrative Services
Board of Governors of the Federal Reserve System
Washington, D. C.   20551

Latest reports on research sponsored by the Department of Housing and
Urban Development:

HUD Research (monthly)
U. S. Department of Housing and Urban Development
Office of Policy Development and Research
Washington, D. C.   20410

Articles by national authorities on matters relating to mortgage and real
estate markets:

MGIC Newsletter (monthly)
MGIC Plaza
Milwaukee, Wisconsin   53201

Economists analyze national economic trends of all types. All are readable,
easy to understand, and authoritative, and will help in following real
construction and market trends:

Business in Brief (bi-monthly)
The Chase Manhattan Bank
New York, New York   10015

Business Bulletin (monthly)
The Cleveland Trust Co.
Cleveland, Ohio   44101

Economic Report (monthly except during summer)
Manufacturers Hanover Trust
350 Park Avenue
New York, New York

Review (monthly)
Federal Reserve Bank of St. Louis
P.O. Box 442
St. Louis, Missouri   63116
(This letter frequently presents very easily understood analyses of economic
trends and aspects of newer economic theories.)

1976 Savings and Loan Fact Book (annual)
U. S. Savings and Loan League
111 E. Wacker Drive
Chicago, Illinois   60601

U. S. Financial Data (weekly)
Federal Reserve Bank of St. Louis
P.O. Box 442
St. Louis, Missouri   63166
(This helps keep track of weekly changes in interest rates and other changes in
money markets which will affect mortgage market volume and rates.)

Real Estate Report (quarterly)
Real Estate Research Corp.
72 W. Adams
Chicago, Illinois   60603

U. S. Department of Commerce
Bureau of the Census
1970 Census of Population and Housing
(Population and housing characteristics of cities by census tracts)
Supt. of Documents
U. S. Government Printing Office
Washington, D. C.   20402 or any
Department of Commerce Field Office
These are for sale. Citations for particular volumes are available at any state college or university library. When in almost any large city with a major federal office building, you should visit the government book store where you will find displays of many kinds of government publications which will be of interest.

Miscellaneous Information

For the latest tax laws affecting real estate:

Your Federal Income Tax, 1976 (or current year) edition and *Tax Guide for Small Business*
Supt. of Documents
U. S. Government Printing Office
Washington, D. C.   20402 or
Local Internal Revenue Service Office

FHA Techniques of Housing Market Analysis
Supt. of Documents
U. S. Government Printing Office
Washington, D. C.   20402

GLOSSARY

abstract of title. A legal history of the claim of ownership, prepared by a lawyer, public official, or abstract company.

acceleration clause. A provision in a mortgage which gives the lender the right, under certain conditions, to demand immediate payment of the entire outstanding balance of the mortgage. Typical conditions are sale of the property or other actions on the part of the borrower which might impair the lender's security.

active (or general) partner. An investor in a *syndicate* who plays an active part in organizing and managing the affairs of the syndicate.

advance commitment. See *regular take-out commitment.*

adverse possession. Two or more persons claim title to a property.

agency. The relationship between a principal and the principal's appointee whereby the appointee acts on behalf of the principal in dealings with a third party.

allocation commitment. A permanent investor allocates a certain dollar amount to purchase acceptable mortgage loans from an *originator,* usually a *mortgage banker.* The terms of this commitment are less specific than for a *regular take-out commitment.*

balloon payment mortgage. The periodic payments are largely interest. When the mortgage matures, a large payment of principal is required in order for the borrower to avoid foreclosure.

bankable commitment. A permanent investor agrees to purchase mortgages which meet standards of acceptability with respect to property characteristics, borrower characteristics, loan-to-value ratio, and interest rate. This agreement, or commitment to purchase, enables the loan *originator,* usually a *mortgage banker,* to get interim financing from a commercial bank. Thus, the commitment is said to be bankable.

beneficiary of a trust deed. The lender, since the trustee arrangement is for the security of the lender's interests.

building residual. An appraisal technique used when the value of the land is known and the value of the building is to be derived by capitalizing the income remaining after assigning a portion of income to the land.

401

business cycle shading. The shaded area of a chart which covers the period from the peak in economic activity through the next trough in activity.

caveat emptor. Let the buyer beware.

closing costs. The expenses incurred by a borrower at the time the loan is paid. Closing costs may include tax stamps, prepaid taxes and insurance, appraisal fees, legal fees, *points,* and a flat fee charged by the lenders.

commitment. See *allocation commitment, regular take-out commitment, standby commitment,* and *take-out commitment.*

condemnation. The taking of private property for the public good.

constant. The base for computing the periodic (usually monthly or annual) mortgage payment per $1,000 of the face amount of the loan. The constant depends on the maturity of the loan and on the interest rate.

constant card. A wallet-sized card which tabulates the constants for each interest rate and maturity in years.

construction loans. Loans to provide money for the labor and materials necessary to build real property.

contingency loans. Loans which will be made only on the occurrence of a specific future event, such as the completion of certain phases of construction.

conventional mortgage. A mortgage not insured by any governmental organization, although it may be insured by a private company. With the revitalization of private mortgage insurance, this term has lost much of its value.

conveyance. Any transfer of title to real property.

cost of capital. A weighted average of the costs, in terms of percentage per year, of debt and equity capital. From the investor's viewpoint, the cost of equity capital should include a risk premium. The cost of debt capital should be the effective interest rate, i.e., the rate adjusted for taxes, fees, and charges spread over the expected time before prepayment.

dedication of property. Arises when a private owner sets aside property for public use and the governmental authorities accept the offer.

deed. A written instrument used in transferring interests in real property.

deficiency judgment. After foreclosure and sale under the terms of a *mortgage* or *trust deed,* any balance remaining due to the lender is a deficiency. A deficiency judgment gives the lender the right to proceed against the personal property of the borrower in order to recover the deficiency.

direct farmers home administration loan. A loan extended by the *Farmers Home Administration* to an eligible borrower.

direct VA loan. A loan extended by the *Veterans' Administration* to an eligible borrower who is usually located in a rural area.

discount rate. The interest rate which the Federal Reserve charges commercial banks for borrowing from it; the rate used to determine the present value of an income stream.

discounting. The process of determining the present value of a future income stream.

disintermediation. This occurs when investors withdraw funds from financial intermediaries in order to invest directly in credit market instruments. For example, savings might be withdrawn from an S&L in order to purchase a short-term bond issued by Fannie Mae or one of the other federal housing credit institutions.

easements. Permission to persons other than the owner to cross over the property or use it in a specific way.

effective interest rate. The rate to the borrower or debt adjusted for fees and charges. Since fees and charges are one-shot expenditures, they must be spread over the expected life of the loan.

eminent domain. The right of a government to compel sale of private property for public interest in return for payment to the private owner.

escheat. The return of private property to the state when there is no known private owner.

escrow. Deposit of all of the legal documents relating to the sale and financing of a property with a third person, an escrow agent, who sees that the terms of the contract are appropriately carried out.

extensions less repayments. The gross amount of new loans made, less the repayment of existing loans. This is the net change in outstanding loans.

Fannie Mae. See *Federal National Mortgage Association*.

Farmers Home Administration (FmHA). A federal agency which helps farmers to secure housing.

Federal Deposit Insurance Corporation (FDIC). An arm of the federal government which insures deposits (up to specified limits) at commercial banks and mutual savings banks. The FDIC exercises regulatory authority over banks which elect the insurance coverage.

Federal funds rate. The interest rate which commercial banks pay to each other for deposits at the Federal Reserve. These funds can be transferred electronically for short periods of time (e.g., overnight).

Federal Home Loan Mortgage Corporation (Freddie Mac). A governmental organization designed to buy and sell mortgages, particularly conventional mortgages, and issue financial instruments backed by these mortgages. It can subsidize the secondary mortgage market by buying on terms favorable to the seller.

Federal National Mortgage Association (Fannie Mae). A quasi-governmental organization (privately owned but with governmentally appointed directors) designed to buy and sell mortgages and issue bonds and other securities backed by its portfolio of mortgages.

Federal Savings and Loan Insurance Corporation (FSLIC). An arm of the federal government which insures deposits (up to specified limits) at savings and loans. Created in 1934 as a counterpart of the FDIC, the FSLIC also exercises regulatory authority over S&L's which elect insurance coverage.

fee simple. The highest form of ownership. Permits the use of the property in any way which will not interfere with the rights of others and within the limits established by the state.

FHA-insured mortgage. The federal government, through the Federal Home Administration, has guaranteed the repayment of the mortgage.

finder's fee. A fee paid by a lender to a broker or other party who brings a borrower to the lender. The fee is usually not obligatory; practices as to the amount, if any, depend on the region of the country.

Freddie Mac. See *Federal Home Loan Mortgage Corporation.*

gap financing. A junior mortgage used in connection with the *split-level takeout.* When only the lower level is achieved, the gap financing brings the total amount up to the highest level of financing.

general partner. See *active partner.*

Ginnie Mae. See next entry.

Government National Mortgage Association (Ginnie Mae). An arm of the Department of Housing and Urban Development designed to buy and sell mortgages and to provide a subsidy to the mortgage market by absorbing a loss on these activities.

gross national product (GNP). The sum of the dollar value of all sales to final users of goods and services.

high-powered money. Deposits that commercial banks keep with the Federal Reserve System. These deposits serve as required reserves against time and checking accounts; i.e., a stipulated percentage of time and checking account balances must be held as deposits at the Federal Reserve. Thus, each dollar of high-powered money supports many dollars of time and checking accounts.

hypothecate. To pledge property as security for a loan without delivering title to the lender.

impounds. Reserves for payment of property taxes and insurance when due. These funds are collected with the borrower's monthly remittance. When impounds are collected, a part is usually collected at the time of closing.

interest-only mortgage. The borrower pays only interest until the maturity of the loan, when a *balloon payment* of principal is required. This type of loan usually has a short maturity (i.e., 5 to 10 years).

interim financing. Short-term loans designed to bridge the gap between the time money is needed (e.g., for construction) and the time a permament debt or equity investor is found (e.g., the completed property is sold).

joint tenancy. An estate of two or more persons who hold ownership in the same degree.

judgment lien.   Arises from lawsuits in which damages have been awarded and the courts use the property as a guarantee that the damages will be paid.

junior mortgage.   In default, the loan secured by a junior mortgage can claim only the residual after the more senior noteholders have been paid in full. Thus, a junior (or second) mortgage is much riskier than a first mortgage.

land residual.   A property appraisal technique which assumes that the value of the building is known. Some of the net income from the property is assigned to the building and the rest is capitalized to find land value.

leaseback arrangements.   A form of financing in which a property owner sells the property with provisions to enter into a lease for the continued use of the property.

leasehold.   The economic and legal rights held by the lessee.

leasehold estate.   The right to use property during the period of a lease, subject to the legal terms of the lease.

liens.   Created whenever property is pledged as security for a debt or other obligation. A claim on the value of property which is exercised only if the specified monetary obligation is not met from other sources.

life estate.   Gives use of property only during the user's lifetime or for a shorter fixed period of time.

life tenant.   One who has been given a life estate. The life tenant may use or lease the estate as long as the interests of successors are not damaged.

limited partner.   An investor in a syndicate who does not take an active interest in management. The liability of passive investors is limited to the amount of their investment.

liquidity of a financial instrument.   The ability to sell the financial instrument at a reasonable price within a reasonably short period of time.

loan commitment.   See *take-out commitment.*

loan extensions.   The total amount of new loans made to borrowers.

loan repayment.   The total principal amount repaid to a lender. Most is repaid as part of installment payments, refinancing, or sale of the property before loan maturity.

M_1.   Currency and demand deposits in the hands of the nonbank public. This is the money supply.

M_2.   Time deposits at commercial banks, exclusive of large-denomination certificates of deposit, plus M_1.

M_3.   Time deposits at thrift institutions plus M_2.

mechanics' lien.   Claim for payment when materials or labor have been furnished for the construction or repair of real property and the amounts due have not been paid. See *liens.*

mortgage.   A contract which pledges real property as security for a loan.

mortgage banker.   An institution which brings together the buyer and seller of mortgages and is compensated with the differential between bid and asked prices. Not to be confused with the *mortgage company*.

mortgage company. An institution with a large part of its business in originating and servicing mortgages which are sold to other investors. A mortgage company cannot accept deposits from the public.

Mortgage Guarantee Insurance Corporation (MGIC). The first private mortgage insurance company to be opened after the Great Depression. Still the largest private mortgage insurance company.

mortgage origination. The process of extending a mortgage loan to a borrower (the mortgagor). This involves borrower analysis and property analysis as well as the processing of legal mortgage and loan documents. See *originator*.

mortgagee. The person or institution which lends money secured by a property.

mortgagor. The property buyer who offers property as collateral in order to obtain a mortgage loan.

moving average. When numbers are arranged over time (e.g., quarterly profits) groups of them can be averaged in an interlocking fashion. For example, a two-quarter moving average of quarterly profits averages the first two numbers, then the second and third numbers, then the third and fourth numbers, and so forth.

Mutual Mortgage Insurance Fund (MMIF). The pool of funds kept by the Federal Housing Administration for payment of claims arising under *FHA-insured mortgages*.

negative leverage. This occurs when additional debt decreases the return to the equity investor. Negative leverage implies that the interest rate on debt is greater than the rate of return on equity.

open-end mortgage. The amount which can be borrowed under the same mortgage at future times is left open to negotiation, subject only to a maximum amount which is stipulated in the mortgage agreement.

opportunity cost. A cost incurred because the best alternative is foregone. The best alternative may be an investment which is no more risky but yields a higher return. If materials are purchased at one price when they could be purchased at a lower price, an opportunity cost is incurred.

options on property. The prospective buyer makes a small down payment (perhaps 5 or 10 per cent) for the right to acquire the property at a given price during a given time period. If the time period lapses, the prospective buyer forfeits the down payment.

originator. The institution or individual which lends money directly to a borrower. The loan contract and the mortgage agreement can then be sold to other parties who become investors in but not originators of the loan. See *mortgage origination*.

package mortgage. A mortgage agreement which includes both real and personal property.

participation loans. A group of lenders agree to buy shares of a loan or pool of loans so as to share the risk. The seller retains a share, eliminating the need to transfer the loan documents and reassuring purchasers as to the quality of the loan.

percentage lease. The lessee, an income-producing business, agrees to pay the lessor a fixed percentage of annual sales or a flat dollar amount annually, whichever is greater.

points. A one-shot fee charged by mortgage lenders. Two points means 2 per cent of the principal amount of the loan, payable at the time of closing. Points alter the *effective interest rate*.

police power. All regulations necessary to protect public health, welfare, safety, and morals.

prepayment penalty. A fee paid by the borrower if the borrower initiates early repayment of a debt.

primary mortgage market. The market in which the buyer of a property obtains a loan with the property as collateral.

prime business rate. The rate which commercial banks charge their least risky borrowers.

prime mortgage rate. The contract rate charged a fully qualified buyer with a highly desirable property.

private property. The exclusive right of one or more persons to possess, control, enjoy, and dispose of an economic good.

private secondary mortgage market. Private institutions and individuals buy and sell mortgages without going through institutions such as Fannie Mae, Ginnie Mae, or Freddie Mac.

property residual. A property appraisal technique which discounts the cash flows from the property up to a certain point in time. The estimated residual value of the property at that time is then discounted back to the present and added to the present value of the cash flows.

purchase money mortgage. The seller of the property takes a *mortgage* or *trust deed* as partial payment for the property.

quitclaim deed. The seller who transfers title through a quitclaim deed relinquishes any claim to the property without warranting that there is any claim to relinquish.

real GNP. Gross national product stated in terms of the dollar value of some base year so as to take out the effects of inflation on GNP.

real property. Land and all things permanently attached to the land.

regular take-out commitment. The permanent investor agrees to buy mortgages, usually from a mortgage banker, on specific properties. The sale from the loan originator to the permanent investor takes place as soon as possible after the mortgages are originated. Often called an "advance commitment."

regulation-Q interest ceilings. The Federal Reserve Board's regulation which limits the maximum interest rate which banks can pay depositors.

revolving line of warehousing credit. A commercial bank agrees to make an interim loan collateralized by acceptable mortgages as long as the total amount of all such loans does not exceed a predetermined maximum. A large number of mortgages can be financed through this device, provided that the amount in the warehouse at any one time does not exceed the limit on the credit line.

risk premium. A part of the interest rate which compensates the lender for risk. For example, a one per cent risk premium might be added to a risk-free interest rate of 6 per cent.

secondary financing. A loan secured by a *junior mortgage.*

secondary mortgage market. The market where a person or institution which holds a mortgage sells it to another person or institution. The property owner (*mortgagor*) is not consulted in this transaction.

service property. A property, such as a church, which is not readily marketable and which does not provide rental income.

servicing function. The servicing of a mortgage—a clerical function which does not involve risk taking. It involves billing, collecting payments, processing defaults, and sometimes handling payments of insurance and property tax. If the servicing agent is different from the mortgagee, the agent is compensated with a fee, usually some percentage (e.g., .4 per cent) of the outstanding principal.

special assessment. A property tax which arises when a government service or facility is being created for the benefit of a limited number of property holders.

specialized mortgage lenders. A term applied to savings and loan associations and to mutual savings banks because the large majority of their assets are held as mortgage loans.

special-purpose property. Property intended for a specific business use and not readily adaptable to other uses.

spendable return. The cash flow to the equity investor after all expenses and taxes have been paid.

split-level takeout. In construction financing, the permanent lender makes a commitment to loan a given amount but only if a specified level of occupancy or rental income is exceeded. A lesser amount (the second level or tier) is loaned if the property fails to achieve the specified level of occupancy or rental income.

standby commitment. A permanent investor agrees, for a fee, to stand ready to purchase mortgages, but only after a considerable time (e.g., 6–9 months) has elapsed since origination and only at a considerable discount from the face value of the mortgages. The originating institution, usually a mortgage banker, will pay a fee for these commitments since they are *bankable commitments.* In construction financing, a standby commitment is a *take-out commitment* with such a high interest rate that it is unlikely to be funded.

syndication. Typically a small number of investors (often fewer than 100) who combine for organizing and managing a specific investment. Syndicates contain provisions for dissolution when their investment objectives are achieved.

take-out commitment. A commitment on the part of a permanent lender, such as an insurance company, to purchase a mortgage loan. When this commitment is exercised, the loan *originator,* usually a *mortgage banker,* is taken out of the deal. In construction financing, a take-out commitment is any commitment to make a permanent mortgage on the completed property.

tenancy at sufferance. Created whenever a tenant continues to occupy a property after expiration of a legal lease agreement.

tenancy at will. Created whenever there is an agreement between the landlord and the tenant that the occupancy may be terminated whenever either party wishes to do so.

tenancy in common. An estate held by two or more persons, each with an undivided interest.

title insurance. Insurance against losses occasioned by defects or encumbrances on a title, but only such defects as are not excepted in the insurance policy. The value of title insurance is greatly reduced (few claims are paid) by the limited nature of the defects which are covered.

trading area. For a retail business, the geographical area over which it delivers a large percentage of its goods.

trust deed. The seller conveys title to a third party, the *trustee,* who has power of sale but only in the event of the borrower's default on loan payments or other terms of the mortgage.

trustee. A person or corporation taking responsibility to protect the interests of others as spelled out in the trust agreement.

usury laws. Restrictions on the amount of interest which lenders can charge.

VA-insured or -guaranteed mortgage. The federal government, through the Veterans' Administration, guarantees the payment of a large percentage of the mortage. Under the insurance program, the entire mortgage is covered.

variable maturity mortgage. A form of the variable rate mortgage in which the monthly payment is supposed to be held constant but the amount credited to interest changes with market conditions. If more of the payment is credited to interest and less to principal, the maturity must be lengthened.

variable payment mortgage. The monthly payment changes, with the amount of the change depending on interest rates or ability to repay.

variable rate mortgage. A normal mortgage or trust deed in which the lender may change the rate of interest at specified times.

warehousing commitment. A commercial bank agrees to provide temporary (*interim*) financing secured by any mortgage which meets well agreed standards as to quality of property, loan-to-value ratio, and ability of borrower to repay.

warehousing loan. A temporary (*interim*) loan made by a commercial bank to a mortgage lender and secured by a mortgage. The mortgage documents go to the commercial bank where they are said to be warehoused until the loan is sold to a permanent investor. The proceeds from this sale pay off the commercial bank loan so that the mortgage documents can be released to the permanent investor.

whole loan sale. The loan originator sells the entire loan (as opposed to a *participation* in the loan) on the *secondary market*, retaining only the servicing contract and some part of the origination fees or *points*. Whole loans generally pay higher interest than participations because the buyer encounters higher processing costs and greater risk that the selling institution is not selling its best quality loans.

wraparound (blanket) mortgage. A number of properties or property rights offered as security for a single debt.

INDEX